PRIVATE LIBRARIES IN RENAISSANCE ENGLAND

A Collection and Catalogue of Tudor and Early Stuart Book-Lists

Volume IV

PLRE 87–112

MEDIEVAL & RENAISSANCE
TEXTS & STUDIES

VOLUME 148

PRIVATE LIBRARIES IN RENAISSANCE ENGLAND

A Collection and Catalogue of Tudor and Early Stuart Book-Lists

Volume IV
PLRE 87–112

R. J. FEHRENBACH
General Editor

E. S. LEEDHAM-GREEN
Editor in the United Kingdom

MEDIEVAL & RENAISSANCE TEXTS & STUDIES
Binghamton, New York
1995

The publication of this volume has been supported by a grant from the National Endowment for the Humanities, an independent federal agency.

© Copyright 1995
Center for Medieval and Early Renaissance Studies
State University of New York at Binghamton

Library of Congress Cataloging-in-Publication Data

Private libraries in Renaissance England : a collection and catalogue of Tudor and early Stuart book-lists / R. J. Fehrenbach, general editor, E. S. Leedham-Green, editor in the United Kingdom.
  v. 1 — (Medieval & renaissance texts & studies : v. 87, 105, 117, 148)
  Includes bibliographical references and index.
  Contents: v. 1. PLRE 1-4. — v. 2. PLRE 5-66. — v. 3. PLRE 67-86. — v. 4. PLRE 87-112
  ISBN 0-86698-099-7, v. 1; ISBN 0-86698-151-9, v. 2; ISBN 0-86698-170-5, v. 3; ISBN 0-86698-188-8, v. 4.
  1. Private libraries—England—History—1400-1600—Sources. 2. Private libraries—England—History—17th-18th centuries—Sources. 3. Books and reading—England—History—16th century—Sources. 4. Books and reading—England—History—17th century—Sources. 5. Private libraries—England—Catalogs—Bibliography. 6. Book collecting—England—History—Sources. 7. Library catalogs—England—Bibliography. I. Series.
Z997.2.G7P75 1994
017'.1'0942—dc20   91-18418
                                                            CIP

This book is made to last.
It is set in Baskerville, smythe-sewn,
and printed on acid-free paper
to library specifications

Printed in the United States of America

Table of Contents

Table of Annotated Book-lists by PLRE Number — vii
Table of Annotated Book-lists by Owner — ix
Contributing Editors — x
Advisory Editors — xii
Acknowledgments — xiii
Common Abbreviations
   Sources — xiv
   Degrees — xx

Introduction — xxi

Annotated Book-lists — 1

Appendices
   PLRE Cumulative Catalogue — 295
   APND Lists in Preparation — 314
   Additions and Corrections, PLRE Addresses — 315

Indices
   Authors and Works — 317
   Editors and Compilers — 336
   Translators — 338
   Stationers — 339
   Places of Publication — 342
   Dates of Publication — 347

Mark Hubert Curtis
1920–1994

Table of Annotated Book-lists by PLRE *Number*

PLRE 87: Thomas Morgan (inventory 1570) *Scholar (student)*
    W. P. GRIFFITH
PLRE 88: William Stocker (inventory c.1570) *Scholar (M.A.)*
    E. S. LEEDHAM-GREEN & ALAIN A. WIJFFELS
PLRE 89: Thomas Thornbury (d.1570) *Scholar (probably student)*
    J. S. CRAIG
PLRE 90: Tichborne (inventory 1570, partly 1569) *Scholar (probably B.C.L.)*
    E. S. LEEDHAM-GREEN & ALAIN A. WIJFFELS
PLRE 91: John Beddow (inventory 1571, partly 1577) *Scholar (schoolmaster) M.A.*
    CHARLES A. HUTTAR
PLRE 92: Robert Hart (d.1571) *Scholar (M.A.)*
    RICHARD OVENDEN
PLRE 93: Robert Hooper (inventory 1571) *Scholar (M.A.)*
    KATY HOOPER
PLRE 94: Lewis Jones (d.1571) *Scholar (B.A.)*
    W. P. GRIFFITH
PLRE 95: Thomas Maudesley (d.1571) *Scholar (B.A.)*
    WILLIAM M. ABBOTT
PLRE 96: Jerome Reynolds (d.1571) *Scholar, Physician (M.A., perhaps B.M.)*
    R. J. FEHRENBACH & MORDECHAI FEINGOLD

PLRE 97: John Reynolds (d.1571) *Scholar (M.A.)*
    R. J. FEHRENBACH & MORDECHAI FEINGOLD
PLRE 98: Austin (inventory 1572) *Probably Scholar*
    J. S. CRAIG
PLRE 99: William Battbrantes (d.1572) *Scholar (probably student)*
    CHRISTINA M. COYNE
PLRE 100: John Mitchell (d.1572) *Servant*
    KATY HOOPER
PLRE 101: Thomas Neale (d.1572) *Scholar (student)*
    ANN R. MEYER
PLRE 102: William Smallwood (inventory 1572) *Scholar (M.A.)*
    E. S. LEEDHAM-GREEN
PLRE 103: Henry Hutchinson (d.1573) *Scholar (B.A.)*
    MARGERY H. SMITH, C.S.J.
PLRE 104: William Kettelby (inventory 1573) *Scholar (M.A.)*
    GRADY A. SMITH
PLRE 105: Richard Lanham (inventory 1573) *Scholar (B.A.)*
    R. J. FEHRENBACH
PLRE 106: Walter Dyllam (inventory 1575) *Scholar (student)*
    R. J. FEHRENBACH
PLRE 107: Nicholas Lombard (d.1575) *Scholar (M.A.)*
    JOHN B. GABEL
PLRE 108: Richard Lye (d.1575) *Manciple*
    E. S. LEEDHAM-GREEN
PLRE 109: James Powell (d.1575) *Scholar (M.A.)*
    RICHARD J. PANOFSKY
PLRE 110: Philip Johnson (d.1576) *Scholar (B.Th.)*
    D. V. N. BAGCHI
PLRE 111: Richard Slatter (inventory 1576) *Scholar (M.A.)*
    RUDOLPH P. ALMASY
PLRE 112: John Tatham (d.1576) *Scholar (M.A.)*
    CHARLES A. HUTTAR

Table of Annotated Book-lists by Owner

Austin (inventory 1572)	PLRE 98
William Battbrantes (d.1572)	PLRE 99
John Beddow (inventory 1571, partly 1577)	PLRE 91
Walter Dyllam (inventory 1575)	PLRE 106
Robert Hart (d.1571)	PLRE 92
Robert Hooper (inventory 1571)	PLRE 93
Philip Johnson (d.1576)	PLRE 110
Lewis Jones (d.1571)	PLRE 94
William Kettelby (inventory 1573)	PLRE 104
Richard Lanham (inventory 1573)	PLRE 105
Nicholas Lombard (d.1575)	PLRE 107
Richard Lye (d.1575)	PLRE 108
Thomas Maudesley (d.1571)	PLRE 95
John Mitchell (d.1572)	PLRE 100
Thomas Morgan (inventory 1570)	PLRE 87
Thomas Neale (inventory 1572)	PLRE 101
James Powell (d.1575)	PLRE 109
Jerome Reynolds (d.1571)	PLRE 96
John Reynolds (d.1571)	PLRE 97
Richard Slatter (inventory 1576)	PLRE 111
John Tatham (d.1576)	PLRE 112
Thomas Thornbury (d.1570)	PLRE 89
Tichborne (inventory 1570, partly 1569)	PLRE 90

Contributing Editors

WILLIAM M. ABBOTT
Assistant Professor of History, Fairfield University

RUDOLPH P. ALMASY
Associate Dean of Academic Affairs, Eberly College of Arts and Sciences
West Virginia University

D. V. N. BAGCHI
Lecturer in Theology, University of Hull

CHRISTINA M. COYNE
Assistant Editor, *Private Libraries in Renaissance England*

J. S. CRAIG
Assistant Professor of History, Simon Fraser University

R. J. FEHRENBACH
Professor of English, College of William and Mary

MORDECHAI FEINGOLD
Professor of Science Studies
Virginia Polytechnic Institute and University

JOHN B. GABEL
Professor of English, Emeritus, Ohio State University

CONTRIBUTORS

W.P. GRIFFITH
Lecturer, School of History and Welsh History
University of Wales, Bangor

KATY HOOPER
Special Collections Librarian, Sydney Jones Library
University of Liverpool

CHARLES A. HUTTAR
Professor of English, Hope College

E. S. LEEDHAM-GREEN
Deputy Keeper of the Archives
and Fellow of Darwin College, Cambridge

ANN R. MEYER
Javits Fellow, Department of English, University of Chicago

RICHARD OVENDEN
Curator, Department of Printed Books,
National Library of Scotland

RICHARD J. PANOFSKY
Associate Vice Chancellor for Academic Affairs
University of Massachusetts, Dartmouth

MARGERY H. SMITH, C.S.J.
Professor of English, College of St. Catherine

GRADY A. SMITH
Independent Scholar

ALAIN A. WIJFFELS
Professor of Legal History in the University of Leiden

Advisory Editors

Peter W. M. Blayney
Mark H. Curtis † 1994
W. Speed Hill
Arthur F. Kinney
Nati H. Krivatsy
F. J. Levy
James K. McConica
David McKitterick
W. B. Stephens
Laetitia Yeandle

Assistant Editor

Christina M. Coyne

Consulting Editor for the Oxford Project

Simon Bailey

Editorial and Research Assistants

Susan Martin-Joy
Rives Nicholson

Acknowledgments

As with previous volumes, my chief indebtedness is to the Contributing Editors whose work appears in the following pages. Their knowledge and resourcefulness have been equaled only by their patience and good humor in meeting the demands and addressing the quirks of a system that must serve both the printed book and an electronic database. This volume, like the two preceding it, has been generously supported by the National Endowment for the Humanities, which sustained the work of PLRE with a second award in 1994 following an earlier grant in 1991. I am grateful for the agency's continued support and encouragement.

As the project has grown, so also have the circle of individuals and the number of libraries and institutions generously assisting and supporting PLRE, which, at its core, has always been an enterprise of scholarly collaboration. To all, especially to those named in the preceding pages, I give my thanks, but most particularly to my indispensable colleague, Elisabeth Leedham-Green. Finally, with this volume I remember with affection and special appreciation Mark Curtis, who committed a part of his rich and vigorous life as educator, scholar, and historian to help establish the work of PLRE. It was a commitment for which I will always be deeply grateful.

Williamsburg, Virginia   R.J.F.
May, 1995

Common Abbreviations

SOURCES

A&R   A. F. Allison and D. M. Rogers. *A Catalogue of Catholic Books in English Printed Abroad or Secretly in England 1558–1640.* Bognor Regis, 1956 [Reprints 1964 and 1968].

Adams   H. M. Adams. *Catalogue of Books Printed on the Continent of Europe, 1501–1600, in Cambridge Libraries.* 2 volumes. Cambridge, 1967.

Alumni Cantabrigienses — John Venn and John Archibald Venn. *Alumni Cantabrigienses: A Biographical List of All Known Students, Graduates and Holders of Office at the University of Cambridge from the Earliest Times to 1751, Part I.* 4 volumes. Cambridge, 1922–1927 [Reprint 1974].

Alumni Oxonienses — Joseph Foster, compiler. *Alumni Oxonienses: The Members of the University of Oxford, 1500–1714, Their Parentage, Birthplace, and Year of Birth* ... 4 volumes. Oxford, 1891–1892.

Arber   *A Transcript of the Registers of the Company of Stationers of London,* edited by Edward Arber. 5 volumes. London/Birmingham, 1875–1894 [Reprint 1967].

Athenae Cantabrigienses — C. H. Cooper and T. Cooper. *Athenae Cantabrigienses*. 3 volumes. Cambridge and London, 1858-1913 [Reprint 1967].

Athenae Oxonienses — Anthony à Wood, with additions by Philip Bliss. *Athenae Oxonienses: An Exact History of All the Writers and Bishops Who Have Had Their Education in the University of Oxford. To Which Are Added the Fasti, or Annals of the Said University.* 5 volumes. London, 1813-1820.

Aureliensis — *Index Aureliensis: Catalogus librorum sedecimo saeculo impressorum.* Baden-Baden, 1965-1982 [incomplete].

Benzing   Josef Benzing. *Lutherbibliographie Verzeichnis der gedruckten Schriften Martin Luthers bis zu dessen Tod.* Baden-Baden, 1966.

Bezzel   Irmgard Bezzel. *Erasmusdrucke des 16. Jahrhunderts in Bayerischen Bibliotheken.* Stuttgart, 1979.

BCI   E. S. Leedham-Green. *Books in Cambridge Inventories: Booklists from Vice-Chancellor's Court Probate Inventories in the Tudor and Stuart Periods.* 2 volumes. Cambridge, 1986.

BL   *General Catalogue of Books Printed to 1955* [in the British Library].

BN   *Catalogue Général des Livres Imprimés de la Bibliothèque Nationale* [Paris].

Boase   C. W. Boase, ed. *Register of the University of Oxford.* Volume 1 (1449-1463; 1505-1571). Oxford, 1885.

Bodleian   *Catalogus librorum impressorum Bibliothecae Bodleianae in Academia Oxoniensi.* 4 volumes. Oxford, 1843-1851.

BRUC   A. B. Emden. *A Biographical Register of the University of Cambridge to 1500.* Cambridge, 1963.

Brunet   Jacques-Charles Brunet. *Manuel du libraire et de l'amateur de livres.* 6 volumes. Paris, 1860-1865 [Reprint 1922] (Supplements, 2 volumes, 1878-1880).

BRUO   A. B. Emden. *A Biographical Register of the University of Oxford to AD 1500.* 3 volumes. Oxford, 1957-1959.

BRUO2   A. B. Emden. *A Biographical Register of the University of Oxford AD 1501 to 1540.* Oxford, 1974.

BSB   *Bayerische Staatsbibliothek alphabetische Katalog 1501-1840.* 60 volumes. Munich, New York, London, Paris, 1987-1990.

BT   Elly Cockx-Indestege and Geneviève Glorieux. *Belgica Typographica 1541-1600. Catalogus librorum impressorum ab anno MDXLI ad annum MDC in regionibus quae nunc Regni Belgarum partes sunt.* Nieuwkoop, 1968.

CBEL	George Watson, editor. *The New Cambridge Bibliography of English Literature [600–1660].* Volume 1. Cambridge, 1974.
Clark	Andrew Clark, ed. *Register of the University of Oxford.* Volume 2. 4 parts (1571–1622). Oxford, 1887–1889.
Clessius	Joannes Clessius. *Unius seculi; eiusque virorum literatorum monumentis tum florentissimi, tum fertilissimi, ab anno Dom. 1500 ad 1602. Nundinarum autumnalium inclusive elenchus consummatissimus librorum.* Frankfurt am Main, 1602.
Cockle	Maurice J. D. Cockle. *A Bibliography of Military Books up to 1642.* Second edition. London, 1957 [Reprint 1978].
Copinger	W. A. Copinger. *Supplement to Hain's Repertorium Bibliographicum* [with supplements]. London, 1895 [–1914] [Reprints 1926 and 1950].
Cranz	F. Edward Cranz. *A Bibliography of Aristotle Editions, 1501–1600.* Second edition, with addenda and revisions by Charles B. Schmitt. Baden-Baden, 1984.
CSPD	*Calendar of State Papers: Domestic Series.*
CSPD, *Addenda–Calendar of State Papers: Domestic Series, Addenda, 1580–1625*	
CTC	*Catalogus Translationum et Commentarium: Medieval and Renaissance Latin Translations and Commentaries.* Eds. Paul Oskar Kristeller, F. Edward Cranz, and Virginia Brown. Volumes 1–7. Washington, D.C., 1960–1992 [incomplete].
DM	T. H. Darlow and H. F. Moule. *Historical Catalogue of the Printed Editions of the Holy Scripture in the Library of the British and Foreign Bible Society.* [English and Non-English] 2 volumes. London, 1903–1911. [See DMH following.]
DMH	T. H. Darlow and H. F. Moule (with revisions by A. S. Herbert). *Historical Catalogue of the Printed Editions of the Holy Scripture in the Library of the British and Foreign Bible Society.* [English; Volume 1 of DM revised] London, 1968.
DNB	*Dictionary of National Biography.*
Durling	Richard J. Durling. "A Chronological Census of Renaissance Editions and Translations of Galen." *Journal of the Warburg and Courtauld Institutes* (1961), 24:230–305.
EUL	*Catalogue of the Printed Books in the Library of the University of Edinburgh.* 3 volumes. Edinburgh, 1918–1923.
Gardy	Frédéric Gardy. *Bibliographie des oeuvres théologiques, littéraires, historiques et juridiques de Théodore de Bèze.* Geneva, 1960.
Goff	F. R. Goff. *Incunabula in American Libraries: A Third Census* [with supplements]. New York, 1973 [Revised 1964 edition].

Greg	W. W. Greg. *A Bibliography of the English Printed Drama to the Restoration*. 4 volumes. London, 1939–1959 [Reprint 1970].
GW	*Gesamtkatalog der Wiegendrucke*. 9 volumes. Leipzig/Stuttgart, 1925–1938, 1968–1991 [incomplete].
Hain	L. Hain. *Repertorium Bibliographicum*. 2 volumes. Stuttgart, 1826–1838, 1891 [Reprints 1948 and 1966].
HC *1509–1558*	S. T. Bindoff, editor. *The House of Commons 1509–1558 (The History of Parliament)*. 3 volumes. London, 1982.
HC *1558–1603*	P. W. Hasler, editor. *The House of Commons 1558–1603 (The History of Parliament)*. 3 volumes. London, 1981.
HMC	*Historical Manuscripts Commission*.
IGI	*Indice generale degli incunaboli della biblioteche d'Italia*. 6 volumes. Rome, 1943–1981 [incomplete].
Jayne	Sears Jayne. *Library Catalogues of the English Renaissance*. Reissue with new preface and notes. Godalming, 1983.
Keen	Ralph Keen. *A Checklist of Melanchthon Imprints Through 1560*. Sixteenth Century Bibliography 27. St. Louis, 1988.
Ker	N. R. Ker. "The Provision of Books," in *The Collegiate University*, edited by James McConica. Volume 3 of *The History of the University of Oxford*, General Editor, T. H. Aston. Oxford, 1986.
Klaiber	Wilbirgis Klaiber. *Katholische Kontroverstheologen und Reformer des 16. Jahrhunderts*. Münster, 1978.
Köhler	W. Köhler. *Bibliographia Brentiana*. Berlin, 1904 [Reprint 1963].
Labarre	Albert Labarre. *Bibliographie du Dictionarium d'Ambrogio Calepino (1502–1779)*. Baden-Baden, 1975.
Madan	Falconer Madan. *Oxford Books: A Bibliography of Printed Works Relating to the University and City of Oxford or Printed or Published There*. 3 volumes. Oxford, 1895–1931 [Reprint 1964].
McConica	James McConica. "Elizabethan Oxford: The Collegiate Society," in *The Collegiate University*, edited by James McConica. Volume 3 of *The History of the University of Oxford*, General Editor, T. H. Aston. Oxford, 1986.
NK	Wouter Nijhoff and M. E. Kronenberg. *Nederlandshe Bibliographie van 1500 tot 1540*. The Hague, 1923–1966.
NLM6	Richard J. Durling. *A Catalogue of Sixteenth Century Printed Books in the National Library of Medicine*. Bethesda, Maryland, 1967.
NUC	*National Union Catalogue. Pre-1956 Imprints*.
OED	*The Oxford English Dictionary*. 20 volumes. Second edition. Prepared by J. A. Simpson and E. S. C. Weiner. Oxford, 1989.

Oates	J. C. T. Oates. *A Catalogue of the Fifteenth-Century Printed Books in the University Library, Cambridge.* Cambridge, 1954.
Ong	Walter J. Ong, S. J. *Ramus and Talon Inventory. A Short-Title Inventory of the Published Works of Peter Ramus (1515–1572) and of Omer Talon (ca. 1510–1562) in Their Original and in Their Variously Altered Forms.* Cambridge, Massachusetts, 1958.
PCC	*Prerogative Court of Canterbury.*
Pell	M. Pellechet and M. L. Polain. *Catalogue général des incunables des bibliothèques publiques de France.* 26 volumes. Lichtenstein, 1970 [Reprint].
Polain	Marie Louis Polain. *Catalogue de livres imprimés au XVe siècle des bibliothèques de Belgique.* 4 volumes [and supplements]. Brussels, 1931–1978.
Proctor	Robert Proctor. *An Index to the Early Printed Books in the British Museum: From the Invention of Printing to the Year MD.* 2 volumes [and supplements]. London, 1898–1906 [several reprints in the 1920s].
RRstc	James J. Murphy. *Renaissance Rhetoric: A Short-Title Catalogue of Works on Rhetorical Theory from the Beginning of Printing to A.D. 1700, with Special Attention to the Holdings of the Bodleian Library, Oxford.* New York and London, 1981.
Shaaber	M. A. Shaaber. *Check-list of Works of British Authors Printed Abroad, in Languages Other Than English, to 1641.* New York, 1975.
Staedtke	Joachim Staedtke. *Heinrich Bullinger Bibliographie.* Volume 1. Zürich, 1972.
STC	A. W. Pollard, G. R. Redgrave, W. A. Jackson, F. S. Ferguson, and Katherine F. Pantzer. *A Short-title Catalogue of Books Printed in England, Scotland, and Ireland and of English Books Printed Abroad, 1475–1640.* Second edition. 3 volumes. London, 1976–1991.
VD16	*Verzeichnis der im deutschen Sprachbereich erschienenen Drucke des XVI. Jahrhunderts.* 19 volumes. Stuttgart, 1983–1992 [incomplete].
VHc	Ferdinand Vander Haeghen. *Bibliographie des oeuvres de Josse Clicthove.* Ghent, 1888.
VHe	Ferdinand Vander Haeghen. *Bibliotheca Erasmiana.* Ghent, 1893 [Reprints in 1961, 1972, and 1990].

Wellcome   *A Catalogue of Printed Books in the Wellcome Historical Medical Library.* Volumes 1–2. London, 1962.
Wing   Donald Wing. *Short-title Catalogue of Books Printed in England, Scotland, Ireland, Wales, and British America and of English Books Printed in Other Countries: 1641–1700.* Revised edition. 3 volumes. New York, 1972–1988.

DEGREES

B.A.	Bachelor of Arts
M.A.	Master of Arts
B.C.L.	Bachelor of Civil Law
B.Cn.L.	Bachelor of Canon Law
B.Gram.	Bachelor of Grammar
B.M.	Bachelor of Medicine
B.Th.	Bachelor of Theology
D.C.L.	Doctor of Civil Law
D.Cn.L.	Doctor of Canon Law
D.U.L.	Doctor of Civil and Canon Law (LL.D.)
D.M.	Doctor of Medicine
D.Th.	Doctor of Theology

Introduction

With this volume, PLRE continues publication of 162 book-lists[1] contained in the inventories taken between 1507 and 1653 under the jurisdiction of the Chancellor of Oxford University (exercised by the Vice-Chancellor), mostly for the purposes of probate. The lists are published in chronological order (see **Order** under *Methodology and Format* below); twenty-six lists, dating from 1570 to 1576, appear in the present volume to bring the total of Oxford lists edited in PLRE to 108 (Volume 2 of PLRE [1993] contains sixty-two lists, and Volume 3 [1994] contains twenty lists). The remaining lists will be published in Volumes 5 through 7. Like all book-lists in this Oxford series, the lists edited here are found in manuscripts in the Oxford University Archives housed in the Bodleian, specifically in the probate records and the Chancellors's Registers. These records have been made available on microfilm by Research Publications under the title *The Social History of Property and Possessions: Part I: Inventories and Wills, Including Renaissance Library Catalogues, from the Bodleian Library, Oxford, 1436–1814* (Reading, England, 1990).

A team of nearly fifty international scholars, working from transcrip-

---

[1] This number differs from the total given in Volume 1; in editing, several lists were identified as printer's stock or as books borrowed from colleges, not personally owned books.

tions of the manuscripts made by Mr. Walter Mitchell, M.A. (sometime Assistant to the Keeper of the University Archives), has been enlisted to edit the 162 lists. By granting PLRE permission to use his transcriptions, a labor of many years, Mr. Mitchell has immeasurably reduced the time required to make this information available to the scholarly community. This professional generosity places the PLRE project and scholars working in the Tudor and early Stuart periods greatly in Mr. Mitchell's debt.

The purpose and three-part design of PLRE has been described in its first volume, to which the reader is referred for details (PLRE, Volume 1, pp. xvi–xviii). In brief, however, Part 1 of PLRE is the published form of annotated book-lists associated with Tudor and early Stuart men and women; PLRE 87–112 are contained in this volume. Part 2 is in electronic form and is a cumulative and more detailed catalogue of those lists and others (Appended, or APND lists) previously published elsewhere. Information from the complete database is available upon request and is provided on a cost basis from the General Editor and from the Editor in the United Kingdom. The publishers are developing a CD-ROM that will contain the entire database. Part 3, the PLRE Cumulative Catalogue, is a series of indices and concordances to the complete PLRE database. This Cumulative Catalogue, which appears near the end of each volume of PLRE, is regularly enlarged and revised to incorporate newly edited book-lists.

Errors and Corrections

Anyone with even a passing acquaintance with early book-lists knows that their fragmentary and too often simply illegible entries make identifying books an extremely difficult task. Further, details of these early books resist uniformity, even when the works are identifiable; yet this information must be uniformly entered into a database to meet the categorical requirements of PLRE's design and purpose. However methodical and careful the labor, providing error-free information under such conditions is more to be wished than realized. Happily, however, the ease with which a database can be corrected promises that any misdirection PLRE may inadvertently provide will be temporary, and will encourage PLRE's users to become part of the scholarly collaboration that has always been central to the project. The editors of PLRE ask, therefore, that errors noted and corrections proposed be forwarded (with supporting evidence for the corrections) to either address found in the Appendix.

Methodology and Format

Identification and Annotation. Identification of items, the annotations, and the bio-bibliographical introductions preceding the book-lists are the work of diverse scholars and reflect their individual research and study. But collaboration, intending to provide a reasonable uniformity, is routine at all editorial stages of the PLRE project. Consistency is necessary to avoid offering confusing information when the results of research conducted by individual scholars are combined; it is also required to meet the practical demands of a searchable database. For example, editorial consultation would discourage identifying a late sixteenth-century manuscript entry of *Elucidarius poeticus* as the school text written by Johann Gast and issued, apparently, in a single edition (1544) to the disregard of the widely published encyclopedic work of the same name by Hermann Torrentinus, appearing as it did in at least a dozen editions before 1600. If, however, a Contributing Editor has good reason to question whether such an entry represents the Torrentinus title, the Gast work, or Robert Estienne's book, another popular work of that same name, the Torrentinus identification would carry one of the standard PLRE qualifying terms, *probable* or *perhaps*. Understandably, annotations to such an item may also vary from one Contributing Editor to another.

Among the most troublesome entries to identify with consistency and uniformity are the appearances, by name only, of various widely published authors such as Virgil, Quintilian, Horace, Terence, Sallust, Lucian, and Homer. On occasion, context and supplementary information (e.g., *cum commento*) will help to identify these entries as *Works*, but generally editors choose to qualify such items with *probable* or *perhaps* if they do not list them as *Unidentified*. Similarly, when an entry consists of the name of an author popularly associated with one particular title, that work is assumed in the absence of a clear connection to one of his less well-known works, with a qualification often attached. Thus, an entry of "Agostino Dati" will usually result in an identification of *Elegantiolae*, and an entry of "Theodorus, *Gaza*" will normally result in an identification of *Institutiones grammaticae*, both usually qualified. Such differences as may appear in identifications and commentary, then, reflect the regard that PLRE has for reasonable disagreement among scholars, particularly in an area of research where the primary material is so often fragmentary and imprecise.

Order. The book-lists are presented in chronological order by year of the owner's death, or, if the date of death is unknown, by year of an owner's will if extant, and then alphabetically within each year. In some cases, however, the dates of death and a will are unknown; in others, documents and biographical sources disagree about the dates; and in still others, such dates are irrelevant (e.g., an inventory of books may have been compiled for purposes other than evaluating an owner's estate, with the owner dying years later). In these cases, other information, such as the date of the inventory, is used to determine the place of a book-list in PLRE order. An explanation of the determining date is parenthetically appended to each owner's name in the Table of Contents. For more complete information about the owners' dates of deaths, wills, and inventories, readers are directed to the individual introductions and to the PLRE database.

Introduction. Each book-list is preceded by an introductory essay treating biographical and bibliographical matters relating to the owner and the collection. The introduction is not intended to provide a complete analysis of the book-list, and even less a full study of the owner's life. Except where two dates are provided (e.g., 25 February 1587/88), all dates are given in new style.

Names of owners have been regularized according to modern forms with, in many cases, variant spellings provided. Such alternate forms are derived from published sources such as BRUO, BRUO2, and *Alumni Oxonienses*; whenever the form given in BRUO or BRUO2 (the standard authorities on members of Oxford University to 1540) differs from the adopted PLRE form, it is listed first among the variants and identified. The name of the owner at the head of the introduction is followed by: the owner's profession and appropriate academic degrees (if any), the kind of source the list of books is taken from (inventory, receipt, will, etc.), and the date of that book-list.

For nearly all of these Oxford men happening to die in residence at whatever stage of their academic career, PLRE has chosen to use the generic term "scholar" to indicate their presumed avocations at the time of death and to distinguish graduates still at the University from those who had gone out into the world. Most of them would have been at least in minor orders, and a good many of them supported in their studies by the revenue of one or more benefices, but they are not here designated "clerics" except where there is some evidence that they were actively serving a cure. (Similarly, medical graduates are not designated "physician" in the absence of evidence for their actually having practiced as such.) Instead their status is indicated either by the term "student," for those who had not yet graduated, or by their degree or degrees. A Doctor of Theology who had pursued the conventional course would previously have graduated B.A., M.A., and B.Th. The dates, and any other details, of these earlier degrees will, when documented, be found in the introductions to each list, but in the headings the senior degree alone will usually be found. Two degrees are given where neither is significantly senior to the other (as in the case of a Doctor of both Civil and Canon Law), where more than one senior Faculty is involved (as in the case of a theologian having also qualified in Canon Law), or when holding certain degrees together indicates the exercise of an option (it was, for example, possible to proceed to medical degrees either via the arts course or not: where a Bachelor of Medicine had previously graduated M.A., both degrees are shown).

Classmarks and Transcriptions. The Oxford University Archives classmark of the document containing the book-list and the source of any previously published transcriptions of the list are appended to the introduction.

Reference List. Placed between the introduction and the annotated entries and serving both, a reference list provides a bibliography of works cited in each (except for the sources found in the Common Abbreviations). The form used in the reference list is the Author-Date System of the *Chicago Manual of Style*, 13th ed., 1982, 399–435.

The List of Books. The book-list is presented, with clarifying emendations, as it appears in the manuscript. Each entry is preceded by its assigned PLRE Number.

Entries. Each entry is composed of some or all of the following:[2]

> **PLRE Number Book-list entry**
> Name of author (alternative name of author). *Title of work*. Other contributors. Place of publication: stationer(s), date or range of dates.
> STC status. Annotations. Language(s) of book. Cost or appraised value and date of same. Current location of the book.[2]

---

[2] PLRE has attempted to avoid the use of signs and symbols; this design is most prominently seen in the use of *perhaps* and *probable* (or *probably*) to convey degrees of doubt, and of commonly employed abbreviations, such as *c.* and *et seq.*

PLRE Number. A PLRE Number is always composed of at least two numbers separated by a period. The number preceding the period identifies the place of the book-list within the PLRE catalogue, and the number following the period identifies the individual entries within that book-list. Thus, the forty-seventh item in the third book-list published in PLRE is assigned *3.47*. A PLRE Number that carries an extension (beginning with a colon) identifies an entry in the book-list that represents two or more works. If published separately, the works are assigned numeric extensions (e.g., *3.48:1* and *3.48:2*); if published together in one volume, they are assigned letters (e.g., *3.49:A* and *3.49:B*). Entries that contain unidentified multiple works are assigned an appropriate range extension (e.g., *3.50:1-4* would be used to identify "four bookes of verse"). If the number of works listed is unknown, the extension given is "multiple" (e.g., *3.51 multiple* would be used to identify "divers small bookes"). PLRE numbers in APND lists are preceded by *Ad*, as in *Ad4.36*.

Book-list entry. Within certain limits, book-lists are transcribed to reproduce as faithfully as possible the entries as they appear in the manuscript. The letters *u/v* and *i/j* are regularized and modernized, and thorn is transcribed *th*. Readily identifiable contractions and abbreviations are not altered (e.g., *agt, Mr,* and *wch*), but the less common ones, along with unusual or ambiguous spellings, are followed by an emendation placed in square brackets (e.g., *The trades inclease* is transcribed as *The trades inclease* [*increase*]). Damaged or otherwise illegible portions of the manuscript are treated similarly (e.g., *fil us* [to represent a hole between the *l* and the *u* in the manuscript] is transcribed as *fil*us* [*filius*]). Where an item is recorded as an object of bequest in a Latin will, its accusative form is retained.

Name of author (alternative name of author). Names are STC forms; for names not appearing in the STC, forms are taken from a list of Uniform Names developed by PLRE. Uniformity, as well as ease of recognition, is the goal of PLRE in establishing names. But 1) in cases where the established name differs from the form in the entry and may cause confusion for the user, and 2) in cases where two different forms make virtually equal claims for recognition among scholars, parenthetical alternative forms are given. Examples: *Nicolas Des Gallars* is followed by *(Nicolaus Salicetus), John Holywood* by *(Joannes Sacrobosco),* and *Nicolaus Tudeschis* by *(Panormitanus).*

On occasion, the name of an editor will appear in this place, his role appropriately identified. *Unidentified* is used when the author cannot be identified from the entry (which is different from an identified work having been published anonymously).

Title of work. The title of a work (short title, usually terminating with the first full stop) is entered when known. Often, however, the precise title is impossible to determine from the truncated and abbreviated entries commonly found in early book-lists. Further, the standard bibliographical sources (e.g., BL, Goff, Adams), on which Contributing Editors usually depend for determining titles, frequently modify the actual titles. The main principle here, then, must be to identify the *work* rather than a particular title, especially when a work has gone through several editions with varied titles. As with names, uniformity is essential if titles in the PLRE database are to be selected for analysis. Accordingly, a Uniform Titles list has been developed by PLRE along the following principles: 1) a work that exists in a single edition is identified by its short title; 2) a work that exists in two or more editions that bear only slightly varying titles is identified by one of these titles; 3) a work that exists in several editions with widely varied titles is identified by an artificial title, a) in a construction to reflect one or more of the existing titles, but b) often in a construction designed to describe the work without any attempt to simulate a title. Artificial titles are always enclosed in square brackets. Livy's [*Historiae Romanae decades*] is an example of the first kind of artificial title mentioned above (3a), and [*Aristotle–Ethica: commentary*] by Walter Burley is an example of the latter (3b). *Unidentified* is provided when the precise work represented by the entry cannot be determined.

Other contributors. The names of translators, editors, compilers, and illustrators (their contributions appropriately described) are found here. The forms used follow the same principles described in the section *Name of author* above.

Place of publication. If an entry is identified as a single edition of a single work, the city of publication is provided, regularized and modernized. If the entry represents a work of more than one edition printed in more than one city, one of three general locations is provided: *Britain* (if the identified printing houses were all in the British Isles), *Continent* (if the identified printing houses were all located on the Continent), and *Britain or Continent* (if editions were known to have been issued from different presses located in the British Isles and on the Continent). If a work is completely unidentified, the phrase *Place unknown* is used; where the place of publication of an identified book is unknown, the phrase *Place not given* is used. For non-extant manuscripts, the phrase used is *Provenance unknown* in accordance with the generally less precise geographical origins of most surviving manuscripts. The phrase should not be interpreted as relating to previous ownership.

Stationer(s). When an entry represents a specific, identifiable edition, every stationer involved in the publication of the book (printer, publisher, bookseller) is supplied. But since Contributing Editors generally rely upon bibliographical sources rather than a copy of the identified book for this information, the forms of presentation differ. Accordingly, varied forms will be found, such as: "G. Eld for L. Lisle" and "per Johannem Barbier, expensis Dionisii Roce," but also the non-distinguishing "George Bishop, Ralph Newberie, and Robert Barker"; the same stationer will appear in various constructions: "ap. J. Dayum," but elsewhere "John Day" and "J. Daye." All stationers, however, are accessible by uniform names in the database.

When a work is identified as having been published in a single city, but the precise edition of several possibilities issued by different printing houses cannot be determined, the phrase *different houses* is given. If the place of publication is identified as *Britain, Continent,* or *Britain or Continent*—signifying the impossibility of determining a precise place of publication—the impossibility of determining the stationer obviously follows and this section is left blank. *Stationer unknown* is used when a work is completely unidentified or when the printer, publisher, or bookseller for a known book has not been identified by bibliographers.

Date or range of dates. If a precise date of publication is known, it is provided. If two or more editions of different dates are possibilities, either a range of dates (given as, for example, *1562–1573*) or the phrase *date indeterminable* is provided. NOTE: except for works listed in the STC and in Shaaber (which together offer for English authors a practical comprehensiveness if not absolute inclusiveness) date ranges must be understood to be at best a guide. The range represents the limit known to the Contributing Editor who has consulted a number of bibliographical sources, but the chance that at least one earlier or later edition exists unknown to the Contributing Editor remains a possibility. The same reservation also applies to works presented as a sole edition, and doubts, therefore, must be harbored even when a single date is given. A work, however, that is known to have gone through several editions over several years understandably invites questions about any attempt to assign a date range with certainty (excepting the few authors for whom comprehensive censuses exist). Such uncertainty is particularly a problem with authors who were widely published during this period (Aristotle, Saint Augustine, Cicero, Duns, *Scotus*, Peter Lombard, and Virgil, to name but a few).

STC status. A variety of self-explanatory phrases appear in this section, but the primary purpose of this information is to identify the work represented as an STC (or Wing) book. When a work is *known* to have been published both in England and on the Continent, and the edition cannot be identified, its STC (or Wing) number and its non-STC status are both cited. If, however, an entry is unidentified, nothing can be determined about its place of publication; therefore, the phrase *STC/non-STC status unknown* is used. When a work issued in more than one edition is identified as an STC (or Wing) book, but the precise edition cannot be determined, only the first possible STC (or Wing) number is given, and *et seq.* is appended.

Here also is indicated whether an entry is considered to be something other than a printed book, e.g., a manuscript or a book of blank leaves intended for use as a notebook. An entry is assumed to be a printed book unless clear evidence is provided to the contrary (the use of terms and phrases such as *scriptus, books of parchment, written sermons*, or *a book of clean paper*).

Annotations. Here Contributing Editors furnish whatever information they believe will be useful and instructive in connection with the entry. All citations are abbreviated according to the *Chicago Manual of Style*'s Author-Date System (Chapter 15); full bibliographical sources are found in the Common Abbreviations and in the Reference Lists appended to the individual introductions to book-lists.

Language(s). The language (or languages) of the book is given here. If multiple, the languages are listed, without punctuation, in alphabetical order and in the order of probability. Thus, *English Greek Latin* will be found if all are known to have been employed, but *Latin Greek (probable) English (perhaps)* when doubts of varying degrees exist. Sometimes the word "or," expressing further doubt about which language was employed, is entered. Thus, *English (probable) or Latin (perhaps)* will be found.

Cost or appraised value and date of same. Either 1) the amount the owner paid for the book represented or 2) its appraised value as estimated by the compiler of the book-list is furnished here; the date when the amount was paid or when the appraisal was made is usually limited to a year, which always precedes the day and month when they are given.

Current location of the book. This information is restricted to the physical book cited in the book-list and should not be misunderstood to identify locations of other copies of the book. Whenever possible, the repositories are cited as they appear in the STC (1:xlix–liii), identified by name, not by symbol.

PRIVATE LIBRARIES IN RENAISSANCE ENGLAND

A Collection and Catalogue of Tudor and Early Stuart Book-Lists

Volume IV

PLRE 87–112

Thomas Morgan. Scholar (student): Inventory. 1570

W. P. GRIFFITH

We cannot be at all certain as to the identity of Thomas Morgan of Gloucester Hall or of his status there. It is possible, but unlikely, that he may previously have been an unattached student. One Thomas Morgans [*sic*] was recorded in 1562 as being a student residing in the town under the supervision of William Boldman of St. Peter Le Bailey. Unfortunately, the university matriculation registers had still not been placed on a sound footing by the time of Morgan's inventory, and the other university records seem silent about him too. Moreover, no useful details survive from Gloucester Hall sources.

From his name, one would expect that Morgan was of Welsh origins, perhaps from South Wales like his namesakes who matriculated at Oxford during the mid-1570s. It was certainly the case that the newly formed Gloucester Hall drew its students from the west of England and the Welsh borders. Its principal for most of the 1560s, William Stock, was a Herefordshire man. In later years, Welsh students were to form between ten and fifteen percent of the registered admissions. At this time the hall was reputed to be a hotbed of recusants, and, its not being clear that the inventory was drawn up on decease, possibly Thomas Morgan was one of those who left either to escape persecution or, at least, to follow his faith in a safer environment (see Loach 1986, 381–82, as well as PLRE 81, George and Simon Digby; PLRE 90, Tichborne; PLRE 102, William Smallwood; PLRE 105, Richard Lanham; and PLRE 106, Walter Dyllam). The surname Morgan is more closely associated with the south of Wales than anywhere else, and among the most illustrious families who bore this name in the sixteenth century was the Morgan family of Pencoed, Monmouthshire, who, with their many cadet lines, were very influential. If this student were of a gentry background, then the genealogical evidence offers several possibilities. Among the most plausible are that Thomas Morgan was the second son of Henry Morgan of Gwernyclepa, Monmouthshire, or the fourth son of Harri Morgan of Muddlescombe, Carmarthenshire (see Clark 1886, 329; Dwnn 1841, 219). However, there is nothing in Morgan's slender inventory to indicate that he came from a particularly well-off background. It is just as likely that, like his namesakes in 1575, he was of modest means, one of several such people in those years who were sent to Oxford to acquire a smattering of higher learning in the hope of improving slightly the quality of the clergy within the Elizabethan Church in Wales. A Thomas Morgan became rector of Panteg, Monmouthshire on 22 June 1570, but no further details of him survive (Bradney 1923, 121).

The contents of his very small book-list indicate that Morgan was very much an undergraduate, following the religious devotions with his primer and improving his Latin style through the study of Erasmus. The *Dialogues* of Lucian (in Latin very probably) are by far the most interesting item, indicating that the lively humanist interest in this author had reached the universities.

Oxford University Archives, Bodleian Library: Hyp.B.16.

§

Bradney, Joseph Alfred. 1923. *A History of Monmouthshire from the Coming of the Normans into Wales Down to the Present Time.* Vol. 3, Pt. 2. London: Mitchell Hughes and Clarke.

Dwnn, Lewys. 1841. *Heraldic Visitations of Wales and Part of the Marches,* ed. S. R. Meyrick. Vol. 1. Llandovery: William Rees.

Clark, George Thomas. 1886. *Limbus patrum Morganiae et Glamorganiae, Being the Genealogies of the Older Families of the Lordships of Morgan and Glamorgan.* London: Wyman and Sons.

Loach, Jennifer. 1986. "Reformation Controversies," in *The Collegiate University,* edited by James McConica. Vol. 3 of *The History of the University of Oxford,* gen. ed., T.H. Aston. Oxford: Oxford Univ. Press, pp. 363-96.

§

87.1	copia verborum	
87.2	Colloquium erasmi	
87.3	dialogi Luciani	
87.4	a englyshe prer [primer]	

§

87.1 copia verborum
Desiderius Erasmus. *De duplici copia verborum ac rerum*. Britain or Continent: date indeterminable.
STC 10471.4 *et seq.* and non-STC. The date-range for STC is 1528–1569. *Language(s)*: Latin. Appraised at 6d in 1570.

87.2 Colloquium erasmi
Desiderius Erasmus. *Colloquia*. Britain or Continent: date indeterminable.
STC 10450.6 *et seq.* and non-STC. Given the greater number of Continental editions, it is likely that this item was published abroad. *Language(s)*: Latin. Appraised at 6d in 1570.

87.3 dialogi Luciani
Lucian, *of Samosata*. Probably [*Dialogues–Selected*]. Britain or Continent: date indeterminable.
STC 16891 *et seq.* and non-STC. Conceivably the *Works*, but the appraisal seems low. Given that Erasmus features in 87.1 and 87.2, this may be his edition. *Language(s)*: Latin Greek (perhaps). Appraised at 1d in 1570.

87.4 a englyshe prer [primer]
[*Liturgies–Latin Rite–Hours and Primers–Salisbury and Reformed*]. Britain: date indeterminable.
STC 15986 *et seq.* From 1534. Perhaps the King's Primer (STC 16034), which was in English and Latin. Note also the existence of a volume of private meditations, *A prymmer or boke of private prayer* (STC 20373 *et seq.*). *Language(s)*: English Latin (perhaps). Appraised at one farthing in 1570.

William Stocker. Scholar (M.A.): Inventory. c. 1570

E. S. LEEDHAM-GREEN and ALAIN A. WIJFFELS

William Stocker, Master of Arts and late commoner in Broadgates Hall (later to evolve into Pembroke College), is recorded only as the owner of the goods inventoried, goods which, apart from his books, comprise only a rather fine bed, three tables (one of them large), two chests, two chairs, the hangings of his chamber and, unusually, of his study, and a black leather mail. The absence from the list of any of the usual smaller items may, like the absence of any valuations, be a reflection merely of the compilers' haste. On the other hand, it is possible that Stocker had not died but simply left, covertly or otherwise, and had failed to make arrangements for the disposal of his bulkier possessions.

His books consist very largely of standard texts in civil and canon law, with a few residual natural philosophy texts from his M.A. course (88.10, 88.12, 88.16, 88.18, and 88.21), and a small number of theology texts (88.8, 88.19, 88.20, 88.22, and 88.23), two of them Scotist (88.19-20).

Oxford University Archives, Bodleian Library: Hyp.B.18.

§

88.1	the course of the cannon lawe, contaynynge iii bookes cum glossa
88.2	Hebereda super Clementinis
88.3	Dominicus super Sexto libro Decretalium
88.4	Consilia Alexandri de Torphates
88.5	Tabula Prepositi super 4° Decretalium
88.6	Bartholus super 1a parte Digesti novi
88.7	Petrus Egidius, Cath'
88.8	Aurelius Augustinus
88.9	Ambrosius Calepinus

88.10	Questiones Johannis Canonici super 8o libris Phisicorum
88.11	** Calepinus
88.12	Introductio in libros Phisicorum
88.13	Codex Justiniani cum glossa
88.14	Bartholus super tribus libris Codicis
88.15	Autentica cum glossa
88.16	Introductio in libros Phisicorum
88.17	Gaget*nus
88.18	Bricott super Phisica
88.19	a old Duns of distiches and questions
88.20	Scotus super lo libro Sentenciarum
88.21	Albertus de celo et mundo
88.22	Scrutinium Scripturarum
88.23	Speculum Humane Vite ad Paulum Pontificem

§

88.1 the course of the cannon lawe, contaynynge iii bookes cum glossa
Corpus juris canonici. Continent: date indeterminable.
Language(s): Latin.

88.2 Hebereda super Clementinis
Unidentified. [*Clementines: commentary*]. (*Corpus juris canonici*). Continent: date indeterminable.
The author's name is apparently corrupt. Perhaps Francesco Zabarella, Cardinal. *Language(s)*: Latin.

88.3 Dominicus super Sexto libro Decretalium
Dominicus à Sancto Geminiano. [*Decretales: commentary*]. (*Corpus juris canonici*). Continent: date indeterminable.
Language(s): Latin.

88.4 Consilia Alexandri de Torphates
Unidentified. Continent (probable): date indeterminable.
Almost certainly not an STC book. If on law, perhaps a corrupt form of Alessandro Tartagni, *Consilia*. *Language(s)*: Latin.

88.5 Tabula Prepositi super 4° Decretalium
Joannes Antonius de Sancto Georgio (Prepositus Alexandrinus). [*Decretum: commentary*]. Continent: date indeterminable.
The entry is probably taken from the heading to the index (*tabula*) preceding, in this copy, the actual work: the *Commentari super quarto decretalium*, a commentary on the fourth book of the *Liber Extra*. But this could be a detached quire. *Language(s)*: Latin.

88.6 Bartholus super 1a parte Digesti novi

Bartolus, *de Saxoferrato*. [*Digestum novum (Part 1): commentary*]. (*Corpus juris civilis*). Continent: date indeterminable.
Language(s): Latin.

88.7 Petrus Egidius, Cath'

Peter Gilles (Petrus Aegidius). Unidentified. Continent: date indeterminable.

Gilles, the friend of Erasmus, was the author of a *Summa sive argumenta legum diversorum imperatorum* which might, perhaps, have been described as a "Catena" and would not be out of place in this collection. The entry might, on the other hand, indicate his *Threnodia sive lugubris Cantio, in funus Imperatoris Caesaris Dominis Maximiliani*. *Language(s)*: Latin.

88.8 Aurelius Augustinus

Augustine, *Saint*. Unidentified. Continent: date indeterminable.
Language(s): Latin.

88.9 Ambrosius Calepinus

Ambrogio Calepino. *Dictionarium*. Continent: 1502–1569.

Some editions contained vernacular languages by the date of this inventory. See also 88.11. *Language(s)*: Greek Latin.

88.10 Questiones Johannis Canonici super 8o libris Phisicorum

Joannes, *Canonicus*. [*Aristotle–Physica: commentary*]. Continent: 1475–1520.
Language(s): Latin.

88.11 ** Calepinus

Ambrogio Calepino. *Dictionarium*. Continent: 1502–1569.

Some editions contained vernacular languages by the date of this inventory. See also 88.9. *Language(s)*: Greek Latin.

88.12 Introductio in libros Phisicorum

Unidentified. [*Aristotle–Physica: commentary*]. Continent: date indeterminable.

See also 88.16. *Language(s)*: Latin.

88.13 Codex Justiniani cum glossa

Justinian I. *Codex*. (*Corpus juris civilis*). Continent: date indeterminable.
Gloss by Franciscus Accursius. *Language(s)*: Latin.

88.14 Bartholus super tribus libris Codicis

Probably Bartolus, *de Saxoferrato*. [*Codex: commentary* (part)]. Continent: date indeterminable.

On the last three books of the *Codex*, known through early modern editions as a separate collection: "tres libri." *Language(s)*: Latin.

88.15 Autentica cum glossa
Justinian I. *Novellae constitutiones. (Corpus juris civilis)*. Continent: date indeterminable.

The reading might rather be "Autenticum." *Language(s)*: Latin.

88.16 Introductio in libros Phisicorum
Unidentified. [*Aristotle–Physica: commentary*]. Continent: date indeterminable.

See also 88.12. *Language(s)*: Latin.

88.17 Gaget*nus
Gaeitanus, *de Thienis*. Unidentified. Continent: date indeterminable.

Perhaps his commentary on Aristotle's *Physica*. See preceding and following, as well as 88.10 and 88.12. Another possibility is his commentary on Aristotle's *De caelo*; see 88.21. *Language(s)*: Latin.

88.18 Bricott super Phisica
Thomas Bricot. [*Aristotle–Physica: commentary*]. Continent: date indeterminable.

Language(s): Latin.

88.19 a old Duns of distiches and questions
John Duns, *Scotus*. Unidentified. Continent: date indeterminable.

Perhaps one of the epitomes of the *Quaestiones quodlibetales* such as the *Questiones abbreviate* or Gulielmus Gorris's *Scotus pauperum*, but some version of, for example, the *quaestiones* on Aristotle's *Logica* cannot be ruled out. *Language(s)*: Latin.

88.20 Scotus super 1o libro Sentenciarum
John Duns, *Scotus*. [*Sentences I: commentary*]. Continent: date indeterminable. *Language(s)*: Latin.

88.21 Albertus de celo et mundo
Unidentified. [*Aristotle–De caelo: commentary*]. Continent: date indeterminable.

Either Albertus Magnus or Albertus, *de Saxonia*. *Language(s)*: Latin.

88.22 Scrutinium Scripturarum
Paulus, *de Sancta Maria*. *Scrutinium scripturarum*. Continent: date indeterminable.

Language(s): Latin.

88.23 Speculum Humane Vite ad Paulum Pontificem

Rodericus Sanctius. *Speculum vite humane.* Continent: date indeterminable.

Several editions carry the name of the dedicatee, Pope Paul II, in a prominent place on the title page. *Language(s)*: Latin.

Thomas Thornbury. Scholar (probably student): Probate Inventory. 1570

J. S. CRAIG

Little has survived to shed any light upon Thomas Thornbury of Magdalen Hall, who, when he died in 1570, left a tiny collection of typical student texts. He may have been related to one William Thornbury of Buckinghamshire who matriculated at Magdalen Hall in 1606 (*Alumni Oxonienses*, 4:1479).

Oxford University Archives, Bodleian Library: Hyp.B.19.

§

89.1   a short dixonarie
89.2   epitome Colloquiorum
89.3   theodorus gasus
89.4   castigaciones Rivii
89.5   epistole ciceronis

§

89.1 a short dixonarie
   John Withals. Probably *A shorte dictionarie for yonge begynners*. London: (different houses), 1553–1568.
   STC 25874 *et seq. Language(s)*: English Latin. Appraised at 1d in 1570.

89.2 epitome Colloquiorum
   Desiderius Erasmus. [*Colloquia–Epitome*]. Britain or Continent: date indeterminable.
   STC 10461 and non-STC. *Language(s)*: Latin. Appraised at 1d in 1570.

89.3 theodorus gasus
Theodorus, *Gaza*. Probably [*Institutiones grammaticae*]. Continent: date indeterminable.
Language(s): Latin. Appraised at 2d in 1570.

89.4 castigaciones Rivii
Joannes Rivius. *Castigationes plurimorum ex Terentio locorum*. Continent: 1532–1536.
Language(s): Latin. Appraised at 4d in 1570.

89.5 epistole ciceronis
Marcus Tullius Cicero. [*Selected works–Epistolae*]. Continent: date indeterminable.
Perhaps, however, his repeatedly printed *Epistolae ad familiares*. *Language(s)*: Latin. Appraised at 1d in 1570.

Tichborne. Scholar (probably B.C.L.): Inventory. 1570 (partly 1569)

E. S. LEEDHAM-GREEN and ALAIN A. WIJFFELS

"Mr Tycheborne, Gloucester Hall" is the bald appellation of the owner of the books listed below. Two inventories of them were drawn up, one on 4 November 1569 and the other on 10 October 1570; neither claims to be an inventory on decease and, indeed, the earlier plainly states that it is an inventory of goods arrested, presumably because Tichborne had removed himself without leaving either a forwarding address or any indication that he intended to return. We recall that such behavior was a peculiarly common trait among the inmates of Gloucester Hall (see PLRE 81, George and Simon Digby; PLRE 87, Thomas Morgan; PLRE 102, William Smallwood; PLRE 105, Richard Lanham; and PLRE 106, Walter Dyllam).

It is very tempting indeed, however, to identify this "M*aste*r Tychborne," sojourning at so familiar a staging post for Catholic Europe, with the Edward Tichborne, who came up to New College from St. Peter's, Winchester, and was a fellow there from 1556 to 1566 before proceeding Bachelor of Civil Law on 4 June 1567. The hypothesis gains strength when it is recalled that from New College there fled to the Low Countries between 1558 and 1560 Nicholas Sanders, John Rastell, Thomas Stapleton and John Fowler (Buxton and Williams 1979, p. 49). On the other hand, it is well to remember that many college statutes made little or no allowance for the study of law so that migration to a hall was a frequent expedient of academic lawyers (Barton 1986, 278, n. 3).

The two lists, of 1569 and 1570, were drawn up independently with the books in a different order and differently identified. The great majority of them appear in both lists. As neither list pretends to include all Tichborne's goods—both contain books only—it cannot be assumed either that those occurring only in 1569 had been disposed of by 1570 or that those occurring only in the 1570 list had been acquired since 1569. Since a single *terminus ad quem* was required when allotting Tichborne to his place in the chronological sequence, we have, therefore, chosen 1570. The 1569 list bears no appraisals, presumably because at that date it had not yet been decided that the books were to be disposed of by sale; its compiler, however, was the more careful of the two in describing the books. We have, accordingly, used the 1569 list as the basis for the list below, borrowing the valuations from the 1570 list and inserting the 1570 version of the title in the annotations.

Tichborne's books display a serious pursuit of law, especially civil law, enlivened by an enjoyment of classical literature, including poetry (90.31, 90.42, 90.48, 90.58, 90.65, and 90.70) and the ancient historians (90.14, 90.34, 90.71, and perhaps 90.17). He had also a scattering of theological texts along with more elementary texts (90.25 and 90.79), which he might have used for teaching. His texts in rhetoric (90.19, 90.45, and 90.66) may be of the same status—remnants of earlier studies or tools for teaching, or may represent the proper avocation of a practicing lawyer.

Oxford University Archives, Bodleian Library: Hyp.B.19.

§

Barton, John. 1986. "The Faculty of Law," in *The Collegiate University*, ed. James McConica. Vol. 3 of *The History of the University of Oxford*, gen. ed., T.H. Aston. Oxford: Oxford Univ. Press.

Buxton, John, and Penry Williams, eds. 1979. *New College, Oxford, 1379–1979*. Oxford: Oxford Univ. Press.

§

90.1	Instituciones Juris
90.2	digestum novum de tortis
90.3	barnardus super 6to libro decretalium
90.4	Instituciones Calvini
90.5	4a pars Anthonii
90.6	Summa Angelica
90.7	pandectarum liber vicesimus
90.8	pandectarum libri quinquaginta
90.9	2a pars Rapsodie historiarum
90.10	petrus antesignanus
90.11	regule cum suis ampliationibus
90.12	practica doctoris gwidonis pape
90.13	Tullius de natura deorum
90.14	plutarcus
90.15	etimologiarum divisionum expositiones juris

90.16	2a pars decretalium
90.17	berrocius
90.18	a greke boke
90.19	Colloquium Erasmi
90.20	digestorum seu pandectarum tricessimus
90.21	Elenchus questionum sacrarum
90.22	loci Juris communes
90.23	a grek boke
90.24	leonis augutini constitutiones
90.25	dialectica Joanis Cesarii
90.26	divi aurelii augustini
90.27	a paper boke written
90.28	assertionis lutheranae confutatio
90.29	decretalium epistolarum Gregorii pape
90.30	Codicis domini justiniani principis
90.31	horatius flachus
90.32	novellarum constitutionum domini Justiniani
90.33	codicis domini Justiniani Principis
90.34	suetonius
90.35	natura brevium In frenche
90.36	Petri Ravennatis
90.37	Joachimi Hoperi Phrysii Jureconsulti
90.38	andreae dominici flocci florentini
90.39	loci argumentorum
90.40	the latin Psalmes in myter
90.41	plutarchus
90.42	Plautus
90.43	decretorum 2a pars causa 33
90.44	flores omnium pene doctorum
90.45	marci tulii ciceronis de oratore
90.46	sextus decretalium
90.47	cornelius
90.48	ovidius de tristibus
90.49	digestorum seu pandectarum pars 7a
90.50	digestorum seu pandectarum pars 5a
90.51	digestorum seu pandectarum pars 2a
90.52	digestorum seu pandectarum pars 6a
90.53	boetius de philosophie
90.54	Institutiones juris domini Justiniani
90.55	a paper boke
90.56	compendium Clementis romani pontificis de rebus gestis peregrinationibus et predicationibus Sancti petri
90.57	bartramus de corpore et Sanguine domini
90.58	pithagorae carmina aurea. phocilidae poema admonitorium. theognidis Gnomologia. Coluthi helenae raptus. Triphiodori de

	excidio troiae. omnia Grecolatina in uno volumine expressa
90.59	3a pars summae Antonini
90.60	commentaria Alceati de summa trinitate de sacrosancta ecclesia
90.61	responsa sive consilia nicholae Eurardi
90.62	practica et theorica causarum criminalium Jacobi de novello
90.63	flores collecti per Rowlandinum Bononiensem Juris professorem
90.64	quinquaginta libri digestorum seu pandectarum
90.65	flores poetarum
90.66	demosthenis oratio contra Aeschinem Grece
90.67	interpretatio Erasmi in psalmum lxxxv
90.68	Joachimi Hopperi in libros pandectarum dispositio
90.69	tabellionum libri duo
90.70	dictionarium poeticum
90.71	herodianus Grecolatine
90.72	liber de diversis regulis Juris cum interpretatione francisci Jammesii textoris
90.73	decretales epistolae a Gregorio 9o pontifice collectae
90.74	legum procheiron collectum per constantinum harmenopulam
90.75	Sextus decretalium per bonifacium octavum pontificem
90.76	institutionum juris canonici libri quatuor
90.77	a paper booke
90.78	progimnasmata fori
90.79	Grecae literaturae dragmata
90.80	commentarii Stephani Bodei in institutiones
90.81	decretalium epistolarum Gregorii liber tertius
90.82	a little greke booke
90.83	decreta scriptorum ecclesiasticorum conciliorum et romanorum pontificum
90.84	libellus de vera deo inserviendi methodo
90.85	institutiones Justiniani
90.86	Jus canonicum 5 voluminibus
90.87	chrisostomus de modo orando
90.88	olfaricius
90.89	nemesius de natura hominis
90.90	marcus tullius de pho..a le..a [philosophia?]
90.91	Responsio demissa
90.92:1-6	Six bookes of the text of the civill law worth xvi d. a pece
90.93	Baldwinus in institutiones

§

90.1 Instituciones Juris

Justinian I. *Institutiones*. (*Corpus juris civilis*). Continent: date indeterminable. Taken to correspond with *Instituciones Juris Justiniani* (1570:9), although it might rather be the *Instituciones in parvo volumine* (1570:56), appraised at 2d, which is here arbitrarily taken as representing 90.85 below. See also 90.54. *Language(s)*: Greek Latin. Appraised at 16d in 1570.

90.2 digestum novum de tortis
Justinian I. *Digestum novum. (Corpus juris civilis).* Venice: Baptista de Tortis, 1498-1499.

See Hain 9595-96 and Goff J572-73. Corresponds with 1570:2, *digestum novum de tortis*. *Language(s)*: Latin. Appraised at 2s 6d in 1570.

90.3 barnardus super 6to libro decretalium
Unidentified. Continent: date indeterminable.

Corresponds with 1570:1, *Barnardus super 6tum decretalium*. Bernardus, *Compostellanus*, Junior, published lectures on the first book of the *Decretales*, and Bernardus Bottonus (*Parmensis*) wrote on the first five books in *Casus longi super quinque libros decretalium*; no commentary on the *Sextus liber* has been found attributed to either of them or to any other "Bernardus." *Language(s)*: Latin. Appraised at 3s 4d in 1570.

90.4 Instituciones Calvini
Jean Calvin. *Institutio Christianae religionis*. Continent: date indeterminable.

Not appraised. Not listed in 1570. *Language(s)*: Latin.

90.5 4a pars Anthonii
Antoninus, *Archbishop of Florence*. [*Summa theologica* (part)]. Continent: date indeterminable.

Taken to correspond with half of 1570:5, *duo libri Antonini*. See also 90.59. *Language(s)*: Latin. Appraised with one other at 3s 4d in 1570.

90.6 Summa Angelica
Angelus de Clavasio. *Summa Angelica*. Continent: date indeterminable.

Corresponds with 1570:6, *Summa angelica*. *Language(s)*: Latin. Appraised at 16d in 1570.

90.7 pandectarum liber vicesimus
Justinian I. *Digesta* (part). *(Corpus juris civilis)*. Continent: date indeterminable.

Some editions of the *Digesta* begin with Book 20 (Florence: L. Torrentinus, 1533, for one), but Book 20 is not known to have been published separately at this date. It is possible that the entry is taken from the running-head of part 1 of the set of which other parts appear at 90.49-52 below. Not separately identifiable in the 1570 inventory, but see 90.51 and 90.92 below. Not appraised. *Language(s)*: Latin.

90.8 pandectarum libri quinquaginta

Justinian I. *Digesta. (Corpus juris civilis)*. Continent: date indeterminable. Taken to correspond with 1570:3, *tres libri digestorum*. See also 90.64. *Language(s)*: Latin. Appraised at 6s in 1570.

90.9 2a pars Rapsodie historiarum

Marcus Antonius Sabellicus (Marcus Antonius Coccius, *Sabellicus*). [*Enneades–Posterior pars*]. Continent: date indeterminable.

Corresponds to 1570:8, *2a pars Sabellici. Language(s)*: Latin. Appraised at 16d in 1570.

90.10 petrus antesignanus

Nicolaus Clenardus and Petrus Antesignanus. *Institutiones ac meditationes in graecam linguam, cum scholiis et praxi P. Antesignani*. Continent: 1557–1569.

Corresponds with 1570:33, *gramatica cleonardi. Language(s)*: Greek Latin. Appraised at 6d in 1570.

90.11 regule cum suis ampliationibus

Probably Bartholomaeus Socinus. *Regulae et fallentiae juris*. Continent: date indeterminable.

Full title reads: *Regulae cum suis ampliationibus....* Taken to correspond with 1570:66, *Regulae juris per Bart' Sonim'*, but other identifications are conceivable, such as Joannes Bernardus Diaz, *Fallentiae, seu de regulis juris cum suis amplificationibus liber. Language(s)*: Latin. Appraised at 6d in 1570.

90.12 practica doctoris gwidonis pape

Guido Papa. [*Consilia*]. Continent: date indeterminable.

Taken to correspond with 1570:65, *concilia guidonis papae*. The word "practica" appears in the long title of some editions of the *Consilia. Language(s)*: Latin. Appraised at 2s in 1570.

90.13 Tullius de natura deorum

Marcus Tullius Cicero. *De natura Deorum*. Continent: date indeterminable.

The *De natura deorum* was frequently the first item in the second volume of Cicero's collected philosophical works, and it is possible that this entry corresponds with 90.90 below (1570:45). Not appraised. *Language(s)*: Latin.

90.14 plutarcus

Plutarch. [*Vitae parallelae–Epitome*]. Continent: date indeterminable.

Taken arbitrarily to correspond with 1570:22, *epithomi plutharki*, rather than with 1570:37, *plutharci opuscula*, for which see 90.41 below. *Language(s)*: Latin Greek (perhaps). Appraised at 12d in 1570.

90.15 etimologiarum divisionum expositiones juris
Unidentified. Continent (probable): date indeterminable.
Probably not an STC book. Corresponds with 1570:48, *Etimologia Juris*. *Language(s)*: Latin. Appraised at 5d in 1570.

90.16 2a pars decretalium
Gregory IX, *Pope. Decretales* (part). *(Corpus juris canonici)*. Continent: date indeterminable.
Not separately identifiable in the 1570 inventory, but see note to 90.86. See 90.81 for what may be part of the same set of the *Decretales* and 90.29 and 90.73 for another set. Not appraised. *Language(s)*: Latin.

90.17 berrocius
Perhaps Augustinus Beroius. Unidentified. Continent: date indeterminable.
It is assumed that this entry corresponds with 1570:14, *berosus*, which might suggest Berosus' *De antiquitatibus*. Nearer to the entry here, however, would be Francesco Barozzi (Barocius) the geometer. If a legal author is to be sought, the likeliest candidate is probably Augustinus Beroius. The entry *berosus* in the 1570 inventory carries easily the highest valuation in that list, and Beroius's two folio volumes of commentaries on the *Decretales* (Lyon, Nicolaus Bacccaneus, 1550/51) or his four folio volumes of *Consilia* (Bologna, Giovanni Rossi, 1567) are far likelier to have been so appraised than anything by either of the other authors. *Language(s)*: Latin. Appraised at 10s 3d in 1570.

90.18 a greke boke
Unidentified. Place unknown: stationer unknown, date indeterminable.
STC/non-STC status unknown. Corresponds to 1570:28, *liber grecus*. The repeated vagueness of this entry may perhaps be accounted for by the loss of the title-page. *Language(s)*: Greek. Appraised at 4d in 1570.

90.19 Colloquium Erasmi
Desiderius Erasmus. *Colloquia*. Britain or Continent: date indeterminable.
STC 10450.6 *et seq.* and non-STC. Corresponds with 1570:57, *Colloquium erasmi*. *Language(s)*: Latin. Appraised at 4d in 1570.

90.20 digestorum seu pandectarum tricessimus
Justinian I. *Digesta* (part). *(Corpus juris civilis)*. Continent: date indeterminable.
See 90.7. Perhaps an unidentified edition of book 30 of the *Digesta* alone, but just possibly part 3 of the set of which parts appear at 90.49-52. Not appraised. Not separately identifiable in the 1570 inventory, but see 90.92. *Language(s)*: Latin Greek (perhaps).

90.21 Elenchus questionum sacrarum
Unidentified. Continent (probable): date indeterminable.

Probably not an STC book. Corresponds to 1570:39, *questiones* [*sic*] *elenchi*. *Language(s)*: Latin. Appraised at 2d in 1570.

90.22 loci Juris communes
Unidentified. Continent (probable): date indeterminable.

Probably not an STC book. Corresponds with 1570:47, *loci juris communis*. There are several possibilities including (if the correct reading is "communes" rather than "communis") Mattheus Gribaldus and Marcus Mantuae (Benavides). *Language(s)*: Latin. Appraised at 6d in 1570.

90.23 a grek boke
Unidentified. Place unknown: stationer unknown, date indeterminable.

STC/non-STC status unknown. See 90.18, entry and annotation. The 1570 inventory does not repeat this item, but see notes to 90.87 and 90.89. Not appraised. *Language(s)*: Greek.

90.24 leonis augutini constitutiones
Leo I, *Emperor of the East* and others. *Constitutiones novellae. (Corpus juris civilis)*. Translated by Henricus Agylaeus. Continent: date indeterminable.

Corresponds with 1570:54, *constituciones leonis*. The full title begins *Imp. Leonis Augusti constitutiones novellae.* . . . *Language(s)*: Latin. Appraised at 8d in 1570.

90.25 dialectica Joanis Cesarii
Joannes Caesarius, *Juliacensis. Dialectica*. Continent: date indeterminable.

Joannes Murmellius's commentary on Aristotle's *Categoriae* was issued with most Renaissance editions of the *Dialectica*. Not appraised; not listed in the 1570 list. *Language(s)*: Latin.

90.26 divi aurelii augustini
Augustine, *Saint. De natura et gratia*. Continent: date indeterminable.

Equated, perhaps rashly, with 1570:49, *augustus* [*sic*] *de gratia et natura*, the only Augustine entry in that list. *Language(s)*: Latin. Appraised at 4d in 1570.

90.27 a paper boke written
Unidentified. Provenance unknown: date indeterminable.

Manuscript. Not appraised; not listed in the 1570 inventory. Perhaps a notebook. *Language(s)*: Unknown.

90.28 assertionis lutheranae confutatio
John Fisher, *Saint and Cardinal. Assertionis Lutheranae confutatio*. Continent: 1523–1564.

Corresponds to 1570:21, *Roffensis*. *Language(s)*: Latin. Appraised at 16d in 1570.

90.29 decretalium epistolarum Gregorii pape

Gregory IX, *Pope. Decretales* (part). *(Corpus juris canonici)*. Continent: date indeterminable.

Taken, with 90.73, as corresponding to 1570:10, *Epistole decretales collecte per gregorium in 2bus*, but see also 90.81. *Language(s)*: Latin. Appraised with one other at 20d in 1570.

90.30 Codicis domini justiniani principis

Justinian I. *Codex. (Corpus juris civilis)*. Continent: date indeterminable.

Taken as corresponding to 1570:4, *codex justiniani*. But see another copy at 90.33. *Language(s)*: Latin. Appraised at 3s in 1570.

90.31 horatius flachus

Quintus Horatius Flaccus. Perhaps [*Works*]. Continent: date indeterminable.

Corresponds to 1570:40, *odee horatii*, and perhaps, in the light of this and of the low valuation, one of the editions containing only the Odes and the Epodes. *Language(s)*: Latin. Appraised at 2d in 1570.

90.32 novellarum constitutionum domini Justiniani

Justinian I. *Novellae constitutiones. (Corpus juris civilis)*. Continent: date indeterminable.

Corresponds to 1570:12, *Novellae constituciones Justiniani*. See also 90.24. *Language(s)*: Latin Greek (perhaps). Appraised at 12d in 1570.

90.33 codicis domini Justiniani Principis

Justinian I. *Codex. (Corpus juris civilis)*. Continent: date indeterminable.
Not appraised, but see 90.30 and 90.92. *Language(s)*: Latin.

90.34 suetonius

Caius Suetonius Tranquillus. *De vita Caesarum*. Continent: date indeterminable.

Corresponds to 1570:26, *suetonius*. *Language(s)*: Latin. Appraised at 6d in 1570.

90.35 natura brevium In frenche

Natura brevium. London: (different houses), 1494–1566.

STC 18385 *et seq.* Corresponds to 1570:34, *natura brevium*. *Language(s)*: Law French. Appraised at 4d in 1570.

90.36 Petri Ravennatis

Petrus Ravennas (Pietro Tommai). Unidentified. Continent: date indeterminable.

Taken to correspond with 1570:51, *compendium petri Revennatis*. Either the *Compendium juris canonici* or the *Compendium juris civilis*. *Language(s)*: Latin. Appraised at 6d in 1570.

90.37 Joachimi Hoperi Phrysii Jureconsulti
Joachim Hopper. *Ad Justinianum de obligationibus* πειθανῶν. *(Corpus juris civilis)*. Louvain: apud M. Rotarium, 1553.

Corresponds to 1570:61, *hopperus de obligatio[nibus]*. *Language(s)*: Latin. Appraised at 6d in 1570.

90.38 andreae dominici flocci florentini
Andreas Dominicus Floccus (Lucius Fenestella). Probably *De magistratibus sacerdotiisque Romanorum*. Continent: date indeterminable.

Corresponds with 1570:42, *Andreas flocus*. *Language(s)*: Latin. Appraised at 4d in 1570.

90.39 loci argumentorum
Unidentified. Continent: date indeterminable.

Several possibilities, including the *Loci argumentorum legales* of Nicolaus Everardus, *of Middelburg*. Corresponds precisely with 1570:30. *Language(s)*: Latin. Appraised at 14d in 1570.

90.40 the latin Psalmes in myter
Marco Antonio Flaminio. [*Psalms: paraphrase*]. (*Bible–O.T.*). Continent: date indeterminable.

A verse paraphrase. Taken to correspond with 1570:24, *psalterium flaminii*. *Language(s)*: Latin. Appraised at 12d in 1570.

90.41 plutarchus
Plutarch. [*Selected works*]. Continent: date indeterminable.

Taken as corresponding with 1570:37, *plutharci opuscula*, but see 90.14. *Language(s)*: Latin (probable) Greek (perhaps). Appraised at 2d in 1570.

90.42 Plautus
Titus Maccius Plautus. *Comoediae*. Continent: date indeterminable.

Corresponds precisely with 1570:19. *Language(s)*: Latin. Appraised at 20d in 1570.

90.43 decretorum 2a pars causa 33
Gratianus, *the Canonist*. *Decretum* (part). (*Corpus juris canonici*). Continent: date indeterminable.

Not appraised; not found as such in the 1570 list, but see note to 90.86. *Language(s)*: Latin.

90.44 flores omnium pene doctorum
Thomas, *Hibernicus*. [*Flores omnium fere doctorum*]. Continent: 1483–1567.

Corresponds with 1570:16, *flores doctorum.* See Shaaber T40–52. *Language(s)*: Latin. Appraised at 20d in 1570.

90.45 marci tulii ciceronis de oratore
Marcus Tullius Cicero. *De oratore.* Continent: date indeterminable.
Corresponds with 1570:17, *Tullii de oratore. Language(s)*: Latin. Appraised at 12d in 1570.

90.46 sextus decretalium
Boniface VIII, Pope. *Sextus liber Decretalium. (Corpus juris canonici–Liber Sextus).* Continent: date indeterminable.
Not appraised; not identifiable in 1570 inventory, but see note to 90.86. For another copy see 90.75. *Language(s)*: Latin.

90.47 cornelius
Publius Cornelius Tacitus. Unidentified. Continent: date indeterminable.
Probably not an STC book. Taken as corresponding with 1570:25, *Cornelius tacitus,* but it could be another "cornelius." There is little chance that this is one of the several English editions of Tacitus, but, given the abbreviated entries, the chance exists. *Language(s)*: Latin (probable). Appraised at 20d in 1570.

90.48 ovidius de tristibus
Publius Ovidius Naso. *Tristia.* Continent: date indeterminable.
Corresponds precisely with 1570:43. *Language(s)*: Latin. Appraised at 2d in 1570.

90.49 digestorum seu pandectarum pars 7a
Justinian I. *Digesta* (part). *(Corpus juris civilis).* Continent: date indeterminable.
Not appraised; not separately identifiable in the 1570 inventory. See also 90.7, 90.8, 90.20, 90.50–52 and 90.64. *Language(s)*: Greek Latin.

90.50 digestorum seu pandectarum pars 5a
Justinian I. *Digesta* (part). *(Corpus juris civilis).* Continent: date indeterminable.
Not appraised; not separately identifiable in the 1570 inventory. See also 90.7, 90.8, 90.20, 90.49, 90.51–52 and 90.64. *Language(s)*: Greek Latin.

90.51 digestorum seu pandectarum pars 2a
Justinian I. *Digesta* (part). *(Corpus juris civilis).* Continent: date indeterminable.
Not appraised; not separately identifiable in the 1570 inventory. See also 90.7, 90.8, 90.20, 90.49–50, 90.52 and 90.64. *Language(s)*: Greek Latin.

90.52 digestorum seu pandectarum pars 6a
Justinian I. *Digesta* (part). *(Corpus juris civilis)*. Continent: date indeterminable.
Not appraised; not separately identifiable in the 1570 inventory. See also 90.7, 90.8, 90.20, 90.49-51 and 90.64. *Language(s)*: Greek Latin.

90.53 boetius de philosophie
Anicius M.T.S. Boethius. *De consolatione philosophiae*. Continent: date indeterminable.
Corresponds with 1570:20, *boetius de philosophia*. *Language(s)*: Latin. Appraised at 6d in 1570.

90.54 Institutiones juris domini Justiniani
Justinian I. *Institutiones. (Corpus juris civilis)*. Continent: date indeterminable.
See further copies at 90.1 and 90.85 and the notes there appended. Not appraised, as not certainly identifiable in the 1570 inventory. *Language(s)*: Greek Latin.

90.55 a paper boke
Unidentified. Provenance unknown: date indeterminable.
Manuscript. Not appraised; not listed in the 1570 inventory. Perhaps a notebook. *Language(s)*: Unknown.

90.56 compendium Clementis romani pontificis de rebus gestis peregrinationibus et predicationibus Sancti petri
Clement I, *Saint, Pope*. *De rebus gestis, peregrinationibus atque concionibus Petri*. Translated by Joachim Perion. Paris: (different houses), 1555.
Corresponds with 1570:53, *Epitomi clementis*. *Language(s)*: Latin. Appraised at 8d in 1570.

90.57 bartramus de corpore et Sanguine domini
Ratramnus, *Monachus* (Bertramus, *Corbiensis*). *De corpore et sanguine Domini*. Continent: 1531-1541.
Corresponds with 1570:50, *barteramus de corpore domine*. *Language(s)*: Latin. Appraised at 2d in 1570.

90.58 pithagorae carmina aurea. phocilidae poema admonitorium. theognidis Gnomologia. Coluthi helenae raptus. Triphiodori de excidio troiae. omnia Grecolatina in uno volumine expressa
Pythagoras, Phocylides, Theognis, Coluthus, Tryphiodorus and St. Nilus. *En lector, librum damus vere areum; planeo scholasticum, quo continentur haec Pythagorae carmina aurea. Phocylidae poema admonitorium. Theognidis gnomologia. Coluthi Helenae raptus. Tryphiodori de Troiae excidio*. Edited and translated by Michael Neander, *of Sorau*. Basle: per Joannem Oporinum, 1559.

Entered in the 1570 inventory as, simply, *carmina pithagorae. Language(s)*: Greek Latin. Appraised at 20d in 1570.

90.59 3a pars summae Antonini
Antoninus, *Archbishop of Florence.* [*Summa theologica* (part)]. Continent: date indeterminable.

Taken to correspond with half of 1570:5, *duo libri Antonini.* See also 90.5. *Language(s)*: Latin. Appraised with one other at 3s 4d in 1570.

90.60 commentaria Alceati de summa trinitate de sacrosancta ecclesia
Andrea Alciati. *Ad rescripta principum commentarii.* Continent: date indeterminable.

Taken to correspond with 1570:7, *Aulceatus. Language(s)*: Latin. Appraised at 3s in 1570.

90.61 responsa sive consilia nicholae Eurardi
Nicolaus Everardus, *of Middelburg. Consilia sive responsa.* Louvain: Excudebat Servatius Sassenus sibi, et haeredibus Arnoldi Birckmanni, 1554.

Corresponds with 1570:62, *Eurardi concilia. Language(s)*: Latin. Appraised at 2s 6d in 1570.

90.62 practica et theorica causarum criminalium Jacobi de novello
Jacobus Novellus. [*Practica et theorica causarum criminalium*]. Continent: 1549–1558.

Taken to correspond with 1570:18, *practica Jacobi. Language(s)*: Latin. Appraised at 10d in 1570.

90.63 flores collecti per Rowlandinum Bononiensem Juris professorem
Rolandinus, *de Passageriis.* [*Flores ultimarum voluntatum*]. Continent: date indeterminable.

Corresponds with 1570:31, *flores voluntatum Rolandi. Language(s)*: Latin. Appraised at 6d in 1570.

90.64 quinquaginta libri digestorum seu pandectarum
Justinian I. *Digesta. (Corpus juris civilis).* Continent: date indeterminable.

Not appraised, as not certainly identifiable in the 1570 inventory, but see 90.92. For another copy see 90.8 and the note there.

90.65 flores poetarum
Flores poetarum. Continent: date indeterminable.

Corresponds precisely with 1570:27. *Language(s)*: Latin. Appraised at 12d in 1570.

90.66 demosthenis oratio contra Aeschinem Grece
Demosthenes. [*Selected works–Orations*]. Continent: date indeterminable.

Taken to correspond with 1570:52, *oratio demostines*. Almost certainly an edition of the *Orationes adversariae* with the speeches of Aeschines as well as those of Demosthenes. *Language(s)*: Greek. Appraised at 2d in 1570.

90.67 interpretatio Erasmi in psalmum lxxxv

Desiderius Erasmus. *Concionalis interpretatio, plena pietatis, in Psalmum LXXXV*. Basle: in officina Frobeniana (apud Joannem Hervagium et Hieronymum Frobenium), 1528.

Corresponds with 1570:46. *Language(s)*: Latin. Appraised at 4d in 1570.

90.68 Joachimi Hopperi in libros pandectarum dispositio

Joachim Hopper. *Dispositio in libros pandectarum. (Corpus juris civilis)*. Cologne: 1558–1562.

Corresponds with 1570:54, *dispositio in pandactas*. *Language(s)*: Latin. Appraised at 2d in 1570.

90.69 tabellionum libri duo

Ars notariatus sive tabellionum libri 2. Continent: date indeterminable.

Taken as corresponding to 1570:15, *ars notariatus*. *Language(s)*: Latin. Appraised at 14d in 1570.

90.70 dictionarium poeticum

Charles Estienne. [*Dictionarium historicum ac poeticum*]. Continent: date indeterminable.

Corresponds to 1570:35, *dixionarium poeticum*. *Language(s)*: Latin. Appraised at 4d in 1570.

90.71 herodianus Grecolatine

Herodian. [*Historiae*]. Continent: date indeterminable.

Corresponds to 1570:23, *haerodianus de gestis imperatorum*. *Language(s)*: Greek Latin. Appraised at 14d in 1570.

90.72 liber de diversis regulis Juris cum interpretatione francisci Jammesii textoris

Franciscus Jammetius Textor. *Commentarius in XLIIII leges*. Paris: apud A. Parvum, 1549.

Corresponds to 1570:60, *franciscus Jannettus de regulis juris*. *Language(s)*: Latin. Appraised at 6d in 1570.

90.73 decretales epistolae a Gregorio 9o pontifice collectae

Gregory IX, *Pope. Decretales. (Corpus juris canonici)*. Continent: date indeterminable.

Taken, with 90.29, as corresponding to 1570:10, *Epistole decretales collecte per gregorium in 2bus*, but see also 90.81. *Language(s)*: Latin. Appraised with one other at 20d in 1570.

90.74 legum procheiron collectum per constantinum harmenopulam
Constantine Harmenopoulos, Πρόχειρον, *sive Epitome juris civilis. (Hexabiblos)* Continent: date indeterminable.

Corresponds to 1570:67, *legum procheiron*. *Language(s)*: Latin (probable) Greek (perhaps). Appraised at 12d in 1570.

90.75 Sextus decretalium per bonifacium octavum pontificem
Boniface VIII, *Pope. Sextus liber Decretalium. (Corpus juris canonici–Liber Sextus)*. Continent: date indeterminable.

For another copy see 90.46. Not appraised, as not certainly identifiable in the 1570 list, but see note to 90.86. *Language(s)*: Latin.

90.76 institutionum juris canonici libri quatuor
Perhaps Giovanni Paolo Lancelotto. *Institutiones juris canonici*. Continent: date indeterminable.

Corresponds to 1570:36, *instituciones Juris canonici*. *Language(s)*: Latin. Appraised at 8d in 1570.

90.77 a paper booke
Unidentified. Provenance unknown: date indeterminable.

Manuscript. Not appraised; not listed in the 1570 inventory. Perhaps a notebook. *Language(s)*: Unknown.

90.78 progimnasmata fori
Johann Oldendorp. *Actionum forensium progymnasmata*. Continent: 1539–1566.

Corresponds precisely to 1570:38. *Language(s)*: Latin. Appraised at 2d in 1570.

90.79 Grecae literaturae dragmata
Joannes Oecolampadius. *Graecae literaturae dragmata*. Continent: date indeterminable.

Taken to correspond to 1570:55, *oecolampadius*. *Language(s)*: Greek Latin. Appraised at 2d in 1570.

90.80 commentarii Stephani Bodei in institutiones
Stephanus Bodeus. *In quatuor institutionum imperialium libros commentarii*. Paris: apud Sebastianum Nivellium sub Ciconis, via Jacobea, 1555.

Taken to correspond with 1570:63, *Bodeus in institutiones*. *Language(s)*: Latin. Appraised at 3s 4d in 1570.

90.81 decretalium epistolarum Gregorii liber tertius
Gregory IX, *Pope. Decretales* (part). *(Corpus juris canonici)*. Continent: date indeterminable.

Not appraised, as not certainly identifiable in the 1570 inventory; see, however, the note to 90.86, and also 90.16, 90.29 and 90.73 and the notes there. *Language(s)*: Latin.

90.82 a little greke booke
Unidentified. Place unknown: stationer unknown, date indeterminable.
STC/non-STC status unknown. Not appraised; not readily identifiable in the 1570 list. *Language(s)*: Greek.

90.83 decreta scriptorum ecclesiasticorum conciliorum et romanorum pontificum
Unidentified. Continent (probable): date indeterminable.
Probably not an STC book. Which compendium of canon law cannot be determined. Not appraised, as not identifiable in the 1570 list. *Language(s)*: Latin.

90.84 libellus de vera deo inserviendi methodo
Alonso, *of Madrid*. *Libellus aureus de vera Deo apte inserviendi methodo. Speculum illustrium personarum*. Translated by Joannes Hentensius. Louvain: apud Petrum Zangrium Tiletanum, 1560.
Not appraised, as not found in the 1570 list. *Language(s)*: Latin.

90.85 institutiones Justiniani
Justinian I. *Institutiones. (Corpus juris civilis)*. Continent: date indeterminable.
Taken, a little arbitrarily, as corresponding to 1570:56, *Instituciones in parvo volumine*, but see also 90.1 and 90.54. *Language(s)*: Greek Latin. Appraised at 2d in 1570.

90.86 Jus canonicum 5 voluminibus
Unidentified. Continent: date indeterminable.
The first of eight items occurring only in the 1570 list. Either a distinct *Cursus juris canonici* not featured in the 1569 inventory or a group of canon law texts that might include items 90.16, 90.43, 90.46, 90.75 and 90.81 above, none of them separately listed in the 1570 inventory. See also 90.83. *Language(s)*: Latin. Appraised at 6s 8d in 1570.

90.87 chrisostomus de modo orando
John, *Chrysostom, Saint*. [*De orando Deum*]. Continent: date indeterminable.
Conceivably identifiable with the second unspecified Greek book (90.23) in the 1569 inventory. *Language(s)*: Greek (perhaps) Latin (perhaps). Appraised at 1d in 1570.

90.88 olfaricius
Unidentified. Continent (probable): date indeterminable.

Probably not an STC book. It is just possible that Albericus, *de Rosate*, a popular commentator on the *Codex* and the *Digesta*, is intended. *Language(s)*: Latin (probable). Appraised at 6d in 1570.

90.89 nemesius de natura hominis
Nemesius, *Bishop*. *De natura hominis*. Continent: date indeterminable.

Another candidate for possible correspondence with 90.23 above. *Language(s)*: Greek (perhaps) Latin (perhaps). Appraised at 6d in 1570.

90.90 marcus tullius de pho..a le..a [philosophia?]
Marcus Tullius Cicero. [*Selected works–Philosophica*]. Continent: date indeterminable.

Perhaps to be identified with 90.13 above. *Language(s)*: Latin. Appraised at 6d in 1570.

90.91 Responsio demissa
Unidentified. Place unknown: stationer unknown, date indeterminable. STC/non-STC status unknown. *Language(s)*: Latin. Appraised at 4d in 1570.

90.92:1–6 Six bookes of the text of the civill law worth xvi d. a pece
Unidentified. Continent (probable): date indeterminable.

Probably not an STC book. Either a discrete *Corpus juris civilis* or, perhaps, a group of assorted texts including some of 90.7, 90.20, 90.33, 90.49–52, 90.54, and 90.64 above. *Language(s)*: Latin (probable). Appraised as a group at 4s 16d in 1570.

90.93 Baldwinus in institutiones
Franciscus Balduinus. *Commentarii in libros quatuor Institutionum juris civilis*. Paris: apud Jacobum Dupuys, 1554.

Language(s): Latin. Appraised at 6s in 1570.

John Beddow. Scholar (schoolmaster) (M.A.): Inventory. 1571 (partly 1577)

CHARLES A. HUTTAR

Le Neve's *Fasti* records that in July 1558 "John Bedo an eminent grammarian, who had publicly instructed youths in grammar for four years in this university, was admitted to inform and instruct in that faculty" (*Athenae Oxonienses*, 5 [*Fasti*]:i.154), being awarded the degree Bachelor of Grammar. Thus when he went on to the Bachelor of Arts (16 February 1563), he had already been usher of Magdalen College School for some eight years. He proceeded Master of Arts in July 1566 and left Magdalen early in 1571 to become master of the college's school in Brackley, Northants., where he died six years later (*Alumni Oxonienses*, 1:99; more in Boase, 237, 250; Clark, 2:i.8 and 2:ii.8; Bloxam 1863, 3:124-25). His promotion to Brackley, with approximately a doubling of salary (Orme 1989, 57, 125), may represent an established career path, for his successor in the usher's position, Roger Webster, also succeeded him at Brackley (Stanier 1940, 113). In Beddow's first year at Brackley, the college moved there from Oxford to escape the plague and stayed for several months (Macray 1897, 2:43).

His name is variously recorded as Beddoe, Bedo, Bedoe, Bedoo, Bedow, and, posthumously, Bede, though it may be doubted whether the last is an actual variant of the name (Macray 1897, 2:82) or a mistake resulting from confusion with an earlier Master of Brackley, Robert Bede (1552-1558). He is also to be distinguished from a contemporary John Beddoe who was a fellow of Oriel College, and to whom, by another interpretation of the documents, the 1558 B.Gram. has been assigned (*Alumni Oxonienses*, 1:99).

Most of the books in this collection relate more to his profession of teaching than to scholarship or general interest. There are a Latin-English (91.2) and an English-Latin dictionary (91.34)—the former by the man under whom Beddow taught for thirteen years and the latter clearly announced on the title page as "for young beginners"—as well as a forerunner of both, "Calepine" (91.40:A). There are four humanist works on grammar. There are half a dozen texts of Cicero, with and without commentaries, three of

Horace, two of Virgil, and a handful of other Latin literary texts. Some theological writings, both Catholic and Protestant, round out the collection. Five of the books are by Erasmus. Only two (91.2 and 91.34) can be definitely identified as from English presses. However, 91.2 and possibly 91.1 and 91.13 have Magdalen associations.

This inventory and appraisal of Beddow's goods, dated 23 February 1571, were made not at his death but upon his moving from Oxford to Brackley. It includes, besides the books listed, the usual furnishings, linens, and utensils, and also £11 16d in coins. It was drawn up by John Goode, beadle of the Civil Laws, and Henry Crosse, beadle of Divinity, but its purpose is not known.

A manuscript inventory dated 15 April 1577 records that on his (presumably recent) death, Beddow left as a "legacie to the schole" several books, including one not in the 1571 inventory and perhaps acquired later (91.40). The document lists: "Virgil with sondrie commentaries, Horace with a commentarie, Calepyn with onomasticon deorum. &c" (Macray 1897, 2:82; reproduced in Forrester 1950, plate facing p.25).

Oxford University Archives, Bodleian Library: Hyp.B.10.
Magdalen College Archives, EL/6 (Ledger F), fol. 302^v.

§

Bloxam, John Rouse. 1853-85. *A Register of . . . Magdalen College.* 8 vols. Oxford: W. Graham.

Forrester, Eric G. 1950. *A History of Magdalen College School, Brackley, Northamptonshire, 1548-1949.* Buckingham: N.p.

Macray, William Dunn. 1894-1915. *A Register of the Members of St. Mary Magdalen College, Oxford: From the Foundation of the College.* 8 vols. London: Oxford Univ. Press.

Orme, Nicholas. 1989. *Education and Society in Medieval and Renaissance England.* London: Hambledon Press.

Stanier, R. S. 1940. *Magdalen School: A History of Magdalen College School Oxford.* Oxford Historical Society, N.S. Vol. 3. Oxford: Clarendon Press.

§

91.1	cornu copia
91.2	coopers dixonarie
91.3	mallius maleficarum
91.4	silve morales
91.5	epistoli tullii
91.6	terentius cum commento
91.7	epistole tullii cum commento
91.8	polliciani opera
91.9	oratius cum commento
91.10	valerius maximus
91.11	martialis
91.12	Rethorica tullii
91.13	officia tullii
91.14	officia tullii cum commento
91.15	luctantius
91.16	georgica cum commento
91.17	de fine seculi
91.18	officina textoris
91.19	colloquia erasmi
91.20	magnus alaxandrinus
91.21	enchiridion militis Christiani
91.22	sermones horati cum commento
91.23	vita romana
91.24	textoris 2us Thomas [tomus]
91.25	dispanterius
91.26	oratio ilirica
91.27	titillmannus in paulum
91.28	de prima rerum origine
91.29	oratius
91.30	erasmus de pronuncacione
91.31	apologia erasmi
91.32	grammatica linacri
91.33	vergilius cum commento
91.34	abiedarium anglice latine
91.35	orationes tullii
91.36	aulus gelius
91.37	Raberius de constructione
91.38 multiple	a great many of other smale bookes
91.39	Epitomie plutarchi
91.40:A	Calepyn with onomasticon deorum. &c
91.40:B	[See 91.40:A]

§

91.1 cornu copia
Probably Nicolaus Perottus. *Cornucopia*. Continent: date indeterminable. The work of Eustathius on Homer with the same title (ed. Hadrianus Junius, Basle, 1558) should be considered also; it contained a preface by then-exiled Magdalen fellow Laurence Humphrey, addressed "ad praesidem et socios collegii Magdalen. Oxon." *Language(s)*: Greek Latin. Appraised at 20d in 1571.

91.2 coopers dixonarie
Thomas Cooper, *Bishop*. *Thesaurus linguae Romanae et Britannicae*. London: in aed. quondam Bertheleti, per H. Wykes, 1565.
STC 5686. Cooper became master of the Magdalen College School in 1549 and remained in this position (except for the last year of Mary's reign) through most of Beddow's tenure as usher, leaving in 1567 when he gained clerical preferment as Dean of Christ Church. *Language(s)*: English Latin. Appraised at 6s 8d in 1571.

91.3 mallius maleficarum
Jacob Sprenger and Heinrich Kraemer. *Malleus Maleficarum*. Continent: date indeterminable.
Language(s): Latin. Appraised at 12d in 1571.

91.4 silve morales
Silvae morales. Compiled by Jodocus Badius, *Ascensius*. Lyon: Johann Trechsel, 1492.
Extracts from Virgil, Horace, Juvenal, Mantuan and others. Goff B3. *Language(s)*: Latin. Appraised at 16d in 1571.

91.5 epistoli tullii
Marcus Tullius Cicero. Perhaps [*Selected works–Epistolae*]. Continent: date indeterminable.
The widely published *Epistolae ad familiares* is also a possibility. See also 91.7. *Language(s)*: Latin. Appraised at 6d in 1571.

91.6 terentius cum commento
Publius Terentius, *Afer*. [*Works*]. Britain or Continent: date indeterminable.
STC 23885.3 *et seq.* and non-STC. *Language(s)*: Latin. Appraised at 8d in 1571.

91.7 epistole tullii cum commento
Marcus Tullius Cicero. [*Selected works–Epistolae*]. Continent: date indeterminable.
See also 91.5. *Language(s)*: Latin. Appraised at 12d in 1571.

91.8 polliciani opera
Angelus Politianus (Angelo Ambrogini). [*Works*]. Continent: date indeterminable.

In the manuscript entry, *pars* is inserted above the line. It may refer rather to the previous entry. If it refers to this entry, it may indicate a damaged book, or else part of a multi-volume edition. There was a three-volume edition: Lyon, 1533. *Language(s)*: Latin. Appraised at 10d in 1571.

91.9 oratius cum commento
Quintus Horatius Flaccus. Probably [*Works*]. Continent: date indeterminable.

The relatively high appraised value points to this rather than 91.22 as the Horace which was part of Beddow's legacy to his school (see Introduction). *Language(s)*: Latin. Appraised at 3s 4d in 1571.

91.10 valerius maximus
Valerius Maximus. *Facta et dicta memorabilia*. Continent: date indeterminable.

Language(s): Latin. Appraised at 6d in 1571.

91.11 martialis
Marcus Valerius Martialis. *Epigrammata*. Continent: date indeterminable. *Language(s)*: Latin. Appraised at 4d in 1571.

91.12 Rethorica tullii
Marcus Tullius Cicero. [*Selected works–Rhetorica*]. Continent: date indeterminable.

Conceivably the widely published *Rhetorica ad Herennium* then believed to be Cicero's. *Language(s)*: Latin. Appraised at 8d in 1571.

91.13 officia tullii
Marcus Tullius Cicero. *De officiis*. Continent (probable): date indeterminable.

Probably not an STC book, but see STC 5278 *et seq*. This work is commonly the leading title in collections of Cicero's works. The two pre-1571 printings in STC are bilingual, with English translation by Robert Whittinton, who was one of Beddow's illustrious predecessors at Magdalen College School. See 91.14 which, with its commentary, is definitely not an STC book. *Language(s)*: Latin English (perhaps). Appraised at 2d in 1571.

91.14 officia tullii cum commento
Marcus Tullius Cicero. *De officiis*. Continent: date indeterminable.
See 91.13. *Language(s)*: Latin. Appraised at 10d in 1571.

91.15 luctantius
Lucius Coelius Lactantius. Probably [*Works*]. Continent: date indeterminable.

Language(s): Latin. Appraised at 12d in 1571.

91.16 georgica cum commento
Publius Virgilius Maro. [*Georgics*]. Continent: date indeterminable. *Language(s)*: Latin. Appraised at 8d in 1571.

91.17 de fine seculi
Heinrich Bullinger. *De fine seculi et juditio venturo Domini nostri Jesu Christi.* Basle: per Joannem Oporinum, 1557.
Staedtke no. 320; sole Latin edition. *Language(s)*: Latin. Appraised at 2d in 1571.

91.18 officina textoris
Joannes Ravisius (Textor). [*Officina*]. Continent: date indeterminable.
Perhaps the first volume of a two-volume set, the second appearing at 91.24. Also, either entry may represent the *Epitome*. *Language(s)*: Latin. Appraised at 12d in 1571.

91.19 colloquia erasmi
Desiderius Erasmus. *Colloquia.* Britain or Continent: date indeterminable. STC 10450.6 *et seq.* and non-STC. By 1571 there were more than 100 editions. *Language(s)*: Latin. Appraised at 8d in 1571.

91.20 magnus alaxandrinus
Quintus Curtius Rufus. *De rebus gestis Alexandri Magni.* Continent: date indeterminable.
Language(s): Latin. Appraised at 8d in 1571.

91.21 enchiridion militis Christiani
Desiderius Erasmus. *Enchiridion militis Christiani.* Continent (probable): date indeterminable.
Probably not an STC book, but see STC 10479 *et seq.* The English translation, first published in 1533, retains the Latin title. *Language(s)*: Latin (probable) English (perhaps). Appraised at 10d in 1571.

91.22 sermones horati cum commento
Quintus Horatius Flaccus. *Sermones sive Satirae.* Continent: date indeterminable.
See 91.9. *Language(s)*: Latin. Appraised at 8d in 1571.

91.23 vita romana
Unidentified. Continent (probable): date indeterminable.
Almost certainly not an STC book. Possibilities include Joannes Baptista Egnatius, *De Caesaribus* (one edition of which, Lyon, 1560, appeared with the title *Vitae Romanorum imperatorum aut principum*); Dr. Robert Barnes, *Vitae Romanorum pontificum* (Shaaber B242 [1536] *et seq.*); Herodian [*Historiae*]; and Bartolomeo Platina and others, *Historia de vitis pontificum.* If the

entry is a description rather than a title, the *Lives* of Suetonius and even Plutarch are also possible. *Language(s)*: Latin. Appraised at 12d in 1571.

91.24 textoris 2us Thomas [tomus]
Joannes Ravisius (Textor). [*Officina*]. Continent: date indeterminable.
Perhaps the second volume of a two-volume set, the first appearing at 91.18, or perhaps the equally popular *Epitome*. *Language(s)*: Latin. Appraised at 6d in 1571.

91.25 dispanterius
Jean Despautère. Unidentified. Place unknown: stationer unknown, date indeterminable.
STC/non-STC status unknown. STC lists twelve editions or issues of four different books by Despautère—nearly all published in Scotland. Adams D330-67 displays a wider range of titles and editions from Continental presses. His collected works appeared in 1537 (Adams D338) under the title *Commentarii grammatici*. *Language(s)*: Latin. Appraised at 6d in 1571.

91.26 oratio ilirica
Probably Matthias Flacius, *Illyricus*. Unidentified. Continent: date indeterminable.
The *Disputatio de originali peccato et libero arbitrio, inter M. Flacium Illyricum, et V. Strigelium*, 1562-1563, is a possibility (see Adams F563-64). *Language(s)*: Latin. Appraised at 12d in 1571.

91.27 titillmannus in paulum
Franz Titelmann. Probably [*Epistles: commentary and text*]. (*Bible–N.T.*). Continent: 1528-1554.
A less likely possibility is Titelmann's *Collationes quinque super epistolam Pauli ad Romanos* (Antwerp, 1529). *Language(s)*: Latin. Appraised at 8d in 1571.

91.28 de prima rerum origine
Gulielmus Pastregicus. *De originibus rerum libellus*. Edited by Michael Angelo Biondo. Venice: [impressum per Nicolaum de Bascarinis], 1547.
Language(s): Latin. Appraised at 6d in 1571.

91.29 oratius
Quintus Horatius Flaccus. Probably [*Works*]. Continent: date indeterminable.
See also 91.9. *Language(s)*: Latin. Appraised at 8d in 1571.

91.30 erasmus de pronuncacione
Desiderius Erasmus. *De recta pronuntiatione* [and others]. Continent: 1528-1558.
Language(s): Greek Latin. Appraised at 10d in 1571.

91.31 apologia erasmi
 Desiderius Erasmus. Unidentified. Continent: date indeterminable.
 Several works by Erasmus have titles beginning with the word *Apologia*. *Language(s)*: Latin. Appraised at 8d in 1571.

91.32 grammatica linacri
 Thomas Linacre. Probably *Rudimenta grammatices*. Translated by George Buchanan. Britain or Continent: 1525?–1566.
 STC 15636 *et seq.* and non-STC. See Shaaber L202-27. There were over twenty editions (mostly Continental) of George Buchanan's translation from the original English. Conceivably, however, the entry could refer to Linacre's *Progymnasmata grammatices vulgaria* (STC 15635), which appeared in a single edition published by John Rastell in 1512. *Language(s)*: Latin. Appraised at 4d in 1571.

91.33 vergilius cum commento
 Publius Virgilius Maro. Probably [*Works*]. Britain or Continent: date indeterminable.
 STC 24788 and non-STC. STC 24813 *et seq.* (the *Bucolics* with commentary) are also remote possibilities, but the appraisal suggests a larger work and also identifies this entry with the "Virgil with sondrie commentaries" which Beddow left to Brackley School (see Introduction). *Language(s)*: Latin. Appraised at 2s 6d in 1571.

91.34 abiedarium anglice latine
 Richard Huloet. *Abcedarium Anglico Latinum, pro tyrunculis*. London: [S. Mierdman] ex officina Gul. Riddel, 1552.
 STC 13940. *Language(s)*: English Latin. Appraised at 2s 6d in 1571.

91.35 orationes tullii
 Marcus Tullius Cicero. [*Selected works–Orations*]. Continent: date indeterminable.
 Language(s): Latin. Appraised at 6d in 1571.

91.36 aulus gelius
 Aulus Gellius. *Noctes Atticae*. Continent: date indeterminable.
 Language(s): Latin. Appraised at 4d in 1571.

91.37 Raberius de constructione
 William Lily. *De octo partium orationis constructione*. Commentary by Junius Rabirius. Continent: date indeterminable.
 Originally written by Lily, but edited and emended extensively by Erasmus. Many Continental editions contain commentaries written by Rabirius. *Language(s)*: Latin French (perhaps). Appraised at 4d in 1571.

91.38 multiple   a great many of other smale bookes
Unidentified. Place unknown: stationer unknown, date indeterminable. STC/non-STC status unknown. *Language(s)*: Unknown. Appraised at 7d in 1571.

91.39 Epitomie plutarchi
Plutarch. [*Vitae parallelae–Epitome*]. Continent: date indeterminable.
Darius Tyber's epitome was the standard. *Language(s)*: Latin. Appraised at 6d in 1571.

91.40:A Calepyn with onomasticon deorum. &c
Ambrogio Calepino. *Dictionarium*. Basle: (different houses), 1544–1575 (composite publication).
From a 1577 inventory after Beddow's death (Macray 1897, 2:82; Forrester 1950, plate facing p. 25); see Introduction. Several vernacular languages possible. Not appraised. *Language(s)*: Greek Latin.

91.40:B [See 91.40:A]
Conrad Gesner. *Onomasticon*. [Composite publication].
Issued with every Basle Calepine from 1544 in a composite volume. From a 1577 inventory after Beddow's death (Macray 1897, 2:82; Forrester 1950, plate facing p. 25); see Introduction. Not appraised. *Language(s)*: Greek Latin.

Robert Hart. Scholar (M.A.): Probate Inventory. 1571

RICHARD OVENDEN

Robert Hart (Harte, Hert, Herte), a fellow of St. John's College Oxford, died sometime before 10 March 1571 (the date at which this probate inventory was compiled), probably on 22 February. Foster (*Alumni Oxonienses* 2:664, followed by Stevenson and Salter 1939, 336) draws on the Catalogue of Fellows compiled by Christopher Wren (Librarian 1609-1610) which erroneously refers to his death on 22 February 1572, at which time Wren thought Hart was 24 years old, giving a date of birth in 1548. His age as stated by Wren may well be incorrect, and in any case his error would give a date of birth in 1546. Wren states that he was born in London and educated in Kent (Stevenson and Salter 1939, 336), but he does not appear in the published records of Tonbridge School, an establishment closely linked to St. John's at the time.

The university records are more reliable, however, and first give notice of him in 1565/6 where he is referred to as being in residence as a student in St. John's (Clark 2.ii: 28). He supplicated for a grace to be admitted to the B.A. on 26 March 1566, and was admitted on 6 April. He determined for the degree in Lent of 1567. He supplicated for the M.A. on 8 March 1570, was licensed on 19 April, and incepted on 10 July 1570 (Boase, 261). The date of his matriculation is not known, but was presumably in 1563, seven years before he took the M.A., and before the matriculation statute of 1564/5, which required the names of all those who enjoyed the privileges of the university to be registered (Gibson 1931: lxxxii, 391-95).

After a probationary period as a scholar, Hart became a "fellow" at St. John's, a term at the college which held no distinction between senior members and *discipuli*, and records survive of payments to Hart as a fellow for the period Michaelmas 1568 to Michaelmas 1569 (Stevenson and Salter 1939, 171). Once he had incepted as a Master, Hart was eligible for the lectureship in Rhetoric held by Edmund Campion, and he was duly appointed, allowing Campion to leave on travel. He held this post until his death in the following year (Stevenson and Salter 1939, 189 and 321). The college statutes required all fellows to take holy orders once they had completed their term as a regent, but as Hart held a lectureship, he was exempt (in accordance with the statutes).

The number and value of his personal effects, for a man so young, suggest that he came from a relatively prosperous family. Although he had been a fellow for three years by the time of his death, his stipend alone could not have been generous enough for him to amass the items listed in his inventory, as the college was experiencing its leanest years during the 1560s and early 1570s (the full impact of White's benefaction was not felt until 1572 [Stevenson and Salter 1939, 192]). Thus the payments recorded to him for the year 1568-1569 were less than were due to him by the statutes. Significantly, the first item listed is "a payer of virgynalls" placing Hart with the small number of men in sixteenth-century Oxford who owned musical instruments (Caldwell 1986, 208). Hart was not afraid to show off what he had, to judge from the expensive collection of rings, a few fine clothes, and some gold and silver plate. The value of his possessions and the elaborate arrangements for his obsequies suggest a young man of means, and not afraid of ostentation.

Not surprisingly, much of the content of his book-list corresponds closely to the works stipulated in both the university statutes and those of the college, which in fact follow closely Bishop Fox's statutes for Corpus Christi College. Following the university's Nova Statuta of 1564/5 for example, Hart read Linacre for grammar, Cicero for rhetoric, Aristotle and Porphyry for logic, Tunstall for arithmetic, and John Holywood (Sacrobosco) for astronomy (Fletcher 1986, 172-81).

The college statutes were even more specific, and here we see a very close parallel, not really surprising for one who had so recently graduated and who was now lecturing to undergraduates. In logic, the college statutes specify reading in Caesarius, Aristotle, Porphyry, and Rodolphus Agricola (Stevenson and Salter 1939, 452-53), all of which were owned by Hart. Likewise, the statutes stipulated a number of works for the study of rhetoric, and here again Hart's own collection included almost all of the required reading: Cicero's works, Hermogenes' rhetoric, the orations and declamations of Quintilian (required to prepare students for the M.A., see Fletcher 1986, 193-94), the works of Isocrates, Trapezuntius, Sallust, Virgil, and the *De conscribendis epistolis* of Brandolinus (Schmitt 1983, 79).

In addition to the studies ordered by the statutes of both the university and college, Hart no doubt prescribed reading in his favorite classical authors, and it may be that the editions of classical literature—drama, poetry, but in particular the ancient historians—that are present in number in the inventory formed the basis of this extra reading (McConica 1979, 293). A large number of classical authors are in fact mentioned in the St. John's and Corpus statutes (for the St. John's Statutes see Stevenson and Salter 1939, 452-53, and for those of the Corpus, Ward 1843, 99-101).

Those which also appear in Hart's inventory include Sallust, Valerius Maximus, Suetonius, Virgil, Terence, and Plautus. The Greek authors include Isocrates, Lucian, Aristophanes, and Demosthenes, but Plato, who is mentioned in the Corpus, but not the St. John's Statutes, is not present in Hart's list. There are in fact few unusual Greek texts present, with the standard grammars and dictionaries, such as those of Calepinus and Ceporinus, predominating.

Tantalizingly, he owned one text in Hebrew: an edition of two books of the Old Testament edited by David Kimchi, suggesting he was one of the relatively few men at Oxford who were familiar with the language. Certainly only a handful of the private libraries known about from the period contain Hebrew books (Jones 1983, 278-80).

The importance of Aristotle in mid/late-sixteenth century Oxford is reflected by the presence of several editions and many commentaries on his work, but what is found is both the "new" Aristotle, and a combination of medieval translations and commentaries. Thus we find in addition to Metochita, Donato Acciaioli, and Lefévre d'Étaples, other authors more commonly found in the late medieval university: John Major, Walter Burley, and the (by 1571) uncommon Gaietanus, *de Thienis*, and Joannes Buridanus. The old medieval grammar of the university, Priscian, is not found in his list, suggesting that Hart was keen to concentrate on the humanistic grammar of Linacre, and the Greek grammarians. The absence of the works of Ramus and his followers from Hart's inventory is less surprising in an Oxford list than it would have been for Cambridge at this time as Platonic studies were slower in general to catch on.

The remainder of the booklist provides a few clues to Hart's other interests. The medical works, such as Paulus, *Aegineta*, and the *Regimen Sanitatis Salernitatum*, were really only introductory texts. Likewise the scientific texts (besides those stipulated for the study of astronomy) are somewhat basic, the *Testamentum artem chymicam complectens* of Ramón Lull being the only unusual work in this genre. Hart's books give little away with respect to his theological views; several works by Jeronimo Osorio da Fonseca, *Bishop of Silves*, are present, but they cannot be considered controversial, nor can the presence of works by Erasmus, or St. John, *Chrysostom* raise any eyebrows. A life of Reginald Pole, who had only died in 1558, is unusual, but may be explained away as contemporary history.

Oxford University Archives, Bodleian Library: Hyp.B.14.

§

Caldwell, John. 1986. "Appendix: Music in the Faculty of Arts" in *The Collegiate University*, ed. James McConica. Vol. 3 of *The History of the University of Oxford*, gen. ed. T.H. Aston. Oxford: Oxford Univ. Press.

Fletcher, J.M. 1986. "The Faculty of Arts" in *The Collegiate University*, ed. James McConica. Vol. 3 of *The History of the University of Oxford*, gen. ed. T.H. Aston. Oxford: Oxford Univ. Press.

Gibson, Strickland. 1931. *Statuta Antiqua Universitatis Oxoniensis*. Oxford: Clarendon Press.

Jones, G. Lloyd. 1983. *The Discovery of Hebrew in Tudor England: A Third Language*. Manchester: Manchester Univ. Press.

McConica, James K. 1979. "Humanism and Aristotle in Tudor Oxford," *English Historical Review* 94:291-317.

Schmitt, Charles B. 1983. *John Case and Aristotelianism in Renaissance England*. Kingston and Montreal: McGill–Queen's Univ. Press.

Stevenson, W.H. and H.E. Salter. 1939. *The Early History of St. John's College Oxford*. Oxford: Oxford Historical Society.

Ward, G.R.M. 1843. *The Foundation Statutes of Bishop Fox for Corpus Christi College in the University of Oxford, A.D., 1517*. London: Longman, Brown, Green and Longmans.

§

92.1	Biblia latina in folio
92.2	lexicon grecolatinus
92.3	Metochites in Aristotelis philosofiam
92.4	Aristotelis ppia [philosophia] in 4o grece
92.5	Margaret Ppia [Philosophia]
92.6	Trafezatii rhetor [rhetorica] in 4
92.7	Osorius de gloria
92.8	Osorius de nobilitate
92.9	Osorius de justicia
92.10	Toxites in ad herrenium
92.11	opera Ciceronis in 9 volum [voluminibus]
92.12	epistolae familiares Ciceronis plat
92.13	Virgilius in 8o
92.14	Isocrates orat [orationes] cum epistolis grece
92.15	Donatus in ethica Aristot
92.16	Quintilliani Institutiones
92.17	Ringelbergii opera
92.18	dialectica Perionii
92.19	introductiones Fabri in Ethicam Aristotelis

92.20	Johes Major in Ethica Aristot
92.21	Testamentum Novum grece
92.22	magister Sentenciarum
92.23	Problemata Aristotelis et Alexandri
92.24	loci communes Eckii
92.25	testamentum Lull
92.26	Lullius de divina essentia
92.27	Vita Reginaldi Polae
92.28	liber grece
92.29	Eobanus Hesius de tuanda valetudine
92.30	Arithmetica Recordi anglice
92.31	Johes de Bosco
92.32	Hunteri tabule
92.33	epistole Vintonie et Cheke de pnun [pronuntione] grece
92.34	Plutarchi vite duobus voluminibus
92.35	Honestella [Fenestella]
92.36	Riccius de imitacione
92.37	Exercitacio Lingue Latine
92.38	chartaceus
92.39	Hermogines retorica
92.40	Omfhalius de elocutione
92.41	arithmetica
92.42	Surius de rebus in orbe gestis
92.43	Brandolinus conscribendis de epistolii
92.44	Salustus
92.45	tragedie Senece
92.46	Strabo de sita [situ] orbis
92.47	opera Ovidii tribus vulu [voluminibus] plast
92.48	Terencius plast
92.49	Suetonius de vitis Cesarum
92.50	Laertius de vitis philosophorum
92.51	Lactantius
92.52	Appianus de civilibus
92.53	Plautus
92.54	Agripa in Artem Brevem Lullii
92.55	dialogorum sacrorum Castall [Castallionis]
92.56	L. Flores [Florus]
92.57	Beroaldus in Cic Philippica
92.58	Quintus Curtius
92.59	Ceporini graeca gramatica
92.60	Aeschinis et Demosthenis orat graece
92.61	Morias Encomion
92.62	apophthegmata Erasmi
92.63	gramatica Linacri
92.64	Horatius

92.65	Commentaria Caesaris
92.66	Elegantae Vallae
92.67	Justinus
92.68	Caietanus in Arist
92.69	Organum Aris
92.70	Arithmetica Tonstalli
92.71	Politica Arist: Screnvei
92.72	Ascentius in Salustium
92.73	Buridanus in Ethica Arist:
92.74	Plinii Naturalis historia
92.75	Beroaldus in Asinum Aureum Apulei
92.76	Damascenus de orthodoxa fide
92.77	Burleus in phisica Arist:
92.78	Albertus de Saxonia de caelo
92.79	Rodolphus de inventione dialec
92.80	epistolae Manutii
92.81	Isodorus de summo bono
92.82	Antesignanus in Cleon [Cleonardi] grammaticam
92.83	schemata Susembrote
92.84	gramat Ceporini
92.85	gramat Cleonardi
92.86	dialectica Tetellmani
92.87	Valerius Max:
92.88	Plutarchus de liberis educandis graece
92.89	Silvius in orat [orationem] pro Ligario
92.90	Macropedii rudimenta in graecam linguam
92.91	Gramatica graeca Ceporini graece
92.92	Demostenes contra Leptinum graece
92.93	Aristophanii Plutus graece
92.94	Pontalionis de quantitate sillabarum
92.95	Institutiones imperiales cum casibus
92.96	Formulare instrumentorum
92.97	Luciani dialogi deorum
92.98	Regimen Sanitatis Salerni
92.99	Pauli Aegineti pharmaca simplicia
92.100	Homiliae Chrisostomi graece
92.101	Amonius in Porphirium
92.102	Joel et Malachias hebraice
92.103	Vintonensis ad M. Bucerum
92.104	Repertorium Alphabeticum
92.105	Terentius
92.106	Colloquia Erasmi
92.107	Grammatica Sulpitii
92.108	Flores Senecae
92.109	Exercitationes Guidonis Juvenalis

92.110 Regii de lingua latina comment. tres
92.111 Scematismus artium per Thomam Frisium
92.112 Epistolae P. Bembi
92.113 Longolii
92.114 Grammatica Valerii Ultraict:
92.115 Grammatica Regia
92.116 Macrobius
92.117 Casparus Contarenus
92.118 Proclus de spera
92.119 Tusculanae Quaestiones
92.120 Commentarius in duas orationes Ciceronis
92.121 Valentinus Eritheus
92.122 Petrus Guntherus
92.123 Jeronimus Regius
92.124 Cornelius Tacita [Tacitus]
92.125 Borcerus in metora
92.126 Dialectica Erasmi
92.127 Copia Verborum
92.128:A Dialectica Cesarii
92.128:B [See 92.128:A]
92.129 Palingenius
92.130 Osorii epistola contra haddonum
92.131 Valerii dialect [dialectica]
92.132:1 Capelinus cum cornu copia
92.132:2 [See 92.132:1]
92.133 Valentinus
92.134 Aristot Ethica
92.135 Serebeus orator

§

92.1 Biblia latina in folio
The Bible. Continent: date indeterminable.
Language(s): Latin. Appraised at 20d in 1571.

92.2 lexicon grecolatinus
Unidentified [dictionary]. Continent: date indeterminable.
Language(s): Greek Latin. Appraised at 2s 6d in 1571.

92.3 Metochites in Aristotelis philosofiam
Theodorus, *Metochita. In Aristotelis universam naturalem philosophiam paraphrasis.* Basle: per Nicolaum Bryling, 1562.
Language(s): Latin. Appraised at 3s in 1571.

92.4 Aristotelis ppia [philosophia] in 4o grece
Aristotle. Unidentified. Continent: date indeterminable.
This entry could represent several different works by Aristotle. *Language(s)*: Greek. Appraised at 2s 8d in 1571.

92.5 Margaret Ppia [Philosophia]
Gregor Reisch. *Margarita philosophica*. Continent: date indeterminable.
Language(s): Latin. Appraised at 2s in 1571.

92.6 Trafezatii rhetor [rhetorica] in 4
Georgius Trapezuntius. [*Rhetorica*]. Continent: date indeterminable.
This title contains much of the rhetorical work of Cicero and Hermogenes. Editions from 1472, but the earliest editions in quarto are in the sixteenth century. *Language(s)*: Latin. Appraised at 14d in 1571.

92.7 Osorius de gloria
Jeronimo Osorio da Fonseca, *Bishop*. *De gloria*. Florence: apud Laurentium Torrentinum, 1552.
The 1571 edition of his *Selected works* with *De gloria* leading is too late since Hart died in 1570, old style. *Language(s)*: Latin. Appraised at 16d in 1571.

92.8 Osorius de nobilitate
Jeronimo Osorio da Fonseca, *Bishop*. *De nobilitate civili libri II. De nobilitate christiana libri III*. Continent: 1542–1552.
Language(s): Latin. Appraised at 16d in 1571.

92.9 Osorius de justicia
Jeronimo Osorio da Fonseca, *Bishop*. *De justitia*. Venice: ex officina Jacobus Ziletus impensis Joannes Gryphius, 1564.
Language(s): Latin. Appraised at 20d in 1571.

92.10 Toxites in ad herrenium
Michael Toxites. [*Cicero (spurious)–Rhetorica ad Herennium: commentary and text*]. Basle: Joannes Oporinus (with different houses), 1556–1568.
Language(s): Latin. Appraised at 12d in 1571.

92.11 opera Ciceronis in 9 volum [voluminibus]
Marcus Tullius Cicero. [*Works*]. Continent: date indeterminable.
Language(s): Latin. Appraised at 3s 4d in 1571.

92.12 epistolae familiares Ciceronis plat
Marcus Tullius Cicero. *Epistolae ad familiares*. Continent: date indeterminable.

Perhaps *plat* indicates "platus" or "flat," that is, in sheets, or less likely, "Plantin." *Language(s)*: Latin. Appraised at 12d in 1571.

92.13 Virgilius in 8o
Publius Virgilius Maro. Perhaps [*Works*]. Britain or Continent: date indeterminable.
STC 24787 *et seq.* and non-STC. *Language(s)*: Latin. Appraised at 14d in 1571.

92.14 Isocrates orat [orationes] cum epistolis grece
Isocrates. [*Works*]. Continent: date indeterminable.
Greek title. *Language(s)*: Greek. Appraised at 12d in 1571.

92.15 Donatus in ethica Aristot
Donatus Acciaiolus. [*Aristotle–Ethica: commentary*]. Continent: date indeterminable.
Treated as the independently published commentary; it could be an edition with Acciaiolus's commentary. *Language(s)*: Latin. Appraised at 20d in 1571.

92.16 Quintilliani Institutiones
Marcus Fabius Quintilianus. *Institutiones oratoriae*. Continent: date indeterminable.
Language(s): Latin. Appraised at 12d in 1571.

92.17 Ringelbergii opera
Joachimus Fortius Ringelbergius. [*Works*]. Lyon: (different houses), 1531–1556.
This work covers virtually all fields of human knowledge, including the occult arts, for which this book was placed on the *Index* in 1559. It was no doubt for the large sections on grammar, rhetoric, and dialectics that Hart owned the work. *Language(s)*: Latin. Appraised at 2s in 1571.

92.18 dialectica Perionii
Joachim Perion. *De dialectica*. Continent: 1544–1554.
Language(s): Latin. Appraised at 12d in 1571.

92.19 introductiones Fabri in Ethicam Aristotelis
Jacobus Faber, *Stapulensis*. [*Aristotle–Ethica: commentary and text*]. Continent: 1494–1560.
Most editions of this compendium of Aristotle's text carry Faber's commentary. *Language(s)*: Latin. Appraised at 8d in 1571.

92.20 Johes Major in Ethica Aristot
Joannes Major. *Ethica Aristotelis peripateticorum principis cum Joannis Majo-*

ris commentariis. Aristotle's text was translated by Joannes Argyropoulos. Paris: Vaenundantor cuius impressa sunt Jodoco Badio et in societatem accepto Joannes Parvo, 1530.
Language(s): Latin. Appraised at 16d in 1571.

92.21 Testamentum Novum grece
[*Bible–N.T.*]. Continent: date indeterminable.
Greek title. *Language(s)*: Greek. Appraised at 8d in 1571.

92.22 magister Sentenciarum
Peter Lombard. *Sententiarum libri IIII*. Continent: date indeterminable.
Language(s): Latin. Appraised at 6d in 1571.

92.23 Problemata Aristotelis et Alexandri
Aristotle (spurious). *Problemata*. Continent: date indeterminable.
This work was falsely attributed to Alexander, *Aphrodisiensis* and Aristotle. The editions were accompanied by the commentaries of various Renaissance authors. See CTC 1:126–34. *Language(s)*: Latin. Appraised at 6d in 1571.

92.24 loci communes Eckii
Joannes Eckius. *Enchiridion locorum communium adversus Lutheranos*. Britain or Continent: 1525–1567.
STC 7481.4 and non-STC. *Language(s)*: Latin. Appraised at 8d in 1571.

92.25 testamentum Lull
Ramón Lull. *Testamentum artem chymicam complectens*. Cologne: apud Joannem Byrckmannum, 1566.
Language(s): Latin. Appraised with one other at 14d in 1571.

92.26 Lullius de divina essentia
Ramón Lull. Perhaps *De secretis naturae*. Continent: date indeterminable.
Widely printed; appraised by the compiler with the preceding, also a work on magic and alchemy. But consider Lull's *De conficiendo divino elixire* as well. *Language(s)*: Latin. Appraised with one other at 14d in 1571.

92.27 Vita Reginaldi Polae
Lodovico Beccadelli. *Vita Reginaldi Poli, Cardinalis*. Translated by Andreas Dudith, *Bishop*. Venice: ex officina Dominici Guerrei et Joannes Baptistae fratrum, 1563.
Language(s): Latin. Appraised at 4d in 1571.

92.28 liber grece
Unidentified. Place unknown: stationer unknown, date indeterminable.
STC/non-STC status unknown. *Language(s)*: Greek. Appraised at 4d in 1571.

92.29 Eobanus Hesius de tuanda valetudine

Helius Eobanus, *Hessus*. [*De tuenda bona valetudine*]. Continent: date indeterminable.

Often found with the commentary of Johann Placotomus, and some editions contain additional works. Not appraised. *Language(s)*: Latin.

92.30 Arithmetica Recordi anglice

Robert Record. *The ground of artes teachyng the worke and practise of arithmetike*. London: R. Wolfe, 1543-1570.

STC 20797.5 *et seq.* Not appraised. *Language(s)*: English.

92.31 Johes de Bosco

John Holywood (Joannes Sacrobosco). Unidentified. Continent: date indeterminable.

His *Sphaera mundi* was by far his most widely published work, but his *Algorismus* would also fit the context. *Language(s)*: Latin. Appraised at 4d in 1571.

92.32 Hunteri tabule

Probably Joannes Honterus. *Rudimenta cosmographica*. Continent: date indeterminable.

Some editions carry "cum tabellis geographicus" on the title page. *Language(s)*: Latin. Appraised at 4d in 1571.

92.33 epistole Vintonie et Cheke de pnun [pronuntione] grece

Sir John Cheke. *De pronuntiatione graecae*. Edited by Caelius Augustinus Curio. Basle: per Nicolaum Episcopium juniorem, 1555.

Contains Stephen Gardiner's (Bishop of Winchester) *Disputationes*. *Language(s)*: Greek Latin. Appraised at 8d in 1571.

92.34 Plutarchi vite duobus voluminibus

Plutarch. *Vitae parallelae*. Continent: date indeterminable.

This entry could represent several specific editions or possibly a composite set, from different editions. *Language(s)*: Latin (probable) Greek (perhaps). Appraised at 20d in 1571.

92.35 Honestella [Fenestella]

Andreas Dominicus Floccus (Lucius Fenestella). *De magistratibus sacerdotiisque Romanorum*. Continent: date indeterminable.

Some of the editions of this work also contain the *De magistratibus et sacerdotis et praeterea de diversis legibus romanarum* of Pomponius Laetus. *Language(s)*: Latin. Appraised at 4d in 1571.

92.36 Riccius de imitacione

Bartholomaeus Riccius. *De imitatione libri tres*. Continent: 1545-1557. *Language(s)*: Latin. Appraised at 3d in 1571.

92.37 Exercitacio Lingue Latine
Probably Joannes Lodovicus Vives. [*Familiarium colloquiorum formulae, sive linguae latinae exercitatio*]. Continent: date indeterminable.
Language(s): Latin. Appraised at 2d in 1571.

92.38 chartaceus
Unidentified. Provenance unknown: date indeterminable.
Manuscript. *Chartaceus*, i.e., made of paper. *Language(s)*: Unknown. Appraised at 4d in 1571.

92.39 Hermogines retorica
Hermogenes. *Ars rhetorica*. Continent: date indeterminable.
Language(s): Latin. Appraised at 6d in 1571.

92.40 Omfhalius de elocutione
Jacobus Omphalius. *De elocutionis imitatione ac apparatu*. Continent: date indeterminable.
Language(s): Latin. Appraised at 6d in 1571.

92.41 arithmetica
Unidentified. Place unknown: stationer unknown, date indeterminable.
STC/non-STC status unknown. Works by Humphrey Baker, by Robert Recorde, and by Cuthbert Tunstall were all variously cited by compilers of book-lists as *Arithmetica*; see BCI 2:70, 2:659, and 2:760. Many Continental publications carry this word as part of a Latin title. Tunstall appears elsewhere in this list (92.70) and therefore is probably not intended here. *Language(s)*: Latin (probable) English (perhaps). Appraised at 4d in 1571.

92.42 Surius de rebus in orbe gestis
Laurentius Surius. *Commentaria brevis rerum in orbe gestarum*. Continent: 1566-1568.
Language(s): Latin. Appraised at 18d in 1571.

92.43 Brandolinus conscribendis de epistolii
Aurelius Brandolinus (Lippus). *De ratione scribendi*. Continent: 1549-1565.
The editions often append the letter-writing treatises of Vives, Celtis, Hegendorff, and Strebaeus. *Language(s)*: Latin. Appraised at 16d in 1571.

92.44 Salustus
Caius Sallustius Crispus. Unidentified. Place unknown: stationer unknown, date indeterminable.
STC/non-STC status unknown. *Language(s)*: Latin. Appraised at 8d in 1571.

92.45 tragedie Senece
Lucius Annaeus Seneca. *Tragoediae*. Continent: date indeterminable. *Language(s)*: Latin. Appraised at 6d in 1571.

92.46 Strabo de sita [situ] orbis
Strabo. [*Geographia*]. Continent: date indeterminable. *Language(s)*: Latin. Appraised at 10d in 1571.

92.47 opera Ovidii tribus vulu [voluminibus] plast
Publius Ovidius Naso. [*Works*]. Continent: date indeterminable.

The word *plast* in this entry possibly stands for *platus* (flat), implying that the item was still in sheets, although the high valuation might suggest that the item was bound but in *paste* boards. The 1570 *Opera* published in London (STC 18926.1) was not in three volumes. *Language(s)*: Latin. Appraised at 6s in 1571.

92.48 Terencius plast
Publius Terentius, *Afer*. [*Works*]. Britain or Continent: date indeterminable.

STC 23885 *et seq.* and non-STC. The entry *plast* perhaps stands for *platus* (flat) meaning the item was still in sheets. See also 92.105. *Language(s)*: Latin. Appraised at 12d in 1571.

92.49 Suetonius de vitis Cesarum
Caius Suetonius Tranquillus. *De vita Caesarum*. Continent: date indeterminable.
Language(s): Latin. Appraised at 10d in 1571.

92.50 Laertius de vitis philosophorum
Diogenes Laertius. [*De vita et moribus philosophorum*]. Continent: date indeterminable.
Language(s): Latin Greek (perhaps). Appraised at 10d in 1571.

92.51 Lactantius
Lucius Coelius Lactantius. Unidentified. Place unknown: stationer unknown, date indeterminable.

STC/non-STC status unknown. Possibly an edition of the *Opera* or the *Divinarum institutionum*. *Language(s)*: Latin. Appraised at 12d in 1571.

92.52 Appianus de civilibus
Appian, *of Alexandria*. [*Historia Romana*]. Continent: date indeterminable. *Language(s)*: Latin. Appraised at 16d in 1571.

92.53 Plautus
Titus Maccius Plautus. Unidentified. Continent: date indeterminable. *Language(s)*: Latin. Appraised at 10d in 1571.

92.54 Agripa in Artem Brevem Lullii
Henricus Cornelius Agrippa. *In artem brevem Raymundi Lullii*. Continent: 1531–1568.
Language(s): Latin. Appraised at 6d in 1571.

92.55 dialogorum sacrorum Castall [Castallionis]
Sebastian Castalio. *Dialogorum sacrorum libri quatuor*. Britain or Continent: date indeterminable.
STC 4770 and non-STC. *Language(s)*: Latin. Appraised at 4d in 1571.

92.56 L. Flores [Florus]
Lucius Annaeus Florus. Probably [*Epitomae de Tito Livio bellorum omnium annorum*]. Continent: date indeterminable.
Not appraised. *Language(s)*: Latin.

92.57 Beroaldus in Cic Philippica
Philippus Beroaldus, *the Elder*. [*Cicero–Philippicae: commentary*]. Continent: date indeterminable.
Editions usually contained commentaries by others (Franciscus Maturantius and Georgius Trapezuntius). Some sources, *Aureliensis* among them, say the Beroaldus is *the Younger*. *Language(s)*: Latin. Appraised with one other at 8d in 1571.

92.58 Quintus Curtius
Quintus Curtius Rufus. *De rebus gestis Alexandri Magni*. Continent: date indeterminable.
English translations appeared from 1553, none of which is likely to be intended here. *Language(s)*: Latin. Appraised with one other at 8d in 1571.

92.59 Ceporini graeca gramatica
Jacobus Ceporinus. *Compendium grammaticae graecae*. Continent: 1522–1565.
Other copies at 92.84 and 92.91. *Language(s)*: Greek Latin. Appraised at 4d in 1571.

92.60 Aeschinis et Demosthenis orat graece
Aeschines and Demosthenes. [*Selected works–Orations*]. Continent: date indeterminable.
Not appraised. *Language(s)*: Greek.

92.61 Morias Encomion
Desiderius Erasmus. *Moriae encomium*. Continent: 1511–1551.
Language(s): Latin. Appraised at 6d in 1571.

92.62 apophthegmata Erasmi
Desiderius Erasmus. *Apophthegmata*. Continent: 1531–1570.
Language(s): Latin. Appraised at 10d in 1571.

92.63 gramatica Linacri
Thomas Linacre. *Rudimenta grammatices*. Translated by George Buchanan. Britain or Continent: 1525 (probable)–1566.
STC 15636 and non-STC. Shaaber L202-27. The early Pynson editions were also in English. Possibly also the *Linacri progymnasmata grammatices vulgaria* (1512) STC 15635. *Language(s)*: Latin English (perhaps). Appraised at 12d in 1571.

92.64 Horatius
Quintus Horatius Flaccus. Probably [*Works*]. Continent: date indeterminable.
Language(s): Latin. Appraised at 10d in 1571.

92.65 Commentaria Caesaris
Caius Julius Caesar. *Commentarii*. Continent: date indeterminable.
Language(s): Latin. Appraised at 8d in 1571.

92.66 Elegantae Vallae
Laurentius Valla. *Elegantiae*. Continent: date indeterminable.
Language(s): Latin. Appraised at 8d in 1571.

92.67 Justinus
Trogus Pompeius and Justinus, *the Historian*. [*Epitomae in Trogi Pompeii historias*]. Continent: date indeterminable.
Some of the editions also contain the *Gesta Romanorum* of Florus. *Language(s)*: Latin. Appraised at 6d in 1571.

92.68 Caietanus in Arist
Unidentified. [*Aristotle–Unidentified: commentary*]. Continent: date indeterminable.
This entry could represent one of several different commentaries on specific works of Aristotle if Gaietanus, de Thienis is the author. It could, however, be a work by Thomas de Vio Caietanus whose commentaries on Aristotle's logic appeared in several editions by the date of this inventory, a book complementing the next item, an edition of the *Organon*. *Language(s)*: Latin. Appraised at 16d in 1571.

92.69 Organum Aris
Aristotle. *Organon*. Continent: date indeterminable.
Language(s): Greek (probable) Latin (perhaps). Appraised at 6d in 1571.

92.70 Arithmetica Tonstalli
Cuthbert Tunstall, *Bishop*. *De arte supputandi libri quattuor*. Britain or Continent: 1522-1554.

STC 24319 and non-STC. See notes to 92.41. *Language(s)*: Latin. Appraised at 12d in 1571.

92.71 Politica Arist: Screnvei
Aristotle. *Politica*. Continent: date indeterminable.

Perhaps the translation by Joannes Ludovicus Strebaeus, conceivably intended by *Screnvei*. *Language(s)*: Latin. Appraised at 14d in 1571.

92.72 Ascentius in Salustium
Caius Sallustius Crispus. [*Works*]. Edited by Jodocus Badius, *Ascensius*. Continent: 1504-1564.

An edition of the works of Sallust with the commentary of Jodocus Badius, *Ascensius*. *Language(s)*: Latin. Appraised at 8d in 1571.

92.73 Buridanus in Ethica Arist:
Joannes Buridanus. [*Aristotle–Ethica: commentary*]. Continent: 1489-1518. *Language(s)*: Latin. Appraised at 12d in 1571.

92.74 Plinii Naturalis historia
Pliny, *the Elder*. *Historia naturalis*. Continent: date indeterminable. *Language(s)*: Latin. Appraised at 16d in 1571.

92.75 Beroaldus in Asinum Aureum Apulei
Philippus Beroaldus, *the Elder*. [*Apuleius–Metamorphoses: commentary and text*]. Continent: 1500-1536.

Language(s): Latin. Appraised at 20d in 1571.

92.76 Damascenus de orthodoxa fide
John, *of Damascus, Saint*. *De fide orthodoxa*. Continent: date indeterminable.

This work seems not to have appeared alone; it appears in several editions of various *Selected works*, sometimes leading. *Language(s)*: Greek (probable) Latin (perhaps). Appraised at 2s in 1571.

92.77 Burleus in phisica Arist:
Walter Burley. [*Aristotle–Physica: commentary*]. Continent: 1476-1524. *Language(s)*: Latin. Appraised at 2s in 1571.

92.78 Albertus de Saxonia de caelo
Albertus, *de Saxonia*. [*Aristotle–De caelo: commentary*]. Continent: 1481-1562.

Language(s): Latin. Appraised at 20d in 1571.

92.79 Rodolphus de inventione dialec
Rodolphus Agricola. *De inventione dialectica*. Continent: 1515-1570.
Language(s): Latin. Appraised at 4d in 1571.

92.80 epistolae Manutii
Paolo Manuzio. [*Epistolae*]. Continent: date indeterminable.
From 1558. *Language(s)*: Latin. Appraised at 8d in 1571.

92.81 Isodorus de summo bono
Isidore, *Saint, Bishop of Seville*. *De summo bono*. Continent: date indeterminable.
Language(s): Latin. Appraised at 4d in 1571.

92.82 Antesignanus in Cleon grammaticam
Nicolaus Clenardus. [*Institutiones linguae graecae*]. Continent: date indeterminable.
See also 92.85 below. *Language(s)*: Greek Latin. Appraised at 16d in 1571.

92.83 schemata Susembrote
Joannes Susenbrotus. *Epitome troporum ac schematum*. Britain or Continent: 1535?-1570.
STC 23437 *et seq.* and non-STC. Some editions carry a Greek title. *Language(s)*: Greek Latin. Appraised at 2d in 1571.

92.84 gramat Ceporini
Jacobus Ceporinus. *Compendium grammaticae graecae*. Continent: 1522-1565.
Some editions also contain the *Georgicon* of Hesiod. Other copies at 92.59 and 92.91. *Language(s)*: Greek Latin. Appraised with one other at 8d in 1571.

92.85 gramat Cleonardi
Nicolaus Clenardus. [*Institutiones linguae graecae*]. Continent: date indeterminable.
See also 92.82 above. *Language(s)*: Greek Latin. Appraised with one other at 8d in 1571.

92.86 dialectica Tetellmani
Franz Titelmann. [*Dialectica*]. Continent: date indeterminable.
This entry represents either his *Compendium dialecticae* or the *Dialecticae considerationis libri sex*. *Language(s)*: Latin. Appraised at 6d in 1571.

92.87 Valerius Max:
Valerius Maximus. *Facta et dicta memorabilia*. Continent: date indeterminable.
Language(s): Latin. Appraised at 3d in 1571.

92.88 Plutarchus de liberis educandis graece
Plutarch (spurious). Περὶ παιδῶν ἀγωγῆς *(De educatione puerorum)*. Continent: date indeterminable.
Language(s): Greek. Appraised at 2d in 1571.

92.89 Silvius in orat [orationem] pro Ligario
Franciscus Sylvius, *of Amiens*. [*Cicero–Pro Ligario: commentary and text*]. Continent: 1539–1542.
Language(s): Latin. Appraised at 1d in 1571.

92.90 Macropedii rudimenta in graecam linguam
Georgius Macropedius. *Graecarum institutionum rudimenta*. Paris: apud T. Richardum, 1554.
Language(s): Greek Latin. Appraised at 1d in 1571.

92.91 Gramatica graeca Ceporini graece
Jacobus Ceporinus. *Compendium grammaticae graecae*. Continent: 1522–1565.
Other copies at 92.59 and 92.84. *Language(s)*: Greek Latin. Appraised at 4d in 1571.

92.92 Demostenes contra Leptinum graece
Demosthenes. *Adversus Leptinem*. Continent: date indeterminable.
Greek editions were published in 1526, 1551, 1559, and 1569, at least, but the entry could represent a composite publication with *In Midiam* in 1567, also in Greek. *Language(s)*: Greek Latin (perhaps). Appraised at 2d in 1571.

92.93 Aristophanii Plutus graece
Aristophanes. Πλοῦτος *(Plutus)*. Continent: date indeterminable.
Low valuation for a diglott. *Language(s)*: Greek Latin (perhaps). Appraised at 2d in 1571.

92.94 Pontalionis de quantitate sillabarum
Pantaleon Barteleone Raverinus. *De ratione quantitatis syllabariae liber*. Continent (probable): date indeterminable.
Almost certainly not an STC book. The sole edition known is Lyon, 1575–1576 (see BCI 2:657), but there must have been an earlier edition. For another pre-1575–1576 copy, see PLRE 103.65. *Language(s)*: Latin. Appraised at 3d in 1571.

92.95 Institutiones imperiales cum casibus
Probably Justinian I. *Institutiones. (Corpus juris civilis)*. Continent: date indeterminable.
This entry may also represent the *Institutiones imperiales* of Joachim Hop-

per, 1560 and 1565 (VD16 C5202 and C5204). *Language(s)*: Latin. Appraised at 8d in 1571.

92.96 Formulare instrumentorum
Unidentified. Continent: date indeterminable.

Probably not an STC book. The most likely possibilities are: *Formulare instrumentorum cui subjectum est opusculum ars notariatus nuncupatum* and Petrus Dominicus de Mussis, *Formularium instrumentorum*. *Language(s)*: Latin. Appraised at 4d in 1571.

92.97 Luciani dialogi deorum
Lucian, *of Samosata*. *Deorum dialogi*. Continent: date indeterminable. *Language(s)*: Greek Latin. Appraised at 4d in 1571.

92.98 Regimen Sanitatis Salerni
[*Regimen sanitatis Salernitatum*]. Britain or Continent: date indeterminable.

STC 21596 *et seq.* and non-STC. The Latin-English version of this text contains the Latin title. *Language(s)*: Latin English (perhaps). Appraised at 1d in 1571.

92.99 Pauli Aegineti pharmaca simplicia
Paulus, *Aegineta*. *Pharmaca simplicia*. Edited by Otto Brunfels. Continent: 1531-1532.

Also contains a version of the *De ratione victus* translated by Gulielmus Copus. *Language(s)*: Latin. Appraised at 4d in 1571.

92.100 Homiliae Chrisostomi graece
John, *Chrysostom, Saint*. [*Homiliae*]. Continent: date indeterminable.

Because Cheke's 1543 edition of two homilies issued in London (STC 14634) is in both Greek and Latin, it is not thought to be intended here. *Language(s)*: Greek. Appraised at 1d in 1571.

92.101 Amonius in Porphirium
Ammonius, *Hermiae*. [*Porphyrius, of Tyre–Isagoge: commentary*]. Continent: date indeterminable.

Language(s): Greek Latin. Appraised at 4d in 1571.

92.102 Joel et Malachias hebraice
David Kimchi. *Joel et Malachias cum commentario. (Bible–O.T.)*. Edited by Sebastian Muenster. Basle: ex officina Henrici Petri, 1530.

Title in Hebrew. *Language(s)*: Hebrew Latin. Appraised at 1d in 1571.

92.103 Vintonensis ad M. Bucerum
Stephen Gardiner, *Bishop*. *Ad Martinum Bucerum*. Continent: 1544-1546. Shaaber G7-11. *Language(s)*: Latin. Appraised at 1d in 1571.

92.104 Repertorium Alphabeticum
Unidentified. Continent (probable): date indeterminable.

Probably not an STC book. Conrad Leontorius's *Repertorium alphabeticum sententiarum* (1508) is a possibility, but the entry is much too general to make such a specific identification. *Language(s)*: Latin. Appraised at 2d in 1571.

92.105 Terentius
Publius Terentius, *Afer*. [*Works*]. Britain or Continent: date indeterminable. STC 23885.3 *et seq.* and non-STC. See also 92.48. *Language(s)*: Latin. Appraised at 1d in 1571.

92.106 Colloquia Erasmi
Desiderius Erasmus. *Colloquia*. Britain or Continent: date indeterminable. STC 10450.6 *et seq.* and non-STC. *Language(s)*: Latin. Appraised at 2d in 1571.

92.107 Grammatica Sulpitii
Joannes Sulpitius. *Grammatica*. Britain or Continent: date indeterminable. STC 23425 *et seq.* and non-STC. *Language(s)*: Latin. Appraised at 1d in 1571.

92.108 Flores Senecae
Lucius Annaeus Seneca. [*Selections–Flores selecti*]. Continent: date indeterminable.

Language(s): Latin. Appraised at 2d in 1571.

92.109 Exercitationes Guidonis Juvenalis
Guido Juvenalis. Perhaps *Interpretatio in Laurentii Vallae Elegantias latinae linguae*. Continent: 1490–1508.

Language(s): Latin. Appraised at 4d in 1571.

92.110 Regii de lingua latina comment. tres
Hieronymus Regius. *Linguae latinae commentarii tres*. Venice: (different houses), 1568–1570?

Another copy at 92.123. *Language(s)*: Latin. Appraised at 6d in 1571.

92.111 Scematismus artium per Thomam Frisium
Unidentified. Continent (probable): date indeterminable.

Probably not an STC book. Perhaps Thomas Joannes Freigius, or even an attempt at "Gemmam Frisium" (Reiner Gemma, *Frisius*). *Language(s)*: Latin (probable). Appraised at 8d in 1571.

92.112 Epistolae P. Bembi
Pietro Bembo. [*Epistolae*]. Continent: date indeterminable.

Language(s): Latin. Appraised at 8d in 1571.

92.113 Longolii
Christophorus Longolius. Unidentified. Continent: date indeterminable. Gilbert Longolius is but a slim possibility. *Language(s)*: Latin. Appraised at 10d in 1571.

92.114 Grammatica Valerii Ultraict:
Cornelius Valerius. *Grammaticum institutionum libri IIII*. Continent: 1557–1567.
The entry refers to Valerius's Utrecht origins. *Language(s)*: Latin. Appraised at 10d in 1571.

92.115 Grammatica Regia
William Lily. *Institutio compendiaria totius grammaticae*. Britain or Continent: 1540–1570.
STC 15610.5 *et seq*. This work was known under several variant titles. *Language(s)*: Latin English (perhaps). Appraised at 4d in 1571.

92.116 Macrobius
Ambrosius Aurelius Theodosius Macrobius. *In somnium Scipionis. Saturnalia*. Continent: 1472–1565.
Not all editions carry the *Saturnalia*. *Language(s)*: Latin. Appraised at 4d in 1571.

92.117 Casparus Contarenus
Gasparo Contarini. Unidentified. Continent: date indeterminable. *Language(s)*: Latin. Appraised at 2d in 1571.

92.118 Proclus de spera
Diadochus Proclus. *Sphaera*. Britain or Continent: date indeterminable. STC 20398.3 and non-STC. *Language(s)*: Latin. Appraised at 1d in 1571.

92.119 Tusculanae Quaestiones
Marcus Tullius Cicero. *Quaestiones Tusculanae*. Continent: date indeterminable.
Language(s): Latin. Appraised at 6d in 1571.

92.120 Commentarius in duas orationes Ciceronis
Unidentified. [*Cicero–Selected works–Orations: commentary*]. Continent: date indeterminable.
The two orations are unidentifiable. *Language(s)*: Latin. Appraised at 1d in 1571.

92.121 Valentinus Eritheus
Valentinus Erythraeus. Unidentified. Continent: date indeterminable.
Probably a commentary on one of the rhetorical works of Cicero. *Language(s)*: Latin. Appraised at 20d in 1571.

92.122 Petrus Guntherus

Petrus Guntherus. *De arte rhetorica libri duo*. Continent: 1521-1568. The 1568 edition carries a commentary by Valentinus Erythraeus; see the preceding. *Language(s)*: Latin. Appraised at 10d in 1571.

92.123 Jeronimus Regius

Hieronymus Regius. *Linguae latinae commentarii tres*. Venice: (different houses), 1568-1570?
Another copy at 92.110. Not appraised. *Language(s)*: Latin.

92.124 Cornelius Tacita [Tacitus]

Publius Cornelius Tacitus. Unidentified. Continent: date indeterminable. Not appraised. *Language(s)*: Latin.

92.125 Borcerus in metora

Unidentified. Place unknown: stationer unknown, date indeterminable.
STC/non-STC status unknown. Perhaps a commentary on Aristotle's *Meteora*, with either Dacus or Anicius M.T.S. Boethius having a hand in it. *Language(s)*: Unknown. Appraised at 20d in 1571.

92.126 Dialectica Erasmi

Erasmus Sarcerius. *Dialectica*. Continent: 1537-c.1549
Language(s): Latin. Appraised at 2d in 1571.

92.127 Copia Verborum

Probably Desiderius Erasmus. *De duplici copia verborum ac rerum*. Britain or Continent: date indeterminable.
STC 10471.4 *et seq.* and non-STC. Falling as it does between two "Dialecticas," this entry could also conceivably represent the *Partitiones dialecticae* (1560-1563), the *Partitiones logicae* (1561), or the *Partitiones rhetoricae* (1561) of Bernhard Cop (or Copius). *Language(s)*: Latin. Appraised at 2d in 1571.

92.128:A Dialectica Cesarii

Joannes Caesarius, *Juliacensis*. *Dialectica*. Continent: date indeterminable.
Language(s): Latin. Appraised [composite volume] at 4d in 1571.

92.128:B [See 92.128:A]

Joannes Murmellius. [*Aristotle-Categoriae: commentary*]. Continent: date indeterminable.
Language(s): Latin. Appraised [composite volume] at 4d in 1571.

92.129 Palingenius

Marcellus Palingenius (Pietro Angelo Manzolli [Stellatus]). *Zodiacus vitae*. Britain or Continent: date indeterminable.
STC 19138.5 and non-STC. *Language(s)*: Latin (probable) English (perhaps). Appraised at 6d in 1571.

92.130 Osorii epistola contra haddonum
Jeronimo Osorio da Fonseca, *Bishop*. *In Gualterum Haddonum magistrum libellorum supplicum libri tres*. Continent: 1567–1569.
More likely, the 1569 edition, the long title of which contains "*Praefixa est epistola*," but since the exchange with Walter Haddon involved more than one published epistle, the reference could point to either edition. *Language(s)*: Latin. Appraised at 8d in 1571.

92.131 Valerii dialect [dialectica]
Cornelius Valerius. *Tabulae totius dialectices*. Continent: 1548–1570.
Language(s): Latin. Appraised at 10d in 1571.

92.132:1 Capelinus cum cornu copia
Probably Ambrogio Calepino. *Dictionarium*. Britain or Continent: 1502–1571.
STC 6832.1 *et seq.* and non-STC. Likely to contain several other languages as well; see Labarre. Perhaps bound with the next. *Language(s)*: Greek Latin. Appraised with one other at 16d in 1571.

92.132:2 [See 92.132:1]
Nicolaus Perottus. *Cornucopia*. Continent: date indeterminable.
Perhaps bound with the preceding. *Language(s)*: Latin. Appraised with one other at 16d in 1571.

92.133 Valentinus
Unidentified. Continent (probable): date indeterminable.
Probably not an STC book. This entry may refer to a work by Joannes Valentinus Gentilis, Valentinus Erythraeus, or Valentinus Polidamus. *Language(s)*: Unknown. Appraised at 10d in 1571.

92.134 Aristot Ethica
Aristotle. *Ethica*. Britain or Continent: date indeterminable.
STC 752 *et seq.* and non-STC. *Language(s)*: Latin. Appraised at 20d in 1571.

92.135 Serebeus orator
Jacobus Ludovicus Strebaeus. Unidentified. Continent: date indeterminable.
Possibilities include *De partibus oratoria M.T. Ciceronis* and *De electione et oratoria collocatione verborum*. *Language(s)*: Latin. Appraised at 2s in 1571.

Robert Hooper. Scholar (M.A.): Probate Inventory. 1571

KATY HOOPER

Robert Hooper (Hoper, Howper) was admitted Bachelor of Arts on 10 October 1558 and proceeded Master of Arts on 28 May 1560. Though he was to become master of Balliol on 26 March 1563, a position he held until 1570, he was never a fellow of the college. Foster (*Alumni Oxonienses*, 2:742) suggests that he may have been rector of Fuggleston St. Peter in Wiltshire from 1559 to 1571, but there is no supporting evidence for his claim except the information in Wood (1786, 84) that Robert Hooper's father was John Hooper of New Sarum. The paucity of facts relating to the son's life and career is borne out in John Jones's description of him as a master who "guided the college through difficult times until 1570, without leaving any trace of his character or affections behind him" (Jones 1988, 74). He died intestate; the inventory of his goods is dated 12 January 1571.

None of the books owned by Hooper appears to survive in Balliol library, and it is not possible to identify any of them with the books recorded *ex incerta donatione* in the Benefactors' Register. It is a small collection of mainly scholastic texts, mostly in Latin and published on the Continent.

Oxford University Archives, Bodleian Library: Hyp.A.14.

§

Jones, John. 1988. *Balliol College: A History 1263-1939*. Oxford: Oxford Univ. Press.

Wood, Anthony à. 1786. *The History and Antiquities of the Colleges and Halls in the University of Oxford*. Edited by John Gutch. Oxford: Clarendon Press.

§

93.1	a latayne bible
93.2	senica
93.3	a great paper booke
93.4	monicus Charthusianus de vita jesu christi
93.5	frobenius
93.6	Samsonus super psalmos
93.7	Aristotels naturalia
93.8	lucianus
93.9	Johannes Scotus super metaphisicis
93.10	Burleus super ethicis
93.11	faber stapulensis uppon logycke
93.12	Johannes Janduno super phisica
93.13	petrus de abbano
93.14	paulus venetius
93.15	organon Aristotelis
93.16	Thomas aquinus super ethica
93.17	petrus de abano super librum problematum Aristotelis
93.18	Johannes mer [magister] de magistris
93.19	Dionysius Carthusianus
93.20	Thomas Aquinus
93.21	iiia pars Personi
93.22	Jeronimus in vitis patrum
93.23	Ludalphus de vita christi
93.24	resolucio theologorum
93.25	opus questionum divi augustini
93.26	Isikius in liviticum
93.27	Jacobus de voragine
93.28	distructiorum viciorum
93.29	liber Sententiarum
93.30	distructiorium viciorum agayne
93.31	Johannes Beda in petrum stabulensum
93.32	petrus bartherius
93.33	aureum rosarium theologie
93.34	Sermones Nicholaii de bloni
93.35	Nicholaus cusa
93.36	ludalphus de vita christi
93.37	concordantiae majores alias biblie
93.38	monacus Carthusianus
93.39	Franciscus lewkettus in Johannem duns
93.40	flos theologie
93.41	Epistole Jeronimi
93.42	rationale divinorum
93.43	5a pars lyre

93.44	Comentarii Stephani lingue latine
93.45	exemplaria brevium regis galliae
93.46	Josephus de antiquitatibus
93.47	Calepinus
93.48	opera ovidii
93.49	Capreolus
93.50	organon Aristotelis
93.51	bricott in phisicam
93.52	Sermones dormi securi
93.53	Sermones gagneii
93.54	psalterium hebraicum
93.55	Epithomie totius naturalis philosophie
93.56	Cocleus de concordia religionis
93.57	Novum testamentum latine
93.58	Buckerygerus de sacramento altaris
93.59	apothegmata erasmi
93.60	pighius
93.61	Cassander de baptismo infantium
93.62	Radolphus de Inventione
93.63	Anthonius Corvinus
93.64	Stobeius
93.65	petrus a soto
93.66	Thomas Aquinas contra gentiles
93.67	dorrophei sermones
93.68	Andreas althamerus de consiliacione locorum sacrarum
93.69	Tavernerius de veritate corporis chrisiti
93.70	Agrippa
93.71	gramatica hebraica
93.72	valerius maximus
93.73	faber stapbulensis
93.74	petrus lombardus
93.75	jonas dedicus
93.76	epistolae plinii
93.77	Johannes Aepinus in Evangeliorum assentionis domini

§

93.1 a latayne bible
The Bible. Britain or Continent: date indeterminable.
STC 2055 *et seq.* and non-STC. *Language(s)*: Latin. Appraised at 12d in 1571.

93.2 senica
Lucius Annaeus Seneca. Perhaps [*Works*]. Continent: date indeterminable.

The absence of an appraised value precludes any judgment on the size of the volume. *Language(s)*: Latin.

93.3 a great paper booke
Unidentified. Provenance unknown: date indeterminable.

Manuscript. The notation of the size suggests something other than a personal notebook. *Language(s)*: Unknown. Appraised at 2s 6d in 1571.

93.4 monicus Charthusianus de vita jesu christi
Probably Ludolphus, *de Saxonia* (Carthusiensis). *Vita Jesu Christi*. Continent: date indeterminable.

Possibly an incunable edition, for example that printed at Strassburg, 1474, in which the incipit identifies the author as a Carthusian monk. See also 93.38. Not appraised. *Language(s)*: Latin.

93.5 frobenius
Unidentified. Basle (probable): probably Johann Froben, date indeterminable.

Several possible texts were edited by Froben in Basle in the early sixteenth century, but it is possible that the appraiser's eye was drawn simply to Froben's name as publisher. Other book-lists carry this puzzling entry; see PLRE 67.4 (1558) and PLRE 81.3 (1569). *Language(s)*: Latin (probable) Greek (perhaps). Appraised at 2s in 157i.

93.6 Samsonus super psalmos
Richard Sampson, *Bishop*. [*Psalms: commentary*]. London: (different houses), 1539–1548.

STC 21679 *et seq.* Either the first or the second part of Sampson's commentary on the Psalms with differing titles, but conceivably, from the appraised value, both parts. *Language(s)*: Latin. Appraised at 2s in 1571.

93.7 Aristotels naturalia
Aristotle. *Parva naturalia*. Continent: date indeterminable.

Language(s): Latin (probable) Greek (perhaps). Appraised at 16d in 1571.

93.8 lucianus
Lucian, *of Samosata*. Unidentified. Place unknown: stationer unknown, date indeterminable.

STC/non-STC status unknown. What arrangement of the *Dialogues* (collected, selected, extracts) cannot be determined. Selections from Lucian in Erasmus's translation were printed in London in 1528 and 1531 (STC 16891–92), and in Henry Bullock's translation in Cambridge in 1521 (STC 16896), but Continental editions, both in Latin and Greek, were numerous. The form of the entry seems to preclude Sir Thomas Elyot's English translation of c.1532 (STC 16894). *Language(s)*: Latin (probable) Greek (perhaps). Appraised at 12d in 1571.

93.9 Johannes Scotus super metaphisicis
John Duns, *Scotus*. [*Aristotle–Metaphysica: commentary*]. Venice: (different houses), 1497-1520.
Language(s): Latin. Appraised at 8d in 1571.

93.10 Burleus super ethicis
Walter Burley. [*Aristotle–Ethica: commentary*]. Venice: (different houses), 1481-1521.
Language(s): Latin. Appraised at 8d in 1571.

93.11 faber stapulensis uppon logycke
Jacobus Faber, *Stapulensis*. [*Aristotle–Selected works–Logica: commentary*]. Continent: 1496-1545.
Either his *Introductiones logicales* (Continental editions from 1496-1545) or his *Paraphrases et annotationes in libros logicorum* (Continental editions from 1503-1543). *Language(s)*: Latin. Appraised at 12d in 1571.

93.12 Johannes Janduno super phisica
Joannes de Janduno (Joannes de Gandavo). [*Aristotle–Physica: commentary*]. Continent: 1488-1561.
Language(s): Latin. Appraised at 6d in 1571.

93.13 petrus de abbano
Petrus, *de Abano*. Unidentified. Continent: date indeterminable.
See also 93.17. *Language(s)*: Latin. Appraised at 12d in 1571.

93.14 paulus venetius
Paulus, *Venetus*. Unidentified. Continent: date indeterminable.
Probably one of his commentaries on Aristotle. *Language(s)*: Latin. Appraised at 4d in 1571.

93.15 organon Aristotelis
Aristotle. *Organon*. Continent: date indeterminable.
Language(s): Latin (probable) Greek (perhaps). Appraised at 12d in 1571.

93.16 Thomas aquinus super ethica
Thomas Aquinas, *Saint*. [*Aristotle–Ethica: commentary*]. Continent: date indeterminable.
See also 93.20 and 93.66. *Language(s)*: Latin. Appraised at 16d in 1571.

93.17 petrus de abano super librum problematum Aristotelis
Petrus, *de Abano*. [*Aristotle (spurious)–Problemata: commentary and text*]. Continent: date indeterminable.
See also 93.13. *Language(s)*: Latin. Appraised at 6d in 1571.

93.18 Johannes mer [magister] de magistris
Joannes de Magistris. Unidentified. Continent: date indeterminable. Probably one of his commentaries on Aristotle. *Language(s)*: Latin. Appraised at 4d in 1571.

93.19 Dionysius Carthusianus
Dionysius, *Carthusianus* (Dionysius, *de Rickel*). Perhaps [*Works*]. Continent: date indeterminable.

The appraised value seems too low for the English versions either of his *Vita sacerdotum* (STC 6894) or of the *Speculum aureum* (STC 6894.5-6897.5) then attributed to him. *Language(s)*: Latin. Appraised at 16d in 1571.

93.20 Thomas Aquinus
Thomas Aquinas, *Saint*. Unidentified. Continent: date indeterminable. See also 93.16 and 93.66. *Language(s)*: Latin. Appraised at 12d in 1571.

93.21 iiia pars Personi
Perhaps Joannes Gerson (Jean Charlier de Gerson). [*Works* (part)]. Continent: 1483/84-1520.

There is no identifiable author Persons or Parsons printed before the date of the inventory, while Gerson's *Works* would seem to fit in the context of Hooper's library. *Language(s)*: Latin. Appraised at 12d in 1571.

93.22 Jeronimus in vitis patrum
Jerome, *Saint*. *Vitae patrum*. Continent: date indeterminable.

The English version (STC 14507) published in 1495 is a remote possibility. *Language(s)*: Latin. Appraised at 6d in 1571.

93.23 Ludalphus de vita christi
Ludolphus, *de Saxonia*. *Vita Jesu Christi*. Continent: date indeterminable. For another copy see 93.36. See also 93.4 and 93.38. *Language(s)*: Latin. Appraised at 6d in 1571.

93.24 resolucio theologorum
Nicolaus Denyse. *Resolutio theologorum*. Continent: 1504-1516.

Adams lists a later edition in 1574, but editions do not appear to survive between 1516 and 1574. Appraised at 4d in 1571.

93.25 opus questionum divi augustini
Augustine, *Saint*. *Opus quaestionum*. Continent: date indeterminable. *Language(s)*: Latin. Appraised at 2d in 1571.

93.26 Isikius in liviticum
Hesychius, *of Jerusalem*. *In Leviticum libri septem*. (*Bible–O.T.*). Basle: apud Andreas Cratandrum, 1527.

Language(s): Latin. Appraised at 6d in 1571.

93.27 Jacobus de voragine
Jacobus de Voragine. Probably *Legenda aurea*. Britain or Continent: date indeterminable.
STC 24873 *et seq.* and non-STC. Caxton's English translation saw at least ten editions between 1483 and 1527, but one of the countless Continental Latin editions seems more probable in this collection. His popular *Sermones* also remains a possibility. *Language(s)*: Latin (probable) English (perhaps). Appraised at 4d in 1571.

93.28 distructiorum viciorum
Alexander, *Anglus* (Alexander Carpenter). *Destructorium viciorum*. Continent: date indeterminable.
There is another copy at 93.30. *Language(s)*: Latin. Appraised at 6d in 1571.

93.29 liber Sententiarum
Peter Lombard. *Sententiarum libri IIII*. Continent: date indeterminable. *Language(s)*: Latin. Appraised at 6d in 1571.

93.30 distructiorium viciorum agayne
Alexander, *Anglus* (Alexander Carpenter). *Destructorium viciorum*. Continent: date indeterminable.
There is another copy at 93.28. *Language(s)*: Latin. Appraised at 6d in 1571.

93.31 Johannes Beda in petrum stabulensum
Probably Natalis Beda. *Annotationum in Jacobum Fabrum Stapulensem libri duo*. Continent: 1526.
Includes commentary on Erasmus's paraphrases of the Epistles and Gospels as well as the commentary on Faber's treatment of the Epistles and Gospels. *Language(s)*: Latin. Appraised at 8d in 1571.

93.32 petrus bartherius
Petrus Berthorius. Unidentified. Continent: date indeterminable.
Either the *Dictionarium seu repertorium moralis* or the *Liber Bibliae Moralis*. *Language(s)*: Latin. Appraised at 12d in 1571.

93.33 aureum rosarium theologie
Pelbartus, *de Themeswar*. *Aureum sacrae theologiae rosarium*. Continent: date indeterminable.
A compilation including extracts from Aquinas, Bonaventura, and Duns, Scotus. *Language(s)*: Latin. Appraised at 6d in 1571.

93.34 Sermones Nicholaii de bloni
Nicolaus, *de Blony* (Nicolaus, *de Plove*). [*Sermones*]. Continent: 1491–1498. *Language(s)*: Latin. Appraised at 8d in 1571.

93.35 Nicholaus cusa
Nicolaus de Cusa. Unidentified. Continent: date indeterminable.
Language(s): Latin. Appraised at 4d in 1571.

93.36 ludalphus de vita christi
Ludolphus, *de Saxonia*. *Vita Jesu Christi*. Continent: date indeterminable.
For another copy see 93.23. See also 93.4 and 93.38. Appraised at 6d in 1571.

93.37 concordantiae majores alias biblie
Concordantiae majores biblie. Continent: date indeterminable.
Language(s): Latin. Appraised at 20d in 1571.

93.38 monacus Carthusianus
Probably Ludolphus, *de Saxonia*. Unidentified. Continent: date indeterminable.
See also 93.4, 93.23 and 93.36. *Language(s)*: Latin. Appraised at 6d in 1571.

93.39 Franciscus lewkettus in Johannem duns
Franciscus Lychetus. Probably [*Duns, Scotus–Sentences: commentary*]. Continent: 1512–1520.
Perhaps, however, his commentary on Duns, *Scotus*'s treatment of *Quodlibeta*, of which editions survive 1517–1520, the latter a composite with the above. *Language(s)*: Latin. Appraised at 4d in 1571.

93.40 flos theologie
John Duns, *Scotus*. *Flores totius sacre teologie*. Edited by Philippus Varagius. Milan: per Joannem Jacobum de Ferrariis, 1509.
Language(s): Latin. Appraised at 4d in 1571.

93.41 Epistole Jeronimi
Jerome, *Saint*. *Epistolae*. Continent: date indeterminable.
Language(s): Latin. Appraised at 6d in 1571.

93.42 rationale divinorum
Gulielmus Durandus I, *Bishop of Mende*. *Rationale divinorum officiorum*. Continent: date indeterminable.
Language(s): Latin. Appraised at 2d in 1571.

93.43 5a pars lyre
[*Bible–N.T.–Gospels*]. Edited by Nicolaus de Lyra. Continent: date indeterminable.
With the gloss of Lyra. *Language(s)*: Latin. Appraised at 6d in 1571.

93.44 Comentarii Stephani lingue latine
Unidentified. Continent: date indeterminable.

This entry could represent one of several works: Robert Estienne's *Dictionarium* or Charles Estienne's *Thesaurus* to either Cicero or Priscian. *Language(s)*: Latin. Appraised at 3s 3d in 1571.

93.45 exemplaria brevium regis galliae
Francis I, *King of France*. *Exemplaria literarum quibus Rex Franciscus ad adversariorum maledictis defenditur*. Paris: ex off. (excud.) Rob. Stephani, 1537.

Two editions. Attributed to Guillaume Du Bellay. *Language(s)*: Latin. Appraised at 12d in 1571.

93.46 Josephus de antiquitatibus
Flavius Josephus. *Antiquitates Judaicae*. Continent: date indeterminable.

This entry may represent one of the many editions of the *Works* leading the *De antiquitatibus*. *Language(s)*: Latin Greek (perhaps). Appraised at 12d in 1571.

93.47 Calepinus
Ambrogio Calepino. *Dictionarium*. Continent: 1502-1571.

Several vernacular languages also, depending on the edition. *Language(s)*: Greek Latin. Appraised at 4d in 1571.

93.48 opera ovidii
Publius Ovidius Naso. [*Works*]. Continent: date indeterminable.

Probably not an STC book, but see STC 18926.1. John Kingston's *P. Ovidii Nasonis opera* of 1570, the only book printed in England which could be represented here, in fact contains only the *Metamorphoses* and a life of Ovid. A Continental edition is far more probable. *Language(s)*: Latin. Appraised at 16d in 1571.

93.49 Capreolus
Probably Joannes Capreolus. *Commentaria in IV libros Sententiarum, seu libri IV defensionum theologiae Thomae Aquinatis*. Venice: per Octavianum Scotum, 1483.

In the context of this inventory Joannes Capreolus's commentary on the *Sentences* seems much the likeliest conjecture, but a work by Elia Cavriolo could have been intended. Language(s): Latin. Appraised at 4d in 1571.

93.50 organon Aristotelis
Aristotle. *Organon*. Continent: date indeterminable.
Language(s): Latin. Appraised at 16d in 1571.

93.51 bricott in phisicam
Thomas Bricot. [*Aristotle–Physica: commentary*]. Continent: date indeterminable.

Language(s): Latin. Appraised at 2d in 1571.

93.52 Sermones dormi securi
Sermones dormi secure. Continent: date indeterminable.
This work is sometimes attributed to Joannes, *de Verdena* as compiler. *Language(s)*: Latin. Appraised at 2d in 1571.

93.53 Sermones gagneii
Perhaps Guerricus, *Abbot of Igny.* [*Sermones*]. Edited by Joannes Gagneius. Continent: 1539-1561.
One of Gagneius's biblical commentaries might be so entered. *Language(s)*: Latin. Appraised at 4d in 1571.

93.54 psalterium hebraicum
[*Bible–O.T.–Psalms*]. Continent: date indeterminable.
Language(s): Hebrew. Appraised at 6d in 1571.

93.55 Epithomie totius naturalis philosophie
Perhaps Hieronymus Wildenbergius. [*Aristotle–Selected works–Philosophia naturalis: epitome*]. Continent: 1544-1554.
The early (1496 and 1508) *Epitomata totius philosophia naturalis Aristotelis* by Gerardus de Harderwijck must also be considered. *Language(s)*: Latin. Appraised at 2d in 1571.

93.56 Cocleus de concordia religionis
Joannes Cochlaeus (Johann Dobneck). *Consyderatio de futuro concordiae in religione tractatu.* Ingolstadt: excudebat Alexander Weissenhorn, 1545.
Language(s): Latin. Appraised at 2d in 1571.

93.57 Novum testamentum latine
[*Bible–N.T.*]. Britain or Continent: date indeterminable.
STC 2799 *et seq.* and non-STC. *Language(s)*: Latin. Appraised at 8d in 1571.

93.58 Buckerygerus de sacramento altaris
Michael Bucchinger. *Tyrocinium. De sacro altaris mysterio.* Place not given: stationer unknown, 1554-1555.
Language(s): Latin. Appraised at 6d in 1571.

93.59 apothegmata erasmi
Desiderius Erasmus. *Apophthegmata.* Continent: 1531-1570.
Language(s): Latin. Appraised at 8d in 1571.

93.60 pighius
Albertus Pighius. Unidentified. Continent: date indeterminable.
Language(s): Latin. Appraised at 12d in 1571.

93.61 Cassander de baptismo infantium
Georgius Cassander. *De baptismo infantium*. Cologne: Arnold Birckman, 1563–1566.
Godefridus Cervicornus had a hand in the 1563 edition. *Language(s)*: Latin. Appraised at 6d in 1571.

93.62 Radolphus de Inventione
Rodolphus Agricola. *De inventione dialectica*. Continent: 1515–1570. *Language(s)*: Latin. Appraised at 4d in 1571.

93.63 Anthonius Corvinus
Antonius Corvinus. Unidentified. Continent (probable): date indeterminable.
Probably not an STC book, but see STC 5806. Reyner Wolfe published, in 1550, an anonymous translation of Corvinus entitled *A postill or collection of most godly doctrine upon every gospell through the year* ..., but his Latin works probably enjoyed a wider circulation, at least in academic circles. *Language(s)*: Latin (probable). Appraised at 4d in 1571.

93.64 Stobeius
Joannes Stobaeus. Probably [*Sententiae*]. Continent: 1517–1559. *Language(s)*: Latin Greek (perhaps). Appraised at 8d in 1571.

93.65 petrus a soto
Petrus de Soto. Unidentified. Continent: date indeterminable. *Language(s)*: Latin. Appraised at 6d in 1571.

93.66 Thomas Aquinas contra gentiles
Thomas Aquinas, *Saint*. *Summa contra gentiles*. Continent: date indeterminable.
See also 93.16 and 93.20. *Language(s)*: Latin. Appraised at 2d in 1571.

93.67 dorrophei sermones
Perhaps Dorotheus, *Archimandrite of Palestine, Saint*. [*Sermones*]. Venice: (different houses), 1523–1564.
Language(s): Latin. Appraised at 2d in 1571.

93.68 Andreas althamerus de consiliacione locorum sacrarum
Andreas Althamer. *Conciliatio locorum scripturae*. Continent: 1527–1561. *Language(s)*: Latin. Appraised at 6d in 1571.

93.69 Tavernerius de veritate corporis chrisiti
Joannes Tavernerius. *De veritate corporis et sanguinis Christi in sacramento altaris*. Paris: (different houses), 1548–1558.
Language(s): Latin. Appraised at 2d in 1571.

93.70 Agrippa
Henricus Cornelius Agrippa. Unidentified. Continent (probable): date indeterminable.

Probably not an STC book, but see STC 201 *et seq.*, especially STC 204. On the basis of the valuation, probably a minor work such as *De incertitudine et vanitate scientiarum*, which seems to have had a wider circulation, or at least a wider acknowledged circulation, in the universities than Agrippa's *De occulta philosophia*, for which, in any case, the appraisal seems too low, as it would also be for his *Works*. It is possible, however, that one of his lesser works, either in Latin, or, less probably, in English, is intended. *Language(s)*: Latin. Appraised at 2d in 1571.

93.71 gramatica hebraica
Unidentified. Continent: date indeterminable.

Perhaps one of the grammars of Sebastian Muenster, which had a wide circulation, but possibly a work by Theodore Bibliander, Joannes Campensis, Wolfgang Capito, Nicolaus Clenardus, Elias, *Levita*, David Kimchi, Petrus Martinius, Johann Reuchlin or one of several others. *Language(s)*: Hebrew. Appraised at 2d in 1571.

93.72 valerius maximus
Valerius Maximus. *Faca et dicta memorabilia*. Continent: date indeterminable. *Language(s)*: Latin. Appraised at 2d in 1571.

93.73 faber stapbulensis
Jacobus Faber, *Stapulensis*. Unidentified. Continent: date indeterminable. *Language(s)*: Latin. Appraised at 2d in 1571.

93.74 petrus lombardus
Peter Lombard. *Sententiarum libri IIII*. Continent: date indeterminable. *Language(s)*: Latin. Appraised at 8d in 1571.

93.75 jonas dedicus
Joannes Dedicus. *Questiones moralissime super libros ethicorum*. Oxford: per me. Scolar, 1518.

STC 6458. For Dedicus, see BRUO, 555. *Language(s)*: Latin. Appraised at 4d in 1571.

93.76 epistolae plinii
Pliny, *the Younger*. *Epistolae*. Continent: date indeterminable. *Language(s)*: Latin. Appraised at 4d in 1571.

93.77 Johannes Aepinus in Evangeliorum assentionis domini
Joannes Aepinus. *In evangelium ascensionis Domini enarratio*. Frankfurt am Main: ex officina Petri Brubachii, 1546.

Language(s): Latin. Appraised at 3d in 1571.

Lewis Jones. Scholar (B.A.): Probate Inventory. 1571

W. P. GRIFFITH

Lewis Jones (Johns) was a fellow of All Souls' College, Oxford, at the time of his death towards the end of 1571. No will or grant of probate has survived to date this more precisely, but the inventory of his goods was taken on 21 December 1571. Jones seems to have entered the college during the mid-1560s, presumably as a scholar. Probably it was he who, recorded variously as Jones or Johns, supplicated for the B.A. degree in March 1567 (*Alumni Oxonienses*, 2:824) and who determined for that degree in 1568. He was promoted to the fellows's ranks in 1569, probably as a law fellow, in which status he stood at his death. No further details of his academic career survive.

Jones's origins are also obscure. The college admission books indicate that he was from Wales but there is nothing more specific than that. With a surname like Jones the chances of a clear identification are remote. Yet such a surname was only slowly appearing in Welsh society during the sixteenth century and often, perhaps, less as a deliberate choice on the part of the individual or his family than as a result of clerical convenience. It was not unknown for Welsh students registering at the English universities to have their names transmogrified and for the patronymic, which was the characteristic Welsh form, to be dispensed with. Lewis Jones, therefore, may well have been originally Lewys ab Ieuan or Lewys ap Ieuan, "Ieuan" being the common Welsh form for John, of which "Jones" represents one type of alteration. If that is the case here, then one possible identification emerges, namely that Lewis Jones was Lewys ap Ieuan ap Dafydd of Rhual near Mold in the present day Clwyd, an M.A. not a B.A., who was a younger son of that local gentry family.

One other bit of evidence, however, might lead one to suppose that Jones's origins were in South Wales. Jones left a slenderly valued estate, worth £4 18*s*, but there were also debts owed to him. In 1572, Jones's administrator began and completed a process at the Chancellor's Court to recover them. This administrator was Rice Powell, a member of Christ Church and a Welshman, though his precise place of origin is unknown. In Powell's case, however, it is known he took livings in Pembrokeshire, and it was not unusual for South Wales students in this period to take benefices in their home regions. Since it was often the case that testators chose administrators from their native areas, it is not unreasonable to assume that Jones originated there also. This would explain Jones's attendance at All Souls'. The college held lands in the southwest and regularly promoted students from St. David's diocese into its endowed places.

Though there is no formal record of Jones taking the M.A. degree, his moderately sized inventory of books would suggest that he was at or near that level in his academic career when he died. The books were largely in Latin, but with some in Greek also. Literary texts spanned the elementary to the quite complex, and logic and natural philosophy had their places. Some of the works and the double copies of certain works (94.3 and 94.15; 94.7 and 94.22; 94.8 and 94.10; 94.9 and 94.14) may reflect Jones's duties as a tutor to undergraduates. He possessed, as might be expected, some requisite scriptural sources, but only one work is listed which in any way indicates that he was a student of civil law (94.17).

Oxford University Archives, Bodleian Library: Hyp.B.14.

§

All Souls' College. n.d. (1937?). *All Souls College List of Fellows, 1438-1937.* Oxford: Oxford Univ. Press.

Bartrum, Peter Clement. 1983. *Welsh Genealogies, A.D. 1400-1500.* Vol. 4. Aberystwyth: the National Library of Wales.

Boase, Charles William, ed. 1884. *Register of the University of Oxford.* Vol. 1. Oxford: Oxford Univ. Press.

Morgan, T.J. and Prys Morgan. 1985. *Welsh Surnames.* Cardiff: Univ. of Wales Press.

§

94.1	titus livius 4a et 5a decas
94.2	phisica Aristotelis
94.3	Ovidius metamorphosies
94.4	horatius
94.5	Tytillmanus

94.6	a Introductio to grammer
94.7	Epistolae ciceronis
94.8	copia verborum
94.9	vergilius
94.10	copia verborum
94.11	Instituciones porphirii
94.12	organum aristotelis
94.13	philippica tulli
94.14	vergilius
94.15	ovidius metamorces [metamorphoses]
94.16	agrippa de occultis philosophie
94.17	Angelus aritinus
94.18	epistolae ovidii
94.19	ephemeris Johnes [Johannes] Stadii
94.20	Erasmius de lingua
94.21	agrammer
94.22	epistol** [epistolae] ciceronis cum comto [commento]
94.23	novum testat [testamentum]
94.24	apothegmata erasmi
94.25	pomponius mela
94.26	Rethorica tulli
94.27	grammatica Cleonardi
94.28	Ethica Aristotelis
94.29	a old greke grammer
94.30:1-2	ii grammers
94.31	testament anglice
94.32	ethica melanchthonis
94.33	Sententium ciceronis
94.34	epistolae erasmi
94.35	Salustius
94.36	titilmanni philosophia
94.37	Rethorica valerius
94.38	cornelius valerius
94.39	dialectica caesarius
94.40	colloquium erasmi
94.41	a paper boke

§

94.1 titus livius 4a et 5a decas

Titus Livius. [*Historiae Romanae decades–Selected works*]. Continent: date indeterminable.

It is difficult to identify any separate edition with the specific *decades* noted. See BCI 2:501. *Language(s)*: Latin. Appraised at 12d in 1571.

94.2 phisica Aristotelis
Aristotle. *Physica*. Continent: date indeterminable.
There are several editions with several different commentators, notably those of Averroes, Simplicius, and Augustinus Niphus. *Language(s)*: Latin (probable) Greek (perhaps). Appraised at 8d in 1571.

94.3 Ovidius metamorphosies
Publius Ovidius Naso. *Metamorphoses*. Continent: date indeterminable.
Probably not an STC book, but see STC 18955 *et seq.* If an English edition, then Arthur Golding's translation (STC 18955ff.). See also 94.15. *Language(s)*: Latin (probable) English (perhaps). Appraised at 6d in 1571.

94.4 horatius
Quintus Horatius Flaccus. Probably [*Works*]. Continent (probable): date indeterminable.
Probably not an STC book, but see STC 13797. *Language(s)*: Latin. Appraised at 4d in 1571.

94.5 Tytillmanus
Franz Titelmann. Unidentified. Continent: date indeterminable.
See also 94.36. *Language(s)*: Latin. Appraised at 6d in 1571.

94.6 a Introductio to grammer
Unidentified. Place unknown: stationer unknown, date indeterminable. STC/non-STC status unknown. *Language(s)*: Unknown. Appraised at 8d in 1571.

94.7 Epistolae ciceronis
Marcus Tullius Cicero. [*Selected works–Epistolae*]. Continent (probable): date indeterminable.
Probably not an STC book, but see STC 5295. It is impossible to identify which *Epistolae* precisely are referred to here, and they may differ from those at 94.22. Perhaps the popular *Epistolae ad familiares* is intended. *Language(s)*: Latin. Appraised at 8d in 1571.

94.8 copia verborum
Desiderius Erasmus. *De duplici copia verborum ac rerum*. Britain or Continent: date indeterminable.
STC 10471.4 *et seq.* and non-STC. The date-range for STC editions is 1528–1569. See 94.10 for another copy. *Language(s)*: Latin. Appraised at 2d in 1571.

94.9 vergilius
Publius Virgilius Maro. Probably [*Works*]. Britain or Continent: date indeterminable.

STC 24787 *et seq.* and non-STC. See 94.14 from which this copy perhaps differed. *Language(s)*: Latin. Appraised at 6d in 1571.

94.10 copia verborum
Desiderius Erasmus. *De duplici copia verborum ac rerum*. Britain or Continent: date indeterminable.

STC 10471.4 *et seq.* and non-STC. See also 94.8 for another copy. *Language(s)*: Latin. Appraised at 4d in 1571.

94.11 Instituciones porphirii
Porphyrius, *of Tyre*. [*Isagoge*]. Continent: date indeterminable.

A commentary on and interpretation of Aristotle's logic and therefore an accompanying volume to 94.12. *Language(s)*: Latin (probable) Greek (perhaps). Appraised at 6d in 1571.

94.12 organum aristotelis
Aristotle. *Organon*. Continent: date indeterminable.

Apparently the Latin version in which the *Organon* was most frequently published, and linking naturally with 94.11. *Language(s)*: Latin (probable) Greek (perhaps). Appraised at 8d in 1571.

94.13 philippica tulli
Marcus Tullius Cicero. *Philippicae*. Britain or Continent: date indeterminable.

STC 5311 and non-STC. *Language(s)*: Latin. Appraised at 6d in 1571.

94.14 vergilius
Publius Virgilius Maro. Probably [*Works*]. Britain or Continent: date indeterminable.

STC 24787 *et seq.* and non-STC. See also 94.9. *Language(s)*: Latin. Appraised at 4d in 1571.

94.15 ovidius metamorces [metamorphoses]
Publius Ovidius Naso. *Metamorphoses*. Continent (probable): date indeterminable.

Probably not an STC book, but see STC 18955 *et seq.* If an English edition, Golding's translation (STC 18955ff.). See also 94.3. *Language(s)*: Latin (probable) English (perhaps). Appraised at 8d in 1571.

94.16 agrippa de occultis philosophie
Henricus Cornelius Agrippa. *De occulta philosophia*. Continent: 1531–1567.

The precise edition is difficult to identify, especially since Brunet (1:114–115) cites a 1530 Antwerp edition, the publication of which seems to have been interrupted. The work is apparently rare in students' book-lists. *Language(s)*: Latin. Appraised at 13d in 1571.

94.17 Angelus aritinus
Angelus de Gambellionibus, *Aretinus*. Perhaps *De maleficiis*. Continent: date indeterminable.

If not this commentary on criminal law, his most popular work, perhaps his commentary on Justinian's *Institutes: Lectura super Institutionum libris* (1478–1532). Gambellionibus, an important fifteenth-century law commentator, is probably the only author in the list who reflects Jones's academic status as a law fellow. *Language(s)*: Latin. Appraised at 12d in 1571.

94.18 epistolae ovidii
Publius Ovidius Naso. *Heroides*. Continent (probable): date indeterminable.

Probably not an STC book, but see STC 18939.5 *et seq.* Many editions were available, including the English translation of George Turberville (STC 18939.5). A remote possibility is the *De ponto*, also in the form of verse letters, but this had a far smaller circulation. *Language(s)*: Latin. Appraised at 2d in 1571.

94.19 ephemeris Johnes [Johannes] Stadii
Joannes Stadius. *Ephemerides*. Cologne: Heirs of Arnold Birckman (probable), 1554?–1570.

The first (1554?) edition ran from 1554 to 1557; the second (1556) *ab anno 1554 ad annum 1570*; the third, first issued in 1559, *ab anno 1554 ad annum 1576*, and the most recent (1570) *ab anno 1554 ad annum 1600*. All were issued from Cologne, and all but the 1560 edition, the provenance of which is uncertain, from the press of Arnold Birckman's heirs. *Language(s)*: Latin. Appraised at 16d in 1571.

94.20 Erasmius de lingua
Desiderius Erasmus. *Lingua*. Continent: 1525–1555.
Language(s): Latin. Appraised at 8d in 1571.

94.21 agrammer
Unidentified. Place unknown: stationer unknown, date indeterminable. STC/non-STC status unknown. *Language(s)*: Unknown. Appraised at 6d in 1571.

94.22 epistol** [epistolae] ciceronis cum comto [commento]
Marcus Tullius Cicero. [*Selected works–Epistolae*]. Continent (probable): date indeterminable.

Probably not an STC book, but see STC 5295. See also 94.7. The manuscript entry has "officia" crossed out and replaced by a superscript "epistol**." Perhaps the popular *Epistolae ad familiares*, some editions of which included commentary. *Language(s)*: Latin. Appraised at 2d in 1571.

94.23 novum testat [testamentum]
[*Bible–N.T.*] Britain or Continent: date indeterminable.
STC 2799 *et seq.* and non-STC. *Language(s)*: Latin (probable) Greek (perhaps). Appraised at 6d in 1571.

94.24 apothegmata erasmi
Desiderius Erasmus. *Apophthegmata*. Continent: 1531–1570.
Of the many editions, a Latin one, perhaps one of the many issued in Antwerp, seems likelier here than one of the English translations available to Jones (STC 10443–10444). *Language(s)*: Latin. Appraised at 12d in 1571.

94.25 pomponius mela
Pomponius Mela. *De situ orbis*. Continent: date indeterminable.
A long sequence of editions, several of the later ones published in Paris. *Language(s)*: Latin. Appraised at 4d in 1571.

94.26 Rethorica tulli
Marcus Tullius Cicero (spurious). *Rhetorica ad Herennium*. Continent: date indeterminable.
Conceivably a collection of two or more rhetorical works. *Language(s)*: Latin. Appraised at 6d in 1571.

94.27 grammatica Cleonardi
Nicolaus Clenardus. [*Institutiones linguae graecae*]. Continent: date indeterminable.
Meditationes graecae in artem grammicam is also a possibility, as is his *Tabula in grammaticen Hebraeam*, though improbable in light of the works listed here. A few publications coupled the *Meditationes* and the *Institutiones*. *Language(s)*: Greek Latin. Appraised at 4d in 1571.

94.28 Ethica Aristotelis
Aristotle. *Ethica*. Continent: date indeterminable.
Language(s): Latin (probable) Greek (perhaps). Appraised at 8d in 1571.

94.29 a old greke grammer
Unidentified. Place unknown: stationer unknown, date indeterminable.
STC/non-STC status unknown. *Language(s)*: Greek Latin (perhaps). Appraised at 2d in 1571.

94.30:1–2 ii grammers
Unidentified. Place unknown: stationer unknown, date indeterminable.
STC/non-STC status unknown. *Language(s)*: Latin (probable). Appraised as a pair at 8d in 1571.

94.31 testament anglice
[*Bible–N.T.*] Britain or Continent: 1525–c.1569

STC 2823 *et seq.* The most recent English printing of the New Testament (STC 2873.7) was in the version taken from the Great Bible and appeared c.1569; the Tyndale and Geneva versions, however, cannot be excluded. *Language(s)*: English. Appraised at 12d in 1571.

94.32 ethica melanchthonis
Philipp Melanchthon. [*Aristotle–Ethica: commentary*]. Continent: date indeterminable.

Melanchthon's commentaries on Aristotle's *Ethica* addressed themselves to a varying number of books (see Keen, 142-43). *Language(s)*: Latin. Appraised at 4d in 1571.

94.33 Sententium ciceronis
Marcus Tullius Cicero. [*Selections*]. Continent: date indeterminable.

Perhaps an edition of the popular compilation of Petrus Lagnerius. *Language(s)*: Latin. Appraised at 1d in 1571.

94.34 epistolae erasmi
Desiderius Erasmus. [*Epistolae*]. Continent: date indeterminable. *Language(s)*: Latin. Appraised at 4d in 1571.

94.35 Salustius
Caius Sallustius Crispus. Probably [*Works*]. Britain or Continent: date indeterminable.

STC 21622.2 and non-STC. The only English printing of Sallust (STC 21622.2) by this date had appeared in 1569. *Language(s)*: Latin. Appraised at 2d in 1571.

94.36 titilmanni philosophia
Franz Titelmann. [*Aristotle–Selected works–Philosophia naturalis: commentary*]. Continent: 1530-1571.

See 94.5. *Language(s)*: Latin. Appraised at 4d in 1571.

94.37 Rethorica valerius
Cornelius Valerius. *In universam bene dicendi rationem tabula*. Continent: 1540-1568.

Language(s): Latin. Appraised at 8d in 1571.

94.38 cornelius valerius
Cornelius Valerius. Unidentified. Place unknown: stationer unknown, date indeterminable.

STC/non-STC status unknown. Valerius's *Ethicae, seu de morbis philosophiae brevis descriptio*, a regularly published work, appeared in 1570-71 in an English translation by J. Charlton or Chardon as *The casket of jewels: contaynynge a playne description of morall philosophie* (STC 24583). *Language(s)*: Latin (probable) English (perhaps). Appraised at 8d in 1571.

94.39 dialectica caesarius

Joannes Caesarius, *Juliacensis. Dialectica.* Continent: date indeterminable.

Joannes Murmellius's commentary on Aristotle's *Categoriae* was issued with most Renaissance editions of the *Dialectica*. *Language(s)*: Latin. Appraised at 2d in 1571.

94.40 colloquium erasmi

Desiderius Erasmus. *Colloquia.* Britain or Continent: date indeterminable.

STC 10450.6 *et seq.* and non-STC. Henry Bynneman's London edition of 1571 was the most recent, but there were numerous Continental editions. *Language(s)*: Latin. Appraised at 6d in 1571.

94.41 a paper boke

Unidentified. Provenance unknown: date indeterminable.

Manuscript. Perhaps a notebook or commonplace book of some kind. *Language(s)*: Unknown. Appraised at 2d in 1571.

Thomas Maudesley. Scholar (B.A.): Probate Inventory. 1571

WILLIAM M. ABBOTT

Thomas Maudesley (Maudeslaye, Mawdesley) received the B.A. degree from Oriel College, Oxford, on 21 February 1571 (*Alumni Oxonienses*, 3:992). He died later that year; his inventory is dated 23 December 1571.

Maudesley is not to be confused with the Thomas Mawdesley who received the B.A. from Hart Hall on 30 January 1570, and who may later have been rector of Winterslow, Wiltshire (*Alumni Oxonienses*, 3:992). Richards and Shadwell (1922, 75) conflate the two.

Maudesley's list of seventeen books is strongly centered on classical authors, with Aristotle, and commentaries on Aristotle, comprising roughly half the list. Erasmus is represented with two copies of the *Colloquia*. The only English title is a defense of Anglicanism by John Jewel, Bishop of Salisbury.

Oxford University Archives, Bodleian Library: Hyp.B.16.

§

Evangeliou, Christos. 1988. *Aristotle's Categories and Porphyry*. New York: E.J. Brill.

Richards, George C. and Charles L. Shadwell. 1992. *The Provosts and Fellows of Oriel College Oxford*. Oxford: Blackwell.

§

95.1	Oraciones Tullii cum commento
95.2	Buridanus

95.3   a replye of mr Juell contra Hardingum
95.4   Schola Lovaniensis
95.5   Burleus
95.6   Phisica Aristotelis 1a et 2a
95.7   Niphus super Topica
95.8   Rethorica Ciceronis
95.9   Predicamenta Purphirii
95.10   Ovidius, Metamorphosios
95.11   Dialectica Hunei
95.12   Apothegmata Licostenis
95.13   Hetica Aristotelis
95.14   Colloquie Erasmi
95.15   Formule Colloquiorum
95.16   Wintillbargius
95.17   Organum Aristotelis

§

95.1 Oraciones Tullii cum commento
Marcus Tullius Cicero. [*Selected works–Orations*]. Continent: date indeterminable.
Language(s): Latin. Appraised at 5s in 1571.

95.2 Buridanus
Joannes Buridanus. Probably [*Aristotle–Unidentified: commentary*]. Continent: date indeterminable.
The preponderance of other Aristotelian works and commentaries in the list strongly suggests that the work referred to is one of Buridanus's many commentaries on Aristotle. *Language(s)*: Latin Greek (probable). Appraised at 8d in 1571.

95.3 a replye of mr Juell contra Hardingum
John Jewel, *Bishop*. Probably *A replie unto M. Hardinges answeare*. London: Henry Wykes, 1565–1566.
STC 14606 *et seq*. Jewel's opponent in this tract was Thomas Harding (DNB 24:339); see STC 14600–14609, Shaaber J168, and STC 12758. *Language(s)*: English. Appraised at 2s in 1571.

95.4 Schola Lovaniensis
Commentaria in Isagogen Porphyrii et in omnes libros Aristotelis de dialectica. (*Louvain University*). Louvain: [probably] Servatius Sassenus, 1535–1568.
Sassenus published the 1535 and 1568 editions; bibliographical sources

do not name the publisher of the 1547 and 1553 editions. *Language(s)*: Latin Greek (probable). Appraised at 12d in 1571.

95.5 Burleus
Walter Burley. Probably [*Aristotle–Unidentified: commentary*]. Place unknown: stationer unknown, date indeterminable.

STC/non-STC status unknown. The preponderance of other Aristotelian works and commentaries in the book list strongly suggests that the work referred to is one of Burley's commentaries on Aristotle. Burley commented on a wide range of Aristotelian works, and also on the *Isagoge* of Porphyrius (Hain 1:574–78). *Language(s)*: Latin. Appraised at 2d in 1571.

95.6 Phisica Aristotelis 1a et 2a
Aristotle. *Physica*. Continent: date indeterminable.

1a et 2a is struck out, otherwise this entry would most likely represent the first and second books (alpha and beta) of the *Physica*. Not appraised. *Language(s)*: Greek (perhaps) Latin (perhaps).

95.7 Niphus super Topica
Augustinus Niphus. [*Aristotle–Topica: commentary*]. Continent: 1535–1569. *Language(s)*: Latin Greek (probable). Appraised at 12d in 1571.

95.8 Rethorica Ciceronis
Marcus Tullius Cicero. Probably [*Selected works–Rhetorica*]. Continent: date indeterminable.

This entry may refer to *Rhetorica ad Herennium*, mistakenly but routinely attributed to Cicero. *Language(s)*: Latin. Appraised at 12d in 1571.

95.9 Predicamenta Purphirii
Porphyrius, *of Tyre*. [*Isagoge*]. Continent: date indeterminable.

Porphyry produced two commentaries on Aristotle's *Categories*, only one of which is extant (Evangeliou 1988, 7 and 35–36). This work is the *Isagoge* or *Introduction*. That the compilers of Maudesley's book-list, however, did not use "Isagoge" in their entry suggests that the book may have been *Porphyrii in Aristotelis Praedicamenta*, a Latin translation (NUC 465:683). *Language(s)*: Greek Latin (probable). Appraised at 6d in 1571.

95.10 Ovidius, Metamorphosios
Publius Ovidius Naso. *Metamorphoses*. Continent: date indeterminable. *Language(s)*: Latin. Appraised at 2d in 1571.

95.11 Dialectica Hunei
Augustinus Hunnaeus. *Dialectica, seu generalis logices praecepta*. Continent: 1551–1570.

Language(s): Latin. Appraised at 8d in 1571.

95.12 Apothegmata Licostenis
Conrad Lycosthenes (Conrad Wolffhart). *Apophthegmata.* Continent: 1555–1571.
Language(s): Latin. Appraised at 18d in 1571.

95.13 Hetica Aristotelis
Aristotle. *Ethica.* Britain or Continent: date indeterminable.
STC 752 and non-STC. *Language(s)*: Greek (perhaps) Latin (perhaps). Appraised at 2d in 1571.

95.14 Colloquie Erasmi
Desiderius Erasmus. *Colloquia.* Britain or Continent: date indeterminable.
STC 10450.6 *et seq.* and non-STC. Probably not one of the early editions carrying "formulae" in the title. See the next item, 95.15. *Language(s)*: Latin. Appraised at 4d in 1571.

95.15 Formule Colloquiorum
Desiderius Erasmus. *Colloquia.* Britain or Continent: date indeterminable.
STC 10450.6 *et seq.* and non-STC. Erasmus's *Colloquia* went through many revisions; *Formulae* appeared in the titles of the earliest versions, and had been designed by Erasmus as aids to the teaching of Latin. *Language(s)*: Latin. Appraised at 2d in 1571.

95.16 Wintillbargius
Hieronymus Wildenbergius. Probably [*Aristotle–Unidentified: commentary*]. Continent: date indeterminable.
Given the rest of this library, doubtless one of Wildenbergius's Aristotelian commentaries. *Language(s)*: Latin. Appraised at 6d in 1571.

95.17 Organum Aristotelis
Aristotle. *Organon.* Continent: date indeterminable.
An appraisal of 2s was crossed out. *Language(s)*: Greek (perhaps) Latin (perhaps). Appraised at 20d in 1571.

Jerome Reynolds. Scholar, Physician (M.A., perhaps B.M.): Probate Inventory. 1571

R. J. FEHRENBACH and MORDECHAI FEINGOLD

Jerome Reynolds (Rainolds, Raynolds, Reinolds, Reynoldes) was the eldest son of Richard Reynolds of Pinhoe, Devon. (*Athenae Oxonienses*, 1:614–15). He entered Corpus Christi College c. 1548, graduated B.A. in 1553, and was elected fellow of the college three years later (*Alumni Oxonienses*, 3:1247). After taking his M.A. degree in 1557, Jerome proceeded with the study of theology, but the ascent of Elizabeth to the throne forced Reynolds, an unwavering Catholic, to abandon his intention of becoming a divine (*Athenae Oxonienses*, 1:615). Instead, he obtained the only medical fellowship available at Corpus in early 1559 (Fowler 1893, 372–73) and, five years later, he applied for the degree of Bachelor of Medicine, and a license to practice medicine (*Alumni Oxonienses*, 3:1247). Notwithstanding the shift in his profession, however, Reynolds remained active in defending the old faith. The proceedings of a 1566 visitation of Corpus singled him out as the ring-leader of the opposition party to president Thomas Greenway; he was accused not only of concealing in his room the church plate, vestments and other furniture of the chapel, but also of conspiring to alienate some of the college's property. To these and other accusations, Reynolds retaliated with counter charges against the president but in vain. He was expelled from the college shortly after the visitation (Fowler 1893, 110–23). Over the next few years he probably practiced medicine in Oxford, and at the time of his death in 1571, he was affiliated with Oriel College (*Alumni Oxonienses*, 3:1247).

The books listed here (valued at £26 9s 6d) probably represent only a portion of Reynolds's actual library, as it is unlikely that he owned no classical works. Possibly these were given to one of his younger brothers at Oxford, perhaps the future prominent Catholic apologist William Reynolds, whose education Jerome oversaw during the 1560s (*Athenae Oxonienses*, 1:615). At any rate, the medical section of the collection was not very remarkable, consisting mainly of Galenical and theoretical works. It included Hippocrates' *Opera*, Mesue's *De re medica*, Abulcasis's *Methodus medendi*, Cardan's *Contradicentes medici*, Montanus's *Consultationes medicinales*, Actuarius's *De urinis*, and several works by Galen—including a valuable five-volume edition of the works (valued at £3 6s 8d). Scholastic authors were represented by Duns, *Scotus*, Peter Lombard and Gabriel Biel, while most of the theological works were of the church fathers—Augustine, Chrysostom (Reynolds's favorite), Jerome, Cyprian, Cyril, and Basil—to which were added several Bibles and biblical commentaries, including many of Erasmus's theological works. Only a handful of works pertaining to contemporary theological polemics can be found in the library. There is a scarcity of Protestant works (one Luther, 96.11, and two Bullingers, 96.19 and 96.46), further substantiating Reynolds's Catholicism.

Oxford University Archives, Bodleian Library: Hyp.B.18.

§

Fowler, Thomas. 1893. *The History of Corpus Christi College, with Lists of Its Members*. Oxford: at the Clarendon Press.

Jones, G. Lloyd. 1983. *The Discovery of Hebrew in Tudor England: A Third Language*. Manchester: Manchester Univ. Press.

§

96.1	Alphonses contra herecem
96.2	Lis Christi et Belluae
96.3	Augustinus de civitate Dei
96.4	opera Chrisostomi in 3bus
96.5	postilla Wicelei
96.6	opera Lyrae in vi
96.7	Biblia in magno volumine
96.8	epistole Jeronimi
96.9	decimus tomus Augustini
96.10	opera Ciporani
96.11	postilla Lutheri
96.12	6tus Decretalium
96.13	decreta
96.14	commentaria Fabri in Evangelia
96.15	herbarium viue
96.16	2a pars Bedae in Novum Testamentum
96.17	Gentilis de febribus
96.18	opera Hipocritis

96.19	Orthodoxa Tigurine Ecclesie Ministrorum Confessio
96.20	Philosophia Naturalis Aristotelis
96.21	Arborius in Evangelia
96.22	annotaciones Erasmi in Novum Testamentum
96.23	Parafrases Fabri in Aristotelem
96.24	opera Cirilli
96.25	Novum Testamentum grec et latin
96.26	a French boke
96.27	Theophilactus in Evangelia
96.28	Dionisius in Evangelia
96.29	Theosophia J. Herbarei
96.30	Paraphrases Erasmi in Epistolas
96.31	opera Basilii Magni
96.32	opera Damisceni grec et latin
96.33	Euchimenes in Acta Apostolorum
96.34	Augustinus in psalterium
96.35	opera Bisilii
96.36	opera Jasonis in 2bus
96.37	Mesue de re medica
96.38	Rupartus in duodecim prophetis
96.39	Titilmanus in psalterium
96.40	opera Galeni in 5 voluminibus
96.41	Methodus Medendi Albucacis
96.42	opera Petri Galetini
96.43	Scotus in Sentenias [Sentencias] in 2bus
96.44	Gabriell Biell
96.45	Prima 2e santi Thome
96.46	Bullingerus in Epistolas Pauli
96.47	Isikius in Liviticum
96.48	Methephisica Theophrasti
96.49	Galenus de sanitate tuenda
96.50	Evangelium Matthei hebraici
96.51 multiple	iii French bokes
96.52	concordantie Majoris
96.53	Historia Ecclesiastica
96.54	Leeus contra Calumniis
96.55	Galenus de symtomatum differentiis
96.56	Rabanus de sacramento eucharistie
96.57	Franciscus Marius
96.58	Slotanus
96.59	Albanus Landalis
96.60	Galenus de elementorum facultatibus
96.61	Galenus de locis affectis
96.62	Marcus Antonius
96.63	Compendium Dissidii Hereticorum

96.64	Defensio Ceremoniarum
96.65	Diacosium Martirion
96.66	Micheas hebraic
96.67	Chrisostomus in 2 bus
96.68	Concordantia Evangelica
96.69	Contradicentium Medicorum
96.70	Antydidagma
96.71	loci communes Langmesteri
96.72	Paraphrases in Epistolas Canonicas
96.73	Baculus Pastoralis
96.74	Barnardus de communicacione sacrarum litterarum
96.75	Titilmannus de sacramentis
96.76	Orosius ad Ephesios
96.77	Albartus Patavinus in Evangelia
96.78	Historia Scholastica
96.79	Joannis Crisostomi in Marcum
96.80	Crisostomus in Acta Apostolorum
96.81	Paraprases Erasmi in Paulum
96.82	Titillmannus in epistolas apostolicas
96.83	Petrus Bairius de medendis malis
96.84	a French boke in 4to
96.85	Rofensis adversus Ecolampadium
96.86	textus magistri Senteniarum [Sentenciarum]
96.87	Tractatus Catholice Erudicionis
96.88	Epithomi Gagnei
96.89	Postilla Corvini
96.90	Assertius
96.91	Loricus Demissa
96.92	Controversia Pigii
96.93	Agonologia Christi
96.94	Rofenses contra Lutherum
96.95	Omilia Langmesteri in Evangelia
96.96	Sarcerius in Mattheum
96.97	Johannes Scotus in 3bus
96.98	magister Senteniarum [Sentenciarum]
96.99	Paraphrases Erasmi in 5 voluminibus
96.100	Consultaciones Medicinales in 3bus
96.101	Acarius de urinis
96.102	Chromasius in Mattheum
96.103	Methodus ad Theologiam
96.104	Tannerus de eucharistia
96.105	Anatomia Driandri
96.106	Decaligus hebraic
96.107	Cathaligus Hereticorum
96.108	Loci communes ex Augustino

§

96.1 Alphonses contra herecem
Alfonso de Castro. *Adversus omnes haereses.* Continent: 1534–1565.
Language(s): Latin. Appraised at 3s 4d in 1571.

96.2 Lis Christi et Belluae
Jacobus Palladinus, *de Theramo.* [*Consolatio peccatorum, seu Processus Belial*]. Continent: date indeterminable.
Lis Cristi et Belial appears as a variant title. Many editions, mostly incunabula. *Language(s)*: Latin. Appraised at 6d in 1571.

96.3 Augustinus de civitate Dei
Augustine, *Saint. De civitate Dei.* Continent: date indeterminable.
Language(s): Latin. Appraised at 4s in 1571.

96.4 opera Chrisostomi in 3bus
John, *Chrysostom, Saint.* [*Works*]. Continent: date indeterminable.
Language(s): Latin. Appraised at 13s 4d in 1571.

96.5 postilla Wicelei
Georg Witzell (Georgius Wicelius). [*Postilla*]. Continent: date indeterminable.
Language(s): Latin. Appraised at 5s 4d in 1571.

96.6 opera Lyrae in vi
The Bible. Edited by Nicolaus de Lyra. Continent: date indeterminable.
Glossa ordinaria by Lyra, usually with others contributing. The six-part editions were issued from 1501. *Language(s)*: Latin. Appraised at 20s in 1571.

96.7 Biblia in magno volumine
The Bible. Continent: date indeterminable.
No edition issued from England by the date of this inventory if this represents a folio edition in Latin. *Language(s)*: Latin. Appraised at 3s 4d in 1571.

96.8 epistole Jeronimi
Jerome, *Saint. Epistolae.* Continent: date indeterminable.
Language(s): Latin. Appraised at 6s in 1571.

96.9 decimus tomus Augustini
Augustine, *Saint.* [*Works* (part)]. Continent: date indeterminable.
Language(s): Latin. Appraised at 5s in 1571.

96.10 opera Ciporani
Cyprian, *Saint*. [*Works*]. Continent: date indeterminable.
Language(s): Latin. Appraised at 3s 4d in 1571.

96.11 postilla Lutheri
Martin Luther. [*Postilla*]. Continent: date indeterminable.
Language(s): Latin. Appraised at 4s in 1571.

96.12 6tus Decretalium
Boniface VIII, *Pope*. *Sextus liber Decretalium*. *(Corpus juris canonici)*. Continent: date indeterminable.
Language(s): Latin. Appraised at 5s in 1571.

96.13 decreta
Gratianus, *the Canonist*. *Decretum*. *(Corpus juris canonici)*. Continent: date indeterminable.
Language(s): Latin. Appraised at 6s in 1571.

96.14 commentaria Fabri in Evangelia
Jacobus Faber, *Stapulensis*. [*Gospels: commentary and text*]. *(Bible–N.T.)*. Continent: date indeterminable.
Language(s): Latin. Appraised at 3s 4d in 1571.

96.15 herbarium viue
Otto Brunfels. *Herbarium*. Continent: date indeterminable.
The title-page of the first part reads: *Herbarium vivae eicones*. Language(s): Latin. Appraised at 2s 6d in 1571.

96.16 2a pars Bedae in Novum Testamentum
Beda, *the Venerable*. [*Works* (part)]. Continent: date indeterminable.
The volume of his *Opera* with New Testament commentaries. Language(s): Latin. Appraised at 5s in 1571.

96.17 Gentilis de febribus
Gentile da Foligno. *De febribus*. Continent: date indeterminable.
Solo editions in fifteenth and early sixteenth century, but it sometimes appeared in collections. Language(s): Latin. Appraised at 2s 6d in 1571.

96.18 opera Hipocritis
Hippocrates. [*Works*]. Continent: date indeterminable.
Language(s): Latin Greek (probable). Appraised at 3s in 1571.

96.19 Orthodoxa Tigurine Ecclesie Ministrorum Confessio
Orthodoxa Tigurinae ecclesiae ministrorum confessio. *(Zürich Ministers)*. Translated by Rudolph Walther. Continent: 1545–1565.

One edition each from Zürich and Cologne. *Language(s)*: Latin. Appraised at 12d in 1571.

96.20 Philosophia Naturalis Aristotelis
Aristotle. [*Selected works–Philosophia naturalis*]. Continent: date indeterminable.
Language(s): Latin. Appraised at 3s 4d in 1571.

96.21 Arborius in Evangelia
Joannes Arboreus. *Commentarii in quatuor Domini Evangelistas.* Paris: apud (aere ac sumptu) Joannem Roigny, 1551.
Language(s): Latin. Appraised at 6s 8d in 1571.

96.22 annotaciones Erasmi in Novum Testamentum
Desiderius Erasmus. [*New Testament: commentary*]. Continent: date indeterminable.
Language(s): Latin. Appraised at 16d in 1571.

96.23 Parafrases Fabri in Aristotelem
Jacobus Faber, *Stapulensis.* [*Aristotle–Unidentified: paraphrase*]. Continent: date indeterminable.
Faber wrote paraphrases of the *Logica,* the *Physica,* and the *Philosophia naturalis.* Given the appraisal, perhaps the entry represents more than one. *Parafrases* replaces *Erasmi,* which was struck out. *Language(s)*: Latin. Appraised at 3s 4d in 1571.

96.24 opera Cirilli
Cyril, *of Alexandria, Saint.* [*Works*]. Basle: (different houses), 1528–1566.
Language(s): Latin. Appraised at 3s 4d in 1571.

96.25 Novum Testamentum grec et latin
[*Bible–N.T.*]. Continent: date indeterminable.
Language(s): Greek Latin. Appraised at 2s 6d in 1571.

96.26 a French boke
Unidentified. Continent (probable): date indeterminable.
Probably not an STC book. *Language(s)*: French. Appraised at 12d in 1571.

96.27 Theophilactus in Evangelia
Theophylact, *Archbishop of Achrida.* [*Gospels: commentary and text*]. (*Bible–N.T.*). Continent: date indeterminable.
Language(s): Latin. Appraised at 3s 4d in 1571.

96.28 Dionisius in Evangelia
Dionysius, *Carthusianus* (Dionysius, *de Rickel*). [*Gospels: commentary*]. Continent: date indeterminable.
Language(s): Latin. Appraised at 3s 4d in 1571.

96.29 Theosophia J. Herbarei
Joannes Arboreus. *Theosophia*. Paris: (different houses), 1540-1553 (single edition).
The first two volumes were published in 1540, the third in 1553. *Language(s)*: Latin. Appraised at 3s in 1571.

96.30 Paraphrases Erasmi in Epistolas
Desiderius Erasmus. [*Epistles: paraphrase*]. (*Bible–N.T.*). Continent: date indeterminable.
Conceivably his paraphrases of Paul's Epistles only. *Language(s)*: Latin. Appraised at 16d in 1571.

96.31 opera Basilii Magni
Basil, *Saint, the Great*. [*Works*]. Continent: date indeterminable.
Another copy at 96.35. *Language(s)*: Latin. Appraised at 2s in 1571.

96.32 opera Damisceni grec et latin
John, *of Damascus, Saint*. [*Works*]. Continent: date indeterminable.
Language(s): Greek Latin. Appraised at 4s in 1571.

96.33 Euchimenes in Acta Apostolorum
Oecumenius, *Bishop of Tricca*, compiler. [*Catena patrum in acta et epistolas*]. Continent: date indeterminable.
Language(s): Latin Greek (probable). Appraised at 3s in 1571.

96.34 Augustinus in psalterium
Augustine, *Saint*. [*Psalms: commentary*]. Continent: date indeterminable.
Language(s): Latin. Appraised at 5s in 1571.

96.35 opera Bisilii
Basil, *Saint, the Great*. [*Works*]. Continent: date indeterminable.
Another copy at 96.31. *Language(s)*: Latin. Appraised at 3s 4d in 1571.

96.36 opera Jasonis in 2bus
Jason de Maino. Unidentified. Continent: date indeterminable.
A loose employment of the word *opera*. *Language(s)*: Latin. Appraised at 10s in 1571.

96.37 Mesue de re medica
Joannes Mesue (Yahya Ibn Masawaih). *De re medica*. Translated by Jacques Dubois (Jacobus Sylvius). Continent: 1544-1566.

Could be *Works* or *Selected works* with this title leading. *Language(s)*: Latin. Appraised at 20d in 1571.

96.38 Rupartus in duodecim prophetis
Rupert, *of Deutz*. [*Minor prophets: commentary and text*]. (*Bible–O.T.*). Continent: date indeterminable.
Language(s): Latin. Appraised at 3s in 1571.

96.39 Titilmanus in psalterium
Franz Titelmann. [*Psalms: commentary and text*]. (*Bible–O.T.*). Continent: date indeterminable.
Numerous editions from 1531. *Language(s)*: Latin. Appraised at 4s in 1571.

96.40 opera Galeni in 5 voluminibus
Galen. [*Works*]. Continent: date indeterminable.
The two most celebrated Greek editions of the sixteenth century, the Aldine of 1525 and the Basle edition of 1538, were five-volume sets. But this could be a larger Latin set bound as five. *Language(s)*: Latin Greek (probable). Appraised at £3 6s 8d in 1571.

96.41 Methodus Medendi Albucacis
Abulcasis. *Methodus medendi*. Basle: per Henricum Petrum, 1541.
Language(s): Latin. Appraised at 2s 6d in 1571.

96.42 opera Petri Galetini
Pietro Galatino (Petrus Columna, *Galatinus*). *Opus de arcanis catholicae veritatis*. Continent: date indeterminable.
Language(s): Latin. Appraised at 5s in 1571.

96.43 Scotus in Sentenias [Sentencias] in 2bus
John Duns, *Scotus*. [*Sentences: commentary*]. Continent: date indeterminable.
Whether whole or part cannot be determined. See also 96.97. *Language(s)*: Latin. Appraised at 2s 6d in 1571.

96.44 Gabriell Biell
Gabriel Biel. Unidentified. Continent: date indeterminable.
Likely to be his commentary on Lombard's *Sententiarum IIII* with Duns, *Scotus*'s commentary preceding. *Language(s)*: Latin. Appraised at 12d in 1571.

96.45 Prima 2e santi Thome
Thomas Aquinas, *Saint*. [*Summa theologica–Part II (1)*]. Continent: date indeterminable.
Language(s): Latin. Appraised at 3s 4d in 1571.

96.46 Bullingerus in Epistolas Pauli

Heinrich Bullinger. [*Epistles–commentary and text*]. *(Bible–N.T.)* Zürich: apud Christophorum Froschouerum, 1537-1558.

Bullinger's commentary on Paul's epistles was not published separately but led in his commentary on all epistles. Staedtke nos. 84-87. *Language(s)*: Latin. Appraised at 12d in 1571.

96.47 Isikius in Liviticum

Hesychius, *of Jerusalem*. *In Leviticum libri septem. (Bible–O.T.)*. Edited by Joannes Sichardus. Basle: apud And. Cratandrum, 1527.

Adams H510. *Language(s)*: Latin. Appraised at 2s in 1571.

96.48 Methephisica Theophrasti

Theophrastus. *Metaphysica*. Continent: date indeterminable.

Seems not to have been issued alone; frequently published with Aristotle. *Language(s)*: Latin (probable) Greek (perhaps). Appraised at 8d in 1571.

96.49 Galenus de sanitate tuenda

Galen. *De sanitate tuenda*. Continent: 1517-1559.

Language(s): Latin. Appraised at 8d in 1571.

96.50 Evangelium Matthei hebraici

[*Bible–N.T.–Matthew*]. Continent: 1537-1555.

Probably the Sebastian Muenster edition and Latin translation along with Shem Tob b. Shaprut's Hebrew, but see DM nos. 5088, 5095, and 5096. *Language(s)*: Hebrew Latin (probable). Appraised at 12d in 1571.

96.51 multiple   iii French bokes

Unidentified. Continent (probable): date indeterminable.

Probably not STC books. The compiler had first written *vi French bokes*; he also struck out *3s 4d 12d* as, perhaps, a multiple appraisal. *Language(s)*: French. Appraised at 5s in 1571.

96.52 concordantie Majoris

Unidentified [Biblical concordance]. Continent: date indeterminable.

See, e.g., Adams B1955, B1957-58, B1960. *Language(s)*: Latin. Appraised at 3s 4d in 1571.

96.53 Historia Ecclesiastica

Eusebius, *Pamphili, Bishop*. *Historia ecclesiastica*. Continent: date indeterminable.

Editions from 1474. *Language(s)*: Latin. Appraised at 8d in 1571.

96.54 Leeus contra Calumniis
Edward Lee, *Archbishop of York. Apologia contra quorundum calumnias* [and others]. Continent: 1519 (probable)–1520.
Language(s): Latin. Appraised at 4d in 1571.

96.55 Galenus de symtomatum differentiis
Galen. *De symptomatum differentiis. De symptomatum causis.* Britain or Continent: 1524–1528.
STC 11535 and non-STC. Usually issued with *De morborum differentiis*, with that work leading, but the two editions cited here, which contain only these two works, have *De symptomatum differentiis* leading. *Language(s)*: Latin. Appraised at 2s 4d in 1571.

96.56 Rabanus de sacramento eucharistie
Rabanus Maurus. *De sacramento eucharistae.* Cologne: apud Joannem Quentel, 1551.
Adams R4. *Language(s)*: Latin. Appraised at 12d in 1571.

96.57 Franciscus Marius
Franciscus Marius Grapaldus. *De partibus aedium.* Continent: date indeterminable.
Language(s): Latin. Appraised at 8d in 1571.

96.58 Slotanus
Joannes Slotanus. Unidentified. Continent: date indeterminable.
Language(s): Latin. Appraised at 14d in 1571.

96.59 Albanus Landalis
Alban Langdaile. *Catholica confutatio impiae cuiusdam determinationis N. Ridlei.* Lyon: ex officina Michaëlis Vascosani, 1556.
Sole work; sole edition. *Language(s)*: Latin. Appraised at 8d in 1571.

96.60 Galenus de elementorum facultatibus
Galen. *De alimentorum facultatibus.* Paris: (different houses), 1530–1557.
Conceivably, *Selected works* with this title leading, but the appraisal suggests the single work. The sole Latin edition appeared in 1530; the sole Greek edition was issued in 1557. *Language(s)*: Greek (perhaps) Latin (perhaps). Appraised at 6d in 1571.

96.61 Galenus de locis affectis
Galen. *De locis affectis.* Continent: date indeterminable.
A number of Latin editions from early in the century; a single Greek edition in 1554. *Language(s)*: Latin (probable) Greek (perhaps). Appraised at 6d in 1571.

96.62 Marcus Antonius
Stephen Gardiner, *Bishop* (Marcus Antonius Constantius, *pseudonym*). *Confutatio cavillationum quibus eucharistiae sacramentum ab impiis Capernaitis impeti solet.* Continent: 1552-1554.
Language(s): Latin. Appraised at 12d in 1571.

96.63 Compendium Dissidii Hereticorum
Joannes Bunderius. *Compendium concertationis.* Continent: 1540-1555. See especially Klaiber no. 444. Appraised at 4d in 1571.

96.64 Defensio Ceremoniarum
Joannes Cochlaeus (Johann Dobneck). *Defensio caeremoniarum ecclesiae adversus errores et calumnias trium librorum Ambrosii Moibani.* Ingolstadt: ex officina Alexandri Weissenhorn, 1544.
Language(s): Latin. Appraised at 4d in 1571.

96.65 Diacosium Martirion
John White, *Bishop*. *Diacosiomartyrion.* London: in aed. R. Cali, 1553. STC 25388. *Language(s)*: Latin. Appraised at 6d in 1571.

96.66 Micheas hebraic
Micheas propheta. (Bible–O.T.). Edited by Johann Draconites. Wittenberg: excud. Joannes Crato, 1565.
Part of a series of polyglot editions of single books of the Old Testament. See DM no. 1420 and Adams B1619. *Language(s)*: Chaldaic German Greek Hebrew Latin. Appraised at 6d in 1571.

96.67 Chrisostomus in 2 bus
John, *Chrysostom, Saint*. Unidentified. Place unknown: stationer unknown, date indeterminable.
STC/non-STC status unknown. "Paul contra Paulum 6d" following *Chrisostomus in* is struck out. *Language(s)*: Latin Greek (perhaps). Appraised at 20d in 1571.

96.68 Concordantia Evangelica
Unidentified. Continent (probable): date indeterminable.
Probably not an STC book. Perhaps part of a Biblical concordance, perhaps a Harmonia, some of which carry "concordia" in the title. Calvin's commentary or harmony of the three evangelists, in French only, is a remote possibility, but Calvin seems very out of place in Reynolds's library. Appraised at 8d in 1571.

96.69 Contradicentium Medicorum
Girolamo Cardano. *Contradicentes medici.* Continent: 1545-1565.
Language(s): Latin. Appraised at 6d in 1571.

96.70 Antydidagma
Antididagma seu Christianae et Catholicae religionis propugnatio. (Cologne Cathedral). Continent: 1543-1549.

Said to be mainly the work of Johann Groepper. *Language(s)*: Latin. Appraised at 6d in 1571.

96.71 loci communes Langmesteri
Probably Johann Hoffmeister. *Loci communes rerum theologicarum.* Continent: date indeterminable.

If Hoffmeister, there is nothing to explain the compiler's *Langmesteri*, but the identification is supported by the more than coincidental *Langmesteri* entry at 96.95, which also can be readily identified as a work by Hoffmeister. *Language(s)*: Latin. Appraised at 8d in 1571.

96.72 Paraphrases in Epistolas Canonicas
Desiderius Erasmus. *[Epistles: paraphrase]. (Bible–N.T.)* Continent: 1521-1555.

Language(s): Latin. Appraised at 6d in 1571.

96.73 Baculus Pastoralis
Joannes Franciscus de Pavinis. *Baculus pastoralis.* Paris: (different houses), 1503-1514.

Language(s): Latin. Appraised at 4d in 1571.

96.74 Barnardus de communicacione sacrarum litterarum
Gulielmus Bernardi, *Franciscanus. De sacrarum literarum communicatione.* Paris: apud Vivantium Gaulterot, 1547.

Language(s): Latin. Appraised at 10d in 1571.

96.75 Titilmannus de sacramentis
Probably Franz Titelmann. *Tractatus de expositione mysteriorum missae* [and others]. Continent: 1528-1558.

The compiler, less than diligent with this list (see especially 96.71 and 96.95, as well as the following), might have had one of Tilemannus Heshusius's works on the sacrament in hand instead (*De praesentia corporis Christi in coena domini,* 1560, or *Vera et sanae confessionis de praesentia corporis Christi in coena domini ... defensio,* 1562), either of which would fit the entry, if descriptive, better than the Titelmann. *Language(s)*: Latin. Appraised at 10d in 1571.

96.76 Orosius ad Ephesios
Paulus Orosius. Probably *Historiae adversus paganos.* Continent: date indeterminable.

Almost certainly a mis-hearing of this widely published work. Orosius, who wrote on *Romans,* is not known to have written on *Ephesians. Language(s)*: Latin. Appraised at 6d in 1571.

96.77 Albartus Patavinus in Evangelia

Albertus, *de Padua*. [*Gospels (liturgical): commentary and text*]. *(Bible–N.T.)*. Continent: date indeterminable.
Language(s): Latin. Appraised at 20d in 1571.

96.78 Historia Scholastica

Petrus, *Comestor*. *Historia scholastica*. Continent: date indeterminable. Editions from 1473. *Language(s)*: Latin. Appraised at 10d in 1571.

96.79 Joannis Crisostomi in Marcum

John, *Chrysostom, Saint*. [*Mark, Luke: commentary*]. Continent: 1542–1557. His commentary on *Mark* was not published separately. *Language(s)*: Latin. Appraised at 12d in 1571.

96.80 Crisostomus in Acta Apostolorum

John, *Chrysostom, Saint*. [*Acts: commentary*]. Translated by Desiderius Erasmus. Continent: 1531–1550.
Language(s): Latin. Appraised at 10d in 1571.

96.81 Paraprases Erasmi in Paulum

Desiderius Erasmus. [*Epistles–Paul: paraphrase*]. *(Bible–N.T.)*. Continent: date indeterminable.
Language(s): Latin. Appraised at 4d in 1571.

96.82 Titillmannus in epistolas apostolicas

Franz Titelmann. [*Epistles: commentary and text*]. *(Bible–N.T.)*. Continent: 1528–1554.
Language(s): Latin. Appraised at 12d in 1571.

96.83 Petrus Bairius de medendis malis

Pietro Bairo. *De medendis humani corporis malis enchiridion*. Continent: date indeterminable.
Language(s): Latin. Appraised at 8d in 1571.

96.84 a French boke in 4to

Unidentified. Continent (probable): date indeterminable.
Probably not an STC book. *Language(s)*: French. Appraised at 8d in 1571.

96.85 Rofensis adversus Ecolampadium

John Fisher, *Saint and Cardinal*. *De veritate corporis et sanguinis Christi in eucharistia*. Cologne: (different houses), 1527.
The long title contains: ... *adversus Johannem Oecolampadium*. Three editions in the same year. See Shaaber F71–73 and Klaiber no. 1189. *Language(s)*: Latin. Appraised at 12d in 1571.

96.86 textus magistri Senteniarum [Sentenciarum]
Peter Lombard. *Sententiarum libri IIII*. Continent: date indeterminable. Another copy at 96.98. *Language(s)*: Latin. Appraised at 8d in 1571.

96.87 Tractatus Catholice Erudicionis
Unidentified. Continent (probable): date indeterminable.
Probably not an STC book. *Language(s)*: Latin. Appraised at 6d in 1571.

96.88 Epithomi Gagnei
Joannes Gagneius. *Epitome paraphrastica in epistolam ad Romanos. (Bible–N.T.)*. Paris: apud M. Vascosanum, 1533.
Language(s): Latin. Appraised at 6d in 1571.

96.89 Postilla Corvini
Antonius Corvinus. [*Postilla*]. Continent: date indeterminable.
There is no reason to suspect the 1550 English translation. *Language(s)*: Latin. Appraised at 12d in 1571.

96.90 Assertius
Unidentified. Continent (probable): date indeterminable.
Probably not an STC book. *Language(s)*: Latin. Appraised at 8d in 1571.

96.91 Loricus Demissa
Gerhard Lorich. *De missa publica proroganda*. Mainz (probable): [Ivo Schöffer] excusam expensis autoris, 1536.
The place and stationer are supplied by VD16. *Language(s)*: Latin. Appraised at 8d in 1571.

96.92 Controversia Pigii
Albertus Pighius. *Controversiarum praecipuarum in comitiis Ratisponensibus tractatarum, explicatio*. Continent: 1541–1549.
Language(s): Latin. Appraised at 12d in 1571.

96.93 Agonologia Christi
Unidentified. Continent (probable): date indeterminable.
Probably not an STC book. Perhaps some treatise on the Passion; perhaps a miswriting of "genealogia." *Language(s)*: Latin. Appraised at 10d in 1571.

96.94 Rofenses contra Lutherum
John Fisher, *Saint and Cardinal*. Probably *Assertionis Lutheranae confutatio*. Continent: 1523–1564.
Perhaps, however, *Sacri sacerdotii defensio contra Lutheram* (five editions between 1525 and 1562; Shaaber F95–99), but the *Confutatio* was much more widely published with at least fifteen Latin editions and several Ger-

man editions; see Shaaber F42-64. Some editions contain Luther's *Assertio*. *Language(s)*: Latin. Appraised at 14d in 1571.

96.95 Omilia Langmesteri in Evangelia
Probably Johann Hoffmeister. [*Gospels (liturgical): commentary*]. Continent: date indeterminable.

See the annotation to 96.71. *Language(s)*: Latin. Appraised at 10d in 1571.

96.96 Sarcerius in Mattheum
Erasmus Sarcerius. [*Matthew: commentary*]. Continent: 1538-1544. *Language(s)*: Latin. Appraised at 10d in 1571.

96.97 Johannes Scotus in 3bus
John Duns, *Scotus*. Probably [*Sentences: commentary*]. Continent: date indeterminable.

Perhaps a varied collection of other works; however, the following (96.98) suggests that the above is at least among the works included. See also 96.43. *Language(s)*: Latin. Appraised at 2s in 1571.

96.98 magister Senteniarum [Sentenciarum]
Peter Lombard. *Sententiarum libri IIII*. Continent: date indeterminable. Another copy at 96.86. *Language(s)*: Latin. Appraised at 6d in 1571.

96.99 Paraphrases Erasmi in 5 voluminibus
Desiderius Erasmus. Unidentified. *(Bible–N.T.)*. Continent: date indeterminable.

This is assumed to be a varied collection of some of his many paraphrases, with the Gospels and some of the Epistles the most likely to have been included. *Language(s)*: Latin (probable). Appraised at 5s in 1571.

96.100 Consultaciones Medicinales in 3bus
Joannes Baptista Montanus. [*Consultationes medicinales*]. Continent: date indeterminable.

See Adams M1672-74 and NLM6, nos. 3247-50 (... *centuria prima*, ... *secunda* ... *tertia*). *Language(s)*: Latin. Appraised at 4s in 1571.

96.101 Acarius de urinis
Joannes Actuarius. *De urinis*. Continent: date indeterminable. Editions from 1519. *Language(s)*: Latin. Appraised at 10d in 1571.

96.102 Chromasius in Mattheum
Chromatius, *Saint, Bishop of Aquileia*. *In v and vi caput Matthaei dissertatio*. Basle: per (excud.) Adamum Petrum, 1528.

Language(s): Latin. Appraised at 8d in 1571.

96.103 Methodus ad Theologiam

Probably Desiderius Erasmus. *Methodus: Ratio verae theologiae*. Continent: 1519–1555.

Language(s): Latin. Appraised at 4d in 1571.

96.104 Tannerus de eucharistia

Perhaps Joannes Tavernerius. *De veritate corporis et sanguinis Christi in sacramento altaris*. Paris: (different houses), 1548–1558.

Language(s): Latin. Appraised at 6d in 1571.

96.105 Anatomia Driandri

Joannes Dryander (Joannes Eichmann). [*Anatomia capitas humani*]. Marburg: Eucharius Cervicornus, 1536–1537.

The 1537 edition is enlarged with works by others. *Language(s)*: Latin. Appraised at 4d in 1571.

96.106 Decaligus hebraic

Probably *Alphabetum hebraicum* (part). Continent: date indeterminable.

More than one *Alphabetum hebraicum* and *Alphabetum hebraicum et graecum* included the Decalogue for instruction. See Adams A793 for one of the former, and see Jones 1983 (pp. 252–53) for several of both. *Language(s)*: Hebrew Latin Greek (perhaps). Appraised at 4d in 1571.

96.107 Cathaligus Hereticorum

Bernardus, *de Lutzenburgo*. *Catalogus hereticorum*. Continent: date indeterminable.

Language(s): Latin. Appraised at 4d in 1571.

96.108 Loci communes ex Augustino

Augustine, *Saint*. Unidentified. Continent: date indeterminable.

Several possibilities that might be so described, including Antonius Corvinus (editor), *Augustini et Chrysostomi theologia*, the long title of which contains ... *inque communes locos digesta*. But among the best candidates is Augustine's *Praecipui sacrae scripturae communes loci* (Frankfurt am Main, 1539). *Language(s)*: Latin. Appraised at 4d in 1571.

John Reynolds. Scholar (M.A.): Probate Inventory. 1571

R. J. FEHRENBACH and MORDECHAI FEINGOLD

Very little is known about the life of John Reynolds (Rainolds, Raynolds, Reinolds, Reynoldes), fellow of All Souls'. He graduated B.A. 1562, received his M.A. in 1567, and died four years later (*Alumni Oxonienses* 3:1248).

The modest library of fifty-nine works he owned at the time of his death represents a typical collection of a young Master of Arts who had recently embarked on his theological studies. To a mixture of classical authors—including Quintilian, Aulus Gellius, Livy, Cicero, Quintus Curtius, Lucian, Strabo and Herodian—he had added Valla and the *Epistolae clarorum virorum*, several philosophical textbooks and a few theological works, including such of the Church fathers as St. Bernard, Bruno, *the Carthusian*, Cyprian, as well as Calvin's *Institutes*, John Fisher, Wigandus and Hyperius. In several entries, the compiler rather casually employed the term *opera*.

Oxford University Archives, Bodleian Library: Hyp.B.18.

§

97.1	Biblia Pagneni
97.2	opera Barnardi
97.3	opera Brunonis
97.4	Rophensis de corpore Christi
97.5	opera Cipriani
97.6	opera Aulii Gelii
97.7	opera Quintiliani
97.8	Thomas in Sentenias in duobus voluminibus
97.9	opera Procopii
97.10	Therentius
97.11	opera Livii

97.12	Institutio Calvini
97.13:1-3	tres libri scripti
97.14	Loci Communes Conradi
97.15	opera Fulgoci
97.16	Lyra in 4tuor voluminibus
97.17	Corpus Doctrine Wingagii
97.18	opera Strabonis
97.19	tabulae Aethrei
97.20	Concordantiae Majoris [Majores]
97.21	Josephus in tribus
97.22	Cronica Carionis in 3bus
97.23	Celius 2us in Particiones
97.24	Lactantius
97.25	Hipperius de racione studii
97.26	Responsio Staphilii
97.27	Theophilactus in Paulum
97.28	Lawrentius Valla
97.29	Olphonsius contra hereses
97.30	Halus de judiciis
97.31	Postilla Majoris [Majores]
97.32	Phisica Velcurionis
97.33	Faber in Phisica
97.34	Theophilactus in Evangelium
97.35	Philosophia Foxi
97.36	Quintilianus
97.37	De Officio Pacis
97.38	Dialogus de substantiis phisicis
97.39	Herodianus
97.40	Quintus Curtius
97.41	Hiperius
97.42	Peretius de tradicionibus
97.43	magister Sentenciarum
97.44	Augustinus de philosophia
97.45	Curio in Topica
97.46	Tunstallus
97.47	Lezicius
97.48	Franciscus Belcarius
97.49	Agrippa de vanitate scientiarum
97.50	Declaratio contra Hereses
97.51	Matthias
97.52	Aristotelis De Republica
97.53	Confessio Tillitani
97.54	Epistole Clarorum Virorum
97.55	2a pars Philosophie Ciceronis
97.56	Aristotelis Parva Naturalia

97.57   opusculum Luciani
97.58:1-2   due oraciones
97.59   Tractatus de lamis

§

97.1 Biblia Pagneni
The Bible. Translated by Sanctes Pagninus. Continent: date indeterminable. This, the first modern Latin translation of *The Bible*, appeared in 1528; see DM no. 1608 and Adams B1008. *Language(s)*: Latin. Appraised at 7s in 1571.

97.2 opera Barnardi
Bernard, *Saint*. [*Works*]. Continent: date indeterminable.
Language(s): Latin. Appraised at 8s in 1571.

97.3 opera Brunonis
Bruno, *Carthusian, Saint*. [*Works*]. Paris: venundatur Jodoco Badio Ascensio, 1524.
Language(s): Latin. Appraised at 3s 4d in 1571.

97.4 Rophensis de corpore Christi
John Fisher, *Saint and Cardinal. De veritate corporis et sanguinis Christi in eucharistia*. Cologne: (different houses), 1527.
Three editions in the same year. See Shaaber F71-73. Klaiber, no. 1189. *Language(s)*: Latin. Appraised at 12d in 1571.

97.5 opera Cipriani
Cyprian, *Saint*. [*Works*]. Continent: date indeterminable.
Language(s): Latin. Appraised at 2s 6d in 1571.

97.6 opera Aulii Gelii
Aulus Gellius. *Noctes Atticae*. Continent: date indeterminable.
Language(s): Latin. Appraised at 2s 8d in 1571.

97.7 opera Quintiliani
Marcus Fabius Quintilianus. [*Works*]. Continent: date indeterminable.
See 97.36 for another Quintilian with the same valuation. *Language(s)*: Latin. Appraised at 20d in 1571.

97.8 Thomas in Sentenias in duobus voluminibus
Thomas Aquinas, *Saint*. [*Sentences: commentary*]. Continent: date indeterminable.
Language(s): Latin. Appraised at 2s in 1571.

97.9 opera Procopii

Unidentified. Continent: date indeterminable.

Whether works of history (Procopius, *of Caesarea*) or of theology (Procopius, *of Gaza*) are intended here cannot be determined. The *Opera* of neither author was published by the date of this inventory, and nothing of either had been published in England. *Language(s)*: Latin. Appraised at 3s 4d in 1571.

97.10 Therentius

Publius Terentius, *Afer*. [*Works*]. Britain or Continent: date indeterminable. STC 23885 and non-STC. Single titles are usually identified. *Language(s)*: Latin. Appraised at 8d in 1571.

97.11 opera Livii

Titus Livius. [*Historiae Romanae decades*]. Continent: date indeterminable. *Language(s)*: Latin. Appraised at 2s 6d in 1571.

97.12 Institutio Calvini

Jean Calvin. *Institutio Christianae religionis*. Continent: date indeterminable.

Language(s): Latin. Appraised at 4s in 1571.

97.13:1-3 tres libri scripti

Unidentified. Provenances unknown: dates indeterminable.

Manuscript. Perhaps three personal notebooks. *Language(s)*: Unknown. Appraised at 12d in 1571.

97.14 Loci Communes Conradi

Perhaps Conradus Clingius. *Loci communes theologici*. Continent: 1559–1567.

The widely published *Apophthegmata loci communes* of Conrad Lycosthenes (Wolffhart) is also a possibility, but Clingius fits this collection better. *Language(s)*: Latin. Appraised at 2s 6d in 1571.

97.15 opera Fulgoci

Probably Baptista Fulgosus (Battista Fregoso). *Facta dictaque memorabilia*. Continent: date indeterminable.

Other possibilities include Raphael Fulgosius and St. Fulgentius, *Bishop of Ruspa*, who did, at least, have an *opera* published by the date of this inventory. *Language(s)*: Latin. Appraised at 20d in 1571.

97.16 Lyra in 4tuor voluminibus

Nicolaus de Lyra. [*Postilla*]. *(The Bible: commentary)*. Continent: date indeterminable.

Language(s): Latin. Appraised at 12d in 1571.

97.17 Corpus Doctrine Wingagii
Johann Wigand and Matthias Richter (Matthaeus Judex). Σύνταγμα, seu corpus doctrinae veri et omnipotentis Dei, ex veteri Testamento tantum. Continent: 1558–1568.
Language(s): Latin. Appraised at 3s in 1571.

97.18 opera Strabonis
Strabo. [*Geographia*]. Continent: date indeterminable.
Language(s): Latin. Appraised at 2s in 1571.

97.19 tabulae Aethrei
Valentinus Erythraeus. [*Tabulae in Ciceronem et Sturmium*]. Continent: 1547–1565.
"Aether Sturm" struck out. *Language(s)*: Latin. Appraised at 6d in 1571.

97.20 Concordantiae Majoris [Majores]
Unidentified [Biblical concordance]. Continent: date indeterminable.
See, e.g., Adams B1955, B1957–58, B1960. For another likely "Majores" entered as "Majoris" by the compiler, see 97.31. *Language(s)*: Latin. Appraised at 12d in 1571.

97.21 Josephus in tribus
Flavius Josephus. [*Works*]. Continent: date indeterminable.
Language(s): Latin. Appraised at 4s in 1571.

97.22 Cronica Carionis in 3bus
Johann Carion. *Chronica*. Continent: date indeterminable.
No three-volume edition seems to have been published before 1559. *Language(s)*: Latin. Appraised at 2s 8d in 1571.

97.23 Celius 2us in Particiones
Caelius Secundus Curio. [*Cicero–De partitione oratoria: commentary* (and others)]. Continent: 1556–1567.
Oporinus was involved with the printing of each of the two editions. *Language(s)*: Latin. Appraised at 10d in 1571.

97.24 Lactantius
Lucius Coelius Lactantius. Probably [*Works*]. Continent: date indeterminable.
Language(s): Latin. Appraised at 6d in 1571.

97.25 Hipperius de racione studii
Andreas Gerardus, *Hyperius*. De theologo, sive De ratione studii theologici. Continent: 1556–1562.
Language(s): Latin. Appraised at 12d in 1571.

97.26 Responsio Staphilii

Fridericus Staphylus. *Absoluta responsio in defensionem Apologiae.* Cologne: apud haeredes J. Quentel et G. Calenium, 1563.

Klaiber lists what appears to be an earlier reply (no. 2946), *Altera responsio ...* (without place or date), but it has not been found in any other source, and Klaiber does not give his copy's location. *Language(s)*: Latin. Appraised at 10d in 1571.

97.27 Theophilactus in Paulum

Theophylact, *Archbishop of Achrida.* [*Epistles–Paul: commentary and text*]. (*Bible–N.T.*). Continent: date indeterminable.

Language(s): Latin. Appraised at 8d in 1571.

97.28 Lawrentius Valla

Laurentius Valla. Unidentified. Continent: date indeterminable.

Elegantiae most likely, but the *Works* or other individual titles possible. *Language(s)*: Latin. Appraised at 6d in 1571.

97.29 Olphonsius contra hereses

Alfonso de Castro. *Adversus omnes haereses.* Continent: 1534–1565.

Language(s): Latin. Appraised at 16d in 1571.

97.30 Halus de judiciis

Haly, *Filius Abenragel. De judiciis astrorum.* Continent: date indeterminable.

Language(s): Latin. Appraised at 16d in 1571.

97.31 Postilla Majoris [Majores]

[*Postillae majores*]. Continent: date indeterminable.

Perhaps a Biblical commentary by Joannes Major, but for another probable "Majores" entered as "Majoris" by the compiler, see 97.20. *Language(s)*: Latin. Appraised at 8d in 1571.

97.32 Phisica Velcurionis

Joannes Velcurio. [*Aristotle–Physica: commentary*]. Continent: 1537–1566.

Language(s): Latin. Appraised at 10d in 1571.

97.33 Faber in Phisica

Jacobus Faber, *Stapulensis.* [*Aristotle–Physica: commentary and paraphrase*]. Continent: 1492–1540.

Language(s): Latin. Appraised at 4d in 1571.

97.34 Theophilactus in Evangelium

Theophylact, *Archbishop of Achrida.* [*Gospels: commentary and text*]. (*Bible–N.T.*). Continent: date indeterminable.

Language(s): Latin. Appraised at 10d in 1571.

97.35 Philosophia Foxi
Sebastiano Fox Morzillo. *De naturae philosophia, seu de Platonis et Aristotelis consensione*. Continent: 1551-1560.
Language(s): Latin. Appraised at 8d in 1571.

97.36 Quintilianus
Marcus Fabius Quintilianus. Unidentified. Continent: date indeterminable.
The *Institutiones oratoriae* is probably more likely than the *Declamationes*. The *Works* appear elsewhere in this list (97.7) and therefore are probably not intended here, although both items are given the same valuation. *Language(s)*: Latin. Appraised at 20d in 1571.

97.37 De Officio Pacis
Perhaps Joannes Hessels. *De officio pii et christianae pacis vere amantis viri*. Continent: 1566.
Two editions, one Antwerp, the other Cologne. See Klaiber no. 1516. A more remote possibility is a latinized entry of Sir Anthony Fitzherbert's *Loffice et auctoryte des justyces de peas*, 1538 (STC 10968). *Language(s)*: Latin. Appraised at 4d in 1571.

97.38 Dialogus de substantiis phisicis
Gulielmus, de Conchis. *Dialogus de substantiis physiciis*. Strassburg: excudebat Josias Rihelius, 1567.
Language(s): Latin. Appraised at 6d in 1571.

97.39 Herodianus
Herodian. [*Historiae*]. Continent: date indeterminable.
There is no reason to suspect the 1556? English edition (STC 13221). *Language(s)*: Latin. Appraised at 4d in 1571.

97.40 Quintus Curtius
Quintus Curtius Rufus. *De rebus gestis Alexandri Magni*. Continent: date indeterminable.
One of the several English translations (from 1553, STC 6141.5) is at best only remotely possible. *Language(s)*: Latin. Appraised at 6d in 1571.

97.41 Hiperius
Andreas Gerardus, *Hyperius*. Unidentified. Continent: date indeterminable.
Language(s): Latin (probable). Appraised at 12d in 1571.

97.42 Peretius de tradicionibus
Martin Perez de Ayala, *Archbishop of Valentia*. *De divinis apostolicis, atque ecclesiasticis traditionibus*. Continent: 1549-1562.
Language(s): Latin. Appraised at 20d in 1571.

97.43 magister Sentenciarum
Peter Lombard. *Sententiarum libri IIII.* Continent: date indeterminable. *Language(s)*: Latin. Appraised at 20d in 1571.

97.44 Augustinus de philosophia
Unidentified. Continent (probable): date indeterminable.
Probably not an STC book. One possibility is St. Augustine's *Logica* attributed by GW to Alcuin. *Language(s)*: Latin. Appraised at 20d in 1571.

97.45 Curio in Topica
Caelius Secundus Curio. [*Aristotle–Topica: commentary*]. Continent: date indeterminable.
No edition, translation, commentary of Aristotle's *Topica* by Curio is found in any of the standard bibliographical sources. BCI, however, records a "celius 2us in topica (Aristotelis)" in a 1577 list (BCI 1:325), perhaps a now lost commentary. *Language(s)*: Latin. Appraised at 6d in 1571.

97.46 Tunstallus
Cuthbert Tunstall, *Bishop.* Unidentified. Place unknown: stationer unknown, date indeterminable.
STC/non-STC status unknown. More probably one of his several theological works than his *De arte supputandi libri quattuor* on mathematics. *Language(s)*: Latin. Appraised at 4d in 1571.

97.47 Lezicius
Pierre Lizet. Unidentified. Continent: date indeterminable.
More than one of his theological works would fit this library, perhaps most especially his *Adversum pseudoevangelicam haeresim libri novem*, with editions from Lyon in 1551 and 1552. *Language(s)*: Latin. Appraised at 2d in 1571.

97.48 Franciscus Belcarius
François Beaucaire de Peguillon, *Bishop of Metz.* Unidentified. Continent: date indeterminable.
Language(s): Latin. Appraised at 4d in 1571.

97.49 Agrippa de vanitate scientiarum
Henricus Cornelius Agrippa. *De incertitudine et vanitate scientiarum.* Continent: date indeterminable.
Language(s): Latin. Appraised at 2d in 1571.

97.50 Declaratio contra Hereses
Probably Ruard Tapper. *Declaratio articulorum adversus nostri temporis haereses.* Lyon: (different houses), 1554.
Klaiber, no. 3064. *Language(s)*: Latin. Appraised at 8d in 1571.

97.51 Matthias

Unidentified. Place unknown: stationer unknown, date indeterminable. STC/non-STC status unknown. A number of possibilities, with Matthias Flacius, *Illyricus* prominently among them. *Language(s)*: Latin (probable). Appraised at 8d in 1571.

97.52 Aristotelis De Republica

Aristotle. *Politica*. Continent: date indeterminable.

De replaces *Rhe*, probably the beginning of "Rhetorica" struck out. *Language(s)*: Latin. Appraised at 8d in 1571.

97.53 Confessio Tillitani

Jodocus Ravesteyn (Tiletanus). *Confessionis . . . a ministris, qui in ecclesiam Antwerpiensem . . . confutatio*. Continent: 1566-1568.

Klaiber, no. 2652. *Language(s)*: Latin. Appraised at 6d in 1571.

97.54 Epistole Clarorum Virorum

Probably [*Clarorum virorum epistolae*]. Edited by Johann Reuchlin. Continent: date indeterminable.

Other less widely published works with similar titles may be intended; these include: Joannes Michael Brutus, editor, *Epistolae clarorum virorum quibus veterum auctorum loci complures explicanture tribus libris comprehensae*, (Adams E277), and an Aldine collection of classical writers, *Epistolae clarorum virorum selectae* (Adams E256, E278-79). *Language(s)*: Greek Hebrew Latin. Appraised at 10d in 1571.

97.55 2a pars Philosophie Ciceronis

Marcus Tullius Cicero. [*Selected works–Philosophica*]. Continent: date indeterminable.

Language(s): Latin. Appraised at 6d in 1571.

97.56 Aristotelis Parva Naturalia

Aristotle. *Parva naturalia*. Continent: date indeterminable. *Language(s)*: Latin. Appraised at 10d in 1571.

97.57 opusculum Luciani

Lucian, *of Samosata*. [*Dialogues–Selected*]. Britain or Continent: date indeterminable.

STC 16891 *et seq.* and non-STC. *Language(s)*: Latin. Appraised at 4d in 1571.

97.58:1-2 due oraciones

Unidentified. Continent (probable): date indeterminable.

Probably not STC books. *Language(s)*: Latin. Appraised at 4d in 1571.

97.59 Tractatus de lamis

Ulricus Molitoris. *De lamiis et pythonicis mulieribus*. Continent: date indeterminable.

The 1561 Paris edition carries the title *Tractatus de lamiis et pythonicis*, more likely the item represented here than one of the dozen or so incunables. *Language(s)*: Latin. Appraised at 3d in 1571.

Austin. Scholar (probable): Inventory. 1572

J. S. CRAIG

Little is known of the Austin who possessed this tidy collection of philosophy, grammar and rhetoric, not even his given name. He is described in the inventory taken on 26 January 1572 as "Sir [dominus] Austine of Broadgates in Oxford." The purpose of the inventory is not known: nothing in the inventory indicates that he was deceased, and the significance, if there was any, to the compiler's noting that the inventory was taken in the presence of the principal of Broadgates Hall is now lost. Foster indicates that he might be the William Austin who took his B.A. degree on 23 January 1545 (*Athenae Oxonienses*, 1:46), but there appears to be no compelling reason to accept this identification. Another candidate could well be John Austin, who took his B.A. degree in 1538, his M.A. in 1541 and who was a fellow of All Souls' College in 1538 (*Athenae Oxonienses*, 1:46).

Oxford University Archives, Bodleian Library: Hyp.B.10.

§

98.1	ethica aristotelis
98.2	lexicon in duobus tomus novus
98.3	dialogi Ravicii textoris
98.4	officia ciceronis
98.5	kyliades Homeri
98.6	philosophia Ciceronis
98.7	logica titilmani
98.8	Rethorica valerii
98.9	testamentum grec
98.10	Rodolphus de invencione
98.11	opera virgilii

98.12 castigaciones victorii in Ciceronem
98.13 epistole ciceronis ad atticum
98.14 quedam orationes ciceronis in duobus voluminibus
98.15 institutio valerii de natura philosophie
98.16 arythmetica genefrysii
98.17 exempla venerabilium virorum per eborensem
98.18 gunzagar super kyromansiam
98.19 Renatus de generibus carminum
98.20 theodorus gaza super quibusdam libris Aristotelis

§

98.1 ethica aristotelis
Aristotle. *Ethica*. Britain or Continent: date indeterminable.
STC 752 and non-STC. *Language(s)*: Latin. Appraised at 12d in 1571.

98.2 lexicon in duobus tomus novus
Unidentified [dictionary]. Place unknown: stationer unknown, date indeterminable.
STC/non-STC status unknown. *Language(s)*: Greek (probable) Latin (probable). Appraised at 16s in 1571.

98.3 dialogi Ravicii textoris
Joannes Ravisius (Textor). *Dialogi. Epigrammata*. Continent: 1530–1559. *Language(s)*: Latin. Appraised at 6d in 1571.

98.4 officia ciceronis
Marcus Tullius Cicero. *De officiis*. Continent: date indeterminable.
Conceivably an edition of the *Works*, which title often began with *De officiis*. *Language(s)*: Latin. Appraised at 12d in 1571.

98.5 kyliades Homeri
Homer. *Iliad*. Continent: date indeterminable.
Language(s): Greek (perhaps) Latin (perhaps). Appraised at 16d in 1571.

98.6 philosophia Ciceronis
Marcus Tullius Cicero. [*Selected works–Philosophica*]. Continent: date indeterminable.
Language(s): Latin. Appraised at 12d in 1571.

98.7 logica titilmani
Franz Titelmann. [*Dialectica*]. Continent: date indeterminable.
Language(s): Latin. Appraised at 8d in 1571.

98.8 Rethorica valerii
Cornelius Valerius. *In universam bene dicendi rationem tabula.* Continent: 1557-1568.
Language(s): Latin. Appraised at 8d in 1571.

98.9 testamentum grec
[*Bible–N.T.*]. Continent: date indeterminable.
Language(s): Greek. Appraised at 16d in 1571.

98.10 Rodolphus de invencione
Rodolphus Agricola. *De inventione dialectica.* Continent: date indeterminable.
Language(s): Latin. Appraised at 8d in 1571.

98.11 opera virgilii
Publius Virgilius Maro. [*Works*]. Britain or Continent: date indeterminable.
STC 24787 *et seq.* and non-STC. *Language(s)*: Latin. Appraised at 6d in 1571.

98.12 castigaciones victorii in Ciceronem
Petrus Victorius, *the Elder. Castigationes in M. T. Ciceronis Epistolas.* Basle: Robert Winter, 1540.
Only one edition found in the standard catalogues and bibliographies.
Language(s): Latin. Appraised at 12d in 1571.

98.13 epistole ciceronis ad atticum
Marcus Tullius Cicero. *Epistolae ad Atticum.* Continent: date indeterminable.
Language(s): Latin. Appraised at 12d in 1571.

98.14 quedam orationes ciceronis in duobus voluminibus
Marcus Tullius Cicero. [*Selected works–Orations*]. Continent: date indeterminable.
Language(s): Latin. Appraised at 16d in 1571.

98.15 institutio valerii de natura philosophie
Cornelius Valerius. *Physicae, seu de naturae philosophiae institutio.* Continent: 1567-1568.
Language(s): Latin. Appraised at 4d in 1571.

98.16 arythmetica genefrysii
Reiner Gemma, *Frisius. Arithmeticae practicae methodus facilis.* Continent: 1540-1571.
Language(s): Latin (probable). Appraised at 2d in 1571.

98.17 exempla venerabilium virorum per eborensem

Lucius Andreas Resendius. *Sententia et exempla ex probatissimis quibusque scriptoris collecta*. Continent: 1557–1569.

Resendius, from Evora, was also known as Andreas Eborensis. This may be the second part only, which title (*Exemplorum memorabilium* ...) more closely represents the entry; it may sometimes have been published separately. *Language(s)*: Latin. Appraised at 8d in 1571.

98.18 gunzagar super kyromansiam

Unidentified. Place unknown: stationer unknown, date indeterminable.

STC/non-STC status unknown. *Language(s)*: Latin. Appraised at 6d in 1571.

98.19 Renatus de generibus carminum

René Guillon. *De generibus carminum graecorum*. Continent: date indeterminable.

Language(s): Greek. Appraised at 4d in 1571.

98.20 theodorus gaza super quibusdam libris Aristotelis

Aristotle. Probably [*Selected works–Natural history*]. Edited by Theodorus, Gaza. Continent: date indeterminable.

Language(s): Latin. Appraised at 6d in 1571.

William Battbrantes. Scholar (probably student): Probate Inventory. 1572

CHRISTINA M. COYNE

Little of certainty can be said about William Battbrantes, "late of christes chirch decessed" in March of 1572 when an inventory of his goods was compiled. No one with a remotely similar name appears in *Alumni Oxonienses* or in the list dated 1564/5 in the first university matriculation register showing resident members of Christ Church, including chaplains and singing-men (Clark 2:ii, 11–14). Complicating matters further, Sears Jayne (116) lists him as William Battlet, another name not appearing in either list mentioned above.

His library contains texts from the B.A. and M.A. courses: Cicero's *De finibus*, *De oratore*, and *De officiis* (99.22, 99.23, and 99.25); Aristotle's *Ethica* (99.13); and Seneca's *Works* and *Flores* (99.20, 99.29). Works by Suetonius, Quintilian, Sallust, and Demosthenes further reveal Battbrantes's familiarity with classical literature. One-third of the collection is concerned with theology. Theophylact (99.9 and 99.12), Ignatius (99.16), Augustine (99.27), and Titelmann (99.1 and 99.21) are foremost among the theological authors in the collection. Rounding out Titelmann's traditional Aquinas-based exegesis, volumes of Erasmus and other humanist writers, such as Andreas Resendius (99.6) and Joannes Sturmius (99.31), are found in the library. These texts suggest that Battbrantes had embarked on a study in the faculty of theology, while his possession of the *Codex Theodosianus* (99.2) also suggests advanced study.

One item suggests more about Battbrantes's avocation than it does his studies: the entry "iiii singing books" (99.35:1–4) reveals him as a singer, perhaps one of the singing-men serving the cathedral.

Oxford University Archives, Bodleian Library: Hyp.B.10.

§

99.1   Elucidatio in omnes psalmos
99.2   Codex theodosianus
99.3   glossa Aurea doctoris barthol'
99.4   Salustius
99.5   liber precum
99.6   Sententiae Andreae Eborensis
99.7   siilus Italicus
99.8   Adagiorum liber
99.9   theophilacts in omnes epistolas pauli
99.10   Enchiridion Erasmi
99.11   grammatica greca
99.12   theophilact in evangelia
99.13   ethica Aristotelis
99.14   precepta catonis
99.15   nicholaus de orbellis
99.16   Ignatius Martirus
99.17   Suetonius tranquillus
99.18   Compendium consecrationis
99.19   Quintilianii Ret [Rhetorica]
99.20   Seneca
99.21   Elucidatio in omnes epistolas apostolicas
99.22   Tullius de finibus
99.23   M. tullii Ciceronis de oratore dialogi tres
99.24   Perhrastes seu modi loquendi divinae scripturae Bartholomei Westmeri
99.25   officia tullii
99.26   loci communes rerum theologicarum
99.27   Augusti aurelii soliloquia
99.28   dictionarium poeticum
99.29   flores lucii aenei
99.30   valentinus erythraeus in orationem Ciceronis pro lege manilii
99.31   Jhoannes sturmius de periodis
99.32   demost' oratio V
99.33   nicholaus grimaldus
99.34   Euthicus
99.35:1-4 iiii singing bookes

§

99.1 Elucidatio in omnes psalmos
Probably Franz Titelmann. [*Psalms: commentary and text*]. (*Bible–O.T.*). Continent: 1531–1567.
Language(s): Latin. Appraised at 4s 5d in 1572.

99.2 Codex theodosianus
Theodosius II, *Emperor of the East. Codex Theodosianus.* Continent: date indeterminable.
Language(s): Latin. Appraised at 15d in 1572.

99.3 glossa Aurea doctoris barthol'
Bartholomaeus Fumus. *Summa, sive aurea armilla.* Continent: date indeterminable.
Language(s): Latin. Appraised at 16d in 1572.

99.4 Salustius
Caius Sallustius Crispus. Unidentified. Place unknown: stationer unknown, date indeterminable.
STC/non-STC status unknown. Either his *Works, De bello Jugurthino,* or *De conjuratione Catilinae.* If *Works,* STC 21622.2 is a possibility. *Language(s)*: Latin (probable). Appraised at 6d in 1572.

99.5 liber precum
Unidentified [prayers]. Place unknown: stationer unknown, date indeterminable.
STC/non-STC status unknown. Language(s): Latin. Appraised at 8d in 1572.

99.6 Sententiae Andreae Eborensis
Lucius Andreas Resendius (Andreas Eborensis). *Sententia et exempla ex probatissimis quibusque scriptoris collecta.* Continent: 1557–1569.
Language(s): Latin. Appraised at 20d in 1572.

99.7 siilus Italicus
Silius Italicus. *De bello punico.* Continent: date indeterminable.
Language(s): Latin. Appraised at 6d in 1572.

99.8 Adagiorum liber
Desiderius Erasmus. *Adagia.* Continent: date indeterminable.
Language(s): Latin. Appraised at 12d in 1572.

99.9 theophilacts in omnes epistolas pauli
Theophylact, *Archbishop of Achrida.* [*Epistles–Paul: commentary and text*]. (*Bible–N.T.*). Continent: date indeterminable.
Language(s): Latin. Appraised at 12d in 1572.

99.10 Enchiridion Erasmi
Desiderius Erasmus. *Enchiridion militis Christiani.* Continent: date indeterminable.
English translations (STC 10479 *et seq.*) often carried the Latin title, but

there is no reason to believe that Battbrantes's copy was in English. *Language(s)*: Latin. Appraised at 6d in 1572.

99.11 grammatica greca
Unidentified. Continent: date indeterminable.
Many possibilities, including Clenardus, Ceporinus, and Melanchthon. *Language(s)*: Greek Latin. Appraised at 4d in 1572.

99.12 theophilact in evangelia
Theophylact, *Archbishop of Achrida*. [*Gospels: commentary and text*]. *(Bible— N.T.)*. Continent: date indeterminable.
ADAMS T586. *Language(s)*: Latin Greek (perhaps). Appraised at 12d in 1572.

99.13 ethica Aristotelis
Aristotle. *Ethica*. Britain or Continent: date indeterminable.
STC 752 and non-STC. *Language(s)*: Latin Greek (perhaps). Appraised at 4d in 1572.

99.14 precepta catonis
Dionysius Cato. [*Disticha*]. Britain or Continent: date indeterminable.
STC 4839.4 *et seq.* and non-STC. *Language(s)*: Latin. Appraised at 1d in 1572.

99.15 nicholaus de orbellis
Nicolaus de Orbellis. Unidentified. Continent: date indeterminable.
Language(s): Latin. Appraised at 4d in 1572.

99.16 Ignatius Martirus
Ignatius, *Saint, Bishop of Antioch*. [*Epistolae*]. Continent: date indeterminable.
Editions vary and contain letters by others, including Polycarp and Martial. *Language(s)*: Latin Greek (perhaps). Appraised at 3d in 1572.

99.17 Suetonius tranquillus
Caius Suetonius Tranquillus. Probably *De vita Caesarum*. Continent: date indeterminable.
Language(s): Latin. Appraised at 6d in 1572.

99.18 Compendium consecrationis
Joannes Bunderius. *Compendium concertationis*. Continent: date indeterminable.
Language(s): Latin. Appraised at 8d in 1572.

99.19 Quintilianii Ret [Rhetorica]
Marcus Fabius Quintilianus. Probably [*Works*]. Continent: date indeterminable.
Language(s): Latin. Appraised at 10d in 1572.

99.20 Seneca
Lucius Annaeus Seneca. Perhaps [*Works*]. Continent: date indeterminable.
Language(s): Latin. Appraised at 8d in 1572.

99.21 Elucidatio in omnes epistolas apostolicas
Probably Franz Titelmann. [*Epistles: commentary and text*]. (*Bible–N.T*). Continent: 1528–1554.
Language(s): Latin. Appraised at 4d in 1572.

99.22 Tullius de finibus
Marcus Tullius Cicero. *De finibus*. Continent: date indeterminable.
Language(s): Latin. Appraised at 6d in 1572.

99.23 M. tullii Ciceronis de oratore dialogi tres
Marcus Tullius Cicero. *De oratore*. Continent: date indeterminable.
Language(s): Latin. Appraised at 6d in 1572.

99.24 Perhrastes seu modi loquendi divinae scripturae Bartholomei Westmeri
Bartholomeus Westheimer. *Phrases seu modi loquendi divinae scripturae*. Continent: 1536–1544.
Language(s): Latin. Appraised at 8d in 1572.

99.25 officia tullii
Marcus Tullius Cicero. *De officiis*. Continent: date indeterminable.
Conceivably an edition of Cicero's *Works* with *De officiis* leading. *Language(s)*: Latin. Appraised at 2d in 1572.

99.26 loci communes rerum theologicarum
Unidentified. Continent: date indeterminable.
Author could be either Philipp Melanchthon or Johann Hoffmeister, each of whom published a work with such a title. *Language(s)*: Latin. Appraised at 6d in 1572.

99.27 Augusti aurelii soliloquia
Augustine, *Saint. Soliloquia*. Continent: date indeterminable.
Language(s): Latin. Appraised at 6d in 1572.

99.28 dictionarium poeticum
Unidentified. Continent: date indeterminable.
It is impossible to tell whether this is the work by Hermann Torrentinus

or the work by Charles Estienne, both widely published, though this form of the title makes Estienne's marginally more likely. *Language(s)*: Latin. Appraised at 8d in 1572.

99.29 flores lucii aenei
Lucius Annaeus Seneca. [*Selections–Flores selecti*]. Continent: date indeterminable.
Language(s): Latin. Appraised at 4d in 1572.

99.30 valentinus erythraeus in orationem Ciceronis pro lege manilii
Valentinus Erythraeus. *In orationem M.T.C. pro lege Manilia de Pompeii laudibus annotationes*. Strassburg: excudebat Christianus Mylius, 1556.
Language(s): Latin. Appraised at 16d in 1572.

99.31 Jhoannes sturmius de periodis
Joannes Sturmius. *De periodis*. Strassburg: (different houses), 1550–1567. ADAMS S1991. *Language(s)*: Latin. Appraised at 4d in 1572.

99.32 demost' oratio V
Demosthenes. Unidentified. Continent: date indeterminable.
Which oration or whether *oratio* is an abbreviation for 'orationes' cannot be determined. *Language(s)*: Latin. Appraised at 2d in 1572.

99.33 nicholaus grimaldus
Nicholas Grimald. Unidentified. Continent: date indeterminable.
May be one of his translations of *De officiis*, but more likely one of his own works such as *Christus redivivus, comoedia tragica* (see BCI 2:396 for its appearance in other book-lists). For Grimald's works published before the date of this inventory, see Shaaber G393–95. *Language(s)*: Latin. Appraised at 1d in 1572.

99.34 Euthicus
Augustinus Niphus. Unidentified. Continent (probable): date indeterminable.
Sometimes given as Eutychius Augustus Niphus. Perhaps one of his commentaries on Aristotle. *Language(s)*: Latin (probable). Appraised at 1d in 1572.

99.35:1–4 iiii singing bookes
Unidentified. Place unknown: stationer unknown, date indeterminable.
STC/non-STC status unknown. *Language(s)*: Unknown. Appraised at 4d in 1572.

John Mitchell, Servant: Probate Inventory, 1572

KATY HOOPER

Nothing is known about John Mitchel (Michell) apart from the facts recorded in the inventory of his goods taken on 15 February 1572. He was servant to a Dr. Bayly, probably Walter Bayley, Regius Professor of Medicine, 1561-82 (*Alumni Oxonienses* 1:92).

The dozen books and items of clothing in the inventory were appraised together at 12s 1d—the books representing only 3s 8d of the total, barely more than the value of his coat alone. The identified books are popular medical and scientific works, two of which, a herbal and a work by William Turner, are in English and published in England; the remainder are Latin texts published on the Continent. Aristotle and Pliny are represented, as are such modern authors as Fernel, Ficino, Fuchs, and Chaumette.

Oxford University Archives, Bodleian Library: Hyp.B.16.

§

100.1 Compendium Fussii
100.2 Anthonius Chalmetes Chirurgius
100.3 Paraphrases Philosophie Naturalis
100.4 Marsilius Ficinus
100.5 prima pars Pliniani indicis
100.6 Johannes Fernelius
100.7 a great herball
100.8 Willelmus Turner to Mr Cicell
100.9 liber de secretis nature per Ulstadium
100.10 Anthonius Musa
100.11 multiple   certen other smale bookes of paper

§

100.1 Compendium Fussii
Leonard Fuchs. [*Methodus seu ratio compendiaria perveniendi ad medicinam*]. Continent: 1531–1550.
Likely one of the earlier editions that begin: *Compendiaria*. *Language(s)*: Latin. Appraised at 8d in 1571.

100.2 Anthonius Chalmetes Chirurgius
Antonius Chalmeteus. *Enchiridion chirurgicum*. Continent: 1560–1570. *Language(s)*: Latin. Appraised at 6d in 1571.

100.3 Paraphrases Philosophie Naturalis
Jacobus Faber, *Stapulensis*. [*Aristotle–Selected works–Philosophia naturalis: paraphrase*]. Edited by Jodocus Clichtoveus. Continent: 1492–1541.
Contains paraphrases of various Aristotle texts; most editions carry commentary by Clichtoveus. *Language(s)*: Latin. Appraised at 8d in 1571.

100.4 Marsilius Ficinus
Marsilio Ficino. Unidentified. Continent: date indeterminable.
Likely a medical work. *Language(s)*: Latin. Appraised at 2d in 1571.

100.5 prima pars Pliniani indicis
Joannes Camers (Giovanni Ricuzzi Vellini). *Prima (secunda) pars Pliniani indicis*. Vienna: per H. Vietorum et J. Singrenium sumptibus Leonardi et Luce Alantseae, 1514.
Other editions of the *Historia naturalis* were issued with an index based on Camers's, which had a special title page (e.g., Lyons 1548 and Venice 1558) and was separately paginated, and still others were issued with 1514 index bound with it. A separately printed index (Adams P1572) could have become detached. *Language(s)*: Latin. Appraised at 4d in 1571.

100.6 Johannes Fernelius
Joannes Fernelius. Unidentified. Continent: date indeterminable.
Fernel's collected works were issued under similar titles (*Medicina, Universa medicina, Opera medicinalia*) and it is perhaps one of these to which this entry refers. The valuation, however, may suggest a smaller, single work. *Language(s)*: Latin. Appraised at 2d in 1571.

100.7 a great herball
The grete herball. Britain: 1526–1561.
STC 13176 *et seq*. There were incunable editions which appeared under the title *Arbolayre* (*Wellcome* no.3114) but the wording of this entry suggests a later, English version. The editions were issued from either London or Southwark. *Language(s)*: English. Appraised at 2d in 1571.

100.8 Willelmus Turner to Mr Cicell
William Turner. Perhaps *A new boke of the natures of all wines commonlye used in England*. London: William Seres, 1568.

STC 24360. In the context of this inventory it is possible that the entry represents an imperfect copy of this work which bears a dedication to William Cecil. *Language(s)*: English. Appraised at 2d in 1571.

100.9 liber de secretis nature per Ulstadium
Philippus Ulstadius. *Coelum philosophorum, seu, De secretis naturae*. Continent: 1526–1557.

Language(s): Latin. Appraised at 6d in 1571.

100.10 Anthonius Musa
Antonio Musa Brasavola. Unidentified. Continent: date indeterminable.

Doubtless, one of his pharmaceutical works. *Language(s)*: Latin. Appraised at 4d in 1571.

100.11 multiple   certen other smale bookes of paper
Unidentified. Provenances unknown: dates indeterminable.

Manuscripts. Probably notebooks. Considered by the appraiser to be "nothynge worth." *Language(s)*: Unknown.

Thomas Neale. Scholar (student): Probate Inventory. 1572

ANN R. MEYER

Little is known about Thomas Neale. A native of Northamptonshire, he was born in 1553. When the inventory of his goods was taken in 1572, apparently at his death, he was a demy, or scholar of Magdalen College (*Alumni Oxonienses*, 3:1054).

His few belongings were inventoried as found in the chambers of a fellow of Magdalen, another Northamptonshire man, Thomas Bracebridge (*Alumni Oxonienses*, 1:165; Brasbridge in the DNB and STC), who was to write on both theology and the plague (see STC 3548-3552.5).

In addition to bedding and a chest, Neale owned a modest collection of nine books that included works by Cicero, Lucian and Erasmus, as well as a collection of "lytell old books." There was a Greek grammar, and with the exception of Lucian's dialogues, which were in Greek and Latin, the rest of the identified works were in Latin. Only Erasmus's *De duplici copia ac verborum rerum* could have been published in England.

Oxford University Archives, Bodleian Library: Hyp.B.16.

§

101.1	ius [primus] tomus Philosophie Ciceronis
101.2	2 [secundus] tomus Oracionis Tullii
101.3	Grammatica Ceporini
101.4	Copia Verborum Erasmi
101.5	Dialogi Luciani grece et latine
101.6:1-4	iiii other lytell old bokes

§

101.1 ius [primus] tomus Philosophie Ciceronis
Marcus Tullius Cicero. [*Selected works–Philosophica*]. Continent: date indeterminable.

The first volume of a collection of two or more works in philosophy. *Language(s)*: Latin. Appraised at 6d in 1572.

101.2 2 [secundus] tomus Oracionis Tullii
Marcus Tullius Cicero. [*Selected works–Orations*]. Continent: date indeterminable.

The second volume of a collection of orations. *Language(s)*: Latin. Appraised at 4d in 1572.

101.3 Grammatica Ceporini
Jacobus Ceporinus. *Compendium grammaticae graecae*. Continent: date indeterminable.

Language(s): Greek Latin. Appraised at 4d in 1572.

101.4 Copia Verborum Erasmi
Desiderius Erasmus. *De duplici copia verborum ac rerum*. Britain or Continent: date indeterminable.

STC 10471.4 and non-STC. Language(s): Latin. Appraised at 4d in 1572.

101.5 Dialogi Luciani grece et latine
Lucian, *of Samosata*. [*Dialogues–Selected*]. Continent: date indeterminable.

Conceivably an edition of the *Works*. The editions of Lucian issued in England at the time of this inventory were all in Latin. *Language(s)*: Greek Latin. Appraised at 4d in 1572.

101.6:1–4 iiii other lytell old bokes
Unidentified. Places unknown: stationers unknown, dates indeterminable.

STC/non-STC status unknown. *Language(s)*: Unknown. Appraised as a group of four at 6d in 1572.

William Smallwood. Scholar (M.A.): Inventory. 1572

E.S. LEEDHAM-GREEN

The goods of William Smallwood, M.A. of Gloucester Hall, were listed and valued by the university appraisers on 10 June 1572 in the presence of four B.A.s of the college. There is no indication that Smallwood was deceased, rather that, like so many members of Gloucester Hall, he had quietly melted away, perhaps for religious reasons (see PLRE 81, George and Simon Digby; PLRE 87, Thomas Morgan; PLRE 90, Tichborne; PLRE 105, Richard Lanham; and PLRE 106, Walter Dyllam).

Smallwood had proceeded B.A. in 1554 from Magdalen College but by the time he proceeded to his M.A., between October 1558 and March 1559, he had been installed as one of the founding scholars of Sir Thomas White's new college of St. John's. Although ordained, he was allowed under the college statutes as redrafted in 1562 to be one of the two jurist fellows. Sir Thomas kept a close eye on his foundation and in a letter of 16 November 1563 he orders that Smallwood be removed from his fellowship, as having committed very great and grievous offenses against the statutes, but that he is "to remayn as a borde" until the founder's next visit, after Easter next, should allow him to examine the case (Stevenson and Salter 1939, 416-17). A subsequent letter, of 12 December 1566, reports that Smallwood has been deprived of his fellowship "because he was absent from the college, following the business of other people at the Common Law" (Stevenson and Salter 1939, 422-25). Nonetheless, his friendship with Sir Thomas clearly survived at least until April 1565 when he acted as a witness to the will of his erstwhile benefactor. By the time of Sir Thomas's death in 1567, he had no doubt already taken up quarters in Gloucester Hall. Given Sir Thomas White's known Catholic sympathies and the reputation of Gloucester Hall there are some grounds for suspecting that Smallwood too had Romanist leanings, and the fact that the goods found in the chamber included a pair of virginals and a clavichord might perhaps be taken to indicate that he had left suddenly and not just drifted off leaving his less cherished goods to await in vain his return.

Smallwood's books consist largely, although, *pace* Barton (1986, 278, n. 3), not exclusively, of canon law texts, Gratian's *Decretum* and Gregory's *Decretals* occurring twice each. He also had two dictionaries, a *Book of Common Prayer*, and three theological texts. There are no texts in civil or common law. Deleted entries are not included above as they all seem to be false starts at entries occurring in the list already. It may be that the books listed here do not comprise Smallwood's whole library since the appraisers appended to his inventory a memorandum: "We fownde ii great chestes in the chamber, one beynge locked and certene stuff in hym, wth the wiche we dyd not medle nor open and thother made fast with a rope rownde abowt hym, which we dyd leave full of stuffe and not put in thys inventarie."

Oxford University Archives, Bodleian Library: Hyp.B.18.

§

Barton, John. 1986. "The Faculty of Law," in *The Collegiate University*, edited by James McConica. Volume 3 of *The History of the University of Oxford*, General Editor, T.H. Aston. Oxford: Oxford Univ. Press, pp. 257-83.

Stevenson, W.H., and H.E. Salter. 1939. *The Early History of St. John's College, Oxford*. Oxford Historical Society. Oxford: Clarendon Press.

§

102.1 prima, 2a, 3a, 4a et 5a pars abbatis in tribus voluminibus
102.2 panormitanus, prima, 2a, 3a, 4a et 5a pars in quatuor voluminibus
102.3 concilia abbatis
102.4 quinque libri decretalium gregorii
102.5 1a et 2a pars dominici super 6to Decretalium
102.6 liber Sextus bonifacii
102.7 opera philini in 2
102.8 decreta grasiani in uno volumine
102.9 opera astextani fratris
102.10 Morale Bibliorum
102.11 Etimologia Isidori
102.12 Ambrosius Calepinus
102.13 gratiani decretalia
102.14 gregorii noni decretalia

102.15 2a, 3a pars Vincentii
102.16 A boke of commen prayer
102.17 dionisius carthusianus super Evangelia

§

102.1 prima, 2a, 3a, 4a et 5a pars abbatis in tribus voluminibus
Nicolaus Tudeschis (Panormitanus). [*Decretales: commentary*]. *(Corpus juris canonici)*. Continent: date indeterminable.
Not necessarily an edition originally issued in three volumes. See also 102.2–3. *Language(s)*: Latin. Appraised at 12s in 1572.

102.2 panormitanus, prima, 2a, 3a, 4a et 5a pars in quatuor voluminibus
Nicolaus Tudeschis (Panormitanus). [*Decretales: commentary*]. *(Corpus juris canonici)*. Continent: date indeterminable.
Not necessarily an edition originally issued in four volumes and evidently a less splendid one than the last, valued at 12s although in only three volumes. See also 102.1 and 102.3. *Language(s)*: Latin. Appraised at 10s in 1572.

102.3 concilia abbatis
Nicolaus Tudeschis (Panormitanus). *Consilia*. Continent: date indeterminable.
See also 102.1–2. *Language(s)*: Latin. Appraised at 3s 4d in 1572.

102.4 quinque libri decretalium gregorii
Gregory IX, *Pope*. *Decretales*. *(Corpus juris canonici)*. Continent: date indeterminable.
Another copy at 102.14. *Language(s)*: Latin. Appraised at 5s in 1572.

102.5 1a et 2a pars dominici super 6to Decretalium
Dominicus à Sancto Geminiano. [*Decretales–Liber Sextus: commentary*]. *(Corpus juris canonici)*. Continent: date indeterminable.
The syllables "gra" and "bon" are deleted at the end of the entry, presumably for Gratian and Boniface. *Language(s)*: Latin. Appraised at 12d in 1572.

102.6 liber Sextus bonifacii
Boniface VIII, *Pope*. *Sextus liber Decretalium*. *(Corpus juris canonici)*. Continent: date indeterminable.
Language(s): Latin. Appraised at 12d in 1572.

102.7 opera philini in 2
Felino Maria Sandeo. Probably [*Decretales: commentary*]. *(Corpus juris canonici–Liber Extra)*. Continent: date indeterminable.
Language(s): Latin. Appraised at 9s in 1572.

102.8 decreta grasiani in uno volumine
Gratianus, *the Canonist. Decretum. (Corpus juris canonici)*. Continent: date indeterminable.
See 102.13 for another copy. *Language(s)*: Latin. Appraised at 2s 6d in 1572.

102.9 opera astextani fratris
Astesanus de Ast. Probably *Summa de casibus conscientiae*. Continent: date indeterminable.
Possibly, however, his *Canones poenitentiales*, or a volume with the two works bound together. *Language(s)*: Latin. Appraised at 12d in 1572.

102.10 Morale Bibliorum
Petrus Berthorius. *Liber Bibliae moralis*. Continent: date indeterminable.
Bibliorum replaces *divinorum* in the manuscript. *Language(s)*: Latin. Appraised at 12d in 1572.

102.11 Etimologia Isidori
Isidore, *Saint, Bishop of Seville*. [*Etymologiae*]. Continent: date indeterminable.
Language(s): Latin. Appraised at 8d in 1572.

102.12 Ambrosius Calepinus
Ambrogio Calepino. *Dictionarium*. Continent: date indeterminable.
Perhaps an edition including one or more vernacular languages. *Language(s)*: Greek Latin. Appraised at 18d in 1572.

102.13 gratiani decretalia
Gratianus, *the Canonist. Decretum. (Corpus juris canonici)*. Continent: date indeterminable.
Another copy at 102.8. *Language(s)*: Latin. Appraised at 20d in 1572.

102.14 gregorii noni decretalia
Gregory IX, *Pope. Decretales. (Corpus juris canonici)*. Continent: date indeterminable.
Another copy at 102.4. *Language(s)*: Latin. Appraised at 16d in 1572.

102.15 2a, 3a pars Vincentii
Vincentius, *Bellovacensis* (Vincent, *de Beauvais*). *Speculum major* (part). Continent: date indeterminable.
Language(s): Latin. Appraised at 16d in 1572.

102.16 A boke of commen prayer
[*Liturgies–Church of England–Book of Common Prayer*]. Britain: 1549–1572. STC 16267 *et seq. Language(s)*: English. Appraised at 12d in 1572.

102.17 dionisius carthusianus super Evangelia
Dionysius, *Carthusianus* (Dionysius, *de Rickel*). [*Gospels: commentary*]. Continent: date indeterminable.
Language(s): Latin. Appraised at 20d in 1572.

Henry Hutchinson. Scholar (B.A.): Probate Inventory. 1573

MARGERY H. SMITH, C.S.J.

A Londoner, Henry Hutchinson (Huchenson) was born in 1550 in Moorfields, the son of Agnes and John Hutchinson; the father was clerk of the Merchant Taylors' Company, founders of the Merchant Taylors' School (Hart 1936, "Hutchinson," 1:n.p.) where Richard Mulcaster was the first headmaster. In 1561 Hutchinson was admitted to the school on its opening, having met the requirements laid down by the founders: ". . . First see that they can [repeat] the catechism in English or Latyn & that every [one] of the said two hundreth & fifty schollers can read perfectly & write competently or els lett them not be admytted in no wyse" (Farr 1929, 36).

In 1565 Hutchinson went up to St. John's, Oxford, to read theology. St. John's was founded by a member of the Merchant Taylors' Company, who stipulated that thirty-seven fellowships annually were to be awarded to scholars from the Merchant Taylors' School; Hutchinson's name stands first in the list of Merchant Taylors' fellows at St. John's (Simmonds 1930, 1). In 1569, Hutchinson was granted the B.A. He remained at St. John's as a reader in theology until his death in 1573 at the age of twenty-three; he is buried in the college chapel (*Alumni Oxonienses* 2:778).

The high percentage of Protestant books, many of strident polemical tone, may seem striking; militant Calvinism was not the tone of the college in its foundation days with its Roman Catholic leanings. From 1564 to 1572, however, these tendencies in the only college founded under Mary I were addressed by a president, John Robinson, imported from Cambridge as a *protégé* of William Cecil and John Whitgift, pillars of the moderate-Calvinist orthodoxy. A number of titles have been struck through, leaving one to speculate that these books had been borrowed. Apart from Continental and English polemical tracts and standard Protestant texts, Hutchinson's library is that of a Mulcaster-trained divinity student, acquainted with Hebrew and fluent in Latin and Greek, who dabbled in geography and astronomy.

Oxford University Archives, Bodleian Library: Hyp.B.14.

§

Hart, Mrs. E. P., comp. 1936. *The Register of Merchant Taylor School, 1561-1564*. London: N. p.

Farr, W. C., comp. 1929. *Merchant Taylors' School: Its Origin, History, and Present Surroundings*. Oxford: Blackwell.

Simmonds, Mark J., comp. 1930. *Merchant Taylor Fellows of St. John's*. London: Oxford Univ. Press.

§

103.1	Beroaldus de vitis Cesarum
103.2	foxus actes and monumentes of the churche in two volumes
103.3	Couperes dictionarie of the laste edition
103.4	Bircot super totam logicam
103.5	historia danorum
103.6	Calvin his institutions in englishe
103.7	A greake lexicon in two volumes
103.8	strabonis Cosmographia
103.9	Polidorus Virgill
103.10	Aristophanes grece wth a comment
103.11	Cranmer against Gardiner of transubstantiation
103.12	Juell his defense of the apologie
103.13	Postilla feri de sanctis
103.14	A newe testament in two volumes
103.15	A bible in englishe
103.16	Cosmographia Apiani
103.17	Bernardi oratio de tranquillitate vitae
103.18	Antesignanus grammer
103.19	Plinius de mundi historia
103.20	juells Apologie in english
103.21	Orontius de sphera mundi
103.22	Nowells catachisme in latten
103.23	Joannes Pontanus de rebus caelestibus
103.24	Philo judeus de mundo
103.25	Nowell against dorman
103.26	Interpretatio Carri in philippicas demosthenis
103.27	Peter Martir uppon the sacramente of our lordes supper in englishe

103.28	Ovide de tristibus wth a commente
103.29	Commentarii Caesaris
103.30	Chilias Homeri grece
103.31	Virgilius
103.32	Duae Postillae feri
103.33	Dorbell in philosophiam naturalem
103.34	Monsteri gramatica hebraica
103.35	Diogines laertius de vitis philosophorum
103.36	Paynelles sentences on the scripture
103.37	Anatomie of the masse
103.38	Horatius
103.39	Ovidii metamorphosis
103.40	Ausonius
103.41	Testamentum grece et latine
103.42	sex ciceronis volumina
103.43	Rodolphus Agricola
103.44	Laurentii Vallae elegantiae
103.45	Olynthiasae demosthenis grece, et latine
103.46	Aristotelis aethica
103.47	A Comment uppon the 2 epistle of St paule to the corinthians in englishe
103.48	Senecae tragediae
103.49	Valerius Maximus
103.50	Rami Animadversiones in Aristotelem
103.51	Ceporini Gramatica
103.52	Melanghton in Proverbia
103.53	Questiones Bezae
103.54	Examen theologicum
103.55	Caelius secundus pro authoritate ecclesiae
103.56	Loci communes Melanchton
103.57	Arithmetica Micylli
103.58	Dialogi Luciani grece, et latine
103.59	A booke of sundrie instrumentes
103.60	Talaei rhetorica
103.61	Lactantius firmianus
103.62	Praeces privatae
103.63	Palingenius
103.64	Colloquium erasmi
103.65	Pantaleon de quantitate sillabarum
103.66	Justinus
103.67	Homerus
103.68	three volumes of the olde testament
103.69	Calvini Catechismus grece, et latine
103.70	Gemma Platonis
103.71	Dialogues de Jan loys vives

103.72	Sulpitius Severus
103.73	Lucius Apuleius de aureo Asino
103.74	Argumentum eucharistiae
103.75	Erasmus de misericordia dei
103.76	Valerius de Sphera
103.77	Arithmetica Gemma Phrisii
103.78	Pomponius mela de situ orbis
103.79	Conjecturae de ultimis temporibus
103.80	Ambiani commentarii in tres orationes Ciceronis
103.81	Aristotelis de anima epitome
103.82	Schemata Mosellani
103.83	A godlie admonition of the causes of the counsell of trente
103.84	mr levers sermon preached at Paules Crosse
103.85	An exposition uppon the 5, 6, 7 chapiters of Mathewe
103.86	A battaile against the invocation of sainctes
103.87	An awnswer to mr marshall by mr doctor canfild of the treatise of the crosse
103.88	The reliques of Rome
103.89	Demosthenis orationes duae
103.90	A treatisse betwene the spiritualtye, and temporaltie
103.91	A confutation of the cause of burning of paules steple in london
103.92	The unitie of the churche
103.93	A description of Antechriste
103.94	Christopher Goodman how to obey and disobey
103.95	hunteri Cosmographia
103.96	The summe of divinitie
103.97	A lutinge booke
103.98	Lewis Evans de eucharistia
103.99	certayne paper bookes

§

103.1 Beroaldus de vitis Cesarum

Caius Suetonius Tranquillus. *De vita Caesarum.* Commentary by Philippus Beroaldus, *the Elder.* Continent: date indeterminable.

Editions from as early as 1493, but not all sources agree that the editor is *the Elder* rather than *the Younger* Beroaldus. *Language(s)*: Latin. Appraised at 12d in 1573.

103.2 foxus actes and monumentes of the churche in two volumes

John Foxe, *the Martyrologist. The first (second) volume of the ecclesiasticall history contaynyng the Actes and monumentes of the church.* London: John Day, 1570.

STC 11223. The only two-volume edition to appear before the date of this inventory. *Language(s)*: English. Appraised at 16s in 1573.

103.3 Couperes dictionarie of the laste edition
Thomas Cooper, *Bishop*. *Thesaurus linguae Romanae et Britannicae*. London: [Henry Denham], 1573.
STC 5687. *Language(s)*: English Latin. Appraised at 10s in 1573.

103.4 Bircot super totam logicam
Thomas Bricot. *Textus abbreviatus totius logices Aristotelis*. Continent: date indeterminable.
Language(s): Latin. Appraised at 10d in 1573.

103.5 historia danorum
Saxo, *Grammaticus*. *Gesta Danorum*. Continent: date indeterminable.
Language(s): Latin. Appraised at 6d in 1573.

103.6 Calvin his institutions in englishe
Jean Calvin. *The institution of christian religion*. Translated by T. N[orton]. London: Richard Harrison, 1561–1562.
STC 4415 *et seq*. Reyner Wolfe had a role in printing the first English edition in 1561. *Language(s)*: English. Appraised at 2s 8d in 1573.

103.7 A greake lexicon in two volumes
Unidentified [dictionary]. Continent: date indeterminable.
Language(s): Greek. Appraised at 3s 4d in 1573.

103.8 strabonis Cosmographia
Strabo. [*Geographia*]. Continent: date indeterminable.
Language(s): Latin (probable) Greek (perhaps). Appraised at 16d in 1573.

103.9 Polidorus Virgill
Polydorus Vergilius. Unidentified. Place unknown: stationer unknown, date indeterminable.
STC/non-STC status unknown. Probably either *Anglicae historiae*, the *De inventoribus rerum*, or the English *An abridgement of the notable works of Polidore Vergile*. *Language(s)*: Latin (probable) English (perhaps). Appraised at 3s in 1573.

103.10 Aristophanes grece wth a comment
Aristophanes. [*Works*]. Continent: date indeterminable.
Language(s): Greek. Appraised at 2s in 1573.

103.11 Cranmer against Gardiner of transubstantiation
Thomas Cranmer, *Archbishop*. *An answer of ... Thomas archebyshop of Canterburye, unto a crafty cavillation by S. Gardiner*. London: R. Wolfe, 1551.
STC 5991. The second book of this polemical tract is an answer to Gardiner's on transubstantiation. Gardiner's text is included. *Language(s)*: English. Appraised at 18d in 1573.

103.12 Juell his defense of the apologie

John Jewel, *Bishop*. *A defence of the Apologie of the Churche of Englande.* London: H. Wykes, 1567–1571.

STC 14600 *et seq*. This long title continues *a certaine booke by M. Hardinge*, referring to STC 12762 by Thomas Harding. *Language(s)*: English. Appraised at 16d in 1573.

103.13 Postilla feri de sanctis

Joannes Ferus (Johann Wild, *Prediger zu Mainz*). [*Gospels and Epistles (liturgical): commentary*]. Continent: date indeterminable.
Language(s): Latin. Appraised at 4d in 1573.

103.14 A newe testament in two volumes

[*Bible–N.T.*]. Continent (probable): date indeterminable.

Probably not an STC book, but see STC 2854, 2854.6 and 2866. The only two-volume version of the New Testament printed in England was Erasmus's paraphrase. *Language(s)*: Latin (probable) English (perhaps). Appraised at 12d in 1573.

103.15 A bible in englishe

The Bible. Britain or Continent: date indeterminable.
STC 2063 *et seq*. *Language(s)*: English. Appraised at 2s in 1573.

103.16 Cosmographia Apiani

Peter Apian. *Cosmographia*. Continent: date indeterminable.
Language(s): Latin. Appraised at 2d in 1573.

103.17 Bernardi oratio de tranquillitate vitae

John Bernard. *Oratio pia, religiosa, et solatii plena, de vera animi tranquillitate.* Edited by T. Bernard. London: apud G. Seresium, 1568.

STC 1924. Bernard's book was issued by his brother Thomas after he discovered it among the effects of John following his death. *Language(s)*: Latin. Appraised at 4d in 1573.

103.18 Antesignanus grammer

Nicolaus Clenardus. [*Institutiones linguae graecae*]. Petrus Antesignanus. Continent: date indeterminable.
Language(s): Greek Latin. Appraised at 10d in 1573.

103.19 Plinius de mundi historia

Pliny, *the Elder*. *Historia naturalis*. Continent: date indeterminable.
Language(s): Latin. Appraised at 3d in 1573.

103.20 juells Apologie in english

John Jewel, *Bishop*. *An apologie, or aunswer in defence of the Church of England.* London: R. Wolfe, 1562–1564.

STC 14590 *et seq.* The two editions are translated by two different translators. *Language(s)*: English. Appraised at 2d in 1573.

103.21 Orontius de sphera mundi
Oronce Finé. *De mundi sphaera*. Paris: (different houses), 1542-1555. *Language(s)*: Latin. Appraised at 6d in 1573.

103.22 Nowells catachisme in latten
Alexander Nowell. *Catechismus, sive prima institutio, disciplináque pietatis christianae*. London: R. Wolfii, 1570-1572.

STC 18701 *et seq.* Much more likely the larger catechism since the first shorter catechism appeared in 1573. *Language(s)*: Latin. Appraised at 4d in 1573.

103.23 Joannes Pontanus de rebus caelestibus
Joannes Jovianus Pontanus. *De rebus coelestibus libri XIV*. Continent: date indeterminable.

Perhaps a solo edition, an edition issued in a composite volume as it often was, or a part of Pontanus's *Works*. See Adams P1868 for the latter. *Language(s)*: Latin. Appraised at 2d in 1573.

103.24 Philo judeus de mundo
Philo, *Judaeus*. *De mundo*. Continent: date indeterminable

Often appeared with Aristotle's work of the same name. *Language(s)*: Greek Latin. Appraised at 4d in 1573.

103.25 Nowell against dorman
Alexander Nowell. Unidentified. London: (different houses), 1565-1567.

See STC 18739 *et seq.* Several possibilities among Nowell's Protestant rejoinders to Roman Catholic Thomas Dorman. *Language(s)*: English. Appraised at 2d in 1573.

103.26 Interpretatio Carri in philippicas demosthenis
Demosthenes. *Graecorum oratorum principis, Olynthiacae orationes tres, et Philippicae quatuor*. Translated by Nicholas Carr and edited by Thomas Bing. London: ap. H. Denhamum, 1571.

STC 6577. *Language(s)*: Latin. Appraised at 2d in 1573.

103.27 Peter Martir uppon the sacramente of our lordes supper in englishe
Pietro Martire Vermigli (Peter Martyr). *A discourse or traictise of Petur Martyr Vermill a Florentine, wherin he declared his judgemente concernynge the sacrament of the Lordes supper*. Translated by N. Udall. London: (R. Stoughton [actually E. Whitchurch] for N. Udall), 1550 (probable).

STC 24665. A translation of STC 24673. *Language(s)*: English. Appraised at 10d in 1573.

103.28 Ovide de tristibus wth a commente
Publius Ovidius Naso. *Tristia*. Continent: date indeterminable.
Churchyard's translation of the first three books was published in 1572.
Language(s): Latin. Appraised at 2d in 1573.

103.29 Commentarii Caesaris
Caius Julius Caesar. *Commentarii*. Continent: date indeterminable.
Language(s): Latin. Appraised at 1d in 1573.

103.30 Chilias Homeri grece
Homer. *Iliad*. Continent: date indeterminable.
Language(s): Greek. Appraised at 1d in 1573.

103.31 Virgilius
Publius Virgilius Maro. Probably [*Works*]. Britain or Continent: date indeterminable.
STC 24787 *et seq.* and non-STC. *Language(s)*: Latin. Appraised at 1d in 1573.

103.32 Duae Postillae feri
Joannes Ferus. (Johann Wild, *Prediger zu Mainz*). *Postilla*. Continent: date indeterminable.
Language(s): Latin. Appraised at 6d in 1573.

103.33 Dorbell in philosophiam naturalem
Nicolaus de Orbellis. *Cursus librorum philosophiae naturalis*. Basle: (different houses), 1494–1503.
Language(s): Latin. Appraised at 1d in 1573.

103.34 Monsteri gramatica hebraica
Sebastian Muenster. [*Grammatica hebraica*]. Continent: 1524–1570.
Language(s): Hebrew Latin. Appraised at 2d in 1573.

103.35 Diogines laertius de vitis philosophorum
Diogenes Laertius. [*De vita et moribus philosophorum*]. Continent: date indeterminable.
Language(s): Latin Greek (perhaps). Appraised at 3d in 1573.

103.36 Paynelles sentences on the scripture
Thomas Paynell. *The piththy [sic] and moost notable sayinges of al Scripture*. London: (different houses), 1550–1560.
STC 19494 *et seq. Language(s)*: English. Appraised at 6d in 1573.

103.37 Anatomie of the masse
Agostino Mainardi (Anthoni de Adamo, *pseudonym*). *An anatomi, that is*

to say a parting in peeces of the mass. Strassburg (probable): [Heirs of W. Köpfel], 1556.
STC 17200. *Language(s)*: English. Appraised at 4d in 1573.

103.38 Horatius
Quintus Horatius Flaccus. [*Works*]. Continent: date indeterminable. *Language(s)*: Latin. Appraised at 2d in 1573.

103.39 Ovidii metamorphosis
Publius Ovidius Naso. *Metamorphoses*. Continent: date indeterminable. *Language(s)*: Latin. Appraised at 2d in 1573.

103.40 Ausonius
Decimus Magnus Ausonius. [*Works*]. Continent: date indeterminable. *Language(s)*: Latin. Appraised at 2d in 1573.

103.41 Testamentum grece et latine
[*Bible–N.T.*]. Continent: date indeterminable. *Language(s)*: Greek Latin. Appraised at 8d in 1573.

103.42 sex ciceronis volumina
Marcus Tullius Cicero. Perhaps [*Works* (part)]. Continent: date indeterminable.
Probably not an STC book. Likely an imperfect set of the *Works*, but if, rather, a batch, some of the six volumes could be STC books. *Language(s)*: Latin. Appraised at 3s in 1573.

103.43 Rodolphus Agricola
Rodolphus Agricola. Probably *De inventione dialectica*. Continent: date indeterminable.
His most frequently published work. *Language(s)*: Latin. Appraised at 6d in 1573.

103.44 Laurentii Vallae elegantiae
Laurentius Valla. *Elegantiae*. Continent: date indeterminable. *Language(s)*: Latin. Appraised at 2d in 1573.

103.45 Olynthiasae demosthenis grece, et latine
Demosthenes. *Olynthiacae orationes tres*. Continent: date indeterminable. *Language(s)*: Greek Latin. Appraised at 2d in 1573.

103.46 Aristotelis aethica
Aristotle. *Ethica*. Britain or Continent: date indeterminable.
STC 752 and non-STC. *Language(s)*: Latin. Appraised at 2d in 1573.

103.47 A Comment uppon the 2 epistle of St paule to the corinthians in englishe
Unidentified. [*Epistle 2–Paul: commentary*]. Britain (probable): date indeterminable.
Not found in the STC. *Language(s)*: English. Appraised at 2d in 1573.

103.48 Senecae tragediae
Lucius Annaeus Seneca. *Tragoediae*. Continent: date indeterminable.
Language(s): Latin. Appraised at 2d in 1573.

103.49 Valerius Maximus
Valerius Maximus. *Facta et dicta memorabilia*. Continent: date indeterminable.
Language(s): Latin. Appraised at 3d in 1573.

103.50 Rami Animadversiones in Aristotelem
Pierre de La Ramée. [*Aristotelicae animadversiones*]. Continent: date indeterminable.
Language(s): Latin. Appraised at 6d in 1573.

103.51 Ceporini Gramatica
Jacobus Ceporinus. *Compendium grammaticae graecae*. Continent: 1522–1565.
Language(s): Greek Latin. Appraised at 3d in 1573.

103.52 Melanghton in Proverbia
Philipp Melanchthon. [*Proverbs: commentary*]. Continent: 1525–1572.
Language(s): Latin. Appraised at 2d in 1573.

103.53 Questiones Bezae
Théodore de Bèze. *Quaestionum et responsionum christianarum libellus*. Britain or Continent: 1567–1571.
STC 2036 *et seq.* and non-STC. *Language(s)*: Latin. Appraised at 2d in 1573.

103.54 Examen theologicum
Benedictus Aretius. *Examen theologicum*. Continent: 1570–1573.
Language(s): Latin. Appraised at 3d in 1573.

103.55 Caelius secundus pro authoritate ecclesiae
Caelius Secundus Curio. *Pro vera et antiquae ecclesiae Christi autoritate, in Antonium Florebellum Mutinensem, oratio*. Basle: probably Joannes Oporinus, 1547c.
Language(s): Latin. Appraised at 2d in 1573.

103.56 Loci communes Melanchton

Philipp Melanchthon. [*Loci communes theologici*]. Continent: date indeterminable.

This entry has been struck out in the manuscript and is not appraised. *Language(s)*: Latin.

103.57 Arithmetica Micylli

Jacobus Micyllus, *pseudonym* (Jakob Moltzer). *Arithmetica logistica*. Basle: per (ex off.) Joannem Oporinum, 1555.

Language(s): Latin. Appraised at 2d in 1573.

103.58 Dialogi Luciani grece, et latine

Lucian, *of Samosata*. [*Dialogues–Selected*]. Continent: date indeterminable. *Language(s)*: Greek Latin. Appraised at 3d in 1573.

103.59 A booke of sundrie instrumentes

A book of precedents. London: 1543–1572.

STC 3327 *et seq*. A collection of "instruments" for different legal papers, viz., leases, indentures, etc. The running title is *The boke of sundrye instrumentes*. *Language(s)*: English. Appraised at 4d in 1573.

103.60 Talaei rhetorica

Aldomarus Talaeus (Omer Talon). *Rhetorica*. Continent: date indeterminable.

Generally agreed that Ramus had a major role in the composition of this work. *Language(s)*: Latin. Appraised at 2d in 1573.

103.61 Lactantius firmianus

Lucius Coelius Lactantius (Firmianus). Probably [*Works*]. Continent (probable): date indeterminable.

Probably not an STC book. STC 15118 (1522?) is *Selected works*, which the entry may represent. *Language(s)*: Latin. Appraised at 8d in 1573.

103.62 Praeces privatae

Preces privatae. London: William Seres, 1564–1573.

STC 20378 *et seq*. *Language(s)*: Latin. Appraised at 2d in 1573.

103.63 Palingenius

Marcellus Palingenius (Pietro Angelo Manzolli [Stellatus]). *Zodiacus vitae*. Britain or Continent: date indeterminable.

STC 19138.5 *et seq*. and non-STC. *Language(s)*: Latin (probable) English (perhaps). Appraised at 3d in 1573.

103.64 Colloquium erasmi

Desiderius Erasmus. *Colloquia*. Britain or Continent: date indeterminable.

STC 10450 *et seq*. and non-STC. *Language(s)*: Latin. Appraised at 3d in 1573.

103.65 Pantaleon de quantitate sillabarum
Pantaleon Barteleone Raverinus. *De ratione quantitatis syllabariae liber.* Continent (probable): date indeterminable.
Almost certainly not an STC book. The sole edition known is Lyon, 1575-76 (see BCI 2:657), but there must have been an earlier edition. For another pre-1575-76 copy, see PLRE 92.94. *Language(s)*: Latin. Appraised at 3d in 1573.

103.66 Justinus
Trogus Pompeius and Justinus, *the Historian*. [*Epitomae in Trogi Pompeii historias*]. Britain or Continent: date indeterminable.
STC 24287 *et seq.* and non-STC. The 1564 English abridgement (STC 24290) is unlikely to have been so entered. *Language(s)*: Latin. Appraised at 4d in 1573.

103.67 Homerus
Homer. Perhaps [*Works*]. Continent: date indeterminable.
The appraisal seems low for the complete works. *Language(s)*: Latin (probable) Greek (perhaps). Appraised at 3d in 1573.

103.68 three volumes of the olde testament
[*Bible–O.T.*]. Britain or Continent: date indeterminable.
STC 2350 *et seq.* and non-STC. Whether a three-volume edition, three separate volumes of an incomplete Old Testament, or three different sized volume editions cannot be known. *Language(s)*: Unknown. Appraised at 12d in 1573.

103.69 Calvini Catechismus grece, et latine
Jean Calvin. [*Catechism*]. Geneva: (different houses), 1551-1565.
The title is in Greek. *Language(s)*: Greek Latin. Appraised at 4d in 1573.

103.70 Gemma Platonis
Plato. *Gemmae, sive illustriores sententiae.* Compiled by Niccolò Liburnio. Paris: apud Benedictum Prevost, 1556-1557.
Language(s): Latin. Appraised at 1d in 1573.

103.71 Dialogues de Jan loys vives
Joannes Lodovicus Vives. *Les dialogues.* Continent: date indeterminable.
A French version of *Familiarium colloquiorum formulae, sive linguae latinae exercitatio.* See Brunet 5:1334 and BN. *Language(s)*: French Latin. Appraised at 2d in 1573.

103.72 Sulpitius Severus
Sulpicius Severus. *Sacrae historia.* Continent: 1556-1569.
The *Opera* is too late (1574). *Language(s)*: Latin. Appraised at 1d in 1573.

103.73 Lucius Apuleius de aureo Asino
Lucius Apuleius. [*Metamorphoses*]. Continent: date indeterminable. *Language(s)*: Latin. Appraised at 2d in 1573.

103.74 Argumentum eucharistiae
Unidentified. Place unknown: stationer unknown, date indeterminable. STC/non-STC status unknown. Nothing with such a title has been found, and if the entry is only descriptive, the possibilities are numerous. *Language(s)*: Latin (probable). Appraised with twenty-four others at 2s in 1573.

103.75 Erasmus de misericordia dei
Desiderius Erasmus. *De misericordia Domini*. Continent (probable): date indeterminable.

Probably not an STC book, but see STC 10474 *et seq.* The English translation of Gentian Hervet bears a Latin title. *Language(s)*: Latin (probable). Appraised with twenty-four others at 2s in 1573.

103.76 Valerius de Sphera
Cornelius Valerius. *De sphaera*. Antwerp: (different houses), 1561-1573. *Language(s)*: Latin. Appraised with twenty-four others at 2s in 1573.

103.77 Arithmetica Gemma Phrisii
Reiner Gemma, *Frisius*. *Arithmeticae practicae methodus facilis*. Continent: 1540-1572.

Language(s): Latin. Appraised with twenty-four others at 2s in 1573.

103.78 Pomponius mela de situ orbis
Pomponius Mela. *De situ orbis*. Continent: date indeterminable. *Language(s)*: Latin. Appraised with twenty-four others at 2s in 1573.

103.79 Conjecturae de ultimis temporibus
Andreas Osiander, *the Elder*. *Conjecturae de ultimis temporibus*. Nuremberg: apud Johan Petreium, 1544.

Language(s): Latin. Appraised with twenty-four others at 2s in 1573.

103.80 Ambiani commentarii in tres orationes Ciceronis
Franciscus Sylvius, *of Amiens*. *Commentarii in treis orationes Ciceronis*. Paris: vaenundatur Jodoco Badio, 1529-1534.

The three orations are *Pro Marcello*, *Pro Ligario*, and *Pro Deiotoro*. Four editions in the date range. *Language(s)*: Latin. Appraised with twenty-four others at 2s in 1573.

103.81 Aristotelis de anima epitome
Aristotle. [*De anima–Epitome*]. Continent: date indeterminable.

No "epitome" seems to have been published separately, but see Cranz,

p. 166, for several paraphrases and a collection of Aristotle's epitomes in which *De anima* appears (1500). *Language(s)*: Latin. Appraised with twenty-four others at 2s in 1573.

103.82 Schemata Mosellani

Petrus Schade, *Mosellanus*. *Tabulae de schematibus et tropis* [and others]. Britain or Continent: date indeterminable.

STC 21810.3 and non-STC. The edition from England appeared in 1573. The others are Melanchthon and Erasmus. Language(s): Latin. Appraised with twenty-four others at 2s in 1573.

103.83 A godlie admonition of the causes of the counsell of trente

A godly and necessarye admonition of the decrees and canons of the counsel of Trent. Translated by [Abp. M. Parker?]. London: John Day, 1564.

STC 24265. *Language(s)*: English. Appraised with twenty-four others at 2s in 1573.

103.84 mr levers sermon preached at Paules Crosse

Thomas Lever. *A sermon preached at Pauls crosse, the .xiiii. day of December, ... M.D.L.* Britain: 1551 (probable).

STC 15546 *et seq*. Printed at London and Worcester; reprinted in STC 15551. *Language(s)*: English. Appraised with twenty-four others at 2s in 1573.

103.85 An exposition uppon the 5, 6, 7 chapiters of Mathewe

William Tyndale. *An exposicion uppon the. v.vi.vii. chapters of Mathew*. Britain or Continent: 1533 (probable)–1549 (probable).

STC 24440 *et seq*. *Language(s)*: English. Appraised with twenty-four others at 2s in 1573.

103.86 A battaile against the invocation of sainctes

Jean Veron. *A stronge battery against the idolatrous invocation of the dead saintes, made dialoguewise*. London: H. Sutton for T. Hacket, 1562.

STC 24686. *Language(s)*: English. Appraised with twenty-four others at 2s in 1573.

103.87 An awnswer to mr marshall by mr doctor canfild of the treatise of the crosse

James Calfhill. *An aunswere to the Treatise of the crosse*. London: H. Denham for L. Harryson, 1565.

STC 4368. Answers STC 17496; Calfhill's tract is then responded to by Thomas Marshall in STC 17497. *Language(s)*: English. Appraised with twenty-four others at 2s in 1573.

103.88 The reliques of Rome

Thomas Becon. *The relikes of Rome, concernynge church ware and matters of religion*. London: John Day, c.1560 (probable)–1563 (probable).

STC 1754 *et seq. Language(s)*: English. Appraised with twenty-four others at 2s in 1573.

103.89 Demosthenis orationes duae
Demosthenes. [*Selected works–Orations*]. Continent: date indeterminable. Perhaps, however, Adams D259. *Language(s)*: Latin (probable) Greek (perhaps). Appraised with twenty-four others at 2s in 1573.

103.90 A treatisse betwene the spiritualtye, and temporaltie
Christopher Saint German. *A treatise concernynge the division betwene the spirytualtie and the temporaltie.* London: (different houses), 1532 (probable).

STC 21586 *et seq*. Published anonymously. *Language(s)*: English. Appraised with twenty-four others at 2s in 1573.

103.91 A confutation of the cause of burning of paules steple in london
James Pilkington, *Bishop. The burnynge of Paules church in London in 1561.* London: William Seres, 1563.

STC 19931. Reprints and answers John Morwen's *An addicion*, which seems not to be otherwise extant. *Language(s)*: English. Appraised with twenty-four others at 2s in 1573.

103.92 The unitie of the churche
Perhaps George Joye. *The unite and scisme of the olde chirche.* Antwerp (probable): [Widow of C. Ruremond], 1543.

STC 14830. *Language(s)*: English. Appraised with twenty-four others at 2s in 1573.

103.93 A description of Antechriste
A short description of Antichrist unto the nobilitie of Englande. Emden (probable): [E. van der Erve], c. 1555.

STC 673. Attributed to John Olde, and almost certainly a version of his translation of Rudolph Walther's *Antichristus* at STC 25009. *Language(s)*: English. Appraised with twenty-four others at 2s in 1573.

103.94 Christopher Goodman how to obey and disobey
Christopher Goodman. *How superior powers oght to be obeyd of their subjects: and wherin they may lawfully be disobeyed.* Geneva: J. Crispin, 1558.

STC 12020. *Language(s)*: English. Appraised with twenty-four others at 2s in 1573.

103.95 hunteri Cosmographia
Joannes Honterus. *Rudimenta cosmographica.* Continent: date indeterminable.

Language(s): Latin. Appraised with twenty-four others at 2s in 1573.

103.96 The summe of divinitie

Johann Spangenberg. *The sum of divinitie drawen out of the holy scripture.* Translated by R. Hutten. London: (different houses), 1548–1567.

STC 23004 *et seq.* Published anonymously. *Language(s)*: English. Appraised with twenty-four others at 2s in 1573.

103.97 A lutinge booke

Unidentified. Place unknown: stationer unknown, date indeterminable.

STC/non-STC status unknown. Hutchinson owned a lute, so this item seems appropriate on his inventory of books. This could be STC 15486, a 1568 translation of Adrian Le Roy's book on lute instruction, but Continental printers had produced many editions of lute music before 1573. *Language(s)*: Unknown. Appraised with twenty-four others at 2s in 1573.

103.98 Lewis Evans de eucharistia

Lewis Evans. Probably *A shorte treatyse of the mysterie of the euchariste.* London: Thomas Purfoot, 1569 (probable).

STC 10593. No trace of a Latin edition exists, and nothing in the English edition suggests a prior version. Perhaps the book inventory was written by a clerk familiar with Latin who unconsciously wrote the English title in Latin "shorthand." *Language(s)*: English (probable) Latin (perhaps). Appraised with twenty-four others at 2s in 1573.

103.99 certayne paper bookes

Unidentified. Provenances unknown: dates indeterminable.

Manuscripts. Perhaps personal notebooks. *Language(s)*: Unknown. Appraised at 2s in 1573.

William Kettelby. Scholar (M.A.): Probate Inventory. 1573

GRADY A. SMITH

William Kettelby [Ketilbie, Kettilby, Kettlebie] entered Christ Church in 1563. He is among the students in a 1564/5 list for that college (Clark 2:ii.12), and proceeded B.A. 25 June 1566. After receiving his M.A. on 10 June 1569 he was appointed praelector in astronomy (*Alumni Oxonienses* 2:847). Surviving is a 15 October 1569 dispensation from this obligation for two weeks because of going down (Clark 2:ii.99). Less than four years later he was dead, the probate inventory of his books being made 3 January 1573.

The thrust of Kettelby's studies is clear from the inventory. Fifty-six entries, or well over half of the list, concern medicine, with Galen accounting for at least one fourth of the medical works. Literature, philosophy and theology are well represented; Greek is a noteworthy presence. Interestingly, despite Kettelby's holding a praelectorship in astronomy, only two works (104.16 and 104.33) deal with that subject.

Oxford University Archives, Bodleian Library: Hyp.B.15.

§

Renouard, Philippe. 1908. *Bibliographie des impressions et des oeuvres de Josse Badius Ascensius.* Paris.

§

104.1   dictionarium Eliotti
104.2   montanus de consolacione medicine
104.3   historia Aristotelis

104.4	instituciones fuccii
104.5	fernelius de medendis
104.6	fuccius de curandi racione
104.7	Jobertus valentinus
104.8	gordanus de morborum curacione
104.9	regimen sanitatis salarni
104.10	altera pars montani
104.11	Appiani cosmographia
104.12	arnoldi medici opera
104.13	opera christoferi Avegii
104.14:A	Cesarii dialectica
104.14:B	[See 104.14:A]
104.15	gallenus de curacione per sanguinis emissionem
104.16	alcabitius
104.17	hypocratis opera
104.18	campegius de morborum generibus
104.19	theoria hypocratis
104.20	ventura de lapide philosophica
104.21	anotomia fallopie
104.22	gallenus de constitucione artis medice
104.23	gallenus de victus racione
104.24	methodus medendi galleni
104.25	fuccius de composicione medicamentis
104.26	ars medica galleni que parva dicitur
104.27	gallenus de usu partium
104.28	de hyppocratis dogmatibus
104.29	methodus de febrebus menii
104.30	gallenus de anomaticis administracenibus
104.31	gallenus de compositione pharmacorum localium
104.32	gallenus de aliementorum facultatibus
104.33	orantius de sphera
104.34	organon Aristotelis
104.35	opera ciceronis in 9 voluminibus
104.36	gramatica greca
104.37	epistole ovidii
104.38	crucii gramatica
104.39	Lucius florus de gestis
104.40:1	Salustius et Rodius
104.40:2	[See 104.40:1]
104.41	philostratus de vita apolonii
104.42	cronicon carionis
104.43	Instituciones bullengeri
104.44	Rodulphus agricola
104.45	hisocrates ad nichoclem
104.46	compendium gentie

104.47	epistole bunelli
104.48	Epistole Celii 2i
104.49	Luciani dialogi
104.50	Epistole Ciceronis cum commento
104.51:A	humffredus de nobilitate
104.51:B	[See 104.51:A]
104.52	demostenes de falsa legacione
104.53	hisocrates ad archidamum
104.54	Silvius de medicamentorum dilectu
104.55	gallenus de febribus cum commento giberti
104.56	Rodolecii medici
104.57	diescorides
104.58	dispensatorium cordi
104.59	gallenus de facultatibus simplicum medicamentorum
104.60	hypocratis aphorismi
104.61	dunius de arte medica
104.62	Judeus de victus racione
104.63	Kemptius de Imitando christo
104.64	gentilis de urinis
104.65	victorius de arte medica
104.66	libellus fabrani
104.67	mesue
104.68	Rolandus de medicina
104.69	theophilus de usu partium
104.70	gualterus de arte curativa
104.71	cornelius philosophia
104.72	Rolandus de phlebotomia
104.73	galenus de simptomatum diff
104.74	barnardus de conservacione vite
104.75	bucerus in librum galleni
104.76	a englyshe bible
104.77	Jovellus
104.78	paracellus de gradibus
104.79	Enchiridion Cornatii
104.80	compendium pellitarii
104.81	Calcius de sanitate gubernanda
104.82	Silvius de febrebus
104.83	erasmus de preparacione
104.84	dimostenes
104.85	testamentum grece
104.86	gallenus de naturalibus facultatibus
104.87:1-3	3 paper bokes
104.88	philoretus de urinis
104.89	trivierus de temporibus
104.90	galleni prognosticon

104.91   dimostenis Epistole grece
104.92   Cornelius selsus
104.93   computus de memoria

§

104.1 dictionarium Eliotti
   Sir Thomas Elyot. *The dictionary of syr Thomas Eliot*. London: Thomas Berthelet, 1538–1559.
   STC 7659 *et seq. Language(s)*: English Latin. Appraised at 2s 6d in 1573.

104.2 montanus de consolacione medicine
   Joannes Baptista Montanus. [*Consultationes medicinales*]. Continent: date indeterminable.
   See also 104.10. *Language(s)*: Latin. Appraised at 4s in 1573.

104.3 historia Aristotelis
   Aristotle. *Historia animalium*. Continent: date indeterminable.
   Language(s): Latin. Appraised at 2s in 1573.

104.4 instituciones fuccii
   Leonard Fuchs. *Institutiones medicinae*. Continent: 1555–1572.
   Language(s): Latin. Appraised at 14d in 1573.

104.5 fernelius de medendis
   Joannes Fernelius. Probably *Therapeutices universalis seu medendi rationis libri septem*. Continent: date indeterminable.
   The earlier *Medicina*, which is included in this, is also a possibility. *Language(s)*: Latin. Appraised at 10d in 1573.

104.6 fuccius de curandi racione
   Leonard Fuchs. [*De medendi methodo*]. Continent: 1548–1568.
   Language(s): Latin. Appraised at 16d in 1573.

104.7 Jobertus valentinus
   Laurent Joubert (Valentinus). Perhaps *Medicinae practicae priores libri tres*. Lyon: apud Joannem Gregorium, 1572.
   The phrase *de med racione* is found in the rough copy. *Language(s)*: Latin. Appraised at 4d in 1573.

104.8 gordanus de morborum curacione
   Bernardus de Gordonio. [*Practica, seu Lilium medicinae*]. Continent: date indeterminable.
   Language(s): Latin. Appraised at 12d in 1573.

104.9 regimen sanitatis salarni

[*Regimen sanitatis Salernitatum*]. Britain or Continent: date indeterminable.

STC 21596 and non-STC. All editions published in England by the date of this inventory are in Latin and English. *Language(s)*: Latin English (perhaps). Appraised at 1d in 1573.

104.10 altera pars montani

Probably Joannes Baptista Montanus. Unidentified. Continent: date indeterminable.

There exists more than one writer with a name that could be presented as the entry's *montani*, but see 104.2. *Language(s)*: Latin. Appraised at 4s in 1573.

104.11 Appiani cosmographia

Peter Apian. *Cosmographia*. Continent: date indeterminable.

Gemma, *Frisius* emended virtually half of the approximately two dozen editions published prior to the death of Kettelby. *Language(s)*: Latin. Appraised at 8d in 1573.

104.12 arnoldi medici opera

Arnaldus, *de Villa Nova*. [*Works*]. Continent: date indeterminable. *Language(s)*: Latin. Appraised at 20d in 1573.

104.13 opera christoferi Avegii

Christophorus de Vega. Unidentified. Continent: date indeterminable.

According to bibliographical sources, the earliest edition of Vega's (the name is also written as Christophorus à Vega) *Opera* was not published until 1576, three years after the inventory was made. Most likely this entry refers to separate works of Vega bound together. *Language(s)*: Latin. Appraised at 14d in 1573.

104.14:A Cesarii dialectica

Joannes Caesarius, *Juliacensis*. *Dialectica*. Continent: date indeterminable. *Language(s)*: Latin. Appraised [a composite volume] at 2d in 1573.

104.14:B [See 104.14:A]

Joannes Murmellius. [*Aristotle–Categoriae: commentary*]. [Composite publication].

Almost invariably published with the preceding. *Language(s)*: Latin. Appraised [a composite volume] at 2d in 1573.

104.15 gallenus de curacione per sanguinis emissionem

Galen. *De curandi ratione per venae sectionem*. Continent: 1529–1558. *Language(s)*: Latin. Appraised at 10d in 1573.

104.16 alcabitius
Alchabitius. Unidentified. Continent: date indeterminable.
Language(s): Latin. Appraised at 2d in 1573.

104.17 hypocratis opera
Hippocrates. [*Works*]. Continent: date indeterminable.
Language(s): Latin. Appraised at 2s 4d in 1573.

104.18 campegius de morborum generibus
Symphorien Champier. [*Practica in medicina*]. Continent: date indeterminable.
Language(s): Latin. Appraised at 16d in 1573.

104.19 theoria hypocratis
Jacobus Curio. *Hippocratis ... de naturae temporum anni, et aeris irregularium constitutionum propriis, hominisque omnium aetatum morbis, theoria*. Frankfurt am Main: apud Georgium Corvinum, Sigismundum Feyrabend et haeredes Wigandi Galli, 1569.

Book III of the *Aphorisimi*. *Language(s)*: Greek Latin. Appraised at 14d in 1573.

104.20 ventura de lapide philosophica
Laurentius Ventura. *De ratione conficiendi lapidis philosophici* [and others]. Basle: Petrus Perna, 1571.
Language(s): Latin. Appraised at 20d in 1573.

104.21 anotomia fallopie
Gabriel Fallopius. Probably *Observationes anatomicae*. Continent: 1561–1566.
De humani corporis anatome, compendium, published in Venice in 1571, is a less likely possibility. *Language(s)*: Latin. Appraised at 10d in 1573.

104.22 gallenus de constitucione artis medice
Galen. *De constitutione artis medicae*. Continent: 1531–1552.
Language(s): Latin Greek (perhaps). Appraised at 10d in 1573.

104.23 gallenus de victus racione
Galen. Unidentified. Continent: date indeterminable.
Whether this is Galen's *De attenuante victus ratione*, apparently only published with *De alimentorum facultatibus libri tres* (with the latter leading), his *In Hippocratis de victus ratione privatorum*, or his *In Hippocratis de victus ratione in morbis acutis*, cannot be determined. *Language(s)*: Latin. Appraised at 8d in 1573.

104.24 methodus medendi galleni
Galen. *Methodus medendi*. Translated by Thomas Linacre. Continent: 1519–1553.
Language(s): Latin. Appraised at 14d in 1573.

104.25 fuccius de composicione medicamentis
Leonard Fuchs. *De componendorum medicamentorum ratione*. Continent: 1555–1563.
Rough copy reads *componendis* for *composicione*. *Language(s)*: Latin. Appraised at 12d in 1573.

104.26 ars medica galleni que parva dicitur
Galen. *Ars medica*. Continent: date indeterminable.
Language(s): Latin. Appraised at 8d in 1573.

104.27 gallenus de usu partium
Galen. *De usu partium*. Continent: 1528–1550.
Language(s): Latin Greek (perhaps). Appraised at 12d in 1573.

104.28 de hyppocratis dogmatibus
Galen. [*De Hippocratis et Platonis decretis*]. Continent: 1534–1550.
Some editions read "dogmatis" instead of "decretis." May be *Selected works* with this title leading. *Language(s)*: Latin. Appraised at 14d in 1573.

104.29 methodus de febrebus menii
Ferdinandus de Mena, *Physician. Methodus febrium omnium*. Antwerp: ex officina Christophori Plantini, 1568.
Language(s): Latin. Appraised at 12d in 1573.

104.30 gallenus de anomaticis administracenibus
Galen. *De anatomicis administrationibus*. Continent: 1531–1551.
Also in several collections, with this title leading. *Language(s)*: Latin. Appraised at 10d in 1573.

104.31 gallenus de compositione pharmacorum localium
Galen. *De compositione medicamentorum secundum locos*. Continent: 1535–1561.
Language(s): Latin. Appraised at 12d in 1573.

104.32 gallenus de aliementorum facultatibus
Galen. *De alimentorum facultatibus*. Continent: date indeterminable.
Could be solo edition or leading title of *Selected works*. *Language(s)*: Latin. Appraised at 13d in 1573.

104.33 orantius de sphera
Oronce Finé. *De mundi sphaera*. Paris: (different houses), 1542–1555.
Language(s): Latin. Appraised at 6d in 1573.

104.34 organon Aristotelis
Aristotle. *Organon*. Continent: date indeterminable.
Language(s): Latin. Appraised at 20d in 1573.

104.35 opera ciceronis in 9 voluminibus
Marcus Tullius Cicero. [*Works*]. Continent: 1540–1548.
See Adams C1642–43 for the two editions in nine volumes, conceivably a made-up collection, or part of a larger set. The rough copy of the inventory appraises this item at 10s. *Language(s)*: Latin. Appraised at 9s in 1573.

104.36 gramatica greca
Unidentified. Continent: date indeterminable.
Language(s): Greek Latin. Appraised at 6d in 1573.

104.37 epistole ovidii
Publius Ovidius Naso. *De ponto*. Continent: date indeterminable.
Language(s): Latin. Appraised at 2d in 1573.

104.38 crucii gramatica
Martin Crusius. *Grammatica graeca, cum latina congruens*. Basle: (different houses), 1562–1566.
Language(s): Greek Latin. Appraised at 14d in 1573.

104.39 Lucius florus de gestis
Lucius Annaeus Florus. [*Epitomae de Tito Livio bellorum omnium annorum*]. Continent: date indeterminable.
Language(s): Latin. Appraised at 8d in 1573.

104.40:1 Salustius et Rodius
Caius Sallustius Crispus. Unidentified. Place unknown: stationer unknown, date indeterminable.
STC/non-STC status unknown. Perhaps *Works*, or alternatively *De bello Jugurthino* or *De conjuratione Catiline*. The appraisal is low for more than one, especially since it shares the appraisal with the next with which it is probably bound. Language(s): Latin. Appraised with one other at 6d in 1573.

104.40:2 [See 104.40:1]
Probably Apollonius, *Rhodius. Argonautica*. Continent: 1523–1572.
Probably bound with the preceding. *Language(s)*: Greek (probable) Latin (perhaps). Appraised with one other at 6d in 1573.

104.41 philostratus de vita apolonii
Philostratus. *De vita Apollonii Tyanei*. Continent: date indeterminable.
Language(s): Latin. Appraised at 4d in 1573.

104.42 cronicon carionis
Johann Carion. *Chronica*. Continent: date indeterminable.
Language(s): Latin. Appraised at 6d in 1573.

104.43 Instituciones bullengeri
Heinrich Bullinger. Probably *Institutio eorum qui propter Dominum nostrum Jesum Christum de fide examinantur*. Translated by Josias Simler. Zürich: Christoph Froschouer, 1560.

Brevis ac pia institutio christianae religionis, ad dispersos in Hungaria Ecclesiarum christi ministros, 1559, is a remote possibility. *Language(s)*: Latin. Appraised at 4d in 1573.

104.44 Rodulphus agricola
Rodolphus Agricola. Probably *De inventione dialectica*. Continent: date indeterminable.

Agricola's most widely published work. *Language(s)*: Latin. Appraised at 6d in 1573.

104.45 hisocrates ad nichoclem
Isocrates. *Oratio ad Nicoclem*. Continent: date indeterminable.

Appears leading in many editions in combination with other Isocratic works. *Language(s)*: Latin. Appraised at 1d in 1573.

104.46 compendium gentie
Unidentified. Place unknown: stationer unknown, date indeterminable.

STC/non-STC status unknown. Perhaps something by Gentile da Foligno or by Joannes Guinterius, *of Andernach*, but there are many other possibilities. *Language(s)*: Latin (probable). Appraised at 1d in 1573.

104.47 epistole bunelli
Pierre Bunel. [*Epistolae*]. Continent: 1551–1568.

May include letters by Paolo Manuzio (Manutius) also. *Language(s)*: Latin. Appraised at 2d in 1573.

104.48 Epistole Celii 2i
Caelius Secundus Curio. *Selectarum epistolarum libri duo. Orationum liber unus*. Basle: (different houses), 1533–1570.

Language(s): Latin. Appraised at 3d in 1573.

104.49 Luciani dialogi
Lucian, *of Samosata*. Probably [*Dialogues–Selected*]. Britain or Continent: date indeterminable.

STC 16891 *et seq.* and non-STC. The appraisal seems low for the collected works. *Language(s)*: Latin. Appraised at 4d in 1573.

104.50 Epistole Ciceronis cum commento
Marcus Tullius Cicero. [*Selected works–Epistolae*]. Continent: date indeterminable.

Language(s): Latin. Appraised at 20d in 1573.

104.51:A humffredus de nobilitate

Laurence Humphrey. *Optimates, sive de nobilitate*. Basle: Joannes Oporinus, 1560 (composite publication).

Published with the following. *Language(s)*: Latin. Appraised [a composite volume] at 6d in 1573.

104.51:B [See 104.51:A]

Philo, *Judaeus. De nobilitate*. [Composite publication].

Published with the preceding. *Language(s)*: Latin. Appraised [a composite volume] at 6d in 1573.

104.52 demostenes de falsa legacione

Demosthenes. *De falsa legatione*. Paris: venundatur Jodoco Badio, 1532.

See BN for what is apparently the only edition; confirmed by Philippe Renouard (1908, 2:378), where it is erroneously listed under Demosthenes' *De senectute*. *Language(s)*: Greek Latin. Appraised at 4d in 1573.

104.53 hisocrates ad archidamum

Isocrates. *Archidamus*. Leipzig: in officina Vogeliana, date indeterminable. *Language(s)*: Greek Latin. Appraised at 3d in 1573.

104.54 Silvius de medicamentorum dilectu

Jacques Dubois (Jacobus Sylvius). *De medicamentorum simplicium delectu*. Continent: 1543–1565.

Language(s): Latin. Appraised at 10d in 1573.

104.55 gallenus de febribus cum commento giberti

Hector Gibault. [*Galen–De differentiis febrium: commentary and text*]. Translated by Laurentius Laurentianus. Lyon: apud Gulielmum Rouillium, 1561–1562.

Language(s): Latin. Appraised at 12d in 1573.

104.56 Rodolecii medici

Guillaume Rondelet. Unidentified. Continent: date indeterminable.

The first edition of Rondelet's *Opera omnia medica* was apparently not printed until 1619, but there are still two possibilities: *De materia medicinali et compositione medicamentorum ... methodus*, and *De ponderibus sive de justa quantitate et proportione medicamentorum*. *Language(s)*: Latin. Appraised at 6d in 1573.

104.57 diescorides

Dioscorides. *De medica materia*. Continent: date indeterminable. *Language(s)*: Latin Greek (perhaps). Appraised at 16d in 1573.

104.58 dispensatorium cordi

Valerius Cordus. [*Dispensatorium*]. Continent: 1546-1571.
Language(s): Latin. Appraised at 10d in 1573.

104.59 gallenus de facultatibus simplicum medicamentorum

Galen. *De simplicium medicamentorum facultatibus*. Continent: date indeterminable.

Could be either a solo edition or *Selected works* with this title leading. *Language(s)*: Latin. Appraised at 10d in 1573.

104.60 hypocratis aphorismi

Hippocrates. *Aphorismi*. Continent (probable): date indeterminable.

Probably not an STC book, but see STC 13520. The London printing is a Latin verse adaptation. *Language(s)*: Latin Greek (perhaps). Appraised at 16d in 1573.

104.61 dunius de arte medica

Thaddeus Dunus. Unidentified. Continent: date indeterminable.

The rough copy reads *dunus* for *dunius*. *Language(s)*: Latin. Appraised at 6d in 1573.

104.62 Judeus de victus racione

Unidentified. Continent (probable): date indeterminable.

Probably not an STC book. Perhaps an error in entering Brudus, *Lusitanus, Liber de ratione victus in singulis febribus*. *Language(s)*: Latin. Appraised at 12d in 1573.

104.63 Kemptius de Imitando christo

Thomas, *à Kempis*. *De imitatione Christi*. Continent: date indeterminable.
Language(s): Latin. Appraised at 4d in 1573.

104.64 gentilis de urinis

Aegidius, *Corboliensis*. *De urinis*. Continent: date indeterminable.

Commentary by Gentile da Foligno. Certainly *De urinis*, but whether solo or in the more widespread edition, *De urinis et pulsibus*, cannot be determined. *Language(s)*: Latin. Appraised at 8d in 1573.

104.65 victorius de arte medica

Leonellus de Victoriis. *Practica medicinalis*. Continent: 1545-1561.
Language(s): Latin. Appraised at 12d in 1573.

104.66 libellus fabrani

Perhaps Marcus Fabius Calvus. Unidentified. Continent: date indeterminable.

Calvus translated much of Hippocrates. The rough copy reads *fabiani* for *fabrani*. *Language(s)*: Latin. Appraised at 3d in 1573.

104.67 mesue
Joannes Mesue (Yahya Ibn Masawaih). Unidentified. Continent: date indeterminable.
Language(s): Latin. Appraised at 8d in 1573.

104.68 Rolandus de medicina
Martin Ruland, *the Elder. Medicina practica*. Strassburg: excud. Josias Rihelius, 1564-1567.
Language(s): Latin. Appraised at 8d in 1573.

104.69 theophilus de usu partium
Theophilus, *Protospatharius*. [*Galen–De usu partium–Epitome*]. Continent: 1537-1556.
Language(s): Latin. Appraised at 3d in 1573.

104.70 gualterus de arte curativa
Probably Galen. [*Ad Glauconem*]. Continent: date indeterminable.
The entry *gualterus* is conjectured to be an error for "Galenus" and the work, one of the many editions with the title *De arta curativa ad Glauconem*.
Language(s): Latin. Appraised at 3d in 1573.

104.71 cornelius philosophia
Unidentified. Continent: date indeterminable.
Either Cornelius Valerius or Heinrich Cornelius Agrippa, both of whom wrote works with forms of *philosophia* in the titles, could be intended.
Language(s): Latin. Appraised at 4d in 1573.

104.72 Rolandus de phlebotomia
Martin Ruland, *the Elder. De phlebotomia*. Strassburg: excud. Josias Rihelius, 1567.
Language(s): Latin. Appraised at 4d in 1573.

104.73 galenus de simptomatum diff
Galen. *De morborum et symptomatum differentiis et causis libri sex*. Britain or Continent: 1523-1565.
STC 11535 and non-STC. STC 11531.5 (1522?) is a remote possibility since the entry form is buried in the long title. *Language(s)*: Latin. Appraised at 3d in 1573.

104.74 barnardus de conservacione vite
Bernardus de Gordonio. *Tractatus de conservatione vitae humanae*. Leipzig: imprimebat Joannes Rhamba, curante Ernesto Vogelin, 1570.
Language(s): Latin. Appraised at 6d in 1573.

104.75 bucerus in librum galleni
Unidentified. Place unknown: stationer unknown, date indeterminable.

STC/non-STC status unknown. Clearly a work on Galen, but who is *Bucerus*? Not Martin Bucer. Perhaps an error in writing "Biesius," a stretch, but if Nicolaus Biesius, the item intended is probably *In artem medicam galeni commentarii*. Dominicus Buccius's work on Galen and Hippocrates, *Quaestia III*, is also a possibility. *Language(s)*: Latin. Appraised at 6d in 1573.

104.76 a englyshe bible
The Bible. Britain or Continent: date indeterminable.
STC 2063 *et seq. Language(s)*: English. Appraised at 3s 4d in 1573.

104.77 Jovellus
Chrysostomus Javellus. Unidentified. Continent: date indeterminable.
Language(s): Latin. Appraised at 2d in 1573.

104.78 paracellus de gradibus
Paracelsus. *De gradibus*. Continent: 1562–1572.
Language(s): Latin. Appraised at 6d in 1573.

104.79 Enchiridion Cornatii
Matthias Cornax. *Medicae consultationis apud aegrotos enchiridion*. Basle: per Joannem Oporinum, 1564.
Language(s): Latin. Appraised at 4d in 1573.

104.80 compendium pellitarii
Jacques Peletier. *De peste compendium*. Basle: per Joannem Oporinum, [no date].
NLM6 and BL infer 1560?, WLCM gives 1570? as date. *Language(s)*: Latin. Appraised at 1d in 1573.

104.81 Calcius de sanitate gubernanda
Joannes Katzschius. *De gubernanda sanitate*. Frankfurt am Main: Apud haeredes Christiani Egenolphi, 1557–1570.
Rough copy reads "cattius." *Language(s)*: Latin. Appraised at 2d in 1573.

104.82 Silvius de febrebus
Jacques Dubois (Jacobus Sylvius). *De febribus commentarius ex libris aliquot Hippocratis et Galeni*. Continent: 1554–1561.
Language(s): Latin. Appraised at 6d in 1573.

104.83 erasmus de preparacione
Desiderius Erasmus. *De praeparatione ad mortem*. Continent: 1534–1551.
Date range from VHe. *Language(s)*: Latin. Appraised at 1d in 1573.

104.84 dimostenes
Demosthenes. Unidentified. Place unknown: stationer unknown, date indeterminable.

STC/non-STC status unknown. *Language(s)*: Latin (probable) Greek (perhaps). Appraised at 2d in 1573.

104.85 testamentum grece
[*Bible–N.T.*]. Continent: date indeterminable.
Language(s): Greek. Appraised at 2d in 1573.

104.86 gallenus de naturalibus facultatibus
Galen. *De naturalibus facultatibus*. Britain or Continent: date indeterminable.
STC 11533 and non-STC. Could be one of the several editions of *Selected works* with this title leading. *Language(s)*: Latin. Appraised at 4d in 1573.

104.87:1-3 3 paper bokes
Unidentified. Provenances unknown: dates indeterminable.
Manuscripts. Perhaps notebooks. *Language(s)*: Unknown. Three books appraised at 12d in 1573.

104.88 philoretus de urinis
Theophilus, *Protospatharius*. *De urinis*. Continent: date indeterminable.
Seems not to have been issued separately. See NLM6, nos. 325–332. *Language(s)*: Latin. Appraised at 3d in 1573.

104.89 trivierus de temporibus
Hieremias Triverius. *De temporibus morborum et opportunitate auxiliorum*. Louvain: Servatius Zassenus excud., 1535.
Language(s): Latin. Appraised at 1d in 1573.

104.90 galleni prognosticon
Galen (ascribed). *De prognostica de decubitu infirmorum*. Continent: 1535–1550.
Some editions contain other works. *Language(s)*: Latin. Appraised at 10d in 1573.

104.91 dimostenis Epistole grece
Demosthenes. [*Selected works–Epistolae*]. Continent: date indeterminable.
Language(s): Greek. Appraised at 1d in 1573.

104.92 Cornelius selsus
Aulus Cornelius Celsus. *De re medica*. Continent: date indeterminable.
This work appears on the rough copy rather than the fair copy of the inventory, without an appraisal amount. *Language(s)*: Latin.

104.93 computus de memoria
Unidentified. Place unknown: stationer unknown, date indeterminable.
STC/non-STC status unknown. Appears in rough copy. *Language(s)*: Latin. Appraised at 1d in 1573.

Richard Lanham. Scholar (B.A.): Inventory. 1573

R. J. FEHRENBACH

Richard Lanham (Lanam) was granted a B.A. from Gloucester Hall in February 1573 (*Alumni Oxonienses* 3:873), and an inventory of his goods was made by the university beadle and a stationer on 4 December of the same year. There is nothing in the inventory to suggest that it was compiled at Lanham's death or for debt. Conjecture allows that he may have been among the recusant inhabitants of Gloucester Hall who left Oxford for religious reasons. See Jennifer Loach (1986, 381–82), and also note the inventories of other Gloucester Hall men whose property may have been left behind as a result of a departure from Oxford: PLRE 81 (George and Simon Digby), PLRE 87 (Thomas Morgan), PLRE 90 (Tichborne), PLRE 102 (William Smallwood), PLRE 106 (Walter Dyllam).

The few books cited in Lanham's inventory give no hint of recusancy and are standard fare, however sparse, for a recent B.A.

Oxford University Archives, the Bodleian Library: Hyp.B.15.

§

Jennifer Loach. 1986. "Reformation Controversies," in *The Collegiate University*, edited by James McConica. Vol. 3 of *The History of the University of Oxford*, gen. ed., T.H. Aston. Oxford: Oxford Univ. Press, pp. 363–96.

§

105.1   marcellus palingelius
105.2   Ravicii textus [textoris] dialogi
105.3   orationes demostenes
105.4   terentius

§

105.1 marcellus palingelius
Marcellus Palingenius (Pietro Angelo Manzolli [Stellatus]). *Zodiacus vitae*. Britain or Continent: date indeterminable.
STC 19138.5 *et seq.* and non-STC, and see also STC 19148 *et seq.* English as well as Latin editions were published in England by the date of this inventory. *Language(s)*: Latin (probable) English (perhaps). Appraised at 8d in 1573.

105.2 Ravicii textus [textoris] dialogi
Joannes Ravisius (Textor). *Dialogi. Epigrammata*. Continent: date indeterminable.
Language(s): Latin. Appraised at 6d in 1573.

105.3 orationes demostenes
Demosthenes. Probably [*Selected works*]. Britain or Continent: date indeterminable.
STC 6577 and non-STC. The appraisal seems low for the complete *Works*. *Language(s)*: Latin. Appraised at 6d in 1573.

105.4 terentius
Publius Terentius, *Afer*. Probably [*Works*]. Britain or Continent: date indeterminable.
STC 23885 *et seq.* and non-STC. The appraisal seems low for the complete *Works*, but editions of single plays are usually identified. *Language(s)*: Latin. Appraised at 4d in 1573.

Walter Dyllam. Scholar (student): Inventory. 1575

R. J. FEHRENBACH

Nothing is known of Walter Dyllam, sometime student of Gloucester Hall, except that his goods, or a modest portion of them, were appraised on 12 February 1575 in the house of Roland Thornbury ("Rowlande Thorneboroughe of Magdalene parishe") by university officials. He probably had not died, for although he is referred to as "late scholler in Gloceter Haule," he is not described as deceased. Probably he had recently departed Oxford, and with his likely Irish name (one of the three entries in the inventory is "a Yeryshe rugge blankett") and with Gloucester Hall something of a hotbed of recusants during this period, Dyllam may very well have been among the Gloucester Hall students of the 1560s and 1570s who took leave of Oxford for locations more agreeable to their Roman Catholic sympathies. See Jennifer Loach (1986, 381-82), and see also PLRE 81 (George and Simon Digby), PLRE 105 (Richard Lanham), PLRE 87 (Thomas Morgan), PLRE 102 (William Smallwood), and PLRE 90 (Tichborne) for other young men of Gloucester Hall who may have left Oxford for the same reason. Thornbury, the holder of Dyllam's effects, seems to have had a habit of assisting Gloucester Hall students in ways hardly limited to allowing his house to serve as a repository for their goods. Carl I. Hammer, Jr. (1986, 114, n.1) finds in the Chancery Court records that "on 29 September 1568 Margaret Reade *alias* Tyler confessed 'se habuisse rem et carnaliter cognovisse' Robert Greneway, scholar of Gloucester Hall, in the house of Roland Thornbury in St Mary Magdalen parish, on Saturday 25 September, between seven and eight o'clock in the evening."

Whatever Dyllam took with him, if indeed he had departed Oxford for more congenial places, what he left was unremarkable; aside from the Irish rug, Thornbury stored only one pair of sheets and fourteen books for Dyllam. The books consisted of two dictionaries and twelve other books, apparently less notable than the dictionaries since the stationer and university beadle who served as appraisers did not bother to identify them. The batch appraisal of the books is marred by a tear in the sheet; *vi s.* and a *v* in the pence column are clear, but the valuation may very well have been greater, continuing as with each of the other two entries, in what seems a casually repetitious manner, to register 6*s* 8*d*.

Oxford University Archives, Bodleian Library: Hyp.B.12.

§

Carl I. Hammer, Jr. 1986. "Oxford Town and Oxford University," in *The Collegiate University*, ed. James McConica. Vol. 3 of *The History of the University of Oxford*, gen. ed., T.H. Aston. Oxford: Oxford Univ. Press, pp. 69-116.

Jennifer Loach. 1986. "Reformation Controversies," in *The Collegiate University*, edited by James McConica. Vol. 3 of *The History of the University of Oxford*, gen. ed., T. H. Aston. Oxford: Oxford Univ. Press, pp. 363-96.

§

106.1:1 a old dixionarie of the second edition and a Greke lexicon, wth xii other bookes besides
106.1:2 [See 106.1:1]
106.1:3-15 [See 106.1:1]

§

106.1:1 a old dixionarie of the second edition and a Greke lexicon, wth xii other bookes besides
Unidentified [dictionary]. Place unknown: stationer unknown, date indeterminable.
STC/non-STC status unknown. *Language(s)*: English (perhaps) Latin (perhaps). Appraised with fourteen other books at 6s 8d (probable) in 1575.

106.1:2 [See 106.1:1]
Unidentified [dictionary]. Continent: date indeterminable.
No Greek dictionary had been published in England by the date of this inventory. *Language(s)*: Greek. Appraised with fourteen other books at 6s 8d (probable) in 1575.

106.1:3-15 [See 106.1:1]
Unidentified. Place unknown: stationer unknown, date indeterminable.
STC/non-STC status unknown. *Language(s)*: Unknown. Twelve books appraised with two others at 6s 8d (probable) in 1575.

Nicholas Lombard. Scholar (M.A.): Probate Inventory and Will. 1575

JOHN B. GABEL

Nicholas Lombard (Lambarde, Longbarde, Lumbard(e), Lumbert), a native of Kent, was admitted to the B.A. degree at the university of Oxford in July 1567; he was licensed for the M.A. in March 1572 and incepted in July 1572. He was elected a fellow of Magdalen College (Macray 1897, 185). In the spring of 1575, Lombard was one of six fellows expelled from the college by president Laurence Humphrey for refusing to participate in the election of a dean. Parties on both sides of the dispute corresponded with Lord Burghley and with functionaries in his office throughout June and July of 1575 (CSPD, Elisabeth, 498–501). On August 13, Lombard drew up his will; before the end of the month he was dead. Both the will and an inventory of Lombard's goods, including his books, are extant.

The will specifies that Lombard's books are to go to the son of his "cosen Vicars" with the following exceptions:

> Except I geve to Barbon my musculus[,] bul[in]geres, Calupes, and hyperius Common places, I geve to Tanzly, my Concordance. To Tynly my barnnard. To mr Smyth my Ambrose. as for all the rest my younge [nephew? cosen?] I hope shall in joye them.

Six of the seven works specified here—those by Musculus, Bullinger, Hyperius, St. Bernard, and Ambrose and the concordance—are listed at the very end of the inventory of Lombard's books, along with a seventh work, Calvin's *Institutes* (107.125–31). The word that appears to be "Calupes" in the will (an ink smear makes it indistinct) is certainly not "Calvin." The copyist may have been unable to read the word in Lombard's original and so simply made the best sense he could of it; "CalvIns" in the secretary hand may have been what was misread as "Calupes."

No information on Lombard's "cosen Vicars" or his son has been uncovered. The four legatees named above—John Barbon or Barbone,

Theodore Tansey or Tanzai, Joel Tinley, and Ralph Smith—were Lombard's contemporaries at Magdalen College. Reference is made to each man below in the annotation(s) of the particular book(s) that he was bequeathed.

Of the 133 items in the inventory of Lombard's books, nearly half fall into the categories of theology (some patristic, some medieval, most Renaissance) and biblical studies (a few Hebrew and Greek Bibles, a score of commentaries). About a quarter of the items are works of classical literature and philosophy (particularly Aristotle) and Renaissance commentaries on literature and philosophy (particularly the Aristotle, of course). The rest are standard Renaissance texts on rhetoric, logic, and historiography, and a few volumes of contemporary epistles and *belles lettres*. There are at least three books on medicine, a few on science, and one on law. Most of the books are in Latin; almost all, if not all, were printed on the Continent. The total of the appraised values of the books in the inventory is £14 18*d*.

Oxford University Archives, Bodleian Library, Hyp.A.5 and Hyp.B.15.

§

Macray, William D. 1897. *A Register of the Members of St. Mary Magdalen College, Oxford, from the Foundation of the College. N.S. Vol. 2. Fellows 1522–1575.* London: H. Frowde.

§

107.1	M.T. Cicero .2. volum
107.2	Hieron [Hieronomus] .4. volum
107.3	Theophrasti Metaphysica
107.4	Annotationes August in psal
107.5	Chrysost .2. volum
107.6	Lyra in novum test 2 volum
107.7	Hieron Epist
107.8	Faber stap: in org [organon]
107.9	August in psal
107.10	Ansbertus in Apoc
107.11	Scoti .1. vol sent
107.12	Gerson 3 volum
107.13	Albert .2. volum
107.14	Alexand Anglus dest vitior
107.15	Plinius cum aliis
107.16	Lexicon Vetus
107.17	Niphus Perihermineias
107.18	Niphus in topica

107.19	Aretius in quosdam psal
107.20	Eusebius
107.21	Clementis epist
107.22	Postill Maioris
107.23	Wigandus Vet Test
107.24	Biblia Steph Heb. 3.bus vol
107.25	Math. in Arist
107.26	Longolii Epist
107.27	Test Bezae grecolat
107.28	Staphuli Apollogia
107.29	Erasmi Opuscula
107.30	Comineus
107.31	Ireneus
107.32	Liteltons Tenures
107.33	Cyprian
107.34	Fushius de comp Med
107.35	Homeri Illiades Vallae
107.36	Duo Volum Orat Tullii
107.37	Test grecolat
107.38	Erasmi fragmenta
107.39	Aphrodisei questiones
107.40	Mathisius de Natura
107.41	Mathisius & Perionius
107.42	Arist Magna Moralia
107.43	Erasmi Epist
107.44	Textoris Epitheta
107.45	Chitreus in Lucam
107.46	Caelius Curio
107.47	Hypperii Topica Theol
107.48	Pantaleontis de prosodia
107.49	Quinquerborei Heb gram
107.50	Isaaki Heb gram
107.51	Fushius de medendis morbis
107.52	Schola veneta
107.53:1	Aphrodiseus in Elench & top
107.53:2	[See 107.53:1]
107.54	Martir in Jud [Judices]
107.55	Chimisticum Dorn
107.56	Bernardini Ochini Dial
107.57	Chitreus—genesim
107.58	Corvini postill
107.59	Avenarii Heb gramm
107.60	Pherenarius de cap rellig
107.61	Wigandus in Novum & vet [vetus] test [testamenta] 2 voluminibus
107.62	Westhmeri concill patrum

107.63	Cleonard gramm
107.64	Hipp opusc 2 vol
107.65	Hipp: Theol
107.66	Simon Pauli Postil
107.67	Hemingii Postill
107.68	Collectanea Manlyi
107.69	Melancth in evangelia
107.70	George Walleri Reg vitae
107.71	Spandenbergius postill
107.72	Conciones funeb. [funebrae] Brandelini
107.73	Wigandus in Daniel
107.74	Nicephorus
107.75	Bibliander in prophetas quosdam
107.76	Pontanus
107.77	Paulus Jovius in[?] 4 volum
107.78	Velcurio
107.79	Titelmani philos
107.80	Perionii Dialectica
107.81	Flores Senica
107.82	Elegantiae Vallae
107.83	Politian Misellanea
107.84	Vitruvii Roscii Elocutio
107.85	Lucanus
107.86	Plinius .4. volum
107.87	Hemmingius de lege
107.88	Benediti Anatomice
107.89	T. Livii .5. decas
107.90	Hierocles
107.91	Aulus Gellius
107.92	Hanapi Exempla
107.93	Psalt Campensis
107.94	Flores doctorum
107.95	Epitome chronicorum
107.96	Peucerus de divinationibus
107.97	Maior ad Hebreos
107.98	Examen Melanthonis
107.99	Chitreus in epist Domical [Dominicales]
107.100	Selneccerus in Bezam
107.101	Willichius in Timoth
107.102	Wigandus de imagine Dei
107.103	Bodii Unio dissidentium
107.104	Melancth in orat Tull
107.105	Chitrei reg. Vitae
107.106	Bonfinius de pudicitia
107.107	Paulus Venetus in poster

107.108 Joh Canonicus in phisica
107.109 Ignotus in phisica
107.110 Joh de Celaia
107.111 Opusc August
107.112 Loniceri Compendium in phyisc
107.113 Raymundus Lullius
107.114 Lambini Ethica
107.115 Corn. Agrip de Vanit
107.116 Herberti Chron
107.117 Arist Polit
107.118 Pontanus
107.119 Corderii Comment
107.120 Epist Tullii
107.121 Cardanus de subtillit
107.122 Cardanus de Varietate
107.123 Vitruvius Roscius
107.124 Hessiander
107.125 Bernardus
107.126 Ambros
107.127 Hipp Methodus
107.128 Concordantiae
107.129 Calvini Institut
107.130 Musc Loc Com
107.131 Bullengerius

§

107.1 M.T. Cicero .2. volum

Marcus Tullius Cicero. Unidentified. Place unknown: stationer unknown, date indeterminable.

STC/non-STC status unknown. The high appraisal may indicate a large two-volume set, perhaps of the *Works*, but the entry may also represent two odd volumes from a larger set. *Language(s)*: Latin (probable). Appraised at 20s in 1575.

107.2 Hieron [Hieronomus] .4. volum

Jerome, *Saint*. Unidentified. Continent: date indeterminable.

Commonly issued in nine volumes, but sometimes bound in fewer volumes. *Language(s)*: Latin. Appraised at 20s in 1575.

107.3 Theophrasti Metaphysica

Theophrastus. *Metaphysica*. Continent: date indeterminable.

Seems not to have been issued alone; frequently published with Aristotle. *Language(s)*: Latin (probable) Greek (perhaps). Appraised at 8d in 1575.

107.4 Annotationes August in psal
Augustine, *Saint*. [*Psalms: commentary*]. Continent: date indeterminable. See also 107.9. *Language(s)*: Latin. Appraised at 20d in 1575.

107.5 Chrysost .2. volum
John, *Chrysostom, Saint*. Unidentified. Continent: date indeterminable. *Language(s)*: Latin. Appraised at 10s in 1575.

107.6 Lyra in novum test 2 volum
[*Bible–N.T.*]. Edited by Nicolaus de Lyra. Continent: date indeterminable. *Glossa ordinaria* by Lyra. Appears to be the fifth and sixth volumes of the standard six-volume edition. *Language(s)*: Latin. Appraised at 4s in 1575.

107.7 Hieron Epist
Jerome, *Saint. Epistolae*. Continent: date indeterminable. *Language(s)*: Latin. Appraised at 16d in 1575.

107.8 Faber stap: in org [organon]
Jacobus Faber, *Stapulensis*. [*Aristotle–Selected works–Logica: commentary*]. Continent: date indeterminable. *Language(s)*: Latin. Appraised at 2s in 1575.

107.9 August in psal
Augustine, *Saint*. [*Psalms: commentary*]. Continent: date indeterminable. See also 107.4. *Language(s)*: Latin. Appraised at 20d in 1575.

107.10 Ansbertus in Apoc
Ambrosius Autpertus (Ambrosius, *Ansbertus*). *In Apocalypsim libri decem.* (*Bible–N.T.*). Cologne: per E. Cervicornum impensa G. Hittorpii, 1536. *Language(s)*: Latin. Appraised at 2s 8d in 1575.

107.11 Scoti .1. vol sent
John Duns, *Scotus*. [*Sentences: commentary* (part)]. Continent: date indeterminable. *Language(s)*: Latin. Appraised at 10d in 1575.

107.12 Gerson 3 volum
Joannes Gerson (Jean Charlier de Gerson). Unidentified. Continent: date indeterminable. *Language(s)*: Latin. Appraised at 3s 4d in 1575.

107.13 Albert .2. volum
Probably Albertus Magnus. Unidentified. Place unknown: stationer unknown, date indeterminable. STC/non-STC status unknown. *Language(s)*: Latin. Appraised at 2s 8d in 1575.

107.14 Alexand Anglus dest vitior

Alexander, *Anglus* (Alexander Carpenter). *Destructorium viciorum*. Continent: date indeterminable.

Language(s): Latin. Appraised at 8d in 1575.

107.15 Plinius cum aliis

Unidentified. Place unknown: stationer unknown, date indeterminable.

STC/non-STC status unknown. Whether the elder or younger Pliny is the author here and who or what the "others" may be cannot be determined. *Language(s)*: Latin (probable). Appraised at 3s 4d in 1575.

107.16 Lexicon Vetus

Unidentified [dictionary]. Place unknown: stationer unknown, date indeterminable.

STC/non-STC status unknown. *Lexicon Vetus* is probably a descriptive term, not a title. *Language(s)*: Latin (probable). Appraised at 4s in 1575.

107.17 Niphus Perihermineias

Augustinus Niphus. [*Aristotle–De interpretatione: commentary*]. Continent: date indeterminable.

Language(s): Latin. Appraised at 2s 6d in 1575.

107.18 Niphus in topica

Augustinus Niphus. [*Aristotle–Topica: commentary*]. The text was translated by Niphus. Continent: 1535–1569.

Language(s): Latin. Appraised at 3s 4d in 1575.

107.19 Aretius in quosdam psal

Perhaps Martin Bucer (Aretius Felinus). [*Psalms: commentary and text*]. *(Bible–O.T.)*. Continent: 1529–1554.

The earlier editions of this commentary on all the Psalms were published under the name of Aretius Felinus. But note as a caveat the *quosdam* in the entry. *Language(s)*: Latin. Appraised at 2s 6d in 1575.

107.20 Eusebius

Probably Eusebius, *Pamphili, Bishop*. Unidentified. Continent: date indeterminable.

Others of this name, including Eusebius, *Bishop of Emesa*, are less likely. *Language(s)*: Latin. Appraised at 5s in 1575.

107.21 Clementis epist

Unidentified. Continent: date indeterminable.

The author here may be Pope Clement I (*Epistolae antiquissimae Clementis*, Cologne, 1526) or Pope Clement VII (*Epistolae duae, altera Clementis VII ad Karolum V Imp.*, n.p. 1527 and Cologne, 1527). *Language(s)*: Latin. Appraised at 3s 4d in 1575.

107.22 Postill Maioris
[*Postillae majores*]. *(Bible–N.T.)*. Continent: date indeterminable. *Language(s)*: Latin. Appraised at 16s in 1575.

107.23 Wigandus Vet Test
Johann Wigand and Matthias Richter (Matthaeus Judex). Σύνταγμα, *seu corpus doctrinae veri et omnipotentis Dei, ex veteri Testamento tantum*. Continent: 1558–1575.
Language(s): Latin. Appraised at 4s in 1575.

107.24 Biblia Steph Heb. 3.bus vol [voluminibus]
[*Bible–O.T.*]. Edited by Robert Estienne, *the Elder*. Paris: Robertus Stephanus, date indeterminable.
Conceivably polyglot. *Language(s)*: Hebrew. Appraised at 13s 4d in 1575.

107.25 Math. in Arist
Gerardus Matthisius (Geldrensis). [*Aristotle–Unidentified: commentary*]. Continent: date indeterminable.
This could be any one of the various commentaries Matthisius wrote on Aristotle. For an identifiable work of his, see 107.40. *Language(s)*: Latin. Appraised at 16d in 1575.

107.26 Longolii Epist
Christophorus Longolius. [*Epistolae*]. Continent: date indeterminable. *Language(s)*: Latin. Appraised at 6d in 1575.

107.27 Test Bezae grecolat
[*Bible–N.T.*]. Edited and translated by Théodore de Bèze. Geneva: Henricus Stephanus, 1565–1567.
Language(s): Greek Latin. Appraised at 2s 8d in 1575.

107.28 Staphuli Apollogia
Fridericus Staphylus. *Apologia*. Continent: 1561–1563.
Editions from Cologne and Ingolstadt. *Language(s)*: Latin. Appraised at 6d in 1575.

107.29 Erasmi Opuscula
Desiderius Erasmus. Unidentified. Place unknown: stationer unknown, date indeterminable.
STC/non-STC status unknown. *Language(s)*: Latin. Appraised at 20d in 1575.

107.30 Comineus
Philippe de Comines. Unidentified. Continent: date indeterminable. *Language(s)*: Latin (probable). Appraised at 6d in 1575.

107.31 Ireneus
Probably Irenaeus, *Saint*. Unidentified. Continent: date indeterminable. Works by Joannes Irenaeus and Philotheus Irenaeus were also published during Lombard's lifetime. *Language(s)*: Latin. Appraised at 20d in 1575.

107.32 Liteltons Tenures
Sir Thomas Littleton. [*Tenures*]. Britain or Continent: date indeterminable.

STC 15719 *et seq*. The form of the entry in the inventory suggests that this may be a copy from one of the three editions printed by Richard Tottel in 1557, all entitled *Litletons tenures* (STC 15738-15738.7). One early edition was published in Rouen; the rest were issued in London. *Language(s)*: English or Law French. Appraised at 4d in 1575.

107.33 Cyprian
Cyprian, *Saint*. [*Works*]. Continent (probable): date indeterminable.

Probably not an STC book, but see STC 6152 and 6156-6159.3. *Language(s)*: Latin (probable) English (perhaps). Appraised at 20d in 1575.

107.34 Fushius de comp Med
Leonard Fuchs. *De componendorum medicamentorum ratione*. Continent: 1555-1563.

Language(s): Latin. Appraised at 14d in 1575.

107.35 Homeri Illiades Vallae
Homer. *Iliad*. Translated by Laurentius Valla. Continent: date indeterminable.

Language(s): Latin. Appraised at 6d in 1575.

107.36 Duo Volum Orat Tullii
Marcus Tullius Cicero. [*Selected works–Orations*]. Continent: date indeterminable.

Whether these two volumes are a set, or part of a set, or simply two individual books is impossible to say. *Language(s)*: Latin. Appraised at 16d in 1575.

107.37 Test grecolat
[*Bible–N.T.*]. Continent: date indeterminable.

For another copy of a bilingual New Testament, see 107.27. *Language(s)*: Greek Latin. Appraised at 10d in 1575.

107.38 Erasmi fragmenta
Desiderius Erasmus. Unidentified. Place unknown: stationer unknown, date indeterminable.

STC/non-STC status unknown. Treated as a description of a damaged item. *Language(s)*: Latin (probable). Appraised at 4d in 1575.

107.39 Aphrodisei questiones
Alexander, *Aphrodisiensis*. [*Aristotle–De anima: commentary*]. Continent: date indeterminable.
Language(s): Latin. Appraised at 6d in 1575.

107.40 Mathisius de Natura
Gerardus Matthisius (Geldrensis). [*Aristotle–Selected works–Philosophia naturalis–Epitome: commentary*]. Cologne: (different houses), 1556–1570.
Language(s): Latin. Appraised at 6d in 1575.

107.41 Mathisius & Perionius
Gerardus Matthisius (Geldrensis). [*Aristotle–Unidentified: commentary*]. Text translated by Joachim Perion. Cologne: date indeterminable.
Which of Matthisius's several commentaries on Aristotle's logic, with the text translated into Latin by Perion, cannot be determined. *Language(s)*: Latin. Appraised at 4d in 1575.

107.42 Arist Magna Moralia
Aristotle. *Magna moralia*. Continent: date indeterminable.
Language(s): Latin. Appraised at 8d in 1575.

107.43 Erasmi Epist
Desiderius Erasmus. [*Epistolae*]. Continent: date indeterminable.
Language(s): Latin. Appraised at 4d in 1575.

107.44 Textoris Epitheta
Joannes Ravisius (Textor). [*Epitheta–Epitome*]. Continent: date indeterminable.
Language(s): Latin. Appraised at 6d in 1575.

107.45 Chitreus in Lucam
David Chytraeus. [*Luke: commentary*] (probably a ghost). Continent: date indeterminable.
Chytraeus wrote a number of Biblical commentaries, including one on the Gospel of Matthew, but no record of any on the Gospel of Luke has been found. There is the remote possibility that two items are intended, one by Chytraeus and the other a commentary on Luke by someone else, unidentified. *Language(s)*: Latin. Appraised at 8d in 1575.

107.46 Caelius Curio
Perhaps Caelius Secundus Curio. Unidentified. Continent (probable): date indeterminable.
Probably not an STC book, but see STC 6130. Consider also Caelius Augustinus Curio, a less likely possibility. *Language(s)*: Latin (probable). Appraised at 10d in 1575.

107.47 Hypperii Topica Theol
Andreas Gerardus, *Hyperius. Topica theologica.* Continent: 1564-1573. *Language(s)*: Latin. Appraised at 6d in 1575.

107.48 Pantaleontis de prosodia
Pantaleon Barteleone Raverinus. *De ratione quantitatis syllabariae liber.* Continent (probable): date indeterminable.

Almost certainly not an STC book. The sole edition known is Lyon 1575-76 (See BCI 2:657), which is probably too late for this collection, but there must have been an earlier edition. For two other pre-1575-76 copies, see PLRE 92.94 and PLRE 103.65. *Language(s)*: Latin. Appraised at 4d in 1575.

107.49 Quinquerborei Heb gram
Joannes Quinquarboreus. *De re grammatica Hebraeorum opus.* Paris: (different houses), 1546-1556.

Language(s): Hebrew Latin. Appraised at 10d in 1575.

107.50 Isaaki Heb gram
Joannes Isaac, *Levita. Grammatica hebraea.* Continent: 1557-1570. *Language(s)*: Hebrew Latin. Appraised at 12d in 1575.

107.51 Fushius de medendis morbis
Leonard Fuchs. [*De medendi methodo*]. Continent: 1548-1568. *Language(s)*: Latin. Appraised at 16d in 1575.

107.52 Schola veneta
Probably Academia Veneta. Venice (probable): date indeterminable.

There was a great outpouring of books from the Academia Veneta in 1558-60, including commentaries on the Bible and Aristotle, humanistic works of scholarship, and some original belles lettres. This volume may be the work on the *Topica* published in 1559. See the next item. *Language(s)*: Latin. Appraised at 3s in 1575.

107.53:1 Aphrodiseus in Elench & top
Alexander, *Aphrodisiensis.* [*Aristotle–Sophistici elenchi: commentary*]. Continent: date indeterminable.

Whether two works were bound together or were simply listed together cannot be determined. *Language(s)*: Latin. Appraised with one other at 2s 6d in 1575.

107.53:2 [See 107.53:1]
Alexander, *Aphrodisiensis.* [*Aristotle–Topica: commentary*]. Continent: date indeterminable.

Language(s): Latin. Appraised with one other at 2s 6d in 1575.

107.54 Martir in Jud [Judices]
Pietro Martire Vermigli (Peter Martyr). [*Judges: commentary*]. Zürich: Christoph Froschouer, 1561–1571.
Language(s): Latin. Appraised at 2s 8d in 1575.

107.55 Chimisticum Dorn
Gerard Dorn. [*Chymisticum artificum naturae, theoricum et practicum*]. Frankfurt am Main (perhaps): (stationer unknown), 1568–1569.
Place and printer are apparently not indicated in the book. NUC reports, on what evidence is not indicated, that the work may have been published in Frankfurt. Wellcome says either Leiden or Frankfurt. *Language(s)*: Latin. Appraised at 4d in 1575.

107.56 Bernardini Ochini Dial
Bernardino Ochino. *Dialogi*. Continent: date indeterminable.
Ochino's dialogues were published in various combinations and sometimes individually. It is impossible to know what the present volume contained. *Language(s)*: Latin. Appraised at 2d in 1575.

107.57 Chitreus—genesim
David Chytraeus. [*Genesis: commentary*]. Wittenberg: Johann Crato, 1557–1568.
Language(s): Latin. Appraised at 16d in 1575.

107.58 Corvini postill
Antonius Corvinus. [*Postilla*]. (*Bible–N.T.*). Continent: date indeterminable.
The form of the entry and Lombard's other books make it all but certain that the English edition published in London in 1550 is not intended. *Language(s)*: Latin. Appraised at 12d in 1575.

107.59 Avenarii Heb gramm
Johann Habermann (Joannes Avenarius). [*Grammatica hebraica*]. Wittenberg: (different houses), 1557–1570.
Language(s): Hebrew Latin. Appraised at 16d in 1575.

107.60 Pherenarius de cap rellig
Unidentified. Continent (probable): date indeterminable.
Probably not an STC book. The entry very likely is a garbled *de capitibus religionis*, and represents a catechism or other epitome of doctrine. *Language(s)*: Latin. Appraised at 12d in 1575.

107.61 Wigandus in Novum & vet [vetus] test [testamenta] 2 voluminibus
Johann Wigand. [*Bible* (part): *commentary*]. Continent: date indeterminable.
Wigand wrote on various individual books of the Bible, but I find no record of anything by him specifically of the sort suggested by this entry. *Language(s)*: Latin. Appraised at 2s in 1575.

107.62 Westhmeri concill patrum
Bartholomaeus Westheimer. [*Conciliatio sacrae scripturae et patrum*]. Zürich: 1536-1563.
Language(s): Latin. Appraised at 6d in 1575.

107.63 Cleonard gramm
Nicolaus Clenardus. [*Institutiones linguae graecae*]. Continent: date indeterminable.
Language(s): Greek Latin. Appraised at 3s 4d in 1575.

107.64 Hipp opusc 2 vol
Andreas Gerardus, *Hyperius*. *Opuscula theologica*. Basle: ex officina Oporiniana, 1570-1571 (single edition).

The *Opuscula* of Gerardus was published in two parts, each in its own volume, one dated 1570, the other 1571. The appraisal gives strong evidence that both volumes, in octavo, are represented here. *Language(s)*: Latin. Appraised at 2s 8d in 1575.

107.65 Hipp: Theol
Andreas Gerardus, *Hyperius*. Probably *De theologo, sive De ratione studii theologici*. Basle: Joannes Oporinus, 1556-1572.

Three works of Gerardus have some form of "theologus" in their titles. *De theologo* seems to be the one of them represented by the inventory's *Theol*. *Language(s)*: Latin. Appraised at 16d in 1575.

107.66 Simon Pauli Postil
Simon Paulli, *the Elder*. [*Postilla*]. *(Bible-N.T.)*. Continent: date indeterminable.
Language(s): German. Appraised at 2s in 1575.

107.67 Hemingii Postill
Niels Hemmingsen. [*Gospels (liturgical): commentary*]. Continent (probable): 1562-1569.

Probably not an STC book, but see STC 13061-13062. Given the almost exclusively Latin and Continental nature of the rest of Lombard's books, this is probably from one of the Latin editions published in Leipzig and Wittenberg. But it could be one of the two English editions published by Bynneman in London (1569) that carry "postill" on the title page. *Language(s)*: Latin. Appraised at 16d in 1575.

107.68 Collectanea Manlyi
Joannes Manlius. *Locorum communium collectanea*. Continent: date indeterminable.

Most, if not all, editions also contain a brief medical work, *Libellus medicus variorum experimentorum*. Most of the *loci* are from Melanchthon. *Language(s)*: Latin. Appraised at 18d in 1575.

107.69 Melancth in evangelia
Philipp Melanchthon. [*Gospels (liturgical): commentary and text*]. (*Bible–N.T.*). Continent: date indeterminable.
Language(s): Latin. Appraised at 14d in 1575.

107.70 George Walleri Reg vitae
Georg Walther. *Regulae vitae christianae.* Wittenberg: excudebat Joannes Crato, 1572.
Language(s): Latin. Appraised at 12d in 1575.

107.71 Spandenbergius postill
Johann Spangenberg. [*Gospels and Epistles (liturgical): commentary and text*]. (*Bible–N.T.*). Continent: date indeterminable.

It should be noted that Cyriacus Spangenberg wrote a work in this genre, *Explicationes evangelicorum et epistolarum*, published in Basle by Oporinus, 1564. *Language(s)*: Latin. Appraised at 2s 8d in 1575.

107.72 Conciones funeb. [funebrae] Brandelini
Probably Raphael Brandolinus. Unidentified. Continent: date indeterminable.

Two individual funeral orations of Brandolinus were published, each in its own edition (Rome: 1500 [Goff B1076] and 1501 [Adams B2669]), but no collection is known. Perhaps the compiler grouped the two together here. *Language(s)*: Latin. Appraised at 14d in 1575.

107.73 Wigandus in Daniel
Johann Wigand. *Danielis prophetae explicatio brevis.* Jena: Gunther Huttich, 1571.
Language(s): Latin. Appraised at 18d in 1575.

107.74 Nicephorus
Unidentified. Continent: date indeterminable.

Callistus more likely in this context than others such as Nicephorus, *Blemmida* and Nicephorus, *Chartophylax. Language(s)*: Latin. Appraised at 4s in 1575.

107.75 Bibliander in prophetas quosdam
Theodore Bibliander. Unidentified. Continent: date indeterminable.

I have found no citation of a volume by Bibliander concerned with more than one prophet. *Language(s)*: Latin. Appraised at 14d in 1575.

107.76 Pontanus
Unidentified. Continent: date indeterminable.

This is one of two entries in the inventory accredited to "Pontanus" but not otherwise identified (see 107.118). Several contemporary writers used the name with Joannes Jovianus Pontanus being among the most published. *Language(s)*: Latin. Appraised at 14d in 1575.

107.77 Paulus Jovius in[?] 4 volum

Paolo Giovio, *Bishop*. Unidentified. Continent: date indeterminable.

The four volumes and the appraisal suggest more than one work. *Language(s)*: Latin. Appraised at 5s 6d in 1575.

107.78 Velcurio

Joannes Velcurio. Unidentified. Continent: date indeterminable.

Velcurio wrote commentaries on Aristotle and Livy, both published repeatedly during Lombard's lifetime. *Language(s)*: Latin. Appraised at 8d in 1575.

107.79 Titelmani philos

Franz Titelmann. [*Aristotle–Selected works–Philosophia naturalis: commentary*]. Continent: 1530–1574.

Language(s): Latin. Appraised at 8d in 1575.

107.80 Perionii Dialectica

Joachim Perion. *De dialectica*. Continent: 1544–1554.

Language(s): Latin. Appraised at 8d in 1575.

107.81 Flores Senica

Lucius Annaeus Seneca. [*Selections–Flores selecti*]. Probably edited by Desiderius Erasmus. Continent: date indeterminable.

Language(s): Latin. Appraised at 2d in 1575.

107.82 Elegantiae Vallae

Laurentius Valla. *Elegantiae*. Continent: date indeterminable.

Language(s): Latin. Appraised at 4d in 1575.

107.83 Politian Misellanea

Angelus Politianus (Angelo Ambrogini). *Miscellaneorum centuria una*. Continent: date indeterminable.

Language(s): Latin. Appraised at 4d in 1575.

107.84 Vitruvii Roscii Elocutio

Lucius Vitruvius Roscius. *De commoda ac perfecta elocutione*. Basle: Robert Winter, 1541.

Language(s): Latin. Appraised at 6d in 1575.

107.85 Lucanus

Marcus Annaeus Lucanus. *Pharsalia*. Continent: date indeterminable.

Language(s): Latin. Appraised at 6d in 1575.

107.86 Plinius .4. volum
Unidentified. Continent: date indeterminable.
As with 107.15, it cannot be said which of the two Plinys is the author of this work, although the *Historia naturalis* of *the Elder* would more likely be part of such a multi-volume set than the *Epistolae* of *the Younger* alone. *Language(s)*: Latin. Appraised at 5s in 1575.

107.87 Hemmingius de lege
Niels Hemmingsen. *De lege naturae apodictica methodus*. Wittenberg: (different houses), 1562–1566.
Language(s): Latin. Appraised at 10d in 1575.

107.88 Benediti Anatomice
Alexander Benedictus. *Anatomice sive historia corporis humani*. Continent: 1502–1528.
Language(s): Latin. Appraised at 3d in 1575.

107.89 T. Livii .5. decas
Titus Livius. [*Historiae Romanae decades–Selected works*]. Continent: date indeterminable.
This may be a copy from the 1554 edition printed in Lyon by Sebastian Gryphius, the title of which Adams (L1340) gives as *Decadis quintae libri V*. *Language(s)*: Latin. Appraised at 4d in 1575.

107.90 Hierocles
Hierocles, *of Alexandria*. [*Pythagoras–Carmina aurea: commentary and text*]. Continent: date indeterminable.
A widely published work that sometimes included, mistakenly, the work of the first-century stoic with the same name as the platonist, fifth-century author of this work. Another early writer named Hierocles wrote on veterinary surgery, a subject not likely to have been found in Lombard's library. *Language(s)*: Latin Greek (perhaps). Appraised at 4d in 1575.

107.91 Aulus Gellius
Aulus Gellius. *Noctes Atticae*. Continent: date indeterminable.
Language(s): Latin. Appraised at 16d in 1575.

107.92 Hanapi Exempla
Nicolaus Hanapus. *Exempla sacrae scripturae. (The Bible)*. Continent: date indeterminable.
Given the form of the title in the inventory, there is no reason to think of this as being a copy from either of the two editions printed in England— the 1481 Latin (STC 2993), which does not name Hanapus, or the 1561 English (STC 12742). *Language(s)*: Latin. Appraised at 16d in 1575.

107.93 Psalt Campensis
Joannes Campensis. [*Psalms: paraphrase*]. *(Bible–O.T.).* Britain or Continent: 1532–1565.

STC 2354 and non-STC. Among the possible editions is one printed in Paris in 1534 by F. Regnault at the expense of the London printer Thomas Berthelet. *Language(s)*: Latin. Appraised at 4d in 1575.

107.94 Flores doctorum
Thomas, *Hibernicus*. [*Flores omnium fere doctorum*]. Continent: date indeterminable.

Language(s): Latin. Appraised at 18d in 1575.

107.95 Epitome chronicorum
Achilles Gasser. *Historiarum et chronicorum mundi epitome.* Continent: 1532–1540.

There was a less widely published work, with the title of the entry, by Caspar Ursinus Velius (Henrichus Sellarius, *pseudonym*) that was based on Gasser (Frankfurt, 1533 and 1534 only). *Language(s)*: Latin. Appraised at 2d in 1575.

107.96 Peucerus de divinationibus
Kaspar Peucer. *Commentarius de praecipuis divinationum generibus.* Wittenberg: (different houses), 1533–1572.

Language(s): Latin. Appraised at 20d in 1575.

107.97 Maior ad Hebreos
Georg Meier, *Professor at Wittenberg. Enarratio epistolae ad Hebraeos.* Wittenberg: ex officina Joannis Lufft, 1571.

Language(s): Latin. Appraised at 20d in 1575.

107.98 Examen Melanthonis
Philipp Melanchthon. *Examen eorum qui audiuntur ante ritum publicae ordinationis.* Continent: date indeterminable.

Language(s): Latin. Appraised at 12d in 1575.

107.99 Chitreus in epist Domical [Dominicales]
David Chytraeus. *Dispositiones epistolarum.* Wittenberg: (different houses), 1566–1571.

Language(s): Latin. Appraised at 12d in 1575.

107.100 Selneccerus in Bezam
Nicolaus Selneccer. *Responsio vera et christiana ad Theo: Bezae defensionem et censuram.* Place not given: stationer unknown, 1572.

The book was probably published in Germany. See VD16 and Adams S876. *Language(s)*: Latin. Appraised at 10d in 1575.

107.101 Willichius in Timoth

Jodocus Willich. *Commentaria in utramque ad Timotheum Pauli epistolam. (Bible–N.T.)*. Strassburg: apud Cratonem Mylium, 1542.
Language(s): Latin. Appraised at 3d in 1575.

107.102 Wigandus de imagine Dei

Johann Wigand. *De imagine Dei in homine, et de larva Satanae.* Jena: (stationer unknown), 1572.

Found only in Clessius (25), who does not give the stationer, but another of Wigand's works was published in Jena in 1572 by the widow of Gunther Huttich (see Adams W161). *Language(s)*: Latin. Appraised at 6d in 1575.

107.103 Bodii Unio dissidentium

Herman Bodius, *pseudonym. Unio dissidentium.* Continent: 1525–1557.

STC suggests that "Bodius" is Martin Bucer; Adams prefers Oecolampadius. *Language(s)*: Latin. Appraised at 16d in 1575.

107.104 Melancth in orat Tull

Philipp Melanchthon. Unidentified. Continent: date indeterminable.

The inventory entry is too fragmentary to know whether the work in question is Melanchthon's annotations on *Orator* or *De oratore* or is perhaps his *Lucubrationum in M. Tullii Ciceronis orationes aliquot. Language(s)*: Latin. Appraised at 14d in 1575.

107.105 Chitrei reg. Vitae

David Chytraeus. *Regulae vitae.* Continent: 1555–1573.
Language(s): Latin. Appraised at 6d in 1575.

107.106 Bonfinius de pudicitia

Antonius Bonfinius. *Symposion de virginitate et pudicitia conjugali.* Edited by Joannes Leunclavius. Basle: ex officina Oporiniana, 1572.

Published seventy years after the death of Bonfinius, this was the only existing edition during Lombard's lifetime. *Language(s)*: Latin. Appraised at 6d in 1575.

107.107 Paulus Venetus in poster

Paulus, *Venetus* (Paolus Nicolettus). [*Aristotle–Analytica posteriora: commentary*]. Continent: 1471–1518.
Language(s): Latin. Appraised at 10d in 1575.

107.108 Joh Canonicus in phisica

Joannes, *Canonicus.* [*Aristotle–Physica: commentary*]. Continent: 1475–1520.
Language(s): Latin. Appraised at 4d in 1575.

107.109 Ignotus in phisica
Unidentified. [*Aristotle–Physica: commentary*]. Continent (probable): date indeterminable.
Probably not an STC book. Perhaps the author was unknown to the compiler because the title page was missing. *Language(s)*: Latin. Appraised at 6d in 1575.

107.110 Joh de Celaia
Joannes de Celaya. Unidentified. Continent: date indeterminable.
Language(s): Latin. Appraised at 6d in 1575.

107.111 Opusc August
Augustine, *Saint*. [*Selected works–Opuscula*]. Continent: date indeterminable.
Language(s): Latin. Appraised at 6d in 1575.

107.112 Loniceri Compendium in phyisc
[*Librorum Aristotelis compendium*]. Compiled by Joannes Lonicer. Marburg: in officina Christiani Egenolphi, 1540.
Contains considerably more of Aristotle than the *Physica*, as well as an epithalamium for Joannes Stadius in Greek. See VD16 L2444. *Language(s)*: Greek Latin. Appraised at 10d in 1575.

107.113 Raymundus Lullius
Ramón Lull. Unidentified. Continent: date indeterminable.
Language(s): Latin. Appraised at 12d in 1575.

107.114 Lambini Ethica
Aristotle. *Ethica*. Translated by Dionysius Lambinus. Continent: 1558–1566.
Language(s): Latin. Appraised at 20d in 1575.

107.115 Corn. Agrip de Vanit
Henricus Cornelius Agrippa. *De incertitudine et vanitate scientiarum*. Continent: date indeterminable.
Language(s): Latin. Appraised at 8d in 1575.

107.116 Herberti Chron
Jan Herburt. *Chronica sive historiae Polonicae descriptio*. Basle: ex officina Oporiniana, 1571–1573.
Language(s): Latin. Appraised at 18d in 1575.

107.117 Arist Polit
Aristotle. *Politica*. Continent: date indeterminable.
Language(s): Latin. Appraised at 12d in 1575.

107.118 Pontanus
Unidentified. Continent: date indeterminable.
See annotation to 107.76. *Language(s)*: Latin. Appraised at 6d in 1575.

107.119 Corderii Comment
Mathurin Cordier. [*De corrupti sermonis emendatione*]. Continent: date indeterminable.
Doubtless one of the editions beginning *Commentarius puerorum de quotidiano sermone*. *Language(s)*: Latin. Appraised at 12d in 1575.

107.120 Epist Tullii
Marcus Tullius Cicero. Probably [*Selected works–Epistolae*]. Continent: date indeterminable.
Conceivably the popular *Epistolae ad familiares*. *Language(s)*: Latin. Appraised at 8d in 1575.

107.121 Cardanus de subtillit
Girolamo Cardano. *De subtilitate*. Continent: 1550–1560.
Language(s): Latin. Appraised at 2s in 1575.

107.122 Cardanus de Varietate
Girolamo Cardano. *De rerum varietate*. Continent: 1556–1558.
Language(s): Latin. Appraised at 14d in 1575.

107.123 Vitruvius Roscius
Lucius Vitruvius Roscius. Unidentified. Continent: date indeterminable.
He wrote on education, grammar, and rhetoric. *Language(s)*: Latin. Appraised at 8d in 1575.

107.124 Hessiander
Christoph Herdesianus (Christian Hessiander, *pseudonym*). Unidentified. Continent: date indeterminable.
Any one of several works by this Lutheran theologian might appropriately have been among Lombard's books. In addition to the name Christian Hessiander, Herdesianus employed the names Ambrosius Wolfius, Eusebius Altkircherus, German Beyer von Hall, and Hermannus Pacificus. *Language(s)*: Latin. Appraised at 4d in 1575.

107.125 Bernardus
Probably Bernard, *Saint*. [*Works*]. Continent: date indeterminable.
Lombard bequeathed "To Tynly my barnnard." The recipient was Joel Tinley, a Magdalen College fellow from Kent, as was Lombard (Clark 2.ii:52; Clark 2.iii:27). *Language(s)*: Latin. Appraised at 5s in 1575.

107.126 Ambros
Ambrose, *Saint*. Probably [*Works*]. Continent: date indeterminable.

Lombard bequeathed "To mr Smyth my Ambrose." Ralph Smith was one of the Magdalen fellows expelled from the college in 1575 along with Lombard (Clark 2.ii:37; Clark 2.iii:19; CPSD, 498–501). *Language(s)*: Latin. Appraised at 10s in 1575.

107.127 Hipp Methodus

Andreas Gerardus, *Hyperius*. [*Methodus theologiae sive loci communes*]. Basle: Joannes Oporinus, 1567–1574.

This is one of four books bequeathed to John Barbon, another of the fellows expelled from Magdalen in 1575 (Clark 2.ii:37; Clark 2.iii:47; CPSD, 498–501). It is referred to in the will as "hyperius Common places." Five works by Hyperius are included in the inventory of Lombard's books, all of them in Latin. Whether those who drew up the inventory were correct in supposing that *Methodus theologiae* was the work Lombard had designated "hyperius Common places," I do not know. (An English book called *Two common places taken out of A. Hyperius* [STC 11762] did not appear until 1581; it concerns astrology and magic.) *Language(s)*: Latin. Appraised at 2s in 1575.

107.128 Concordantiae

Unidentified [Biblical concordance]. Continent: date indeterminable.

Lombard specified in his will that "I geve to Tanzly my Concordance." The legatee was, presumably, Theodore Tansey or Tanzai, a fellow at Magdalen College (Clark 2.ii:18; Clark 2.iii:46). *Language(s)*: Unknown. Appraised at 5s in 1575.

107.129 Calvini Institut

Jean Calvin. *Institutio Christianae religionis*. Continent: date indeterminable.

As has been said in the Introduction, this work of Calvin's is what the compilers of the inventory supposed was referred to where the will has what appears to be "Calupes." What the legatee, Robert Barbon, received was a copy of Calvin's *Institutes*. For Barbon, see the annotations to 107.127. *Language(s)*: Latin. Appraised at 2s in 1575.

107.130 Musc Loc Com

Probably Wolfgang Musculus. *Loci communes*. Continent: date indeterminable.

Andreas Musculus also produced a *Loci communes* published during Lombard's lifetime. Lombard left this book, designated in the will simply as "musculus," to John Barbon. For Barbon, see the annotations to 107.127. *Language(s)*: Latin. Appraised at 2s in 1575.

107.131 Bullengerius

Probably Heinrich Bullinger. Unidentified. Continent (probable): date indeterminable.

Probably not an STC book, but see STC 4055. This is another of the four books that Lombard bequeathed to John Barbon. The author may be the less widely published Petrus Bullenger (Pierre Boulenger). For Barbon, see the annotations to 107.127. *Language(s)*: Latin. Appraised at 2s 6d in 1575.

Richard Lye. Manciple: Probate Inventory. 1575

E. S. LEEDHAM-GREEN

Richard Lye, "late manciple of Lyncoll Colledge in Oxon," is as little documented as most college servants of the period. Manciples were, however, or at least had the chance to become, persons of substance. Charged as they were both with the collection of college rents and the provision of many of the college's day-to-day necessities, their path lay open to numerous perquisites. If the manciple of Lincoln College had a stipend of only 26*s* and 8*d* per annum, this was not his sole means of support, and it was, in any case, a more substantial stipend than was accorded to the college bursar. He had rooms in the college, a higher and a lower chamber, and he may also have received livery (Green 1979, 231).

Of Lye himself we may perhaps assume that he was appointed manciple in 1571 on the death from plague of his precessor, Gilbert Bolde. We know also, that when the persistent Romanism of Lincoln finally prompted the bishop, Thomas Cooper, to action in 1574, it was Lye whom the college sent to the rector (i.e., master) of the college, John Bridgewater, then at Wells, with notice of the bishop's intended visitation. Lye came back not with the rector, but with his letter of resignation, and letters under the rector's hand appointing Arthur Atye and John Tatham (PLRE 112) his proctors charged with delivering his letter of resignation to the bishop (Green 1979, 122 and 138).

From his inventory it appears that, like other manciples, he rented out furniture to others: beds, bedsteads, chests, and candlesticks, and several other books are recorded in the rooms of eleven members of the college. The sword recorded in his possession was not his, but he did own one which, for some reason, he had exchanged for it. He seems to have made a testamentary disposition that each be returned to its original owner. He also had a bow and half a dozen arrows, chess-men, a lute chest and other items indicative of modest affluence.

Debts owing to him amounted to £2 3*s* and included at least one outstanding bill for battels: food and drink available for purchase as a supplement to the commons provided by the college. He in turn owed £5 10s 11d to various individuals within and without the college, including 13s 5d to Williams the apothecary, and £3 1s ¼d to the college.

It is conceivable that Lye was, or had been, a student himself: some of his possessions are stated to be in one or other of two studies, but it is also possible that these studies were simply the standing fittings of the rooms allotted to him as manciple.

The inventory was drawn up and appraised not by the usual university authorities but by Anthony Hartley and Hugh Weston, B.A.s of the college, Walter Williams, scholar of the college, and Walter Sheppard, the butler, and, so far as the books are concerned, a pretty mess they made of it. Indeed, various entries appear to have been written by one with little knowledge of books copying from a badly written list of one who had such knowledge. See, for example, 108.47 ("Calaijnus" probably for Calepinus), 108.48 ("Comico Vario" probably for Dominico Nanno) and 108.50 ("Crgan" for Organon).

Oxford University Archives, Bodleian Library: Hyp.B.15.

§

Green, V. H. H. 1979. *The Commonwealth of Lincoln College, 1427–1977*. Oxford: Oxford Univ. Press.

§

108.1	Ekii homiliae
108.2	Brandotinus de ratione scris
108.3	Lradalnus iterum
108.4	Adagia Erasni
108.5	Virglus poeta
108.6	Salustiuus
108.7	Erasmus de ratione concicandi
108.8	Sermones fratris Gabrlis
108.9	Valerius Maxinus
108.10	A grek gramer
108.11	Epigrmata Ulrichi
108.12	Saluistius
108.13	Lodovicus Vives
108.14	Galenus de santetitenda
108.15	J. foxus de Erisarstia
108.16	Andreas de radice Chinae

108.17	Irocretii eratione
108.18	macropednius de consi epii
108.19	oradice Isocratis ad dncum
108.20	Epucures Erasni
108.21	Liber q ii Averi'
108.22	Confabilationes Erasmi
108.23	Ovidiuus faestis
108.24	Arii Contentia
108.25	Justic' historici
108.26	Aris' Organ' 8
108.27	simpolum apostalicum per erasmum
108.28	Grynaeus de utilitate
108.29	solis an other olde lad'
108.30	perrcationes per Erasmum
108.31	Epist Cicorones quedam
108.32	diailiclicae [dialecticae] Valerii
108.33	flores epis Ciceronis
108.34	questionis tartariti in ethica
108.35	Mantanis
108.36	Amonius in porphirium
108.37	Pithy sange of the Scripture
108.38	Larentus Vallius
108.39	Erasmus Rotrodans [Roterodamus]
108.40	trentii em commentario
108.41	Gilberti ducherii
108.42	terentii
108.43	terentii
108.44	Gregoris
108.45	pars i Gregorii
108.46	Comentonis per quersa erationis Ciecronis
108.47	Calaijnus [Calepinus?] Hibraeii
108.48	poleanthea auttore Comico Vario
108.49	brusonis de facetiis
108.50	Crgan'[Organon] Arii
108.51	phisica Aristotelis
108.52	Gratr' despauterii
108.53	Errasni apothe'
108.54	Politico aris'
108.55	Ethica Ariss'
108.56	Sillius poeta Itallius
108.57	phitonis Judei de fabricatione mundi
108.58	Pultisera Navis
108.59	Epis' longolii
108.60	Radolph'
108.61	Toxita in libros ad Her'

108.62	faber in ethica
108.63	Osorius de Justitie
108.64	Catechismus de dicreto
108.65	Pall Vingilios
108.66	Thaurelius de passione Jesu
108.67	Catinus secuen in perlitii Cici
108.68	Justis Martirs appolagia
108.69	Caius plinis secundius
108.70:1	Ciprianius Augustus
108.70:2	[See 108.70:1]
108.71	Coopari Gramatica Greca
108.72	Comentarie Caesaris
108.73	Prinasius Utirenses
108.74	Historia Justini
108.75	Apohthonius
108.76	flores declera'
108.77	flores bibilae
108.78	Terrentiius
108.79	Ciceronis ffia
108.80	Omphalius demitatione
108.81	macropeduus duconscrbiest epii
108.82	copia verborum Oreri [& rerum?]
108.83	Anteris opus
108.84	Urognes de vilii psito
108.85	Instoria Justinii
108.86	Clatechesis Cirilli
108.87	Plutarish Vitam epilone
108.88	the primer in english with genevie salmpes 2
108.89	Ovidinus de arte anandi
108.90	Geneva salmes in frenche
108.91	Erasmus apothagmata in plano pretio
108.92	tres partis philosophie
108.93:1-5	with Mr Pallard v books
108.94:1-5	v bookes in a chest

§

108.1 Ekii homiliae

Joannes Eckius. [*Homiliae*]. Continent: date indeterminable. *Language(s)*: Latin. Appraised at 16d in 1575.

108.2 Brandotinus de ratione scris

Aurelius Brandolinus (Lippus). *De ratione scribendi*. Britain or Continent: 1549-1573.

STC 3542 and non-STC. Possibly containing other works also. *Language(s)*: Latin. Appraised at 16d in 1575.

108.3 Lradalnus iterum

Aurelius Brandolinus (Lippus). Probably *De ratione scribendi*. Britain or Continent: 1549–1573.

STC 3542 and non-STC. The form of the entry seems to suggest another copy of the same work, but another work by the same author remains a possibility. *Language(s)*: Latin. Appraised at 20d in 1575.

108.4 Adagia Erasni

Desiderius Erasmus. *Adagia*. Continent (probable): date indeterminable.

Probably not an STC book, but see STC 10441.5. An edition in Latin and English was published in 1569. *Language(s)*: Latin English (perhaps). Appraised at 16d in 1575.

108.5 Virglus poeta

Publius Virgilius Maro. Probably [*Works*]. Britain or Continent: date indeterminable.

STC 24787 *et seq.* and non-STC. *Language(s)*: Latin. Appraised at 14d in 1575.

108.6 Salustiuus

Caius Sallustius Crispus. Unidentified. Place unknown: stationer unknown, date indeterminable.

STC/non-STC status unknown. Perhaps either *De bello Jugurthino, De conjuratione Catilinae*, or both in *Works*. See also 108.12. *Language(s)*: Latin. Appraised at 10d in 1575.

108.7 Erasmus de ratione concicandi

Desiderius Erasmus. *Ecclesiastes, sive de ratione concionandi*. Continent: 1535–1554.

Language(s): Latin. Appraised at 12d in 1575.

108.8 Sermones fratris Gabrlis

Gabriel Barletta. [*Sermones*]. Continent: date indeterminable.

The form of the entry indicates one of the pre-1540 editions, probably *Sermones Fratris Gabrielis Barelete ... tam quadragesimales quam de sanctis* edited, with additions, by Benedictus, *Brixianus*. There is no edition between 1539 and 1571 when the title takes a different form. *Language(s)*: Latin. Appraised at 6d in 1575.

108.9 Valerius Maxinus

Valerius Maximus. *Facta et dicta memorabilia*. Continent: date indeterminable.

Language(s): Latin. Appraised at 6d in 1575.

108.10 A grek gramer

Unidentified. Continent (probable): date indeterminable.

Probably not an STC book. *Language(s)*: Greek Latin. Appraised at 6d in 1575.

108.11 Epigrmata Ulrichi

Ulrich von Hutten. [*Epigrammata*]. Continent: date indeterminable.

Hutten's epigrams were included in selections of his works issued under a variety of titles, and seem often to have been regarded as the chief item. *Language(s)*: Latin. Appraised at 8d in 1575.

108.12 Saluistius

Caius Sallustius Crispus. Unidentified. Place unknown: stationer unknown, date indeterminable.

STC/non-STC status unknown. Perhaps either *De bello Jugurthino*, *De conjuratione Catilinae*, or both in *Works*. See 108.6. *Language(s)*: Latin. Appraised at 6d in 1575.

108.13 Lodovicus Vives

Joannes Lodovicus Vives. Unidentified. Continent (probable): date indeterminable.

Probably not an STC book. Assuming a Latin edition, none of which was published in England by the date of this inventory. *Language(s)*: Latin (probable). Appraised at 8d in 1575.

108.14 Galenus de santetitenda

Galen. *De sanitate tuenda*. Continent: 1517-1559.

Language(s): Latin Greek (perhaps). Appraised at 10d in 1575.

108.15 J. foxus de Erisarstia

John Foxe, *the Martyrologist*. Syllogisticon hoc est: argumenta, ... de re et materia sacramenti eucharistici. London: J. Daius, 1563?

STC 11249. *Language(s)*: Latin. Appraised at 10d in 1575.

108.16 Andreas de radice Chinae

Andreas Vesalius. *Epistola, rationem modumque propinandi radicis Chynae decocti pertractans*. Continent: 1546-1547.

Perhaps, from the form of the entry, L. Luisini (ed.), *De morbo gallico* (Venice: Jordanus Zilettus, 1566-67), of which the first volume opens with the first few pages of "De radice Chynae, A. Vesalii ad J. Roelants, epistola" *Language(s)*: Latin. Appraised at 12d in 1575.

108.17 Irocretii eratione

Isocrates. [*Selected works–Orations*]. Continent: date indeterminable.

See also 108.19. *Language(s)*: Latin Greek (perhaps). Appraised at 12d in 1575.

108.18 macropednius de consi epii
Georgius Macropedius. *Methodus de conscribendis epistolis*. Continent: date indeterminable.

Another copy at 108.81. *Language(s)*: Latin. Appraised at 10d in 1575.

108.19 oradice Isocratis ad dncum
Isocrates. *Ad Demonicum*. Continent: date indeterminable.

See also 108.17. *Language(s)*: Greek Latin. Appraised at 2d in 1575.

108.20 Epucures Erasni
Desiderius Erasmus. *Epicureus*. With translation into Greek and commentary by Bartholomaeus Caversinus. Antwerp: ex officina Gulielmi Silvii, typographi Regii, 1567.

Bezzel no. 540. Another possibility might be the *Problema et Epicureus* issued in Paris in 1533, or a more general selection here identified from a running head. *Language(s)*: Greek Latin. Appraised at 2d in 1575.

108.21 Liber q ii Averi'
Unidentified. Place unknown: stationer unknown, date indeterminable.

STC/non-STC status unknown. Conceivably Averroes, *Liber qui dicitur destructio destructionum*, but the reading of the manuscript is very uncertain. It is just possible that the last word should be read as "Andri:" *Language(s)*: Latin (probable). Appraised at 6d in 1575.

108.22 Confabilationes Erasmi
Hermannus Schottenius, *Hessus* and Desiderius Erasmus. *Confabulationes tyronum literariorum ad amussim Colloquiorum Erasmi*. Continent: 1525–1560.

Language(s): Latin. Appraised at 2d in 1575.

108.23 Ovidiuus faestis
Publius Ovidius Naso. *Fasti*. Britain or Continent: date indeterminable. STC 18947.5 and non-STC. *Language(s)*: Latin. Appraised at 4d in 1575.

108.24 Arii Contentia
Probably Aristotle. [*Selected works*]. Continent: date indeterminable.

A number of editions of selected works of Aristotle open with the word 'Contenta' (e.g., H. Stephanus, Paris, 1511; Jean Petit, P. le Preux, F. Regnualt and H. Stephanus, all Paris, 1515). *Language(s)*: Latin (probable) Greek (perhaps). Appraised at 6d in 1575.

108.25 Justic' historici
Trogus Pompeius and Justinus, *the Historian*. [*Epitomae in Trogi Pompeii historias*]. Britain or Continent: date indeterminable.

STC 24287 and non-STC. Additional copies at 108.74 and 108.85. See also 108.28. *Language(s)*: Latin. Appraised at 12d in 1575.

108.26 Aris' Organ' 8
Aristotle. *Organon*. Continent: date indeterminable.
See another copy at 108.50. *Language(s)*: Latin Greek (perhaps). Appraised at 7d in 1575.

108.27 simpolum apostalicum per erasmum
Desiderius Erasmus. *Explanatio symboli apostolorum*. Continent: date indeterminable.
Language(s): Latin. Appraised at 6d in 1575.

108.28 Grynaeus de utilitate
Simon Grynaeus. *De utilitate legendae historiae*. Continent: date indeterminable.
Apparently not published separately; most frequently appears with Justinus's *Epitome* in the *Trogi Pompeii historias*. See 108.25, 108.74, and 108.85. *Language(s)*: Latin. Appraised at 7d in 1575.

108.29 solis an other olde lad'
Unidentified. Place unknown: stationer unknown, date indeterminable.
STC/non-STC status unknown. *Language(s)*: Unknown. Appraised at 6d in 1575.

108.30 perrcationes per Erasmum
Desiderius Erasmus. *Precationes*. Continent: date indeterminable.
Language(s): Latin. Appraised at 6d in 1575.

108.31 Epist Cicorones quedam
Marcus Tullius Cicero. [*Selected works–Epistolae*]. Continent: date indeterminable.
Language(s): Latin. Appraised at 2d in 1575.

108.32 diailiclicae [dialecticae] Valerii
Cornelius Valerius. *Tabulae totius dialectices*. Continent: 1548–1575.
Language(s): Latin. Appraised at 2d in 1575.

108.33 flores epis Ciceronis
Marcus Tullius Cicero. [*Epistolae–Selections*]. Continent: date indeterminable.
Language(s): Latin. Appraised at 7d in 1575.

108.34 questionis tartariti in ethica
Petrus Tartaretus. [*Aristotle–Ethica: commentary*]. Continent: date indeterminable.
Most sixteenth-century editions also contained other works. *Language(s)*: Latin. Appraised at 2d in 1575.

108.35 Mantanis
Unidentified. Continent: date indeterminable.

The entry could refer to any of a number of authors printed on the continent named "Montanus" or "Monte" or, indeed, to Baptista Spagnuoli, "Mantuanus." *Language(s)*: Latin (probable). Appraised at 3d in 1575.

108.36 Amonius in porphirium
Ammonius, *Hermiae*. [*Porphyrius, of Tyre–Isagoge: commentary*]. Continent: date indeterminable.

Language(s): Latin. Appraised at 4d in 1575.

108.37 Pithy sange of the Scripture
Thomas Paynell. *The piththy [sic] and moost notable sayinges of al Scripture.* London: (different houses), 1550–1552 (probable).

STC 19494 *et seq. Language(s)*: English. Appraised at 8d in 1575.

108.38 Larentus Vallius
Laurentius Valla. Unidentified. Continent: date indeterminable.

Very probably his *Elegantiae*, but there are other possibilities, including the *Works*, although the valuation would be low for this, or for the more massive forms of the *Elegantiae. Language(s)*: Latin. Appraised at 12d in 1575.

108.39 Erasmus Rotrodans [Roterodamus]
Desiderius Erasmus. Unidentified. Place unknown: stationer unknown, date indeterminable.

STC/non-STC status unknown. *Language(s)*: Latin (probable). Appraised at 10d in 1575.

108.40 trentii em commentario
Publius Terentius, *Afer*. [*Works*]. Britain or Continent: date indeterminable.

STC 23885.3 *et seq.* and non-STC. STC 23885 (1497) does not carry commentary. *Language(s)*: Latin. Appraised at 16d in 1575.

108.41 Gilberti ducherii
Gilbertus Ducherius. Probably *Epigrammata*. Lyon: apud Seb. Gryphium, 1538.

No other work of Ducherius has been found. *Language(s)*: Latin. Appraised at 12d in 1575.

108.42 terentii
Publius Terentius, *Afer*. [*Works*]. Britain or Continent: date indeterminable.

STC 23885 *et seq.* and non-STC. See 108.40, 108.43, and 108.78. *Language(s)*: Latin. Appraised at 10d in 1575.

108.43 terentii
Publius Terentius, *Afer*. Unidentified. Place unknown: stationer unknown, date indeterminable.
STC/non-STC status unknown. The low valuation suggests a single play or selections rather than the *Works*. See also 108.40, 108.42, and 108.78. *Language(s)*: Latin. Appraised at 2d in 1575.

108.44 Gregoris
Unidentified. Continent (probable): date indeterminable.
Probably not an STC book. The entry could refer to Gregory I, Gregory, *Nazianzus*, Gregory, *of Nyssa*, St. Gregory *of Tours* or, less probably, Gregory IX or St. Gregory, *Thaumaturgus* to name no more. The scope is to some extent limited if this entry and the next represent parts of the same work. *Language(s)*: Latin. Appraised at 12d in 1575.

108.45 pars i Gregorii
Unidentified. Continent: date indeterminable.
Possible candidates here are Gregorius, *Ariminensis*, Petrus Gregorius, *Tholosanus*, Gregory, *Nazianzus*, and, especially, Gregory I, all of whom had a work or *Works* issued in several parts. See the preceding. *Language(s)*: Latin (probable) Greek (perhaps). Appraised at 20d in 1575.

108.46 Comentonis per quersa erationis Ciecronis
Marcus Tullius Cicero. Unidentified. Continent: date indeterminable.
Perhaps either the *De optimo genere oratorum* or the *De partitione oratoria*, as annotated by Léger Du Chesne (Leodegarius à Quercu) and first issued in 1544 and 1571 respectively. The entry is, however, so corrupt that it might also be interpreted as, say, "Commentarii super quasdam orationes Ciceronis." *Language(s)*: Latin. Appraised at 2s in 1575.

108.47 Calaijnus [Calepinus?] Hibraeii
Perhaps Ambrogio Calepino. *Dictionarium*. Lyon: Guillaume Rouille and (different houses), 1570–1571.
Only two editions of Calepino with Hebrew were available to Lye by the time of his death in 1575. Rouille alone was responsible for the 1571 edition. See Labarre, nos. 117 and 120. It is possible, however, that "Calepinus," if that is indeed what the entry intends, is here simply a synonym for "dictionarium." The valuation seems low for the polyglot Calepinus suggested above. *Language(s)*: Dutch French German Greek Hebrew Italian Latin Spanish. Appraised at 12d in 1575.

108.48 poleanthea auttore Comico Vario
Perhaps Dominicus Nannus, *Mirabellius*. *Polyanthea*. Continent: date indeterminable.
The identification rests on the assumption that "Comico Vario" is a mis-

transcription of "Dominico Nanno" and, of course, on the word "Poleanthea." If, however, the term is here descriptive, the work intended might have been rather an edition of the *Comicorum Graecorum sententiae* issuing from several Continental presses. *Language(s)*: Greek Latin. Appraised at 2s in 1575.

108.49 brusonis de facetiis
Lucius Domitius Brusonius. *Facetiarum exemplorumque libri VII*. Continent: date indeterminable.
Language(s): Latin. Appraised at 20d in 1575.

108.50 Crgan' [Organon] Arii
Aristotle. *Organon*. Continent: date indeterminable.
See another copy at 108.26. *Language(s)*: Latin (probable) Greek (perhaps). Appraised at 12d in 1575.

108.51 phisica Aristotelis
Aristotle. *Physica*. Continent: date indeterminable.
Language(s): Latin Greek (perhaps). Appraised at 14d in 1575.

108.52 Gratr' despauterii
Jean Despautère. [*Grammatica*]. Continent: date indeterminable.
Language(s): Latin. Appraised at 2s in 1575.

108.53 Errasni apothe'
Desiderius Erasmus. *Apophthegmata*. Continent: 1531–1573.
Date range from VHe. Another copy at 108.91. *Language(s)*: Latin. Appraised at 8d in 1575.

108.54 Politico aris'
Aristotle. *Politica*. Continent: date indeterminable.
Language(s): Latin Greek (perhaps). Appraised at 18d in 1575.

108.55 Ethica Ariss'
Aristotle. *Ethica*. Continent: date indeterminable.
STC 752 and non-STC. *Language(s)*: Latin Greek (perhaps). Appraised at 20d in 1575.

108.56 Sillius poeta Itallius
Silius Italicus. *De bello punico*. Continent: date indeterminable.
Language(s): Latin. Appraised at 12d in 1575.

108.57 phitonis Judei de fabricatione mundi
Philo, *Judaeus*. *De opificio mundi*. Continent: date indeterminable.
Seems not to have been published solo; it leads in several collections.
Language(s): Latin Greek (perhaps). Appraised at 14d in 1575.

108.58 Pultisera Navis
Sebastian Brant. *Stultifera navis*. Continent (probable): date indeterminable.
Probably not an STC book, but see STC 3545 *et seq. Language(s)*: Latin English (perhaps). Appraised at 10d in 1575.

108.59 Epis' longolii
Christophorus Longolius. [*Epistolae*]. Continent: date indeterminable. *Language(s)*: Latin. Appraised at 12d in 1575.

108.60 Radolph'
Unidentified. Continent (probable): date indeterminable.
Probably not an STC book. Possibilities include Rodolphus Agricola, Caspar Rhodolphus (perhaps on logic), but also Rudolph Walther and others. *Language(s)*: Latin. Appraised at 8d in 1575.

108.61 Toxita in libros ad Her'
Michael Toxites. [*Cicero (spurious)–Rhetorica ad Herennium: commentary and text*]. Basle: Joannes Oporinus (with different houses), 1556–1568. *Language(s)*: Latin. Appraised at 14d in 1575.

108.62 faber in ethica
Jacobus Faber, *Stapulensis*. [*Aristotle–Ethica: commentary*]. Continent: date indeterminable.
Either the *Artificialis introductio in X libros Ethicorum*, which contains commentary, or the *Commentarii in X libros Ethicorum*. Numerous editions of each from as early as the fifteenth century. *Language(s)*: Latin. Appraised at 8d in 1575.

108.63 Osorius de Justitie
Jeronimo Osorio da Fonseca, *Bishop*. *De justitia*. Continent: 1564–1574. *Language(s)*: Latin. Appraised at 18d in 1575.

108.64 Catechismus de dicreto
Perhaps *Catechismus ex decreto Concilii Tridentini*. Continent: 1566–1575.
Other catechisms, such as the Palatinate, *Catechismus catholicus qui antea quidem ex decreto Concilii Tridentini scriptus*, remain as remoter possibilities. *Language(s)*: Latin. Appraised at 14d in 1575.

108.65 Pall Vingilios
Probably Marcellus Palingenius (Pietro Angelo Manzolli [Stellatus]). *Zodiacus vitae*. Britain or Continent: date indeterminable.
STC 19138.5 *et seq.* and non-STC. *Language(s)*: Latin (probable) English (perhaps). Appraised at 10d in 1575.

108.66 Thaurelius de passione Jesu

Johann Tauler. *Exercitia super vita et passione Jesu Christi.* Continent: 1565–1572.

We choose to ignore the horrible possibility that Caelius Aurelianus, *De tardis passionibus*, is intended. *Language(s)*: Latin. Appraised at 12d in 1575.

108.67 Catinus secuen in perlitii Cici

Perhaps Caelius Secundus Curio. [*Cicero–De partitione oratoriae: commentary* (and others)]. Continent: 1556–1567.

Another possibility might be the commentary on this same text by M. Rocca Cataneo, but it seems to have been published only in Italian. *Language(s)*: Latin. Appraised at 14d in 1575.

108.68 Justis Martirs appolagia

Justinus, *Martyr.* Perhaps [*Works* (part)]. Continent: date indeterminable.

Either part of his *Opera* or perhaps a separate printing of the *Logos paraeneticos*. *Language(s)*: Latin (probable) Greek (perhaps). Appraised at 15d in 1575.

108.69 Caius plinis secundius

Probably Pliny, *the Elder. Historia naturalis.* Continent: date indeterminable.

Perhaps, given the idiosyncrasies of the scribe, Pliny, *the Younger* (Caius Plinius Caecilius Secundus). *Language(s)*: Latin. Appraised at 12d in 1575.

108.70:1 Ciprianius Augustus

Probably Cyprian, *Saint.* Unidentified. Continent: date indeterminable.

Assuming two items, probably bound together. See the following (108.70:2). *Language(s)*: Latin. Appraised with one other at 12d in 1575.

108.70:2 [See 108.70:1]

Perhaps Augustine, *Saint.* Unidentified. Continent (probable): date indeterminable.

Probably not an STC book. See notes to 108.70:1. *Language(s)*: Latin. Appraised with one other at 12d in 1575.

108.71 Coopari Gramatica Greca

Probably Jacobus Ceporinus. *Compendium grammaticae graecae.* Continent: date indeterminable.

Language(s): Greek Latin. Appraised at 8d in 1575.

108.72 Comentarie Caesaris

Caius Julius Caesar. *Commentarii.* Continent: date indeterminable. *Language(s)*: Latin. Appraised at 12d in 1575.

108.73 Prinasius Utirenses

Primasius, *Bishop of Adrumetum.* Unidentified. Continent: date indeterminable.

Celebrated chiefly for his commentary on Revelation, Primasius was also the author of a commentary on the Pauline epistles. *Language(s)*: Latin. Appraised at 14d in 1575.

108.74 Historia Justini
Trogus Pompeius and Justinus, *the Historian*. [*Epitomae in Trogi Pompeii historias*]. Britain or Continent: date indeterminable.

STC 24287 and non-STC. Additional copies at 108.25 and 108.85. See also 108.28. *Language(s)*: Latin. Appraised at 12d in 1575.

108.75 Apohthonius
Aphthonius, *Sophista. Progymnasmata*. Britain or Continent: date indeterminable.

STC 699 *et seq.* and non-STC. *Language(s)*: Latin. Appraised at 12d in 1575.

108.76 flores declera'
Unidentified. Place unknown: stationer unknown, date indeterminable.

STC/non-STC status unknown. Perhaps the entry is a form of 'Flores decretalium,' but nothing with that title has been found. *Language(s)*: Latin. Appraised at 20d in 1575.

108.77 flores bibilae
Flores Bibliae. (Bible–Selections). Compiled by Thomas, *Hibernicus*. Continent: 1555–1574.

See Shaaber T29–36. *Language(s)*: Latin. Appraised at 16d in 1575.

108.78 Terrentiius
Publius Terentius, *Afer*. [*Works*]. Britain or Continent: date indeterminable.

STC 23885 *et seq.* and non-STC. See 108.40, 108.42, and 108.43. *Language(s)*: Latin. Appraised at 10d in 1575.

108.79 Ciceronis ffia
Marcus Tullius Cicero. Probably *De officiis*. Continent: date indeterminable.

De officiis was the leading title in many editions of Cicero's *Works*, including two printed in England before the date of this inventory. *Language(s)*: Latin. Appraised at 12d in 1575.

108.80 Omphalius demitatione
Jacobus Omphalius. *De elocutionis imitatione ac apparatu*. Continent: 1537–1572.

Language(s): Latin. Appraised at 12d in 1575.

108.81 macropeduus duconscrbiest epii
Georgius Macropedius. *Methodus de conscribendis epistolis*. Continent: date indeterminable.

Another copy at 108.18. *Language(s)*: Latin. Appraised at 12d in 1575.

108.82 copia verborum Oreri [& rerum?]

Probably Desiderius Erasmus. *De duplici copia verborum ac rerum*. Britain or Continent: date indeterminable.

STC 10471.4 *et seq.* and non-STC. *Language(s)*: Latin. Appraised at 12d in 1575.

108.83 Anteris opus

Unidentified. Place unknown: stationer unknown, date indeterminable.

STC/non-STC status unknown. *Language(s)*: Latin (probable). Appraised at 4d in 1575.

108.84 Urognes de vilii psito

Perhaps Diogenes Laertius. [*De vita et moribus philosophorum*]. Continent: date indeterminable.

Language(s): Latin (probable) Greek (perhaps). Appraised at 12d in 1575.

108.85 Instoria Justinii

Trogus Pompeius and Justinus, *the Historian*. [*Epitomae in Trogi Pompeii historias*]. Britain or Continent: date indeterminable.

STC 24287 and non-STC. Additional copies at 108.25 and 108.74. See also 108.28. Appraised at 14d in 1575.

108.86 Clatechesis Cirilli

Cyril, *Jerusalem, Saint. Catechesis*. Continent: 1564.

Editions from Paris, Cologne, and Antwerp in 1564. *Language(s)*: Latin (probable) Greek (perhaps). Appraised at 12d in 1575.

108.87 Plutarish Vitam epilone

Plutarch. [*Vitae parallelae–Epitome*]. Continent: date indeterminable.
Language(s): Latin. Appraised at 12d in 1575.

108.88 the primer in english with genevie salmpes 2

Perhaps [*Liturgy–Church of England–Book of Common Prayer* (with Geneva *Psalms*)]. London: R. Jugge and J. Cawood, 1566.

STC 16297. The identification rests on the assumption that the 2 in the entry is an indication of format and, even more rashly, that the word *primer* is here used anachronistically to describe *The Book of Common Prayer*. Alternatively, what is here represented is a strange combination of the Geneva *Psalms* and a Roman Primer. STC 16297 was issued in two parts. *Language(s)*: English. Appraised at 20d in 1575.

108.89 Ovidinus de arte anandi

Publius Ovidius Naso. *Ars amatoria*. Continent: date indeterminable.
Language(s): Latin. Appraised at 12d in 1575.

108.90 Geneva salmes in frenche
[*Bible–O.T.–Psalms*]. Continent: date indeterminable.
Not all editions of the Geneva version were published in Geneva. See Adams B1482-89. *Language(s)*: French. Appraised at 16d in 1575.

108.91 Erasmus apothagmata in plano pretio
Desiderius Erasmus. *Apophthegmata*. Continent: 1531–1573.
If the last three words of the entry are to be taken as read, the implication might conceivably be that the book was in mint condition "at its full ["pleno" for *plano*] price." On the other hand the eccentricities of this list are such that it might almost as well be one of the early editions, "ex Plutarcho praesertim" or almost anything else. Date range from VHe. Another copy at 108.53. *Language(s)*: Latin. Appraised at 16d in 1575.

108.92 tres partis philosophie
Unidentified. Place unknown: stationer unknown, date indeterminable.
STC/non-STC status unknown. Probably either Aristotle or Cicero. *Language(s)*: Latin. Appraised at 12d in 1575.

108.93:1-5 with Mr Pallard v books
Unidentified. Places unknown: stationers unknown, dates indeterminable.
STC/non-STC status unknown. Not appraised. *Language(s)*: Unknown.

108.94:1-5 v bookes in a chest
Unidentified. Places unknown: stationers unknown, dates indeterminable.
STC/non-STC status unknown. Not appraised. *Language(s)*: Unknown.

James Powell, Scholar (M.A.): Probate Inventory, 1575

RICHARD J. PANOFSKY

James Powell received the B.A. on 26 February 1565, became a fellow of Oriel College in 1565, and received the M.A. on 30 June 1569. In 1570 he was appointed praelector in natural philosophy—an annually renewable academic appointment like today's college lecturer—and was presumably still praelector at his death on 6 June 1575.

Powell's small library of forty-two items reflects interests in natural science and metaphysics (dominated by Aristotle), history (emphasizing Roman), law (both civil and canon), and theology, and it contains some familiar titles in grammar, logic, and rhetoric. The theological titles are common enough, with nothing to suggest Protestant sympathies: two titles from the medieval church (Nicolaus de Lyra and Thomas, *Hibernicus*), a Bible and New Testament, a book of psalms, a prayer book, and a collection of prayers by Erasmus. Also, an unidentified work, "Consolaciones in Afflixionibus" is probably theological. A few titles reflect an interest in moral philosophy, including a Marcus Aurelius. Probably all of Powell's books are in Latin, most or all published on the Continent. Except for Erasmus and Polydore Vergil, there is little suggestion of a humanistic context, and few or none of the works suggest contemporary interests.

Such a list of books is unremarkable for the holder of an M.A. with expertise in natural philosophy—with an old-fashioned bent. Sacrobosco's *Sphaera mundi* (109.41) is a standard medieval school text on astronomy. Even the *Malleus mallificarum* (109.8), a late fifteenth century work on witchcraft, can fit the range of topics encompassed by traditional natural philosophy: "The medieval scientist had to be scientist, metaphysician, historian, theologian, and more, all in one intellect" (Steneck 1976, 146).

Oxford University Archives, Bodleian Library: Hyp.B.17.

§

Steneck, Nicholas H. 1976. *Science and Creation in the Middle Ages*. Notre Dame: Univ. of Notre Dame Press.

§

109.1	Questiones Scoti in Metaphisicam Aristotelis
109.2	Abbutius
109.3	Gabrielis Vironensis
109.4	Phisica Aristotelis
109.5	Polidorus Vergilius
109.6	Dispauterius
109.7	Officia Ciceronis
109.8	Mallius Mallificarum
109.9	Apthonius
109.10	Flores Doctorum
109.11	Therentius
109.12	Lyra
109.13	Melchior
109.14	a old bible
109.15	Cornucopia
109.16	dixionarium trium lingualum [linguarum] tribus linguis conscriptum
109.17	Horatius
109.18	Orationes Tullii tribus voluminibus
109.19	Apothegmata Erasmi
109.20	Instituciones Lingue Grece
109.21	Osorius de st
109.22	Herodian in 2bus [duobus] voluminibus
109.23	Instituciones Juris Civilis
109.24	Epistole Pauli Manutii
109.25	David Salpmes
109.26	Instituciones Juris Canonici
109.27	Commentarii Julii Cesaris
109.28	a prayer boke
109.29	Consolaciones in Afflixionibus
109.30	Epithomi Plutarci
109.31	Logica Sturmii
109.32	Marcus Aurelius
109.33	Historia Hanniball and Scipio
109.34	Historia Justini
109.35	Testamentum Novum
109.36	Valerius Maximus

109.37   Mynisinger
109.38   Velcurio
109.39   Epistolae Tullii
109.40   Precationes Erasmi
109.41   Sphera J. de Sacrobosco
109.42   Salustius

§

109.1 Questiones Scoti in Metaphisicam Aristotelis
John Duns, *Scotus*. [*Aristotle–Metaphysica: commentary*]. Venice: (different houses), 1497–1520.
Language(s): Latin. Appraised at 10d in 1575.

109.2 Abbutius
Probably Nicolaus Tudeschis (Panormitanus). Unidentified. Continent: date indeterminable.

If his commentary on the *Decretales*, probably only a part given this low appraisal. *Language(s)*: Latin. Appraised at 6d in 1575.

109.3 Gabrielis Vironensis
Gabriel Zerbus. Unidentified. Continent: date indeterminable.

Zerbus, sometimes referred to as Veronensis, published on metaphysics and medicine. On the basis of the rest of his collection, Powell is more likely to have owned a work in metaphysics, but his instructorship in natural philosophy makes ownership of a medical work certainly possible. *Language(s)*: Latin. Appraised at 6d in 1575.

109.4 Phisica Aristotelis
Aristotle. *Physica*. Continent: date indeterminable.
Language(s): Latin (probable) Greek (perhaps). Appraised at 12d in 1575.

109.5 Polidorus Vergilius
Polydorus Vergilius. Unidentified. Place unknown: stationer unknown, date indeterminable.

STC/non-STC status unknown. Probably either *Anglicae historia*, the *De inventoribus rerum*, or the English *An abridgement of the notable worke of Polidore Vergile*. *Language(s)*: Latin (probable) English (perhaps). Appraised at 20d in 1575.

109.6 Dispauterius
Jean Despautère. Unidentified. Place unknown: stationer unknown, date indeterminable.

STC/non-STC status unknown. Doubtless, one of his works on Latin grammar and rhetoric: *Syntaxis, Rudimenta, Orthographiae praecepta,* or *Grammatica,* typical manuals for use by those classically educated. *Language(s)*: Latin. Appraised at 6d in 1575.

109.7 Officia Ciceronis
Marcus Tullius Cicero. *De officiis.* Continent: date indeterminable.

The English/Latin version (1558) is but a remote possibility given the form of the entry. Conceivably an edition of the *Works,* titles of which often begin with *De officiis. Language(s)*: Latin. Appraised at 6d in 1575.

109.8 Mallius Mallificarum
Jacob Sprenger and Heinrich Kraemer. *Malleus maleficarum.* Continent: date indeterminable.

The slight value is appropriate for a book of about 130 leaves. *Language(s)*: Latin. Appraised at 2d in 1575.

109.9 Apthonius
Aphthonius, *Sophista. Progymnasmata.* Britain or Continent: date indeterminable.

STC 699 *et seq.* and non-STC. *Language(s)*: Latin. Appraised at 10d in 1575.

109.10 Flores Doctorum
Thomas, *Hibernicus.* [*Flores omnium fere doctorum*]. Continent: date indeterminable.

Language(s): Latin. Appraised at 12d in 1575.

109.11 Therentius
Publius Terentius, *Afer.* Probably [*Works*]. Britain or Continent: date indeterminable.

STC 23885 *et seq.* and non-STC. Less likely the *Vulgaria. Language(s)*: Latin. Appraised at 10d in 1575.

109.12 Lyra
Nicolaus de Lyra. Probably [*Postilla* (part)]. Continent: date indeterminable. A very low valuation for the whole. *Language(s)*: Latin. Appraised at 4d in 1575.

109.13 Melchior
Unidentified. Continent (probable): date indeterminable.

Almost certainly not an STC book. Many possibilities, with Melchior Hittorp the likeliest. His defense of the Roman Catholic liturgy might fit this collection. *Language(s)*: Latin. Appraised at 8d in 1575.

109.14 a old bible
The Bible. Britain or Continent: date indeterminable.

STC 2055 *et seq.* and non-STC. *Language(s)*: Latin (probable) English (perhaps). Appraised at 2s 6d in 1575.

109.15 Cornucopia
Probably Nicolaus Perottus. *Cornucopia*. Continent: date indeterminable.

This comprehensive Latin grammar is a likely enough reference work for Powell's study. The Aldine *Thesaurus cornucopiae*, a grammar and dictionary of Latin and Greek and the product of many scholars, must also be considered; a folio format might explain the item's relatively high valuation at over 3 shillings. *Language(s)*: Latin. Appraised at 3s 4d in 1575.

109.16 dixionarium trium lingualum [linguarum] tribus linguis conscriptum
Probably Robert Estienne, *the Elder*. *Dictionariolum puerorum, tribus linguis Latina, Anglica et Gallica conscriptum*. English text by Jean Veron. London: apud R. Wolfium, 1552.

STC 10555. There is no reason to believe that Powell's edition contained German instead of English. Conceivably Calepine's polyglot dictionary, but the entry approximates the Estienne title closely. *Language(s)*: English French Latin. Appraised at 8d in 1575.

109.17 Horatius
Quintus Horatius Flaccus. Probably [*Works*]. Britain or Continent: date indeterminable.

STC 13784 and non-STC. At the appraised value, which replaces "15d" crossed out, probably not the edition published in London the year before. *Language(s)*: Latin. Appraised at 3d in 1575.

109.18 Orationes Tullii tribus voluminibus
Marcus Tullius Cicero. [*Selected works–Orations*]. Continent: date indeterminable.

Language(s): Latin. Appraised at 3s 4d in 1575.

109.19 Apothegmata Erasmi
Desiderius Erasmus. *Apophthegmata*. Continent (probable): date indeterminable.

Probably not an STC book, but see STC 10443. The exact correspondence of the entry to the full title and the high assessment of value make it likely that this entry refers to a full Latin edition of Erasmus's *Apophthegmata* rather than to Nicholas Udall's Englished selections (STC 10443). *Language(s)*: Latin (probable). Appraised at 16d in 1575.

109.20 Instituciones Lingue Grece
Nicolaus Clenardus. [*Institutiones linguae graecae*]. Continent: date indeterminable.

Language(s): Greek Latin. Appraised at 8d in 1575.

109.21 Osorius de st
Jeronimo Osorio da Fonseca, *Bishop*. Unidentified. Continent: date indeterminable.
This entry was lined through, apparently before it was completed; no appraisal was given. The crossing out obscures *de st*, which could be *de inst*, a truncated "de institutione" for *De regis institutione et disciplina*. *Language(s)*: Latin.

109.22 Herodian in 2bus [duobus] voluminibus
Herodian. [*Historiae*]. Continent: date indeterminable.
Language(s): Latin Greek (perhaps). Appraised at 8d in 1575.

109.23 Instituciones Juris Civilis
Justinian I. *Institutiones.* (*Corpus juris civilis*). Continent: date indeterminable.
Language(s): Greek Latin. Appraised at 6d in 1575.

109.24 Epistole Pauli Manutii
Paolo Manuzio. [*Epistolae*]. Britain or Continent: date indeterminable.
STC 17286 *et seq.* and non-STC. *Language(s)*: Latin. Appraised at 8d in 1575.

109.25 David Salpmes
[*Bible–O.T.–Psalms*]. Britain or Continent: date indeterminable.
STC 2354 *et seq.* and non-STC. *Language(s)*: Latin. Appraised at 6d in 1575.

109.26 Instituciones Juris Canonici
Probably Giovanni Paolo Lancelotto. *Institutiones juris canonici*. Continent: date indeterminable.
The principal edition of canon law in use; but the entry could describe Marcus Cucchus, *Institutionum juris canonici libri quatuor* (with editions between 1563–66). *Language(s)*: Latin. Appraised at 6d in 1575.

109.27 Commentarii Julii Cesaris
Caius Julius Caesar. *Commentarii*. Continent: date indeterminable.
Language(s): Latin. Appraised at 8d in 1575.

109.28 a prayer boke
Unidentified. Place unknown: stationer unknown, date indeterminable.
STC/non-STC status unknown. *Language(s)*: Unknown. Appraised at 2d in 1575.

109.29 Consolaciones in Afflixionibus
Unidentified. Continent (probable): date indeterminable.
Probably not an STC book. Perhaps one of the many late medieval man-

uals of consolation. A long shot is Urbanus Rhegius, *In omnis generis afflictionibus* (1545), a medical treatise that includes "consolationes" near the end of its long title. Classical authors also wrote on this theme. *Language(s)*: Latin. Appraised at 4d in 1575.

109.30 Epithomi Plutarci
Plutarch. [*Vitae parallelae–Epitome*]. Continent: date indeterminable. *Language(s)*: Latin. Appraised at 8d in 1575.

109.31 Logica Sturmii
Joannes Sturmius. [*Dialectica*]. Continent: date indeterminable. *Language(s)*: Latin. Appraised at 6d in 1575.

109.32 Marcus Aurelius
Probably Marcus Aurelius Antoninus. [*De vita sua*]. Continent: date indeterminable.

The popular fictional biography, *The golden boke of Marcus Aurelius* by Antonio de Guevara, is a less likely possibility for this library. *Language(s)*: Latin Greek (perhaps). Appraised at 8d in 1575.

109.33 Historia Hanniball and Scipio
Unidentified. Place unknown: stationer unknown, date indeterminable.

STC/non-STC status unknown. Parts of either Plutarch or Livy would fit the entry, although the relevant sections of their respective works seem not to have been published separately in Latin. The popular translation, primarily out of Livy, by Sir Anthony Cope (STC 5718 *et seq.*, in 1544, 1548, and 1561 editions), *The historie of two the moste noble capitaines of the worlde, Anniball and Scipio*, might have been routinely rendered in Latin by the compiler. *Language(s)*: Latin (probable) English (perhaps). Appraised at 6d in 1575.

109.34 Historia Justini
Trogus Pompeius and Justinus, *the Historian*. [*Epitome in Trogi Pompeii historias*]. Britain or Continent: date indeterminable.

STC 24287 and non-STC. *Language(s)*: Latin. Appraised at 6d in 1575.

109.35 Testamentum Novum
[*Bible–N.T.*]. Britain or Continent: date indeterminable.

STC 2799 *et seq.* and non-STC. *Language(s)*: Latin. Appraised at 12d in 1575.

109.36 Valerius Maximus
Valerius Maximus. *Facta et dicta memorabilia*. Continent: date indeterminable.

Language(s): Latin. Appraised at 8d in 1575.

109.37 Mynisinger

Joachim Mynsinger. Unidentified. Continent: date indeterminable.

His one work in theology, *Enchiridion religiosum*, would fit this collection, but it seems not to have been translated from German into Latin in Powell's lifetime. Virtually everything else of Mynsinger's was on law, including his widely published *Apotelesma*. *Language(s)*: Latin. Appraised at 6d in 1575.

109.38 Velcurio

Joannes Velcurio. [*Aristotle–Physica: commentary*]. Continent: date indeterminable.

Language(s): Latin. Appraised at 12d in 1575.

109.39 Epistolae Tullii

Marcus Tullius Cicero. [*Selected works–Epistolae*]. Continent (probable): date indeterminable.

Probably not an STC book, but see STC 5295. Among the many versions of Cicero's letters, the popularity of the *Epistolae ad familiares*, which includes the 1573 STC 5295, makes it a reasonable possibility. *Language(s)*: Latin. Appraised at 8d in 1575.

109.40 Precationes Erasmi

Desiderius Erasmus. *Precationes*. Continent: date indeterminable.
Language(s): Latin. Appraised at 4d in 1575.

109.41 Sphera J. de Sacrobosco

John Holywood (Joannes Sacrobosco). *Sphaera mundi*. Continent: date indeterminable.

Language(s): Latin. Appraised at 4d in 1575.

109.42 Salustius

Caius Sallustius Crispus. Unidentified. Continent (probable): date indeterminable.

Probably not an STC book, but see STC 21622.2. Perhaps *Works*, which would then make the Latin STC 21622.2 a possibility, or alternatively *De bello Jugurthino* or *De conjuratione Catalinae*. Powell is not likely to have owned a translation in English. *Language(s)*: Latin. Appraised at 8d in 1575.

Philip Johnson. Scholar (B.Th.): Probate Inventory. 1576

D. V. N. BAGCHI

Philip Johnson (B.A. 1566, M.A. 1568, B.Th. 1575) was principal of St. Edmund Hall from 1572 until 1576, the year of his death. A taberdar of The Queen's College in 1566, he was elected fellow in 1569, assuming the principalship of the neighboring and dependent society three years later (*Alumni Oxonienses* 2:815, and McGrath 1921, 1:179–80, 1:280 and 2:297). Shortly before his untimely death, he resigned this post to become domestic chaplain to the new Archbishop of Canterbury, Edmund Grindal (Kelly 1989, 91–92).

Johnson's extensive library of almost three hundred titles, with a total appraised value of £12 16*s* 1*d*, is evidence for the claim that academics of the 1560s and 1570s could acquire more books in their early careers than their predecessors might in a lifetime (Ker, 472). Theological books predominate, and it is clear that Johnson kept himself abreast of the very latest Continental publications. As befits the library of Grindal's *aide-de-camp*, writers of the Reformed tradition slightly outnumber Lutheran authorities, and Hebrew and Greek Bibles and standard patristic texts are well represented; the most valuable item is a volume of John, Chrysostom's *Works* (110.140) appraised at ten shillings. Copies of some of the most important anti-Reformation titles complete this impressive collection.

Oxford University Archives, Bodleian Library: Hyp.B.14.

§

Greenslade, S.L. 1963. *The Cambridge History of the Bible: The West from the Reformation to the Present Day*. Vol. 3. Cambridge: Cambridge Univ. Press.

Kelly, J.N.D. 1989. *St. Edmund Hall: Almost Seven Hundred Years*. Oxford: Oxford Univ. Press.

McGrath, J.R. 1921. *The Queen's College.* 4 Vols. Oxford: Clarendon Press.

§

110.1	Ecclesiastica historia Eusebei
110.2	loci communes Andree musculi
110.3	opera Aristotelis grece
110.4	Christomi [Chrisostomi] opera
110.5	gualterus in Johannem
110.6	Adagia Erasmi
110.7	5tus tomus
110.8	commentaria budei
110.9	gualterus super Lucam
110.10	divus Thomas in epistolas pauli
110.11	augustinus in fratres in heremo
110.12	Ederus
110.13	gualterus in epistolas pauli in Chorintios
110.14	petrus marter in genesim
110.15	gualterus in acta
110.16	Cronologia funcii
110.17	brunus de heretecis
110.18	Clavis scripture
110.19	opera barnardi
110.20	flaccus de vitis pontificum
110.21	marter in reges
110.22	panoplia lundani in 4 Evangelia
110.23	biblia grece
110.24	cornucopia
110.25	Laviterus super prophetis
110.26	lavater in paralipomenon
110.27	Chemniz in consilium tredentinum
110.28	polianthea
110.29	gualterus super marcum
110.30	wolfius in officia ciceronis
110.31	opera Cipriani
110.32	Tomas aquinas super 4 evangelia
110.33	gualterus in prophetas
110.34	petrus marter in romanos
110.35	opera Josephi
110.36	Calvinus in genecem
110.37	Erasmi annotaciones in novum testamentum
110.38	gualterus in romanos
110.39	Calvinus in Eseam
110.40	the pollegi of England

110.41	bullengerus in pocalypsim
110.42	Claudius in omnes epistolas pauli
110.43	hermonia Calvini
110.44	Calinus [Calvinus] in omnes epistolas pauli
110.45	Calvinus in prophetas ger [germanice?]
110.46	Instituciones Calvini
110.47	hemengius in omnes epistolas pauli
110.48	petrus marter in 2 librum samuelis
110.49	buserus in psalmos
110.50	hamelmannus de tradicionibus
110.51	Epit' August'
110.52	politica Aristotelis commento
110.53	biblia pagnini
110.54	Cromerus
110.55	lavater in Josuam
110.56	Calvinus in psalmos
110.57	Calvinus in Ezecheil
110.58	Concilii West'
110.59	grammatica Cevelerii
110.60	bridges supper
110.61	loci Communes hiperii
110.62	loci communes musculi
110.63	opera Clementis
110.64	cronica slidani
110.65	opera epipheni
110.66	ozorius de justicia
110.67	Conciliorum colleccio
110.68	novum testamentum grece et latine
110.69	problemata Aretii
110.70	opuscula hiperii
110.71	Instituciones bullengeri
110.72	Lutherus ad galathas
110.73	opera fulgentii
110.74	Epistole bezi
110.75	opera Justini
110.76	opera justini [Dionysii] ariopagitae
110.77	loci communes melancton
110.78	gardiner de sacramentis
110.79	osorius de institucione regis
110.80	abdias
110.81	Cronica fulgencii
110.82	orationes Isocratis grece et latine
110.83	major in Epistolam ad Ebreos
110.84	philo Judeus de script' [scripturis]
110.85	hiperius de ratione studii

110.86	conciones funebres
110.87	methodus pauli in duobus
110.88	stephanus de sanctis
110.89	instituciones hopperi
110.90	testamentum Erasmi
110.91	summa conciliorum
110.92	opera Irinei
110.93	Enchiridion hemingii
110.94	Epithomi pagnini Ebre' [Ebreici]
110.95	annotaciones Monsteri Ebraice latine
110.96	grammatica Campensis
110.97	omilia Helmesii in 2bus
110.98	postilla spangilbergii in 3bus
110.99	gramatica Monsteri Ebraica
110.100	postilla Roiardi in 4
110.101	Calvinus in Josuam
110.102	Epistole chytrei
110.103	biblia Ebreica in 7m [septem]
110.104	2a pars postille firiensis
110.105	halicarnoseus in 2bus de originibus romanis
110.106	Snoeus in psalmos
110.107	cronica Carionis
110.108	retorica tullii
110.109:1	Thomus 1us philo: Tho: 1us orat: tullii
110.109:2	[See 110.109:1]
110.110	Epistole ad aticum
110.111	garrettus de sacrificio messe
110.112	cronica sleade' [sleadeni]
110.113	meditaciones Augustini
110.114	chitreus in leviticum
110.115	cronica palentini
110.116	chitreus de electione
110.117	chitreus in numerum
110.118	cronica Surii
110.119	chitreus in genesim
110.120	lavater de spectris
110.121	Cathakismus hemingeii
110.122	conciones funebres
110.123	sacrabosco de sphera
110.124	narbrokes confession
110.125	tilimannus de erroribus
110.126	disciplina de verbo dei
110.127	gemephrisius
110.128	questiones besi
110.129	periones de vitis sanctorum

110.130	2a pars orationum tullii
110.131	hessius de sacramentis
110.132	Johannis de sacrabosco
110.133	Chitreus exodum
110.134	Ambrosius in apocalypsim
110.135	Epistole osorii ad reginam
110.136	Exkeus de sacraficio misse
110.137	vita Juelli
110.138	Catakismus noelli
110.139	opera lyri in 7 voluminibus
110.140	opera chrisostimi
110.141	cronica Coclei
110.142	Eckeus in Lutherum
110.143	postilla majoris
110.144	Epistole Augustini
110.145	Thomas aquinas de sentenciis
110.146	boccasius
110.147	dixonarium Eliotti
110.148	boetius
110.149	questiones Augustini
110.150	hollond de ordine heremetarum
110.151	Ludolphus de vita christi
110.152	augustinus in psalmos
110.153	sermones de tempore
110.154	distructorium viciorum
110.155	sententie lombardi
110.156	confutatio hessei
110.157	titilman super matheum
110.158	Lutherus adversus Rophensem
110.159	askhame scholemaster
110.160	Sermones Bartrandi
110.161	opuscula hugonis
110.162	metiorum Aristotelis
110.163	omilia gregorii
110.164	Sermones de tempore
110.165	conciones fabricii ebraice
110.166	opera nisephori
110.167	velcurio in phisicam
110.168	theologia damaseni
110.169	platana de vitis pontificum
110.170	fabule Isopi grece et latine
110.171	eximii doctor
110.172	Sermones pipini
110.173	holcott in proverbia salamonis
110.174	Apophthegmata licostenis

110.175 pallingelius
110.176 Epithomi plutarchi
110.177 polidorus de Inventoribus
110.178 Sermones bartrandi
110.179 Sermones de tempore
110.180 dixionarium poeticum
110.181 omilia ad regem
110.182 Scotus
110.183 Tullii ad herenium cum commento
110.184 omilia heckii
110.185 psalterium grece et hebraice
110.186 osorius de gloria
110.187 philosophia wildenbergii
110.188 exempla licostenis
110.189 Epistole longolii
110.190 Epistole manusii
110.191 Tomus 2us Nisephori
110.192:A similia licostenis
110.192:B [See 110.192:A]
110.193 theophylacke in omnes epistolas pauli
110.194 summa Angelica
110.195 questiones tusculani commento
110.196 tertium volumen orationis tullii
110.197 Sermones de tempore
110.198 historia scholastica
110.199 de laudibus sanctorum
110.200 historia Justini cum commento
110.201 barnardinus de senis
110.202 sermones de voragine
110.203 fabule Isopi grece et latine
110.204 omilia Clitovii
110.205 sententie chytrei
110.206 omilia heckii tomus 2us
110.207 tirosinus de sacro altare
110.208 opus super sententias
110.209 confessio fidei
110.210 Rethorica quinctiliani
110.211 Johnson adversus Hopperum
110.212 confessio fidei
110.213 boemius de moribus gentium
110.214 concilium tridentinum
110.215 haymo in omnes Epistolas pauli
110.216 historiae affricani
110.217 flores Epigrammatum
110.218 proverbia salamonis

110.219	ovidius metamorphoses
110.220	gramatica saeporini
110.221	lucius florus de gestis romanorum
110.222	exembla eborasencia
110.223	brandolinus de conscribendis epistolis
110.224	methodus emingii
110.225	Rupertus de divinis officiis
110.226	granatensis
110.227	Ethica Aristotelis grece
110.228	officia ciceronis
110.229	Sententiae Ciceronis
110.230	ficinus de vita
110.231	problemata Aristotelis
110.232	Innosentius
110.233	particiones Sturmii
110.234	patricius
110.235	basilius de spiritu sancto
110.236	grammatica linacri
110.237	hiperius
110.238	Epigrammata Soteri
110.239	confessio fidei
110.240	de furoribus galliae
110.241	marulus
110.242	apthonius
110.243	concordantiae bibliae
110.244	hiperius de sacra lectione
110.245	Enchiridion Eckii
110.246	perionius de rebus gestis
110.247:1	topica hiperii et antididagma
110.247:2	[See 110.247:1]
110.248	confessio genevensis
110.249	dialectica Setonis
110.250	confessio hofmester
110.251:1	liber poeticus et salust
110.251:2	[See 110.250:1]
110.252	dialogi luciani grece
110.253	albinus in sal***ius [psalmos?]
110.254	Scorus
110.255	Ilia homeri
110.256	philosophia Adriani
110.257	altomerus
110.258	liturgius
110.259	historia selii secundi
110.260	Sententiae in lutherum
110.261	gualterus de quantitate sillabarum

110.262 psalmi titilmani
110.263 fenestella
110.264 copia verborum
110.265 Algerus de eucharistia
110.266 Smyth contra lutherum
110.267 therentius
110.268 Epistole Ciceronis
110.269:1-2 ii paper bookes in folio
110.270 opera Juelli

§

110.1 Ecclesiastica historia Eusebei
Eusebius, *Pamphili, Bishop. Historia ecclesiastica*. Continent: date indeterminable.
Language(s): Latin. Appraised at 4s in 1576.

110.2 loci communes Andree musculi
Andreas Musculus. *Loci communes sacri*. Continent: 1563-1573.
Printed at Erfurt and Leipzig (Adams M2003-2005; VD16 M7181-7183). See also 110.62. *Language(s)*: Latin. Appraised at 3s in 1576.

110.3 opera Aristotelis grece
Aristotle. [*Works*]. Continent: date indeterminable.
Either the Aldus Manutius (Venice, 1495-1498) edition (GW 2334), or, more likely, Erasmus's Basle edition of 1531-1552 (Adams A1730-1733). *Language(s)*: Greek. Appraised at 3s 4d in 1576.

110.4 Christomi [Chrisostomi] opera
John, *Chrysostom, Saint*. [*Works*]. Continent: date indeterminable.
See also 110.140. *Language(s)*: Latin. Appraised at 4s in 1576.

110.5 gualterus in Johannem
Rudolph Walther. [*John: commentary and text*]. (*Bible-N.T.*). Zürich: Christoph Froschouer, 1565-1575.
Language(s): Latin. Appraised at 3s in 1576.

110.6 Adagia Erasmi
Desiderius Erasmus. *Adagia*. Continent: date indeterminable.
Language(s): Latin. Appraised at 8d in 1576.

110.7 5tus tomus
Unidentified. Place unknown: stationer unknown, date indeterminable.
STC/non-STC status unknown. *Language(s)*: Latin (probable). Appraised at 6d in 1576.

110.8 commentaria budei
Gulielmus Budaeus. *Commentarii linguae graecae.* Continent: 1529-1556. See Adams B3093-3097 and VD16 B9086-9088. *Language(s)*: Greek Latin. Appraised at 5s in 1576.

110.9 gualterus super Lucam
Rudolph Walther. [*Luke: commentary and text*]. *(Bible–N.T.).* Zürich: Christoph Froschouer, 1557-1573.
Language(s): Latin. Appraised at 3s 4d in 1576.

110.10 divus Thomas in epistolas pauli
Thomas Aquinas, Saint. [*Epistles–Paul: commentary*]. Continent: date indeterminable.
Language(s): Latin. Appraised at 8d in 1576.

110.11 augustinus in fratres in heremo
Augustine, Saint. *Sermones ad heremitas.* Continent: date indeterminable.
Language(s): Latin. Appraised at 6d in 1576.

110.12 Ederus
Georg Eder. Unidentified. Continent: date indeterminable.
Language(s): Latin (probable). Appraised at 2s in 1576.

110.13 gualterus in epistolas pauli in Chorintios
Rudolph Walther. *In priorem (posteriorem) D. Pauli ad Corinthios epistolam homiliae. (Bible–N.T.).* Zürich: Christoph Froschouer, 1572.
Language(s): Latin. Appraised at 3s in 1576.

110.14 petrus marter in genesim
Pietro Martire Vermigli (Peter Martyr). *In primum librum Mosis, qui vulgo Genesis dicitur, commentarii. (Bible–O.T.).* Zürich: Christoph Froschouer, 1569.
Adams M770. *Language(s)*: Latin. Appraised at 2s 6d in 1576.

110.15 gualterus in acta
Rudolph Walther. [*Acts: commentary and text*]. *(Bible–N.T.).* Continent: date indeterminable.
Printed at Zürich and Lyons (Adams G1385-1389). *Language(s)*: Latin. Appraised at 2s 6d in 1576.

110.16 Cronologia funcii
Johann Funck. *Chronologia.* Continent: date indeterminable.
Language(s): Latin. Appraised at 3s in 1576.

110.17 brunus de heretecis
Conrad Brunus. Unidentified. Continent: date indeterminable.
Either *Libri sex de hereticis in genere*, 1549 (see Adams B2962; VD16 B7202) or, given the appraisal, more likely *Breve introductorium de haereticis, e sex libris eius excerptum*, 1548 (VD17 7203; Klaiber 350). *Language(s)*: Latin. Appraised at 6d in 1576.

110.18 Clavis scripture
Matthias Flacius, *Illyricus*. *Clavis scripturae*. Basle: probably Joannes Oporinus, Eusebius Episcopius, and Paul Quecus, 1567.
Basil Hall (Greenslade 1963, 87) gives 1562 as the *editio princeps* of this work, but that date is not confirmed anywhere else. *Language(s)*: Latin. Appraised at 6s in 1576.

110.19 opera barnardi
Bernard, *Saint*. [*Works*]. Continent: date indeterminable.
It is possible, but very unlikely, that the *Opuscula* (published only as incunables) is meant. See GW 3905-3908. *Language(s)*: Latin. Appraised at 20d in 1576.

110.20 flaccus de vitis pontificum
Matthias Flacius, *Illyricus*. Perhaps *De sectis, dissensionibus, scriptorum et doctorum pontificiorum liber*. Continent: date indeterminable.
Language(s): Latin. Appraised at 12d in 1576.

110.21 marter in reges
Pietro Martire Vermigli (Peter Martyr) and Johann Wolf, *of Zürich*. [*Kings: commentary and text*]. (*Bible–O.T.*). Zürich: Christoph Froschouer, 1566-1571.
Language(s): Latin. Appraised at 4s in 1576.

110.22 panoplia lundani in 4 Evangelia
Willelmus Lindanus, *Bishop*. *Panoplia evangelica*. Continent: 1559-1575. *Language(s)*: Latin. Appraised at 16d in 1576.

110.23 biblia grece
The Bible. Continent: date indeterminable.
Language(s): Greek. Appraised at 4s in 1576.

110.24 cornucopia
Unidentified. Continent: date indeterminable.
Possible authors include Nicolaus Perottus, Eustathius, *Bishop of Thessalonica*, and Joannes Ravisius, *Textor*. *Language(s)*: Latin (probable) Greek (perhaps). Appraised at 6d in 1576.

110.25 Laviterus super prophetis
Ludwig Lavater. Unidentified. Continent: date indeterminable.
Lavater wrote on Ezechiel, Ezra, and Nehemiah. *Language(s)*: Latin. Appraised at 3s 4d in 1576.

110.26 lavater in paralipomenon
Ludwig Lavater. *In libros Paralipomenon sive Chronicorum commentarius. (Bible–O.T.)*. Zürich: Christoph Froschouer, 1573.
Language(s): Latin. Appraised at 2s in 1576.

110.27 Chemniz in consilium tredentinum
Martinus Chemnitius. *Examen concilii Tridentini*. Frankfurt am Main: (different houses), 1566–1574.
It is likely that the 1574 one-volume folio edition is meant at this valuation. See Adams C1438; VD16 C2169. *Language(s)*: Latin. Appraised at 2s in 1576.

110.28 polianthea
Dominicus Nannus, *Mirabellius. Polyanthea*. Continent: date indeterminable. *Language(s)*: Latin. Appraised at 12d in 1576.

110.29 gualterus super marcum
Rudolph Walther. [*Mark: commentary and text*]. *(Bible–N.T.)*. Continent: 1561–1570.
Language(s): Latin. Appraised at 2s in 1576.

110.30 wolfius in officia ciceronis
Marcus Tullius Cicero. *De officiis*. Edited by Hieronymus Wolfius. Continent: date indeterminable.
At least two editions are known to have been issued at Basle (1563 and 1569). *Language(s)*: Latin. Appraised at 2s in 1576.

110.31 opera Cipriani
Cyprian, *Saint*. [*Works*]. Continent: date indeterminable.
Language(s): Latin. Appraised at 12d in 1576.

110.32 Tomas aquinas super 4 evangelia
Thomas Aquinas, *Saint*. [*Gospels: commentary*]. Continent: date indeterminable.
Language(s): Latin. Appraised at 8d in 1576.

110.33 gualterus in prophetas
Rudolph Walther. [*Minor prophets: commentary and text*]. *(Bible–O.T.)*. Zürich: Christoph Froschouer, 1563–1572.
Language(s): Latin. Appraised at 4s in 1576.

110.34 petrus marter in romanos
Pietro Martire Vermigli (Peter Martyr). [*Romans: commentary*]. Continent: 1558–1570.
Language(s): Latin. Appraised at 4s in 1576.

110.35 opera Josephi
Flavius Josephus. [*Works*]. Continent: date indeterminable.
Possibly in Greek (Basle: Froben, 1544). *Language(s)*: Latin (probable). Appraised at 2s in 1576.

110.36 Calvinus in genecem
Jean Calvin. [*Genesis: commentary*]. Continent: date indeterminable.
The entry indicates a separate Genesis commentary, but it is possible that *Mosis libri V, cum J. Calvini commentariis, Genesis seorsum, reliqui quatuor in formam harmoniae digesti* is meant. See Adams C275–276. *Language(s)*: Latin. Appraised at 4s in 1576.

110.37 Erasmi annotaciones in novum testamentum
Desiderius Erasmus. [*New Testament: commentary*]. Continent: date indeterminable.
Language(s): Latin. Appraised at 12d in 1576.

110.38 gualterus in romanos
Rudolph Walther. [*Romans: commentary and text*]. (*Bible–N.T.*). Zürich: Christoph Froschouer, 1566–1572.
Language(s): Latin. Appraised at 12d in 1576.

110.39 Calvinus in Eseam
Jean Calvin. [*Isaiah: commentary*]. Geneva: Joannes Crispinus, 1551–1559.
Language(s): Latin. Appraised at 4s in 1576.

110.40 the pollegi of England
Perhaps John Jewel, *Bishop. An apologie, or aunswer in defence of the Church of England*. London: R. Wolfe 1562–1564.
STC 14590 *et seq. Language(s)*: English. Appraised at 2d in 1576.

110.41 bullengerus in pocalypsim
Heinrich Bullinger. [*Revelation: commentary*]. Basle: (different houses), 1557–1570.
Staedtke, nos. 327–329. *Language(s)*: Latin. Appraised at 12d in 1576.

110.42 Claudius in omnes epistolas pauli
Unidentified. Continent (probable): date indeterminable.
Probably not an STC book. Claudius Guilliaudus wrote such a commentary. Other less likely authors are Claudius Seysell (so Adams) or *Altissido-*

rensis (so BL), *Archbishop of Turin*, and Claude d'Espence, both of whom published commentaries on individual Pauline epistles, but not on the complete corpus, in the sixteenth century. *Language(s)*: Latin (probable). Appraised at 12d in 1576.

110.43 hermonia Calvini
Jean Calvin. *Harmonia*. Geneva: (different houses), 1555-1572. Language(s): Latin. Appraised at 4s in 1576.

110.44 Calinus [Calvinus] in omnes epistolas pauli
Jean Calvin. [*Epistles–Paul: commentary*]. Geneva: (different houses), 1551-1565.
Language(s): Latin. Appraised at 3s in 1576.

110.45 Calvinus in prophetas ger [germanice?]
Jean Calvin. Unidentified. Place unknown: stationer unknown, date indeterminable.

STC/non-STC status unknown. A German translation of Calvin's commentary upon the minor prophets, or of a collection of his commentaries upon the major prophets, or both? Just possibly *Bildenüs eins newen Propheten auss Franckreich herbracht* (Paris: V. Gautherot, 1539; BL), but this is very unlikely in view of the appraised value. Johnson's books give no other evidence of his reading German, and the *ger* could be, perhaps, *gen* for Geneva or even a phonetic abbreviation for Jeremiah, from Calvin's commentary on Jeremiah issued with a commentary on Lamentations (Jeremiah leading) in 1563, and issued alone in 1576. *Language(s)*: German (perhaps) Latin (perhaps). Appraised at 3s in 1576.

110.46 Instituciones Calvini
Jean Calvin. *Institutio Christianae religionis*. Continent (probable): date indeterminable.

Probably not an STC book, but see STC 4414. If, as it appears, a Latin edition, the two 1576 editions (Lausanne, London) are less likely to have been in a collection of one who died in May, 1576, than earlier editions, especially as the 1576 editions are octavo and not likely to have been appraised at 2s. *Language(s)*: Latin. Appraised at 2s in 1576.

110.47 hemengius in omnes epistolas pauli
Niels Hemmingsen. Probably *Commentaria in omnes epistolas Apostolorum, Pauli, Petri, Judae, Johannis, Jacobi, et in eam quae ad Hebraeos inscribitur. (Bible–N.T.)*. Leipzig: Andreas Schneider, typis Voegeliansis, 1572.

Possibly the entry, *omnes epistolas pauli*, is a mistaken assimilation; see 110.42 and 110.44, but the long title, from Adams B1862, does cite Paul first. *Language(s)*: Latin. Appraised at 4s in 1576.

110.48 petrus marter in 2 librum samuelis
Pietro Martire Vermigli (Peter Martyr). [*Samuel: commentary*]. Zürich: Christoph Froschouer, 1564-1575.
Language(s): Latin. Appraised at 2s in 1576.

110.49 buserus in psalmos
Martin Bucer. [*Psalms: commentary and text*]. *(Bible–O.T.).* Continent: 1529-1554.
The Geneva 1554 edition is the likeliest possibility, the others being issued under Bucer's pseudonym, Felinus. *Language(s)*: Latin. Appraised at 5s in 1576.

110.50 hamelmannus de tradicionibus
Hermann Hamelmann. *De traditionibus apostolicis.* Continent: 1555-1568.
Language(s): Latin. Appraised at 12d in 1576.

110.51 Epit' August'
Augustine, *Saint. Omnium operum epitome.* Continent: date indeterminable.
Language(s): Latin. Appraised at 16d in 1576.

110.52 politica Aristotelis commento
Aristotle. *Politica.* Continent: date indeterminable.
Language(s): Latin (probable) Greek (perhaps). Appraised at 8d in 1576.

110.53 biblia pagnini
The Bible. Translated and edited by Sanctes Pagninus. Continent: date indeterminable.
Language(s): Greek Hebrew Latin. Appraised at 2s 6d in 1576.

110.54 Cromerus
Martin Cromer, *Bishop.* Unidentified. Place unknown: stationer unknown, date indeterminable.
STC/non-STC status unknown. *De falsa nostri temporis, et vera Christi religione* is perhaps the most likely identification, given the theological interest of the rest of the collection, followed by *A notable example of God's vengeance uppon a murdering king,* STC 6046. But Cromer was also a prolific historian of Poland. *Language(s)*: Latin (probable) English (perhaps). Appraised at 6d in 1576.

110.55 lavater in Josuam
Ludwig Lavater. [*Joshua: commentary*]. Continent: 1565-1567.
Printed at Zürich by Christoph Froschouer in 1565 and at Leipzig by E. Voegelin in 1567. See Adams L305 and VD16 B3035-3036. *Language(s)*: Latin. Appraised at 8d in 1576.

110.56 Calvinus in psalmos
Jean Calvin. [*Psalms: commentary and text*]. *(Bible–O.T.)*. Geneva: (different houses), 1557–1564.

Probably not an STC book, but see STC 4395. *Language(s)*: Latin. Appraised at 18d in 1576.

110.57 Calvinus in Ezecheil
Jean Calvin. *In viginti prima Ezechielis prophetae capita praelectiones*. Edited by J. Budaeus and C. Jonvillaeus, with preface by Théodore de Bèze. Geneva: François Perrin, 1565.

The only Latin edition by the date of this inventory. *Language(s)*: Latin. Appraised at 18d in 1576.

110.58 Concilii West'
Bartholomaeus Westheimer. [*Conciliatio sacrae scripturae et patrum*]. Continent: 1536–1563.

Language(s): Latin. Appraised at 10d in 1576.

110.59 grammatica Cevelerii
Antonius Rodolphus Cevallerius. Perhaps *Rudimenta hebraicae linguae*. Continent: 1560–1574.

Language(s): Hebrew Latin. Appraised at 16d in 1576.

110.60 bridges supper
Probably John Bridges, *Bishop. The supremacie of christian princes*. London: H. Bynneman for H. Toye, 1573.

STC 3737. The conjecture is that *supper* is an abbreviation or mistranscription for "supremacie." *Language(s)*: English. Appraised at 16d in 1576.

110.61 loci Communes hiperii
Andreas Gerardus, *Hyperius*. [*Methodus theologiae sive loci communes*]. Basle: Joannes Oporinus, 1567–1574.

Language(s): Latin. Appraised at 12d in 1576.

110.62 loci communes musculi
Wolfgang Musculus. *Loci communes*. Continent: 1560–1573.

Possibly another copy of the *Loci communes* of the less well-known Andreas Musculus. See Adams M2003. See 110.2. *Language(s)*: Latin. Appraised at 20d in 1576.

110.63 opera Clementis
Unidentified. Continent: date indeterminable.

It is impossible to say whether the *Opera omnia* of Clement I, *Saint, Pope* or of Clement, *of Alexandria* is meant. See Adams C2114–2118 and C2104–2109 respectively. *Language(s)*: Latin. Appraised at 18d in 1576.

110.64 cronica slidani
Joannes Philippson, *Sleidanus*. Unidentified. Continent (probable): date indeterminable.
Probably not an STC book, but see STC 19848 and 19849. Either *De quatuor summis imperiis*, translated as *A briefe chronicle* (STC 19849) or *De statu religionis et reipublicae, Carolo Quinto, Caesare, commentarii*, translated as *A famous cronicle of our time* (STC 19848). See also 110.112. *Language(s)*: Latin (probable). Appraised at 12d in 1576.

110.65 opera epipheni
Epiphanius, *Bishop of Constantia*. [*Works*]. Basle: Joannes Hervagius, 1544. *Language(s)*: Greek. Appraised at 20d in 1576.

110.66 ozorius de justicia
Jeronimo Osorio da Fonseca, *Bishop*. *De justitia*. Continent: 1564-1572. *Language(s)*: Latin. Appraised at 8d in 1576.

110.67 Conciliorum colleccio
[*Councils of the church*]. Continent: date indeterminable.
Editions of Merlin, Crabbe, Sagittarius, and Surius should be considered. See Adams C2766-2772. *Language(s)*: Latin. Appraised at 6d in 1576.

110.68 novum testamentum grece et latine
[*Bible–N.T.*]. Continent: date indeterminable.
The editions of Erasmus, Bèze, and Montanus should be considered. See Adams B1686-1703. *Language(s)*: Greek Latin. Appraised at 8d in 1576.

110.69 problemata Aretii
Benedictus Aretius. [*Problemata theologica*]. Lausanne: Franciscus Le Preux, 1573-1576.
See EUL 1:144 for these editions. *Language(s)*: Latin. Appraised at 12d in 1576.

110.70 opuscula hiperii
Andreas Gerardus, *Hyperius*. *Opuscula theologica*. Edited by Hieronymus Vietor. Basle: ex officina Oporiniana, 1570-1571 (single edition).
Language(s): Latin. Appraised at 12d in 1576.

110.71 Instituciones bullengeri
Pierre Boulenger. *Institutionum christianarum libri octo*. Paris: Sebastian Nivelle and Guillaume Desboys, 1560-1561.
Language(s): Latin. Appraised at 6d in 1576.

110.72 Lutherus ad galathas
Martin Luther. [*Galatians: commentary*]. Continent: 1519-1563.

It is impossible to determine whether this is the 1519 commentary or the expanded work of 1535. See Benzing 416-426 and 3183-3187. *Language(s)*: Latin. Appraised at 6d in 1576.

110.73 opera fulgentii
Fulgentius, *Bishop of Ruspa*. [*Works*]. Continent: 1519-1574. *Language(s)*: Latin. Appraised at 10d in 1576.

110.74 Epistole bezi
Théodore de Bèze. *Epistolarum theologicarum liber unus*. Geneva: Eustathius Vignon, 1573-1575.
Gardy, nos. 296-98. *Language(s)*: Latin. Appraised at 4d in 1576.

110.75 opera Justini
Justinus, *Martyr*. [*Works*]. Continent: date indeterminable.
Less likely is Robert Stephanus's Greek edition (Paris, 1551); see Adams J494. Possible translators are Joachim Perion (Paris, 1554), Sigmund Gelen (Basle, 1555), and Johann Lang (Basle, 1565). *Language(s)*: Latin (probable). Appraised at 6d in 1576.

110.76 opera justini [Dionysii] ariopagitae
Dionysius *Areopagita*. [*Works*]. Continent: date indeterminable.
Possibly a Greek edition (see Adams D519-520). *Language(s)*: Latin (probable). Appraised at 6d in 1576.

110.77 loci communes melancton
Philipp Melanchthon. [*Loci communes theologici*]. Continent: date indeterminable.
Many editions from 1521; see Keen pp. 84-90 for most. *Language(s)*: Latin. Appraised at 8d in 1576.

110.78 gardiner de sacramentis
Stephen Gardiner, *Bishop*. Unidentified. Place unknown: stationer unknown, date indeterminable.
STC/non-STC status unknown. Possibly either STC 11592, *An explication and assertion of the true Catholic faith, touching the sacrament of the altar* (Rouen [?London]: R. Caly, 1551) or *Confutatio cavillationum quibus sacrosanctum Eucharistiae sacramentum ... impeti solet* (1522, 1554; Shaaber, G13-14). See 110.88 for what may be another copy. *Language(s)*: Latin (probable) English (perhaps). Appraised at 4d in 1576.

110.79 osorius de institucione regis
Jeronimo Osorio da Fonseca, *Bishop*. *De regis institutione et disciplina*. Continent: 1571-1574.
Printed at Lisbon and Cologne. *Language(s)*: Latin. Appraised at 8d in 1576.

110.80 abdias
Abdias, *Bishop of Babylon*. [*De historia certaminis apostolici*]. Continent: 1552-1576.
Sometimes with other works, particularly Joachim Perion's *De rebus gestis apostolorum*. *Language(s)*: Latin. Appraised at 6d in 1576.

110.81 Cronica fulgencii
Unidentified. Continent (probable): date indeterminable.
Probably not an STC book. Just possibly the *Mythologiae* of Fabius Planciades Fulgentius. *Language(s)*: Latin (probable). Appraised at 8d in 1576.

110.82 orationes Isocratis grece et latine
Isocrates. Probably [*Works*]. Continent: date indeterminable.
Language(s): Greek Latin. Appraised at 20d in 1576.

110.83 major in Epistolam ad Ebreos
Georg Meier, *Professor at Wittenberg*. *Enarratio epistolae ad Hebraeos*. Wittenberg: ex officina Joannis Lufft, 1571.
Language(s): Latin. Appraised at 10d in 1576.

110.84 philo Judeus de script' [scripturis]
Philo, *Judaeus*. Unidentified. Continent: date indeterminable.
Language(s): Latin. Appraised at 12d in 1576.

110.85 hiperius de ratione studii
Andreas Gerardus, *Hyperius*. *De theologo, sive De ratione studii theologici*. Continent: 1556-1572.
Printed at Basle and Strassburg. *Language(s)*: Latin. Appraised at 10d in 1576.

110.86 conciones funebres
Unidentified. Place unknown: stationer unknown, date indeterminable.
STC/non-STC status unknown. Among the possibilities are Fridericus Nausea, *Concio funebris* (1539) and Edmund Grindal, *Concio funebris in obitum ... Ferdinandi caesaris* (1564), STC 12378. Just possibly Johnson's own manuscript sermons. See also 110.122. *Language(s)*: Latin. Appraised at 8d in 1576.

110.87 methodus pauli in duobus
Simon Paulii, *the Elder*. *Methodi aliquot locorum doctrinae ecclesiae Dei*. Continent: 1565-1573.
Printed at Rostock and Magdeburg. *Language(s)*: Latin. Appraised at 20d in 1576.

110.88 stephanus de sanctis
Unidentified. Continent (probable): date indeterminable.

Probably not an STC book. A work written or printed by an Estienne? Perhaps a garbled entry representing Stephen Gardiner, *Bishop*, on the sacraments (see Shaaber G13-14). See 110.78. *Language(s)*: Latin (probable). Appraised at 4d in 1576.

110.89 instituciones hopperi
Joachim Hopper. *Institutiones imperiales. (Corpus juris civilis)*. Cologne: apud haered. of Joannis Quentel et Gervinum Calenium, 1560.
Language(s): Latin. Appraised at 10d in 1576.

110.90 testamentum Erasmi
[*Bible–N.T.*]. Edited by Desiderius Erasmus. Continent: 1516-1575.
Language(s): Latin Greek (probable). Appraised at 6d in 1576.

110.91 summa conciliorum
Bartolome Carranza, *Archbishop*. [*Summa conciliorum*]. Continent: 1546-1576.
Language(s): Latin. Appraised at 8d in 1576.

110.92 opera Irinei
Irenaeus, *Saint*. [*Adversus haereses*]. Continent: 1526-1576.
Language(s): Latin. Appraised at 10d in 1576.

110.93 Enchiridion hemingii
Niels Hemmingsen. *Enchiridion theologicum*. Continent: 1559-1568.
Language(s): Latin. Appraised at 4d in 1576.

110.94 Epithomi pagnini Ebre' [Ebreici]
Sanctes Pagninus. *Thesauri linguae sanctae epitome*. Antwerp: Christopher Plantin, 1570-1572.
Normally issued with 110.103. *Language(s)*: Hebrew Latin. Appraised at 8d in 1576.

110.95 annotaciones Monsteri Ebraice latine
Sebastian Muenster. Unidentified. Continent: date indeterminable.
The relatively high appraisal suggests a sizable volume, such as the *Institutio elementaria in Hebraicam linguam* based on the Hebrew grammar of Elias, *Levita*. Compare the cheaper (and therefore shorter?) 110.99. *Language(s)*: Hebrew Latin. Appraised at 8d in 1576.

110.96 grammatica Campensis
Joannes Campensis. [*Grammatica hebraica*]. Continent: 1520-1553.
Based on the Hebrew grammar of Elias, *Levita*. *Language(s)*: Hebrew Latin. Appraised at 4d in 1576.

110.97 omilia Helmesii in 2bus
Heinrich Helmesius. [*Homiliae*]. Continent: date indeterminable.
Language(s): Latin. Appraised at 10d in 1576.

110.98 postilla spangilbergii in 3bus
Johann Spangenberg. [*Gospels and Epistles (liturgical): commentary and text*]. *(Bible–N.T.)*. Continent: 1547–1564.
Language(s): Latin. Appraised at 2s in 1576.

110.99 gramatica Monsteri Ebraica
Sebastian Muenster. [*Grammatica hebraica*]. Continent: date indeterminable.
It is impossible to say which of Muenster's Hebrew grammars is meant. This item is, however, presumably shorter than the more highly appraised 110.95. *Language(s)*: Hebrew Latin. Appraised at 4d in 1576.

110.100 postilla Roiardi in 4
Joannes Royardus. [*Homiliae*]. Continent: date indeterminable.
It is impossible to say which of Royardus's series of homilies is meant. The *Homiliae in omnes Epistolas Dominicales et Festivitates sanctorum* was published in four volumes (Antwerp: J. Graphaeus and J. Steels, 1546–1567). See Klaiber no. 2699. *Language(s)*: Latin. Appraised at 16d in 1576.

110.101 Calvinus in Josuam
Jean Calvin. [*Joshua: commentary*]. Geneva: (different houses), 1564–1575.
Language(s): Latin. Appraised at 6d in 1576.

110.102 Epistole chytrei
David Chytraeus. *Dispositiones epistolarum*. Wittenberg: (different houses), 1563–1576.
Language(s): Latin. Appraised at 6d in 1576.

110.103 biblia Ebreica in 7m [septem]
Biblia sacra Hebraica, Chaldaice, Graece, et Latine. (*The Bible*). Edited by Benito Arias Montano. Antwerp: Christopher Plantin, 1569–1572.
In seven volumes. Usually issued with Pagninus's *Thesauri hebraice linguae epitome grammatices libellus* (see 110.94). *Language(s)*: Chaldaic Greek Hebrew Latin Syriac. Appraised at 7s in 1576.

110.104 2a pars postille firiensis
Probably Joannes Ferus (Johann Wild, *Prediger zu Mainz*). [*Postilla*]. Continent: date indeterminable.
Language(s): Latin. Appraised at 4d in 1576.

110.105 halicarnoseus in 2bus de originibus romanis
Dionysius, *of Halicarnassus*. *Antiquitates sive origines Romanae*. Continent: date indeterminable.
Language(s): Latin. Appraised at 12d in 1576.

110.106 Snoeus in psalmos
Raynerius Snoy, *Goudanus*. [*Psalms: paraphrase and text*]. *(Bible–O.T.)*. Continent: date indeterminable. 1538–1544.
Language(s): Latin. Appraised at 6d in 1576.

110.107 cronica Carionis
Johann Carion. *Chronica*. Continent: date indeterminable.
The 1550 English translation (STC 4626) is but a remote possibility. *Language(s)*: Latin. Appraised at 4d in 1576.

110.108 retorica tullii
Marcus Tullius Cicero. Unidentified. Place unknown: stationer unknown, date indeterminable.
STC/non-STC status unknown. Any of Cicero's rhetorical works, or any combination of them, may be represented. It is most likely to be either part of an *Opera omnia* (see Adams C1638-1657) or the spurious *Rhetorica ad Herennium* (see Adams C1674-1692; 1700-1703; STC 5323.5). *Language(s)*: Latin. Appraised at 6d in 1576.

110.109:1 Thomus 1us philo: Tho: 1us orat: tullii
Marcus Tullius Cicero. [*Selected works–Philosophica*]. Continent: date indeterminable.
First part of the double entry is interpreted to mean the first book of Cicero's philosophical works. *Language(s)*: Latin. Appraised with one other at 8d in 1576.

110.109:2 [See 110.109:1]
Marcus Tullius Cicero. [*Selected works–Orations*]. Continent: date indeterminable.
The second part of the double entry is interpreted to mean the first book of Cicero's orations. See 110.130 and 110.196. *Language(s)*: Latin. Appraised with one other at 8d in 1576.

110.110 Epistole ad aticum
Marcus Tullius Cicero. *Epistolae ad Atticum*. Continent: date indeterminable.
Perhaps, rather, a collection containing the letters *Ad Brutum* and *Ad Quintum fratrem*. *Language(s)*: Latin. Appraised at 4d in 1576.

110.111 garrettus de sacrificio messe
Joannes Garetius. *Sacrificii missae ex Sanctis Patribus assertio*. Continent: 1561-1569.
Language(s): Latin. Appraised at 4d in 1576.

110.112 cronica sleade' [sleadeni]
Joannes Philippson, *Sleidanus*. Unidentified. Continent (probable): date indeterminable.

Probably not an STC book, but see STC 19848 and 19849. Either *De quatuor summis imperiis*, translated as *A briefe chronicle* (STC 19849) or *De statu religionis et reipublicae, Carolo Quinto, Caesare, commentarii*, translated as *A famous cronicle of our time* (STC 19848). See also 110.64. *Language(s)*: Latin (probable). Appraised at 6d in 1576.

110.113 meditaciones Augustini
Augustine, *Saint* (spurious). *Meditationes*. Continent: date indeterminable. *Language(s)*: Latin. Appraised at 4d in 1576.

110.114 chitreus in leviticum
David Chytraeus. [*Leviticus: commentary*]. Wittenberg: (different houses), 1569-1575.
Language(s): Latin. Appraised at 4d in 1576.

110.115 cronica palentini
Unidentified. Continent (probable): date indeterminable.
Probably not an STC book. Possibly a work by the Spanish historian Alfonso Fernandez de Palencia (Alphonus Palentinus) or, less likely, the *Chronographia ecclesiae christianae* of Henricus Pantaleon. *Language(s)*: Latin. Appraised at 6d in 1576.

110.116 chitreus de electione
David Chytraeus. *De lectione historiarum*. Continent: 1563-1565.
Language(s): Latin. Appraised at 4d in 1576.

110.117 chitreus in numerum
David Chytraeus. *In Numeros enarratio*. Wittenberg: Johann Crato, 1572.
Language(s): Latin. Appraised at 4d in 1576.

110.118 cronica Surii
Laurentius Surius. *Commentaria brevis rerum in orbe gestarum*. Continent: 1566-1574.
Four editions of this work, chronicling events from 1500 to 1566, 1567, 1568, and 1574 respectively, were published before the date of the inventory. *Language(s)*: Latin. Appraised at 6d in 1576.

110.119 chitreus in genesim
David Chytraeus. [*Genesis: commentary*]. Wittenberg: Johann Crato, 1557-1576.
Language(s): Latin. Appraised at 4d in 1576.

110.120 lavater de spectris
Ludwig Lavater. *De spectris*. Geneva: (different houses), date indeterminable.
There was an English translation in 1572 (STC 15320). *Language(s)*: Latin. Appraised at 4d in 1576.

110.121 Cathakismus hemingeii
Niels Hemmingsen. *Catechismi quaestiones concinnatae.* Continent: 1562–1570.
Printed at Leipzig and Wittenberg. *Language(s)*: Latin. Appraised at 4d in 1576.

110.122 conciones funebres
Unidentified. Place unknown: stationer unknown, date indeterminable. STC/non-STC status unknown. Just possibly Johnson's own manuscript sermons. See also 110.86 where the possibilities of works by Nausea and by Grindal are mentioned. *Language(s)*: Latin. Appraised at 4d in 1576.

110.123 sacrabosco de sphera
John Holywood (Joannes Sacrobosco). *Sphaera mundi.* Continent: date indeterminable.
See also 110.132. Shaaber H277–H412. *Language(s)*: Latin. Appraised at 2d in 1576.

110.124 narbrokes confession
John Northbrooke. Probably *Spiritus est.... A breefe and pithy summe of the christian faith.* London: J. Kingston for W. Williamson, 1571.
STC 18663. *Language(s)*: English. Appraised at 6d in 1576.

110.125 tilimannus de erroribus
Tilemannus Heshusius. *Sexcenti errores pleni blasphemiis in Deum.* Frankfurt am Main: apud Georgius Corvinum, 1572.
Language(s): Latin. Appraised at 2d in 1576.

110.126 disciplina de verbo dei
Perhaps Walter Travers. *Ecclesiastica disciplina.* Heidelberg: Michael Schirat, 1574.
False imprint reads: Rupellae, excudebat Adamus de Monte. Shaaber T110 and Adams T915. Translated by Thomas Cartwright as *A full and plaine declaration of ecclesiasticall discipline* (STC 24184). *Language(s)*: Latin. Appraised at 2d in 1576.

110.127 gemephrisius
Reiner Gemma, *Frisius.* Unidentified. Continent: date indeterminable.
Probably the *Arithmeticae practicae methodus facilis* or else an astronomical work. *Language(s)*: Latin. Appraised at 2d in 1576.

110.128 questiones besi
Théodore de Bèze. *Quaestionum et responsionum christianarum libellus.* Britain or Continent: 1570–1576.
STC 2036 and non-STC. The English translation, STC 2037–38 (1572,

1574), is a remote possibility. The Second Part (*pars altera*), was first issued in 1576, the year of this inventory. *Language(s)*: Latin. Appraised at 2d in 1576.

110.129 periones de vitis sanctorum
Joachim Perion. *De sanctorum virorum, qui Patriarchae ab Ecclesia appellantur, rebus gestis ac vitis.* Continent: 1555.

Printed at Paris and Cologne. *Language(s)*: Latin. Appraised at 2d in 1576.

110.130 2a pars orationum tullii
Marcus Tullius Cicero. [*Selected works–Orations*]. Continent: date indeterminable.

It is impossible to say which three-volume edition of the *Orationes* this part is from, but the following possible issues were divided into *partes* rather than *volumina*: Adams C1856, 1857–1859, 1861, 1862, 1865, 1867. The expression, however, may be simply descriptive. In either case 110.109:2 and 110.196 may be parts of the same edition. *Language(s)*: Latin. Appraised at 4d in 1576.

110.131 hessius de sacramentis
Unidentified. Place unknown: stationer unknown, date indeterminable.

STC/non-STC status unknown. Perhaps one of Tilemann Heshusius's works on the sacraments, none of which actually carries the phrase *de sacramentis* in the title. See, for example, Adams H460 and H467; see also 110.78. Other possibilities include something by either Helius Eobanus, *Hessus* or Hermannus Schottenius, *Hessus*. *Language(s)*: Latin (probable). Appraised at 2d in 1576.

110.132 Johannis de sacrabosco
John Holywood (Joannes Sacrobosco). Unidentified. Continent: date indeterminable.

Possibly *De sphaera*, or some variant of it, but see also 110.123. *Language(s)*: Latin. Appraised at 2d in 1576.

110.133 Chitreus exodum
David Chytraeus. [*Exodus: commentary*]. Wittenberg: Johann Crato, 1561–1570.

Language(s): Latin. Appraised at 4d in 1576.

110.134 Ambrosius in apocalypsim
Unidentified. [*Revelation: commentary*]. Continent: date indeterminable.

Possibly either the *Expositio super Apocalypsin* of Saint Ambrose or, perhaps less likely, *In Apocalypsim libri decem* of Ambrosius Autpertus (*Ansbertus*). *Language(s)*: Latin. Appraised at 4d in 1576.

110.135 Epistole osorii ad reginam
Jeronimo Osorio da Fonseca, *Bishop*. *Epistola ad Elisabetam, Angliae Reginam*. Continent: 1562-1575.
Two English editions in 1565 (STC 18887-88). *Language(s)*: Latin. Appraised at 2d in 1576.

110.136 Exkeus de sacraficio misse
Joannes Eckius. *De sacrificio missae contra Lutheranos*. Continent: 1526-1562. *Language(s)*: Latin. Appraised at 2d in 1576.

110.137 vita Juelli
Laurence Humphrey. *Joannis Juelli Angli, episcopi Sarisburiensis vita et mors, eiusque; verae doctrinae defensio*. London: apud J. Dayum, 1573.
STC 13963. *Language(s)*: Latin. Appraised at 8d in 1576.

110.138 Catakismus noelli
Alexander Nowell. *Catechismus*. London: (different houses), 1570-1576.
STC 18701 *et seq*. It is impossible to decide which of Nowell's three catechisms is meant, but it is most likely the largest and most scholarly version, the *Catechismus, sive prima institutio, disciplinaque pietatis christianae*. *Language(s)*: Latin Greek (perhaps). Appraised at 4d in 1576.

110.139 opera lyri in 7 voluminibus
Probably *The Bible*. Continent: date indeterminable.
With *glossa ordinaria* by Lyra, usually with others contributing. The seventh volume would be the *Repertorium* if this is indeed the six-part version of the Bible issued from 1501 on, but the seven volumes may not be a single edition and could represent part of the Bible and Lyra's widely issued *Postilla*, conveniently described by the compiler as *opera*. *Language(s)*: Latin. Appraised at 6s in 1576.

110.140 opera chrisostimi
John, *Chrysostom, Saint*. [*Works*]. Continent: date indeterminable.
See also 110.4. *Language(s)*: Latin. Appraised at 10s in 1576.

110.141 cronica Coclei
Joannes Cochlaeus (Johann Dobneck). Unidentified. Continent: date indeterminable.
Just possibly either the *Commentaria (Historia) de actis et scriptis M. Lutheri* or the *Historiae Hussitarum libri duodecim*. *Language(s)*: Latin. Appraised at 12d in 1576.

110.142 Eckeus in Lutherum
Joannes Eckius. Unidentified. Place unknown: stationer unknown, date indeterminable.

STC/non-STC status unknown. A number of possibilities including *De sacrificio missae contra Lutheranos, Enchiridion locorum communium adversus Lutheranos*, and *Prima (-quinta) pars operum contra Ludderum*; at 8d one of the smaller works is more likely. *Language(s)*: Latin. Appraised at 8d in 1576.

110.143 postilla majoris
[*Postillae majores*]. *(Bible–N.T.)*. Continent: date indeterminable.
Sermons by either Joannes Major or Georg Meier, *Professor of Wittenberg* (also known as Georgius Majores) are very remote possibilities. *Language(s)*: Latin. Appraised at 4d in 1576.

110.144 Epistole Augustini
Augustine, *Saint. Epistolae*. Continent: date indeterminable.
See also 110.51. *Language(s)*: Latin. Appraised at 4d in 1576.

110.145 Thomas aquinas de sentenciis
Thomas Aquinas, *Saint*. [*Sentences: commentary*]. Continent: date indeterminable.
Language(s): Latin. Appraised at 6d in 1576.

110.146 boccasius
Giovanni Boccaccio. Unidentified. Continent (probable): date indeterminable.
Probably not an STC book. An English translation is possible, but unlikely. *Language(s)*: Latin (probable). Appraised at 6d in 1576.

110.147 dixonarium Eliotti
Sir Thomas Elyot. *The dictionary of syr Thomas Eliot*. London: Thomas Berthelet, 1538–1559.
STC 7659 *et seq*. *Language(s)*: English Latin. Appraised at 4s in 1576.

110.148 boetius
Anicius M.T.S. Boethius. Perhaps *De consolatione philosophiae*. Continent (probable): date indeterminable.
Probably not an STC book, but see STC 3199 *et seq*. The valuation strongly suggests the *De consolatione philosophiae*. *Language(s)*: Latin (probable). Appraised at 2d in 1576.

110.149 questiones Augustini
Augustine, *Saint. Quaestiones evangeliorum*. Cologne: Joannes Gymnicus, 1529–1530.
VD16 A4230 for the 1530 edition; Villanova University holds the only 1529 edition found. *Language(s)*: Latin. Appraised at 4d in 1576.

110.150 hollond de ordine heremetarum
Unidentified. Place unknown: stationer unknown, date indeterminable. STC/non-STC status unknown. *Language(s)*: Latin. Appraised at 4d in 1576.

110.151 Ludolphus de vita christi
Ludolphus, *de Saxonia*. *Vita Jesu Christi*. Continent: date indeterminable. *Language(s)*: Latin. Appraisal illegible.

110.152 augustinus in psalmos
Augustine, *Saint*. [*Psalms: commentary*]. Continent: date indeterminable. This item is marked with a cross in the margin. *Language(s)*: Latin. Appraisal illegible.

110.153 sermones de tempore
Unidentified [sermons]. Continent: date indeterminable.
See also 110.164, 110.179, and 110.197. The only remote STC possibility is a 1510 collection by Joannes Herolt (Discipulus). *Language(s)*: Latin. Appraised at 4d in 1576.

110.154 distructorium viciorum
Alexander, *Anglus* (Alexander Carpenter). *Destructorium viciorum*. Continent: 1480–1521.
See Shaaber A217–227. *Language(s)*: Latin. Appraised at 4d in 1576.

110.155 sententie lombardi
Peter Lombard. *Sententiarum libri IIII*. Continent: date indeterminable. *Language(s)*: Latin. Appraised at 4d in 1576.

110.156 confutatio hessei
Unidentified. Continent (probable): date indeterminable.
Almost certainly not an STC book. Perhaps either Joannes Hessel's *Confutatio novitiae fidei* or his *Confutatio cujusdam haereticae confessionis Teutonicae*. A more remote possibility is the *Confutatio prolegomenon Brentii* of Stanislaus Hozyusz, *Cardinal*. See Klaiber nos. 1512, 1520, and 1603. *Language(s)*: Latin (probable). Appraised at 6d in 1576.

110.157 titilman super matheum
Franz Titelmann. *Paraphrastica elucidatio in Evangelium secundum Matthaeum*. (*Bible–N.T.*). Antwerp: in officina J. Steelsii; typis S. Coqui, 1545. *Language(s)*: Latin. Appraised at 4d in 1576.

110.158 Lutherus adversus Rophensem
Martin Luther. Unidentified. Continent (probable): date indeterminable.
Probably not an STC book. Perhaps either a slip for "Rophensis adversus

Lutherum," or a reference to Luther's refutation of Henry VIII's *Assertio septem sacramentorum*, which the compiler may have attributed to John Fisher, a common misattribution at the time. *Language(s)*: Latin (probable). Appraised at 4d in 1576.

110.159 askhame scholemaster
Roger Ascham. *The scholemaster or plaine and perfite way of teachyng children, the Latin tong.* London: J. Daye, 1570–1573.
STC 832 *et seq. Language(s)*: English Latin. Appraised at 4d in 1576.

110.160 Sermones Bartrandi
Bertrandus, *de Turre*. [*Sermones*]. Strassburg: (different houses), 1500–1502. See also 110.178. *Language(s)*: Latin. Appraised at 2d in 1576.

110.161 opuscula hugonis
Perhaps Hugo, *de Sancto Victore*. Unidentified. Continent (probable): date indeterminable.
Probably not an STC book. *Language(s)*: Latin (probable). Appraised at 4d in 1576.

110.162 metiorum Aristotelis
Aristotle (spurious). *Meteorologica*. Continent: date indeterminable.
Language(s): Latin. Appraised at 6d in 1576.

110.163 omilia gregorii
Gregory I, *Saint, Pope*. [*Homiliae super Evangeliis*]. Continent: date indeterminable.
Language(s): Latin. Appraised at 4d in 1576.

110.164 Sermones de tempore
Unidentified [sermons]. Continent: date indeterminable.
See also 110.153, 110.179, and 110.197. The only remote STC possibility is a 1510 collection by Joannes Herolt (Discipulus). *Language(s)*: Latin. Appraised at 4d in 1576.

110.165 conciones fabricii ebraice
Unidentified. Continent: date indeterminable.
The possibilities include Wolfgang Fabricius Capito, *Institutionum Hebraicarum libri duo* (Basle, 1518); Theodorus Fabritius, *Institutiones in linguam sanctam* (Cologne, 1528); and works by the hebraicists Gui and Nicolas Le Fèvre de la Boderie. *Language(s)*: Hebrew Latin. Appraised at 4d in 1576.

110.166 opera nisephori
Nicephorus Callistus. *Ecclesiastica historia*. Continent: date indeterminable.

See 110.191 for what is probably the second volume. *Language(s)*: Latin. Appraised at 2d in 1576.

110.167 velcurio in phisicam
Joannes Velcurio. [*Aristotle–Physica: commentary*]. Continent: 1537–1575. *Language(s)*: Latin. Appraised at 6d in 1576.

110.168 theologia damaseni
John, *of Damascus, Saint*. *Theologia*. Paris: Henricus Stephanus, 1507–1519. *Language(s)*: Latin. Appraised at 4d in 1576.

110.169 platana de vitis pontificum
Bartolomeo Platina, Onofrio Panvino, Antonio Cicceralla, and Abraham Bzowski. *Historia de vitis pontificum*. Continent: date indeterminable. *Language(s)*: Latin. Appraised at 6d in 1576.

110.170 fabule Isopi grece et latine
Aesop. *Fabulae*. Continent: date indeterminable.
See also 110.203. *Language(s)*: Greek Latin. Appraised at 3d in 1576.

110.171 eximii doctor
Unidentified. Place unknown: stationer unknown, date indeterminable. STC/non-STC status unknown. Several works beginning *Eximii doctoris* . . . could be intended, perhaps one of the most likely being Erasmus's *Eximii doctoris Hieronymi Stridonensis vita*. *Language(s)*: Latin (probable). Appraised at 4d in 1576.

110.172 Sermones pipini
Guillaume Pepin. [*Sermones*]. Continent: date indeterminable. *Language(s)*: Latin. Appraised at 4d in 1576.

110.173 holcott in proverbia salamonis
Robert Holcot. [*Proverbs: commentary*]. Paris: (different houses), 1510–1518.
Language(s): Latin. Appraised at 4d in 1576.

110.174 Apophthegmata licostenis
Conrad Lycosthenes (Wolffhart). *Apophthegmata*. Continent: 1555–1574. *Language(s)*: Latin. Appraised at 12d in 1576.

110.175 pallingelius
Probably Marcellus Palingenius (Pietro Angelo Manzolli [Stellatus]). *Zodiacus vitae*. Britain or Continent: date indeterminable.
STC 19138.5 *et seq*. and non-STC. *Language(s)*: Latin (probable) English (perhaps). Appraised at 4d in 1576.

110.176 Epithomi plutarchi
Plutarch. [*Vitae parallelae–Epitome*]. Continent: date indeterminable.
Language(s): Latin. Appraised at 4d in 1576.

110.177 polidorus de Inventoribus
Polydorus Vergilius. *De inventoribus rebum*. Continent: date indeterminable.
Language(s): Latin. Appraised at 4d in 1576.

110.178 Sermones bartrandi
Bertrandus, *de Turre*. [*Sermones*]. Continent: 1500–1502.
See also 110.160. *Language(s)*: Latin. Appraised at 4d in 1576.

110.179 Sermones de tempore
Unidentified [sermons]. Continent: date indeterminable.
See also 110.153, 110.164, and 110.197. The only remote STC possibility is a 1510 collection by Joannes Herolt (Disciplus). *Language(s)*: Latin. Appraised at 6d in 1576.

110.180 dixionarium poeticum
Probably Hermann Torrentinus. [*Elucidarius carminum*]. Continent: date indeterminable.
Difficult to distinguish this widely published work from Robert Estienne's work, *Dictionarium historicum ac poeticum*. *Language(s)*: Latin. Appraised at 6d in 1576.

110.181 omilia ad regem
Unidentified. Place unknown: stationer unknown, date indeterminable.
STC/non-STC status unknown. *Language(s)*: Latin (probable). Appraised at 4d in 1576.

110.182 Scotus
John Duns, *Scotus*. Unidentified. Continent: date indeterminable.
Language(s): Latin. Appraised at 4d in 1576.

110.183 Tullii ad herenium cum commento
Marcus Tullius Cicero (spurious). *Rhetorica ad Herennium*. Britain or Continent: date indeterminable.
STC 5323.5 and non-STC. *Language(s)*: Latin. Appraised at 6d in 1576.

110.184 omilia heckii
Joannes Eckius. [*Homiliae*]. Continent: date indeterminable.
See also 110.206. *Language(s)*: Latin. Appraised at 4d in 1576.

110.185 psalterium grece et hebraice
[*Bible–O.T.–Psalms*]. Continent: date indeterminable.

Probably with a Latin translation not noted. *Language(s)*: Greek Hebrew. Appraised at 6d in 1576.

110.186 osorius de gloria
Jeronimo Osorio da Fonseca, *Bishop*. *De gloria*. Continent: date indeterminable.
Conceivably Osorio's *Selected works* with *De gloria* leading. *Language(s)*: Latin. Appraised at 8d in 1576.

110.187 philosophia wildenbergii
Hieronymus Wildenbergius. Perhaps *Totius philosophiae humanae digestio*. Paris: Jean Roigny, 1553.
Possibly, but less likely, the same author's *Totius naturalis philosophiae in Physicam Aristotelis epitome*. *Language(s)*: Latin. Appraised at 4d in 1576.

110.188 exempla licostenis
Lucius Domitius Brusonius. *Facetiarum exemplorumque libri VII*. Edited by Conrad Lycosthenes (Wolffhart). Continent: 1559-1562.
Printed at Basle and Lyon. *Language(s)*: Latin. Appraised at 6d in 1576.

110.189 Epistole longolii
Christophorus Longolius. [*Epistolae*]. Continent: 1533-1570.
The *Epistolae* appeared as early as 1524 in a *Selected works*. *Language(s)*: Latin. Appraised at 4d in 1576.

110.190 Epistole manusii
Paolo Manuzio. [*Epistolae*]. Britain or Continent: 1558-1575.
STC 17286 *et seq.* and non-STC. *Language(s)*: Latin. Appraised at 4d in 1576.

110.191 Tomus 2us Nisephori
Nicephorus Callistus. Probably *Ecclesiastica historia*. Continent: date indeterminable.
Part of a two-volume set; see 110.166 for what is probably the first volume. *Language(s)*: Latin. Appraised at 8d in 1576.

110.192:A similia licostenis
Conrad Lycosthenes (Wolffhart). *Similium loci communes*. Basle: per E. Episcopium et Nicolai fr. haeredes, 1575 (composite publication).
Language(s): Latin. Appraised [a composite volume] at 6d in 1576.

110.192:B [See 110.192:A]
Theodor Zwinger. *Similitudinem methodo*. [Composite publication].
Language(s): Latin. Appraised [a composite volume] at 6d in 1576.

110.193 theophylacke in omnes epistolas pauli
Theophylact, *Archbishop of Achrida*. [*Epistles–Paul: commentary and text*]. (*Bible–N.T.*). Continent: date indeterminable.
Language(s): Latin. Appraised at 6d in 1576.

110.194 summa Angelica
Angelus de Clavasio. *Summa Angelica*. Continent: date indeterminable.
Language(s): Latin. Appraised at 3d in 1576.

110.195 questiones tusculani commento
Marcus Tullius Cicero. *Quaestiones Tusculanae*. Continent: date indeterminable.
This text was published at Paris between 1509 and 1549 with commentaries by P. Beroaldus and G. Valla (see Adams C1797ff.). *Language(s)*: Latin. Appraised at 4d in 1576.

110.196 tertium volumen orationis tullii
Marcus Tullius Cicero. [*Selected works–Orations*]. Continent: date indeterminable.
See the annotation to 110.130. See also 110.109:2. *Language(s)*: Latin. Appraised at 4d in 1576.

110.197 Sermones de tempore
Unidentified [sermons]. Continent: date indeterminable.
See also 110.153, 110.164, and 110.179. The only remote STC possibility is a 1510 collection by Joannes Herolt (Discipulus). *Language(s)*: Latin. Appraised at 4d in 1576.

110.198 historia scholastica
Petrus, *Comestor*. *Historia scholastica*. Continent: date indeterminable.
Language(s): Latin. Appraised at 4d in 1576.

110.199 de laudibus sanctorum
Unidentified. Place unknown: stationer unknown, date indeterminable.
STC/non-STC status unknown. Possibly Robertus Caracciolus, *Bishop*, *Sermones de laudibus sanctorum (Sermones de sanctis)*; apparently all editions incunables, but other collections of *Sermones de sanctis* might very well be so listed from a long title or an incipit. See the collection by Franciscus de Mayronis: *Sermones de laudibus sanctorum et tractatum* (Hain 10531). *Language(s)*: Latin (probable). Appraised at 4d in 1576.

110.200 historia Justini cum commento
Trogus Pompeius and Justinus, *the Historian*. [*Epitomae in Trogi Pompeii historias*]. Britain or Continent: date indeterminable.
STC 24287 and non-STC. The text was published with the commentary

of Sichard at Basle in 1530 (Adams J727), and with that of Philipp Melanchthon and Georg Major (Georg Meier, *Professor at Wittenberg*) at Hagenau in 1533 (Adams J728). STC 24287 also carries commentary. *Language(s)*: Latin. Appraised at 4d in 1576.

110.201 barnardinus de senis
Bernardinus, *of Siena, Saint*. Unidentified. Continent (probable): date indeterminable.

Probably not an STC book, but see STC 1966. *Language(s)*: Latin (probable). Appraised at 2d in 1576.

110.202 sermones de voragine
Jacobus de Voragine. [*Sermones*]. Continent: date indeterminable. *Language(s)*: Latin. Appraised at 2d in 1576.

110.203 fabule Isopi grece et latine
Aesop. *Fabulae*. Continent: date indeterminable.
See also 110.170. *Language(s)*: Greek Latin. Appraised at 4d in 1576.

110.204 omilia Clitovii
Jodocus Clichtoveus. [*Homiliae*]. Continent: date indeterminable. *Language(s)*: Latin. Appraised at 2d in 1576.

110.205 sententie chytrei
David Chytraeus. Unidentified. Continent: date indeterminable.
See BCI 2:208. *Language(s)*: Latin. Appraised at 3d in 1576.

110.206 omilia heckii tomus 2us
Joannes Eckius. [*Homiliae*]. Continent: date indeterminable.
Possibly the second of a four-volume set (Ingolstadt 1536–1540) or of a three-volume set (Paris 1538–1540). See Adams E52–55. See 110.184. *Language(s)*: Latin. Appraised at 4d in 1576.

110.207 tirosinus de sacro altare
Unidentified. Continent (probable): date indeterminable.
Probably not an STC book. Possibly a liturgical manual. *Language(s)*: Latin. Appraised at 4d in 1576.

110.208 opus super sententias
Unidentified. [*Sentences: commentary*]. Continent: date indeterminable. *Language(s)*: Latin. Appraised at 2d in 1576.

110.209 confessio fidei
Unidentified. Place unknown: stationer unknown, date indeterminable. STC/non-STC status unknown. See also 110.212 and 110.239. Presum-

ably one of the many published confessions of Protestant churches on the Continent. *Language(s)*: Latin. Appraised at 4d in 1576.

110.210 Rethorica quinctiliani
Marcus Fabius Quintilianus. *Institutiones oratoriae*. Continent: date indeterminable.
Language(s): Latin. Appraised at 4d in 1576.

110.211 Johnson adversus Hopperum
Henry Joliffe and Robert Jonson. [*Responsio ad articulos Joannis Hoperi*]. Antwerp: ex officina Christophori Plantini, 1564.
Language(s): Latin. Appraised at 4d in 1576.

110.212 confessio fidei
Unidentified. Place unknown: stationer unknown, date indeterminable. STC/non-STC status unknown. Presumably one of the many published confessions of Protestant churches on the Continent. See also 110.209 and 110.239. *Language(s)*: Latin. Appraised at 3d in 1576.

110.213 boemius de moribus gentium
Joannes Boemus. [*Omnium gentium mores, leges et ritus*]. Continent: 1520-1571.

The English translations of various parts (STC 3196.5-3198.5) would almost certainly not be so entered. *Language(s)*: Latin. Appraised at 2d in 1576.

110.214 concilium tridentinum
Probably *Acta Concilii Tridentini*. (*Councils-Trent*). Continent: 1546-1569.
Conceivably, but less likely, the *Canones et decreta Concilii Tridentini*. See Adams C2783-89. *Language(s)*: Latin. Appraised at 2d in 1576.

110.215 haymo in omnes Epistolas pauli
Haymo, *Bishop of Halberstadt*. [*Epistles-Paul: commentary*]. Continent: 1519-1550.
Some editions contain the text. *Language(s)*: Latin. Appraised at 4d in 1576.

110.216 historiae affricani
Optatus, *Saint*. [*De schismate Donatistarum*]. Continent: 1549-1569.
Editio princeps in 1543, but with works by others. *Language(s)*: Latin. Appraised at 4d in 1576.

110.217 flores Epigrammatum
Probably *Anthologia graeca*. Continent: date indeterminable.
Epigrammata graeca is a less likely possibility with this entry, especially since it appears at 110.238. *Language(s)*: Greek Latin. Appraised at 4d in 1576.

110.218 proverbia salamonis
[*Bible–O.T.–Proverbs*]. Continent (probable): date indeterminable.
Probably not an STC book, but see STC 2752 *et seq.* and 2759.7 *et seq.*
Language(s): Latin (probable). Appraised at 2d in 1576.

110.219 ovidius metamorphoses
Publius Ovidius Naso. *Metamorphoses*. Continent: date indeterminable.
Language(s): Latin (probable) Greek (perhaps). Appraised at 3d in 1576.

110.220 gramatica saeporini
Jacobus Ceporinus. *Compendium grammaticae graecae*. Continent: 1539–1553.
Language(s): Greek Latin. Appraised at 3d in 1576.

110.221 lucius florus de gestis romanorum
Lucius Annaeus Florus. [*Epitomae de Tito Livio bellorum omnium annorum*]. Continent: date indeterminable.
Language(s): Latin. Appraised at 3d in 1576.

110.222 exembla eborasencia
Lucius Andreas Resendius (Andreas Eborensis). *Sententia et exempla ex probatissimis quibusque scriptoris collecta*. Continent: 1557–1569.
Language(s): Latin. Appraised at 4d in 1576.

110.223 brandolinus de conscribendis epistolis
Aurelius Brandolinus (Lippus). *De ratione scribendi*. Britain or Continent: 1549–1573.
STC 3542 and non-STC. Editions usually include other works. *Language(s)*: Latin. Appraised at 4d in 1576.

110.224 methodus emingii
Niels Hemmingsen. Unidentified. Continent: date indeterminable.
Either the *De lege naturae apodicta methodus* (see Adams H196–97) or the *De methodis libri duo* (see Adams H199). *Language(s)*: Latin. Appraised at 2d in 1576.

110.225 Rupertus de divinis officiis
Rupert, *of Deutz*. *De divinis officiis*. Cologne: (different houses), 1526–1557.
Earlier editions by Arnold Birckman, the 1557 by his heirs. *Language(s)*: Latin. Appraised at 4d in 1576.

110.226 granatensis
Luis, *de Granada*. Unidentified. Continent: date indeterminable.
The form of the entry would rule out the translation listed in the STC.
Language(s): Latin. Appraised at 2d in 1576.

110.227 Ethica Aristotelis grece
Aristotle. *Ethica*. Continent: date indeterminable.
Language(s): Greek. Appraised at 4d in 1576.

110.228 officia ciceronis
Marcus Tullius Cicero. *De officiis*. Continent: date indeterminable.
Language(s): Latin. Appraised at 2d in 1576.

110.229 Sententiae Ciceronis
Marcus Tullius Cicero. [*Selections*]. Britain or Continent: date indeterminable.
STC 5318.3 and non-STC. *Language(s)*: Latin. Appraised at 4d in 1576.

110.230 ficinus de vita
Marsilio Ficino. [*De triplici vita*]. Continent: date indeterminable.
Language(s): Latin. Appraised at 3d in 1576.

110.231 problemata Aristotelis
Aristotle (spurious). *Problemata*. Continent: date indeterminable.
Language(s): Latin. Appraised at 2d in 1576.

110.232 Innosentius
Unidentified. Place unknown: stationer unknown, date indeterminable.
STC/non-STC status unknown. Innocent III, Innocent IV, and Innocent VIII are all possibilities. *Language(s)*: Latin. Appraised at 2d in 1576.

110.233 particiones Sturmii
Joannes Sturmius. Probably *In partitiones oratorias Ciceronis dialogi*. Continent: 1539–1565.
Possibly the *Partitionum dialectarum libri quatuor*, but rhetoric is more likely in this library. *Language(s)*: Latin. Appraised at 2d in 1576.

110.234 patricius
Unidentified. Continent (probable): date indeterminable.
Probably not an STC book. Perhaps either Francesco Patrizi, *Bishop*, or his namesake, the philosophical writer, both of whose works circulated widely in the universities. *Language(s)*: Latin (probable). Appraised at 4d in 1576.

110.235 basilius de spiritu sancto
Basil, *Saint, the Great*. *Opus argutum De spiritu sancto*. Translated by Desiderius Erasmus. Continent: 1532.
Basle and Paris editions in the same year. *Language(s)*: Latin. Appraised at 2d in 1576.

110.236 grammatica linacri

Thomas Linacre. Probably *Rudimenta grammatices*. Translated by George Buchanan. Britain or Continent: 1525 (probable)–1566.

STC 15636 *et seq.* and non-STC. Widely printed at Antwerp, Basle, London, Lyon, and Paris. The single edition of his *Progymnasmata grammatices vulgaria* (1512) is a far less likely possibility. *Language(s)*: Latin. Appraised at 3d in 1576.

110.237 hiperius

Andreas Gerardus, *Hyperius*. Unidentified. Continent (probable): date indeterminable.

Probably not an STC book, but see STC 11759. *Language(s)*: Latin. Appraised at 2d in 1576.

110.238 Epigrammata Soteri

Epigrammata graeca. Edited by Joannes Soter. Continent: 1525–1544.

Printed at Cologne and Freiburg im Briesgau. See 110.217. *Language(s)*: Greek Latin. Appraised at 2d in 1576.

110.239 confessio fidei

Unidentified. Place unknown: stationer unknown, date indeterminable.

STC/non-STC status unknown. Presumably one of the many published confessions of Protestant churches on the Continent. See also 110.209 and 110.212. *Language(s)*: Latin (probable). Appraised at 4d in 1576.

110.240 de furoribus galliae

François Hotman. *De furoribus Gallicis*. Britain or Continent: 1573.

STC 13844 *et seq.* and non-STC. At least two editions, one from Basle, the other from London, with Edinburgh falsely given in imprint. *Language(s)*: Latin. Appraised at 2d in 1576.

110.241 marulus

Probably Marko Marulic. Unidentified. Continent: date indeterminable.

Michael Tarchaniota Marullus is also a possibility. *Language(s)*: Latin. Appraised at 3d in 1576.

110.242 apthonius

Aphthonius, *Sophista*. *Progymnasmata*. Britain or Continent: date indeterminable.

STC 699 *et seq.* and non-STC. *Language(s)*: Latin. Appraised at 2d in 1576.

110.243 concordantiae bibliae

Unidentified [Biblical concordance]. Continent: date indeterminable. *Language(s)*: Latin. Appraised at 2d in 1576.

110.244 hiperius de sacra lectione
Andreas Gerardus, *Hyperius*. *De sacrae scripturae lectione*. Basle: Joannes Oporinus, 1561-1569.
Language(s): Latin. Appraised at 2d in 1576.

110.245 Enchiridion Eckii
Joannes Eckius. *Enchiridion locorum communium adversus Lutheranos*. Britain or Continent: date indeterminable.
STC 7481.4 and non-STC. *Language(s)*: Latin. Appraised at 2d in 1576.

110.246 perionius de rebus gestis
Joachim Perion. Unidentified. Continent: date indeterminable.
It is impossible to decide which of the author's three works containing "de rebus gestis" in their titles is meant, but the *De rebus gestis, vitisque Apostolorum* is marginally most likely, its title being more consonant with the entry. See 110.129 for one of the other works; the third is *De vita rebusque gestis Jesu Christi*. *Language(s)*: Latin. Appraised at 2d in 1576.

110.247:1 topica hiperii et antididagma
Andreas Gerardus, *Hyperius*. *Topica theologica*. Continent: 1565-1573.
Language(s): Latin. Appraised with one other at 4d in 1576.

110.247:2 [See 110.247:1]
Probably *Antididagma seu Christianae et Catholicae religionis propugnatio*. (*Cologne Cathedral*). Continent: 1544-1549.
Said to be mainly the work of Johann Groepper. *Language(s)*: Latin. Appraised with one other at 4d in 1576.

110.248 confessio genevensis
Probably Théodore de Bèze. *Confessio christianae fidei*. Britain or Continent: 1560-1575.
STC 2006 and non-STC. See BCI 2:90 (Denys 188). *Language(s)*: Latin. Appraised at 3d in 1576.

110.249 dialectica Setonis
John Seton. *Dialectica*. London: (different houses), 1545-1574.
STC 22250 *et seq. Language(s)*: Latin. Appraised at 2d in 1576.

110.250 confessio hofmester
Johann Hoffmeister. Probably *Judicium de articulis Confessionis fidei anno (1530) Augustae exhibitis*. Continent: 1552-1559.
Printed at Mainz and Cologne. See Klaiber no. 1566. *Language(s)*: Latin. Appraised at 2d in 1576.

110.251:1 liber poeticus et salust
Unidentified. Place unknown: stationer unknown, date indeterminable.

STC/non-STC status unknown. *Language(s)*: Latin (probable). Appraised with one other at 2d in 1576.

110.251:2 [See 110.250:1]
Caius Sallustius Crispus. Unidentified. Place unknown: stationer unknown, date indeterminable.
STC/non-STC status unknown. *Language(s)*: Latin. Appraised with one other at 2d in 1576.

110.252 dialogi luciani grece
Lucian, *of Samosata*. Probably [*Works*]. Continent: date indeterminable.
An edition of *Selected works* is also possible. *Language(s)*: Greek. Appraised at 3d in 1576.

110.253 albinus in sal***ius [psalmos?]
Perhaps Alcuin. Unidentified. Continent (probable): date indeterminable.
Probably not an STC book. Possibly *In septem Psalmos poenitentiales et CXVIII. psalmum et in Cantica graduum expositio* (Adams A639). *Language(s)*: Latin. Appraised at 6d in 1576.

110.254 Scorus
Perhaps Antonius Schorus. Unidentified. Continent: date indeterminable.
Less likely, but still possible, is a work by Henricus Schorus (see BCI 2:693). *Language(s)*: Latin. Appraised at 2d in 1576.

110.255 Ilia homeri
Homer. *Iliad*. Continent: date indeterminable.
Language(s): Latin (probable) Greek (perhaps). Appraised at 4d in 1576.

110.256 philosophia Adriani
Hadrianus Castellensis, *Cardinal*. *De vera philosophia*. Continent: 1507–1540.
Language(s): Latin. Appraised at 2d in 1576.

110.257 altomerus
Probably Andreas Althamer. *Conciliatio locorum scripturae*. Continent: 1527–1561.
Language(s): Latin. Appraised at 3d in 1576.

110.258 liturgius
Unidentified. Continent (probable): date indeterminable.
Probably not an STC book. Possibly the *Leitourgikon* of Chrysostom (see Adams L837–844). *Language(s)*: Greek (probable) Latin (perhaps). Appraised at 2d in 1576.

110.259 historia selii secundi
Caelius Secundus Curio. *De bello Melitensi historia nova*. Basle: apud Joannem Oporinum, 1567.
Language(s): Latin. Appraised at 2d in 1576.

110.260 Sententiae in lutherum
Unidentified. Place unknown: stationer unknown, date indeterminable. STC/non-STC status unknown. If not an academic condemnation of Luther (such as those of the universities of Cologne and Louvain [Adams L2078], and Paris [Adams P326, 331]), or a legal condemnation (such as the edict of Worms [Adams C1359]), then conceivably a work based on or in support of Luther. Possibilities include *Insignium sacrae scripturae sententiarum expositiones, quas Martinus Lutherus amicorum bibliis inscribere subinde est solitus* (1548), and *Prophetiae aliquot verae et sententiae insignes ... Martini Lutheri ... de calamitatibus ... Germanis obventuris* (1551?). *Language(s)*: Latin. Appraised at 4d in 1576.

110.261 gualterus de quantitate sillabarum
Rudolph Walther. *De syllabarum et carminum libri duo*. Britain or Continent: 1542-1575.
STC 25011 and non-STC. *Language(s)*: Latin. Appraised at 2d in 1576.

110.262 psalmi titilmani
Franz Titelmann. [*Psalms: commentary and text*]. (Bible–O.T.). Continent: 1531-1573.
Language(s): Latin. Appraised at 2d in 1576.

110.263 fenestella
Andreas Dominicus Floccus (Lucius Fenestella). Unidentified. Continent: date indeterminable.
Language(s): Latin. Appraised at 2d in 1576.

110.264 copia verborum
Desiderius Erasmus. *De duplici copia verborum ac rerum*. Britain or Continent: 1511-1573.
STC 10471.4 *et seq.* and non-STC. *Language(s)*: Latin. Appraised at 2d in 1576.

110.265 Algerus de eucharistia
Alger, *Monk of Cluny*. *De veritate corporis et sanguinis dominici in Eucharistia* [and others]. Continent: 1530-1561.
See Adams J173-175. *Language(s)*: Latin. Appraised at 2d in 1576.

110.266 Smyth contra lutherum
Richard Smith, *Dean*. Unidentified. Continent: date indeterminable.
Language(s): Latin. Appraised at 2d in 1576.

110.267 therentius

Publius Terentius, *Afer*. [*Works*]. Britain or Continent: date indeterminable.

STC 23885 *et seq.* and non-STC. *Language(s)*: Latin. Appraised at 2d in 1576.

110.268 Epistole Ciceronis

Marcus Tullius Cicero. [*Selected works–Epistolae*]. Continent: date indeterminable.

May represent the popular *Epistolae ad familiares*, which was also published in England by the date of this inventory. *Language(s)*: Latin. Appraised at 2d in 1576.

110.269:1-2 ii paper bookes in folio

Unidentified. Provenances unknown: dates indeterminable.

Manuscripts. Perhaps ledgers, but the size may also indicate works in manuscript. *Language(s)*: Unknown. Appraised at 2s in 1576.

110.270 opera Juelli

John Jewel, *Bishop*. Unidentified. London: (different houses), date indeterminable.

No collected work of Jewel was published by the date of this inventory, so the entry must represent a number of separately issued titles. The appraisal compares favorably with other multi-volume entries: see 110.103 at 7s, 110.139 at 6s, and probably 110.18 at 6s and 110.140 at 10s. Since no book so titled could have been in hand, this is an example of the compiler's using Latin for an entry, a characteristic that must be considered when attempting to identify other entries. *Language(s)*: Latin (probable) English (perhaps). Appraised at 6s in 1576.

Richard Slatter. Scholar (M.A.): Inventory. 1576

RUDOLPH P. ALMASY

Richard Slatter (Sclater, Slater, Slatear, Slatier, Slatyer), having proceeded B.A. in 1568 and M.A. in 1572 (Boase, 268), was a fellow of University College when an inventory of "alle suche stuffe as bokes and thinges" found in his study was taken on 21 April 1576. Although the compilers of the inventory twice referred to Slatter as "late" of University College, Foster notes that the inventory was "without averment of decease" and identifies this Richard Slatter with one recorded as a fellow of St. John's College in 1602 (*Alumni Oxonienses* 4:1324 [Sclater]). No other source links the two, and in its varied spellings Slatter is a very common name. Yet, appraisals, absent here, would be expected for an inventory compiled for probate on the owner's decease. Whether the Richard Slatter of University College and the Richard Slatter of St. John's are one cannot be determined, and given that uncertainty, neither can it be determined when the owner of the following list of books died or for what purpose the inventory was compiled.

The small collection consists entirely of theology and Aristotle, with perhaps one book on law. The theology includes at least one volume of Luther's *Works* and perhaps another of the reformer's books. Only one book, a large Bible, is in English.

Oxford University Archives, Bodleian Library: Hyp.B.18.

§

111.1 a great Bible in Englyshe
111.2 Longdobardus in omnes Pauli epistolas
111.3 Calvini Institutio
111.4 Liber Allegoriarum

111.5   Erasmi Paraphrases
111.6   3 et 4 tomus Originis
111.7   Tomus 4us omnium operum Lutheri
111.8   Liber legis de amctionibus [auctionibus?]
111.9   Buridanus in questiones aethecas
111.10 Liber catacius [cartaceus] in folio
111.11 Aristotelis Phisica
111.12 Commentarii Metaphisica Aristotelis

§

111.1 a great Bible in Englyshe
The Bible. Britain or Continent: date indeterminable.
STC 2063 *et seq.* Perhaps a copy of one of the "Great Bibles" (STC 2068 *et seq.*), but more likely the entry simply identifies a large (folio) Bible. See BCI 2:94-98 for the many references to large Latin Bibles as *Biblia magna*. *Language(s)*: English.

111.2 Longdobardus in omnes Pauli epistolas
Peter Lombard. [*Epistles–Paul: commentary and text*]. (*Bible–N.T.*) Paris: (different houses), 1535-1555.
Language(s): Latin.

111.3 Calvini Institutio
Jean Calvin. *Institutio Christianae religionis.* Continent (probable): date indeterminable.
Probably not an STC book, but see STC 4414 and STC 4426.4, which were printed in 1576, the year of this inventory, which was compiled in April. *Language(s)*: Latin.

111.4 Liber Allegoriarum
Unidentified. Continent (probable): date indeterminable.
Probably not an STC book. Various possibilities include Luther's *Allegoriarum, typorum et exemplum veteris et novi testamenti* (Basle, 1561), which would fit Slatter's collection better than, say, much older works of similar titles by Jodocus Badius, *Ascensius* and Hugo, *de Sancto Victore.* For a work definitely by Luther, see 111.7. *Language(s)*: Latin.

111.5 Erasmi Paraphrases
Desiderius Erasmus. [*New Testament: paraphrase*]. (*Bible–N.T.*) Continent: date indeterminable.
Language(s): Latin.

111.6 3 et 4 tomus Originis
Origen. [*Works* (part)]. Continent: date indeterminable.
The 1512 and 1522 Paris editions of Origen's *Opera* by Joannes Parvus and Jodocus Badius, *Ascensius* were published in four volumes. See Adams O279-80. *Language(s)*: Latin.

111.7 Tomus 4us omnium operum Lutheri
Martin Luther. [*Works* (part)]. Continent: date indeterminable.
The fourth volume of Luther's *Works* was published separately in 1552 (Adams L1749 and Benzing 2), in 1570 (Adams L1750), and perhaps in 1574 (Adams L1751). *Language(s)*: Latin.

111.8 Liber legis de amctionibus [auctionibus?]
Unidentified. Continent (probable): date indeterminable.
Probably not an STC book. Perhaps "*actionibus*" instead, and perhaps related to the *Institutes*. *Language(s)*: Latin.

111.9 Buridanus in questiones aethecas
Joannes Buridanus. [*Aristotle–Ethica: commentary*]. Paris: 1489-1518. *Language(s)*: Latin.

111.10 Liber catacius [cartaceus] in folio
Unidentified. Provenance unknown: date indeterminable.
Manuscript. Conceivably a ledger. *Language(s)*: Latin (probable).

111.11 Aristotelis Phisica
Aristotle. *Physica*. Continent: date indeterminable.
There is no indication from Slatter's collection that he knew Greek. *Language(s)*: Latin Greek (perhaps).

111.12 Commentarii Metaphisica Aristotelis
Unidentified. [*Aristotle–Metaphysica: commentary*]. Place unknown: stationer unknown, date indeterminable.
Antonius Andreae's commentary on the *Metaphysics* was printed in England in 1480, though the entry probably represents one of the many Continental publications. *Language(s)*: Latin.

John Tatham. Scholar (M.A.): Probate Inventory. 1576

CHARLES A. HUTTAR

John Tatham (Tatam, Tattam) went to Oxford from the diocese of Lincoln (Fletcher 1974, 250). The size of his library argues against penury; otherwise nothing is known of his family save that an older brother, Thomas, fellow of Lincoln College, had taken degrees in arts (B.A., 1544; M.A. 1548) and supplicated for the B.M. in 1554 (BRUO2, 556–57). Thomas settled in Oxford, marrying an alderman's daughter, and died in 1557 (Wood 1899, 168, 230).

John was elected a probationer fellow of Merton College in 1563 (along with Thomas Bodley), received the B.A. 24 March 1564, and became a full fellow in 1565. In the midst of the squabbles which rent Merton in these years, Tatham seems to have retained the approval of the senior fellows who, in 1567, approved him for presentation for the M.A., though they did not approve some of is peers, and appointed him one of the deans. He was appointed praelector in rhetoric in 1569 and put in charge of the college's gardens ("eligitur hortulanus") for 1573 (*Alumni Oxonienses*, 4:1457; Fletcher 1974, 250; Brodrick 1885, 267; Fletcher 1976, 15, 47).

His administrative talents were recognized in his being chosen in 1573 as one of the university's two proctors along with Edmund Lilley, later to be Vice-Chancellor (Clark 2:ii.55). Not long afterward, the Chancellor of Oxford, the earl of Leicester, faced a crisis at Lincoln College, where recusancy remained strong fifteen years after Elizabeth's accession. Indeed, two successive rectors of Leicester's choosing had gone over to Rome: Francis Babington was deprived in 1563 and fled abroad, and John Bridgewater followed suit in July 1574 (Green 1979, 127–31, 138). Tatham was Leicester's new choice for the position. Already installed in residence at Lincoln, he was chosen to present Bridgewater's resignation to the college and then succeeded as rector almost at once, being confirmed in the position by the college visitor, Thomas Cooper, late Vice-Chancellor and now Bishop of Lincoln (Green 1979, 138–39; *Alumni Oxonienses*, 4:1457). He retained some tutorial duties while rector, in addition to extensive responsibilities in connection with the college's far-flung real estate holdings and with university administration as well as the day-to-day operations of the college (Clark 2:i.247, 2:ii.66n; Green 1979, 150-51, 204, 207, 213). He was, in addition, rector of the parish church in Waterstock, eight miles east of Oxford. But his brief career was nearly over. He died in November 1576 and was buried in the north choir aisle of the collegiate parish church, All Saints', on the 20th (Wood 1899, 211; Clark 2:iv.406) or 30th (*Alumni Oxonienses*, 4:1457).

It is not known whether John Tatham was related to another Thomas Tatham, from Leicestershire, who became a fellow of Merton while John was still at that college (Clark 2:ii.20n, 2:iii.33; Brodrick 1885, 269) and whose 1586 booklist is to appear in PLRE, Volume 6.

During his career at Oxford, John Tatham's library grew to well over 300 volumes (not 900 as given by Ker [473]—see note to 112.222), more than two-thirds of which can be identified in the inventory at least by author. Of this group, at least seventeen were printed in England and up to forty-two others might have been British editions. Ten were written in English, and at least five were English translations, but, as one would expect, the great majority of Tatham's books were in Latin, with a few in Greek and one in Italian. The collection has a strikingly modern bent: well over one-third of the identifiable authors were Tatham's contemporaries, or at least were active in the years of his education and maturity. The rest are about evenly divided between authors of the preceding hundred years and earlier authors, ancient and medieval. Fifteen of Tatham's books were certainly printed in the 1570s, and another seventy or so might have been, though with equal probability they could have been from earlier editions.

His library shelves were well organized, if the inventory is any indication (and it was done so carelessly in other respects that one must suppose the appraisers simply took the books as they came to them). The first twenty volumes or so are nearly all of a theological nature—Bibles, sermons, commonplaces and other handbooks, church fathers, and the like. Then there is a group of Aristotelian texts and commentaries, mostly in natural philosophy. A few lexicographical works are followed by a section of standard classical texts. The next sizable group is of law books, both ecclesiastical (though canon law had not been part of the curriculum for a generation) and civil (112.46-60), followed by theoretical and practical studies of government and of the educational preparation of rulers (112.64-72 [with 112.68 and 112.70 uncertain]; see also 112.26, 112.105-6, and 112.173-77). Then there is more on philosophy and science, some of the latter with a strong magical bent; a section on ethics; and volumes of letters (112.107-17), poetry (112.120, 112.122, 112.124-32), more theology (112.138, 112.140-54 [112.141 uncertain]), history (112.155-63; see also 112.72), and medicine (112.164-66, 112.169; see also 112.99 and 112.102). There are works on grammar and rhetoric (112.172, 112.178-82, 112.184-97, 112.208-10) and logic (112.198-200, 112.202-7, 112.213), with revisionist schools of thought well represented alongside the traditional. Now and then additional volumes on these topics appear outside their groups. Tatham seems to have had an especial fondness, or professional use, for abridgments, epitomes, compendia, digests, handbooks, and collections of excerpts—whether in theology, philosophy, or other subjects. The books of loci communes were standard teaching tools, but they may also—if considered together with such works as 112.19, 112.22, 112.95, 112.103, 112.160, 112.172, 112.190, 112.205-7, and perhaps 112.150, 112.164, 112.203, and 112.221—suggest an interest in the contemporary debates concerning method. Tatham had several books of current religious controversy, with Anglicans, Catholics, and Puritans all represented, but this part of the collection is rather spotty, some major works being omitted. There are, for example, Jewel's *Replie* (112.8) but none of the other works in the Jewel-Harding controversy; Haddon's defense of the English church against Osorius (part of 112.100) but not the work that provoked it, Osorius's open letter to the Queen, although Tatham has three other works by Osorius. On the Continent, French and Swiss reform (112.7, 112.117, 112.140, 112.155, 112.161) interested him more than the Lutheran variety; among Lutherans, his collection leans to those with whom Calvinists might feel some kinship, such as Melanchthon, Peucer, Hemmingsen, and Gerardus, *Hyperius*. A few books reflect the Zürich influence in the Elizabethan settlement (112.3-4, 112.8). Several of Tatham's books have Oxford associations of one sort or another, including 112.4, 112.8, 112.25, 112.27, 112.68, 112.73, 112.100, 112.133, 112.144, 112.149, 112.151, 112.196, and perhaps 112.5.

The inventory was taken 22 December 1576 by Henry Milward, stationer, and Henry Cross, beadle. With one exception (112.58) the first 101 entries and the last five are all in one hand, and 112.102-217 in another. The entries were apparently written in haste, often leading to careless error. In addition to the text here edited (A), the records include a fair copy (B) and a copy of B (C). Textual variants are recorded in the notes.

Oxford University Archives, Bodleian Library: Hyp.B.19.

§

Brodrick, George C. 1885. *Memorials of Merton College, with Biographical Notices of the Wardens and Fellows.* Oxford Historical Society, 4. Oxford: Clarendon Press.

Fletcher, John M., ed. 1974. *Registrum annalium collegii Mertonensis 1521-1567.* Oxford Historical Society, n.s. 23. Oxford: Clarendon Press.

———. 1976. *Registrum annalium collegii Mertonensis 1567-1603.* Oxford Historical Society, n.s. 24. Oxford: Clarendon Press.

Green, Vivian. 1979. *The Commonwealth of Lincoln College 1427-1977*. Oxford: Oxford Univ. Press.

Wood, Anthony. 1899. *Survey of the Antiquities of the City of Oxford*. Ed. Andrew Clark. Volume 3, Addenda and Indexes. Oxford Historical Society, no. 37. Oxford: Clarendon Press.

§

112.1	castalionis Bible
112.2	bible in 4to in englysh
112.3	decadae Bullengeri
112.4	loci communes petri martiris
112.5	loci communes musculi
112.6	Canitius
112.7	Instituciones calvini
112.8	replicatio Juelli
112.9	vita christi
112.10	pars gregorii
112.11	Sermones discipuli
112.12	opera origenis
112.13	1a 2a et 3a pars Ambrosii
112.14	speculum morale
112.15	cronica pant*alii
112.16	**mones [Sermones] parasiensis
112.17	apothegmata licostenes
112.18	loci communes hipperii
112.19	hipperius de studio philoie [philosophie]
112.20	faber stapulensis
112.21	pars augustini
112.22	avoreus in phisica et metaphisica
112.23	paulus venetus
112.24	Johannes canonicus
112.25	scotus super arist elenc
112.26	thomas aquinas super politica
112.27	ocham in phisicam
112.28	phisica Aristois perioni interprete
112.29	phisica Aristotelis Argeropili
112.30	J. canonicus super phisica
112.31	fox super phisica
112.32	dixonarium basilii
112.33	lexicon Ambrosii
112.34	whittgift contra Carter [Cartwright]
112.35	nisolius

112.36	cornucopia latine lingue
112.37	opera Cicer**is
112.38	guido bonatus
112.39	Cineca
112.40	plautus cum comto [commento]
112.41	Adagia Erasmi
112.42	vitae plutharki
112.43	boetius in arithmetica
112.44	albertus magnus
112.45	orat tullii
112.46	vivianus legis peritus
112.47	liber Justiniani
112.48	libellus decretorum
112.49:1-3	tres libri legum
112.50	l**dwode in constituciones Anglie
112.51	maxilanus in regulis juris
112.52	dedacus in decretal
112.53	J acurtius super Institiones
112.54	reforma legum eccliasticarum
112.55	******** super Instituciones
112.56	Lancelottus de jure pontificio
112.57	Instituciones imperiales hoppero authore
112.58	Duarenus
112.59	Epistole decretales gregorii
112.60	libri decretalium bonifacii
112.61	novum testamentum
112.62	Sermones latemeri
112.63	Sermones brodfordi
112.64	Osorius de institucione Regis
112.65	the courteer in englyshe
112.66	Epistole Simiti
112.67	foxius de Institucione Regis
112.68	lodovicus vivus
112.69	Aristo: politica grece
112.70	lorichius
112.71	christian polysye
112.72	viperanus de Rege
112.73	Langthwetes cronacles
112.74	themisteus in Aristot
112.75	paraphrases themistii
112.76	firrerius de immortalitate anime
112.77	carpentarius de natura
112.78	Agrippa de occulta philosophia
112.79	cardanus in ptolomeum
112.80	gardanus de vanitate [varietate]

112.81	Idem de subtilitate
112.82	piuserus de divinitate
112.83	flores Aris
112.84	garseus de meteoris
112.85	foxius de naturis
112.86	faber in phisicam
112.87	velcurio
112.88	vives de officio mariti
112.89	osorius de gloria
112.90	Idem de Justicia
112.91	Ethica melanctonis
112.92	Bonfinius de virginitate
112.93	Agrippa de vanitate scientiarum
112.94	Aulus gelius
112.95	Ringelbergii opera
112.96	Ethica Aristotelis
112.97	pascasius de alea
112.98	Sententie tullii
112.99	gordonius
112.100	haddoni opera
112.101	testamentum grecolatine
112.102	fernelius
112.103	pars 2a hypirii
112.104	hypirii loci communes
112.105	officii ciceronis
112.106	machivell in itali
112.107	guevara epistelles
112.108	golden epistelles by fentun
112.109	manucii epistole
112.110	policiani
112.111	pliniii [sic] epistole
112.112	epistole ciceroni*
112.113	longolius
112.114	Sadoleti epistole
112.115	ascamii epistole
112.116	epistole textoris
112.117	epistole cellii
112.118	enchiridion hemingii
112.119	gortius de figuris
112.120	homeri iliada latine
112.121	augustinus de herecibus
112.122	homiri illias latine
112.123	epitome adagiorum
112.124	homiri illias grece
112.125	horatius

112.126	virgilius
112.127	terentius
112.128	plautus bis
112.129	tragedii cenice
112.130	martial epigram
112.131	ovid metamor
112.132	ovid de tristibus
112.133	grammati linacri
112.134	gram melankto
112.135	a commen gram [grammar]
112.136	collocum erasmi
112.137	valla de lingua la.
112.138	the Secund replye of cartwryght
112.139	berouldi opuscule
112.140	suplitium valentini gentilis
112.141	phylo Judeus
112.142	lombardi sententie
112.143	a syck mans Sawve
112.144	doctor cawfylde agaynst martiall
112.145	homellie Judocii
112.146	lactantius
112.147	ecclesiastica disciplina
112.148	pastor hemingii
112.149	the shyp of Safttye
112.150	compendium theologie
112.151	de adoratione Imaginum
112.152	flaminius in spalmo
112.153	spalterium greco latine
112.154	gerson de immitatione christi
112.155	status gallie
112.156	fabritii histore
112.157	Justinus
112.158	Valerius maxi
112.159	Salustius
112.160	bodinus
112.161	comminei cronicon
112.162	boemus
112.163	Vita plutarchi
112.164	galeni pars
112.165	paracelsus
112.166	ficinus de Vita
112.167	caesars commentar*es
112.168	tunstallus arithmeti
112.169	regiment Sanit*tis
112.170	Biblia Hieronimi

112.171	pollidor Virgill
112.172	epitome Rodolp*i
112.173	xenophon de re puplica
112.174	markcus aurelius
112.175	elyotes governor
112.176	paradinus
112.177	omphalius
112.178	phrasis manutii
112.179	corderius
112.180	scorus de lingua latine
112.181	silvii progimnasmata
112.182	quintilianus
112.183	apiani cosmogra
112.184	melanctonis rethori
112.185	brandolinus
112.186	rethorica ciceronis
112.187	cicero ad herenium
112.188	athoninus
112.189	sturmius de periodis
112.190	hermogines
112.191	trapesuntius
112.192	sturminus in partitionibus
112.193	erasmus de epistolis
112.194	Idem de copie
112.195	Idem de pronuntiatione
112.196	Vivis rethorica
112.197	arisstotilis retho
112.198	organum aristotilis grece
112.199	gorsii dialec
112.200	organum latine
112.201	encomium morie
112.202	perronie dialec
112.203	rodulphi
112.204	valerii tabule
112.205	Rami dialec
112.206	viottus de demonstratione
112.207	dialectica melanctonis
112.208	erithrerius de periedis
112.209	faleti orationis
112.210	orationes demost grec
112.211	aristot metaphys
112.212	Vico merca de animio
112.213	problemata aristo
112.214	compendium philoso
112.215	lucanus

112.216 bebelii facestii
112.217 phisica melanctonis
112.218 oracones demostini
112.219 sambucus
112.220 nunnius
112.221 willikius
112.222 multiple   a great many of lytell bookes in parchment to the nomber of on [one] hundrethe

§

112.1 castalionis Bible
The Bible. Translated by Sebastian Castalio. Basle: (different houses), 1551–1573.

The editions from 1551 to 1556 were produced either by or at the costs of Oporinus; the 1573 edition was by Petrus Perna. *Language(s)*: Latin. Appraised at 5s 4d in 1576.

112.2 bible in 4to in englysh
The Bible. Britain or Continent: 1537–1576.

STC 2065 *et seq*. If the description *in 4to* is reliable, the possibilities begin with the 1537 edition (STC 2065). *Language(s)*: English. Appraised at 5s in 1576.

112.3 decadae Bullengeri
Heinrich Bullinger. *Sermonum decades*. Zürich: Christoph Froschouer, 1549–1567.

Staedtke nos. 179–87. *Language(s)*: Latin. Appraised at 5s in 1576.

112.4 loci communes petri martiris
Pietro Martire Vermigli. *Loci communes*. Edited by Robert Massonius. London: ex typ. J. Kyngstoni, 1576.

STC 24667. The first edition. *Language(s)*: Latin. Appraised at 7s in 1576.

112.5 loci communes musculi
Probably Wolfgang Musculus. *Loci communes*. Continent (probable): 1560–1573.

There was also a *Loci communes* by Andreas Musculus, published in two editions from 1563 to 1573, but the *Loci communes sacrae theologiae* of Wolfgang Musculus was the more popular work. Conceivably Tatham's copy could have been the 1563 English translation (STC 18308) by John Man, the controversial Warden of Merton whose side Tatham supported (see Introduction). *Language(s)*: Latin (probable). Appraised at 5s in 1576.

112.6 Canitius
Petrus Canisius, *Saint*. Perhaps *Authoritates sacrae scripturae*. Continent: 1569–1571.

His more popular work, a catechism (*Summa doctrinae christianae*), would not carry the high appraisal of this, a multi-volume work. *Language(s)*: Latin. Appraised at 6s in 1576.

112.7 Instituciones calvini
Jean Calvin. *Institutio Christianae religionis*. Britain or Continent: date indeterminable.

STC 4414 and non-STC. Apart from translations, the work was not published in England until the year of Tatham's death. He is likely to have had this standard work earlier in his career. *Language(s)*: Latin. Appraised at 4s in 1576.

112.8 replicatio Juelli
John Jewel, *Bishop*. *A replie unto M. Hardinges answeare*. London: H. Wykes, 1565–1566.

STC 14606 *et seq*. The Latin translation of Jewel's *Replie* (STC 14608) did not appear until 1578; hence the inventory entry must refer to the English work—entered in Latin presumably as a mark of its academic stature. See items 112.149 and 112.151 for related works of controversy. *Language(s)*: English. Appraised at 3s in 1576.

112.9 vita christi
Ludolphus, *de Saxonia*. *Vita Jesu Christi*. Continent: date indeterminable. *Language(s)*: Latin. Appraised at 6d in 1576.

112.10 pars gregorii
Probably Gregory I, *Saint, Pope*. [*Works* (part)]. Continent: date indeterminable.

An incomplete set is indicated by *pars*. Of at least fifteen editions during this period, at least five are known in multiple volumes, including the quartos published in Venice, 1571. *Language(s)*: Latin. Appraised at 4d in 1576.

112.11 Sermones discipuli
Joannes Herolt (Discipulus). [*Sermones discipuli*]. Britain or Continent: date indeterminable.

STC 13226 and non-STC. *Language(s)*: Latin. Appraised at 4d in 1576.

112.12 opera origenis
Origen. [*Works*]. Continent: date indeterminable. *Language(s)*: Latin. Appraised at 3s in 1576.

112.13 1a 2a et 3a pars Ambrosii
Ambrose, *Saint*. [*Works*]. Continent: date indeterminable.

Conceivably these three volumes could be a partial set of one of the later editions, 1527–55, in four, five, or six volumes, but only the pre-Erasmian editions were in three "parts," so designated. *Language(s)*: Latin. Appraised at 2s 6d in 1576.

112.14 speculum morale
Unidentified. Continent: date indeterminable.

Either the anonymous early-fourteenth-century compilation, drawn primarily from Aquinas, published alongside the three genuine parts of Vincentius, *Bellovacensis's* (Vincent *de Beauvais*) *Speculum major*, or the *Speculum morale totius sacrae scripturae* of Cardinal Joannes Vitalis de Furno. *Language(s)*: Latin. Appraised at 6d in 1576.

112.15 cronica pant*alii
Heinrich Pantaleon. *Chronographia ecclesiae christianae*. Basle: 1550–1568. *Language(s)*: Latin. Appraised at 8d in 1576.

112.16 **mones [Sermones] parasiensis
Perhaps Paratus. [*Sermones*]. Continent: date indeterminable.

Consider also the *Postillae* of Gulielmus, *Avernus, Bishop of Paris*. *Language(s)*: Latin. Appraised at 4d in 1576.

112.17 apothegmata licostenes
Conrad Lycosthenes (Conrad Wolffhart). *Apophthegmata*. Continent: 1555–1574.

Language(s): Latin. Appraised at 12d in 1576.

112.18 loci communes hipperii
Andreas Gerardus, *Hyperius*. [*Methodus theologiae sive loci communes*]. Basle: Joannes Oporinus, 1567–1574.

See also 112.104; the two might be parts of the same whole. *Language(s)*: Latin. Appraised at 12d in 1576.

112.19 hipperius de studio philoie [philosophie]
Andreas Gerardus, *Hyperius*. *De theologo, sive De ratione studii theologici*. Continent: 1556–1572.

Language(s): Latin. Appraised at 10d in 1576.

112.20 faber stapulensis
Jacobus Faber, *Stapulensis*. Unidentified. Continent: date indeterminable. *Language(s)*: Latin. Appraised at 8d in 1576.

112.21 pars augustini
Augustine, *Saint*. Unidentified. Continent (probable): date indeterminable. Almost certainly not an STC book. Only the 1483? edition of *Excitatio ad*

eleemosynam was published in Latin in England before the date of this inventory as *pars*, likely a part of the *Opera*. *Language(s)*: Latin. Appraised at 4d in 1576.

112.22 avoreus in phisica et metaphisica

Aristotle. [*Works* (part)]. Commentary by Averroes with additions by Leonardo Bruni, *Aretino*. Venice: Bernardinus Stagninus de Tridino, 1489.

"Jhon Tatam procurator Academiae" is written on the flyleaf of the Christ Church copy (McConica 517), which is volume 1 of a five-volume edition. Volume 1 contains the *Physica*, but the *Metaphysica*, named by the compiler, is in the third volume. See GW 2339. The appraisal makes it unlikely that this is the entire five-volume edition. The next item, 112.23, may be a commentary in turn on Averroes. *Language(s)*: Latin. Appraised at 8d in 1576. *Current location*: Christ Church, Oxford, Hyp.I.85.

112.23 paulus venetus

Paulus, *Venetus* (Paulus Nicolettus). Unidentified. Continent: date indeterminable.

Placed as it is among a group of Aristotelian commentaries, mostly on the *Physica*, perhaps his *Expositio super octo libros Physicorum necnon super commento Averrois*. *Language(s)*: Latin. Appraised at 12d in 1576.

112.24 Johannes canonicus

Joannes, *Canonicus*. [*Aristotle–Physica: commentary*]. Britain or Continent: 1475–1520.

STC 14621 and non-STC. The author's only known published work (Shaaber C104-11). See 112.30 for another copy. *Language(s)*: Latin. Appraised at 4d in 1576.

112.25 scotus super arist elenc

John Duns, *Scotus*. [*Aristotle–Sophistici elenchi: commentary*]. Continent: 1493–1520.

Entry struck out in version A and left without an appraised value; not included in version B or C and, therefore, probably not Tatham's book. *Language(s)*: Latin.

112.26 thomas aquinas super politica

Thomas Aquinas, *Saint*. [*Aristotle–Politica: commentary*]. Completed by Petrus de Alvernia. Continent: date indeterminable.

Language(s): Latin. Appraised at 12d in 1576.

112.27 ocham in phisicam

William, *of Occam*. [*Aristotle–Physica: commentary*]. Continent: 1494–1506. Shaaber O16-17. *Language(s)*: Latin. Appraised at 5d in 1576.

112.28 phisica Aristois perioni interprete
Aristotle. *Physica*. Edited and translated by Joachim Perion. Continent: 1549–1576.
Language(s): Latin Greek (perhaps). Appraised at 2s in 1576.

112.29 phisica Aristotelis Argeropili
Aristotle. *Physica*. Translated by Joannes Argyropoulos. Continent: date indeterminable.
In many editions, the *Physica* is followed by other works of Aristotle in translation. *Language(s)*: Latin. Appraised at 4d in 1576.

112.30 J. canonicus super phisica
Joannes, *Canonicus*. [*Aristotle–Physica: commentary*]. Britain or Continent: 1475–1520.
STC 14621 and non-STC. Preceding the entry, the word *questiones* has been struck out, as if the cataloguer had begun to copy the title. See also 112.24. *Language(s)*: Latin. Appraised at 6d in 1576.

112.31 fox super phisica
Unidentified. [*Aristotle–Physica: commentary*]. Continent (probable): date indeterminable.
Probably not an STC book. A puzzling entry, since there is no known work on this subject by the syncretist Sebastiano Fox Morzillo (whose interest in Aristotle is well known and who is represented by other works in Tatham's library), nor by any other writer bearing the name Fox or a name such as Fuchs, Reynard, or Vulpius that might have been anglicized as Fox. It is possible that this is another copy of 112.85. *Language(s)*: Latin. Appraised at 6d in 1576.

112.32 dixonarium basilii
Unidentified [dictionary]. Continent (probable): date indeterminable.
Possibly Basilio Zanchi's *Dictionarium poeticum*, Basilius Faber's *Thesaurus eruditionis scholasticae*, or any of numerous dictionaries published in Basle (see 1589 inventory entry cited in BCI 2:272), though in that case the form ought to be "Basileae." *Language(s)*: Latin. Appraised at 3s 4d in 1576.

112.33 lexicon Ambrosii
Ambrogio Calepino. *Dictionarium*. Continent: 1502–1576.
Perhaps one of the editions with *Lexicon* as well as *Ambrosii* on the title page (Labarre, no. 31–63 *passim*). May include one or more vernacular languages and Hebrew. *Language(s)*: Greek Latin. Appraised at 12d in 1576.

112.34 whittgift contra Carter [Cartwright]
John Whitgift, *Archbishop*. *The defense of the aunswere to the Admonition, against the Replie*. London: Henry Bynneman for Humphrey Toy, 1574.

STC 25430 *et seq.* Two editions in 1574. See annotations to PLRE 4.18. Item 112.138 below is Cartwright's reply. *Language(s)*: English. Appraised at 4s in 1576.

112.35 nisolius
Marius Nizolius. Probably [*Observationes*]. Continent: 1535-1576.

Nizolius's *In M. T. Ciceronem observationes utilissimae* appeared in numerous editions beginning in 1535; from 1559 on, it appeared as *Thesaurus Ciceronianus*. *Language(s)*: Latin. Appraised at 5s in 1576.

112.36 cornucopia latine lingue
Nicolaus Perottus. *Cornucopia*. Continent: date indeterminable. *Language(s)*: Latin. Appraised at 4s in 1576.

112.37 opera Cicer**is
Marcus Tullius Cicero. [*Works*]. Continent (probable): date indeterminable.

Probably not an STC book, but see STC 5265.7 *et seq.* The two pre-1576 editions listed in STC under [*Works*] both carried the title *De officiis* and contained the philosophical writings only, not the letters or orations. At this appraised value, the entry *opera* likely refers to one of the Continental editions of the complete works. *Language(s)*: Latin. Appraised at 12s in 1576.

112.38 guido bonatus
Guido Bonatus. *Decem tractatus astronomiae*. Continent: 1491-1550. *Language(s)*: Latin. Appraised at 20d in 1576.

112.39 Cineca
Lucius Annaeus Seneca. Unidentified. Continent (probable): date indeterminable.

Probably not an STC book, but see STC 22216 and 22222 *et seq.* Probably not a complete *Works* since the word *opera* following *Cineca* is struck out. See also below, 112.129. English translations of a few individual works were published before 1576, some in bilingual editions (STC 22216, 22222-28). *Language(s)*: Latin (probable). Appraised at 8d in 1576.

112.40 plautus cum comto [commento]
Titus Maccius Plautus. *Comoediae*. Continent: date indeterminable.

An initial appraisal, perhaps *iiii*, is struck out, and *xii* added after the *d*. Another Plautus is at 112.128. *Language(s)*: Latin. Appraised at 12d in 1576.

112.41 Adagia Erasmi
Desiderius Erasmus. *Adagia*. Continent: date indeterminable.

Tatham also had the *Epitome* of this work (112.123). The STC editions, all pre-1576, are in English, and titled *Proverbes or adagies*. See also 112.136,

112.193-95, and 112.201 for other works by Erasmus. *Language(s)*: Latin. Appraised at 12d in 1576.

112.42 vitae plutharki
Plutarch. *Vitae parallelae*. Continent: date indeterminable.

The author's name was first spelled *plutarki*, then an *h* was inserted. See below, 112.163, for another copy of Plutarch. *Language(s)*: Latin Greek (perhaps). Appraised at 12d in 1576.

112.43 boetius in arithmetica
Anicius M.T.S. Boethius. *Arithmetica*. Continent: date indeterminable.

In Venetian editions of the 1490s, the *Arithmetica* is followed by *De geometria*, *De musica*, and, in 1499, by other works. There is also an *Epitome* of the work, by Jacobus Faber, *Stapulensis* (editions 1496-1553), as well as an *Arithmetica speculativa . . . in compendia redacta* by the same editor (1533-1553). *Language(s)*: Latin. Appraised at 8d in 1576.

112.44 albertus magnus
Albertus Magnus. Unidentified. Place unknown: stationer unknown, date indeterminable.

STC/non-STC status unknown. *Language(s)*: Latin. Appraised at 4d in 1576.

112.45 orat tullii
Marcus Tullius Cicero. [*Selected works–Orations*]. Continent: date indeterminable.

The denomination on the appraised value is illegible: possibly 4s, but that would be unusually high (see, however, 112.37). Conceivably the abbreviation *orat* could mean a single oration published separately. *Language(s)*: Latin. Appraised at 4d in 1576.

112.46 vivianus legis peritus
Probably Vivianus Tuscus. Unidentified. Continent: date indeterminable.

Several works by this thirteenth-century authority were published in the 1490s in Basle and Freiburg; commentaries on the *Codex*, *Digestum vetus*, and *Infortiatum*, generally were printed separately but sometimes bound together. A less likely possibility is Georgius Viviennus (Joris Vivien), author of a dictionary of terms in both civil and canon law, *Synopsis utriusque juris* (Louvain, 1563), as well as an alphabetized *Epitome* of the Decretals (1571) and more specialized studies in both civil and canon law, 1563-71. *Language(s)*: Latin. Appraised at 6d in 1576.

112.47 liber Justiniani
Justinian I. Unidentified. *(Corpus juris civilis)*. Continent: date indeterminable.

The entry continues with *super* and another word, now illegible; both are struck out. *Language(s)*: Latin. Appraised at 12d in 1576.

112.48 libellus decretorum
Gratianus, *the Canonist*. *Decretum*. (*Corpus juris canonici*). Continent: date indeterminable.
Language(s): Latin. Appraised at 8d in 1576.

112.49:1–3 tres libri legum
Unidentified. Place unknown: stationer unknown, date indeterminable. STC/non-STC status unknown. *Language(s)*: Latin (probable). Appraised at 16d in 1576.

112.50 l**dwode in construciones Anglie
William Lyndewode, *Bishop*. *Constitutiones provinciales*. Britain or Continent: 1483–1557.
STC 17102 *et seq*. The title of the 1557 edition, printed by Thomas Marshe, comes closest to the entry. *Language(s)*: Latin. Appraised at 12d in 1576.

112.51 maxilanus in regulis juris
Dinus de Mugello. *De regulis juris*. Continent: date indeterminable.
Language(s): Latin. Appraised at 4d in 1576.

112.52 dedacus in decretal
Diego Covarruvias a Leyva, *Bishop of Segovia*. Probably [*Decretales–Epitome*]. Continent: 1550–1568.
Preceding the title are the words: "Didaci Covarruvius Toletani" (see NUC 125:362). *Language(s)*: Latin. Appraised at 12d in 1576.

112.53 J acurtius super Institiones
Probably Guido. *Casus longi super Institutis*. Editing attributed to Gulielmus Accursius. Continent: date indeterminable.
The identification of Accursius is complicated by the *J* or *I* which commences the entry. Having no punctuation, it may be a false, mistaken start for "Item" which precedes each entry, or for the title "Institutions." It may also be an initial and the reference could then conceivably be to Jacobus Curtius, author of *Eikaston–id est conjecturalium–Juris Civilis* (Antwerp, 1550; Cologne, 1554) (Adams C3109). *Language(s)*: Latin. Appraised at 6d in 1576.

112.54 reforma legum eccliasticarum
Thomas Cranmer, *Archbishop* (with Walter Haddon, Richard Cox, and others). *Reformatio legum ecclesiasticarum*. Edited by John Foxe, *the Martyrologist*. London: ex off. J. Daii, 1571.

STC 6006. Printed from manuscript nearly twenty years after its composition. *Language(s)*: Latin. Appraised at 6d in 1576.

112.55 ******** super Instituciones
Unidentified. [*Corpus juris civilis: commentary*]. Continent (probable): date indeterminable.

Probably not an STC book. Entry struck out in version A (making the author's name illegible), but the appraised value remains undeleted; entry not included in version B or C. *Language(s)*: Latin. Appraised at 4d in 1576.

112.56 Lancelottus de jure pontificio
Giovanni Paolo Lancelotto. Probably *Institutiones juris canonici*. Continent: date indeterminable.

Language(s): Latin. Appraised at 20d in 1576.

112.57 Instituciones imperiales hoppero authore
Joachim Hopper. *Institutiones imperiales. (Corpus juris civilis)*. Cologne: Heirs of Joannes Quentel and Gervinus Calenius, 1560–1565.

VD16 C5202 and 5204. On the appraised value, see annotation to next item. Includes helps for beginning students ("in gratiam Tyronum"). *Language(s)*: Latin. Appraised with another at 12d in 1576.

112.58 Duarenus
Franciscus Duarenus. Unidentified. Continent: date indeterminable.

Entered (in version A only) interlinearly, in a different hand, between Hopper's *Institutiones* and two works on the *Decretals*. The entry apparently replaces one six lines later, *franciscus duerenus*, which was crossed out before insertion of the appraised value; Duarenus and Hopper were then bracketed with the appraised value of 12d. It is possible, however, to interpret the 12d as applying to Hopper alone and Duarenus as having been left unappraised. Duarenus wrote several works on the law, both civil and canon. *Language(s)*: Latin. Appraised with another at 12d in 1576.

112.59 Epistole decretales gregorii
Gregory IX, *Pope. Decretales. (Corpus juris canonici)*. Continent: date indeterminable.

Epistolae decretales summorum pontificum is the title used, perhaps solely, by Plantin. But this could be one of the other editions bearing the title beginning *Decretales epistolae*. *Language(s)*: Latin. Appraised with another at 5s in 1576.

112.60 libri decretalium bonifacii
Boniface VIII, *Pope. Sextus liber Decretalium. (Corpus juris canonici)*. Continent: date indeterminable.

Language(s): Latin. Appraised with another at 5s in 1576.

112.61 novum testamentum
[*Bible–N.T.*]. Britain or Continent: date indeterminable.

STC 2799 *et seq.* and non-STC, but see STC 2815 *et seq.* Probably in Latin, but the chance of this entry's standing for an English translation is strengthened by the use of Latin for the following two entries, which can only refer to English works. An edition containing Greek (112.101) is explicitly so described. The appraised value is relatively high. *Language(s)*: Latin (probable) English (perhaps). Appraised at 20d in 1576.

112.62 Sermones latemeri
Hugh Latimer, *Bishop*. [*Sermons*]. London: 1549–1575.

STC 15274 *et seq.* Apart from editions of individual sermons, various collections of Latimer's sermons were published. *Language(s)*: English. Appraised with one other at 20d in 1576.

112.63 Sermones brodfordi
John Bradford, *Prebendary of St. Paul's. Two notable sermons, ... the one of repentance, and the other of the Lordes supper*. Edited by Thomas Sampson, *Dean of Christ Church*. London: J. Awdeley and J. Wyght, 1574.

STC 3499.5 *et seq.* Three editions in 1574. *Language(s)*: English. Appraised with one other at 20d in 1576.

112.64 Osorius de institucione Regis
Jeronimo Osorio da Fonseca, *Bishop. De regis institutione et disciplina.* Continent: 1571–1574.

Other works by this author are at 112.89 and 112.90. *Language(s)*: Latin. Appraised at 12d in 1576.

112.65 the courteer in englyshe
Baldassare Castiglione, *Count. The courtyer.* Translated by Sir Thomas Hoby. London: W. Seres, 1561.

STC 4778. *Language(s)*: English. Appraised at 10d in 1576.

112.66 Epistole Simiti
Perhaps Quintus Aurelius Symmachus. [*Epistolae*]. Continent: date indeterminable.

Another possibility is the *Epistolae* of Synesius, *Bishop of Ptolemais*, available in Greek, Latin, and bilingual editions (1499–1558). *Language(s)*: Latin. Appraised at 6d in 1576.

112.67 foxius de Institucione Regis
Sebastiano Fox Morzillo. *De regni regisque institutione.* Antwerp: (different houses), 1556–1566.

Language(s): Latin. Appraised at 6d in 1576.

112.68 lodovicus vivus
Joannes Lodovicus Vives. Unidentified. Place unknown: stationer unknown, date indeterminable.
STC/non-STC status unknown. For other works of Vives owned by Tatham, see 112.88 and 112.196. *Language(s)*: Latin (probable) English (perhaps). Appraised at 6d in 1576.

112.69 Aristo: politica grece
Aristotle. *Politica*. Continent: date indeterminable.
A prior appraisal of 6d is struck out. *Language(s)*: Greek. Appraised at 4d in 1576.

112.70 lorichius
Unidentified. Continent: date indeterminable.
Either Reinhard Lorich or the more widely published Gerhard Lorich; the position of this item in the inventory argues for Reinhard, who wrote on political philosophy. *Language(s)*: Latin. Appraised at 4d in 1576.

112.71 christian polysye
Sir Geoffrey Fenton. *A forme of christian pollicie*. London: H. Middelton for R. Newbery, 1574.
STC 10793a. Translation from Jean Talpin's *La police chrestienne*. *Language(s)*: English. Appraised at 8d in 1576.

112.72 viperanus de Rege
Giovanni Antonio Viperano. *De rege, et regno liber. De historia scribenda liber*. Antwerp: ex officina Christophori Plantini, 1569.
Language(s): Latin. Appraised at 2d in 1576.

112.73 Langthwetes cronacles
Thomas Lanquet. *An epitome of cronicles*. London: (different houses), 1549-1565.
STC 15217 *et seq*. *Language(s)*: English. Appraised at 8d in 1576.

112.74 themisteus in Aristot
Themistius. [*Aristotle–Unidentified: paraphrase*]. Continent: date indeterminable.
Themistius wrote paraphrases of much of Aristotle, including the *Posterior Analytics, Metaphysics, Physics, De anima, De caelo*, and the *Parva naturalia*. See 112.75. *Language(s)*: Latin. Appraised at 6d in 1576.

112.75 paraphrases themistii
Themistius. [*Aristotle–Unidentified: paraphrase*]. Continent: date indeterminable.
See notes for 112.74. *Language(s)*: Latin. Appraised at 6d in 1576.

112.76 firrerius de immortalitate anime
Giovanni Ferrerio, *Piemontese. Academica de animorum immortalitate enarratio*. Paris: ex officina Michaëlis Vasconsani, 1539.
Based on Cicero's *Somnium Scipionis*. *Language(s)*: Latin. Appraised at 2d in 1576.

112.77 carpentarius de natura
Jacobus Carpentarius. [*Aristotle–Physica: commentary and text*]. Paris: ex officina G. Buonii, 1560–1576.
Considering the appraised value, perhaps only part of this two-part work. *Language(s)*: Latin. Appraised at 2d in 1576.

112.78 Agrippa de occulta philosophia
Henricus Cornelius Agrippa. *De occulta philosophia*. Continent: 1531–1567.
Language(s): Latin. Appraised at 12d in 1576.

112.79 cardanus in ptolomeum
Girolamo Cardano. *In Cl. Ptolemaei de astrorum judiciis*. Continent: 1554–1555.
First of three books by Cardano in this inventory. See 112.80-81. *Language(s)*: Latin. Appraised at 8d in 1576.

112.80 gardanus de vanitate [varietate]
Girolamo Cardano. *De rerum varietate*. Continent: 1556–1558.
This work was written as a continuation of 112.81. See also 112.79. *Language(s)*: Latin. Appraised at 12d in 1576.

112.81 Idem de subtilitate
Girolamo Cardano. *De subtilitate*. Continent: 1550–1560.
See 112.79-80. *Language(s)*: Latin. Appraised at 6d in 1576.

112.82 piuserus de divinitate
Kaspar Peucer. *Commentarius de praecipuis divinationum generibus*. Wittenberg: (different houses), 1553–1576.
VD16 P1972-75. Predominantly Latin but contains many headings and quotations in Greek and a sixty-two page glossary of Greek words and sentences. *Language(s)*: Greek Latin. Appraised at 10d in 1576.

112.83 flores Aris
Probably Jacques Bouchereau, compiler. *Flores illustriores Aristotelis*. Continent: 1560–1575.
John Foxall, *Monumentorum*, also known as *Flores e libris Posteriorum Analyticorum Aristotelis*, is a remote possibility. *Language(s)*: Latin. Appraised at 6d in 1576.

112.84 garseus de meteoris
Joannes Garcaeus. *Meteorologia*. Wittenberg: Johann Schwertel, 1568. VD16 G448. See also 112.119. *Language(s)*: Latin. Appraised at 10d in 1576.

112.85 foxius de naturis
Sebastiano Fox Morzillo. *De naturae philosophia, seu de Platonis et Aristotelis consensione*. Continent: 1551-1560.

The 1554 edition contains also his *De philosophici studii ratione*. *Language(s)*: Latin. Appraised at 6d in 1576.

112.86 faber in phisicam
Jacobus Faber, *Stapulensis*. [*Aristotle–Physica: commentary and paraphrase*]. Continent: date indeterminable.

Language(s): Latin. Appraised at 2d in 1576.

112.87 velcurio
Joannes Velcurio. Probably [*Aristotle–Physica: commentary*]. Continent: 1537-1575.

The identification is based on the position of this entry in the inventory. Velcurio also produced works on a range of other subjects, including commentaries on Livy and Erasmus. *Language(s)*: Latin. Appraised at 4d in 1576.

112.88 vives de officio mariti
Joannes Lodovicus Vives. *De officio mariti*. Continent: 1529-1540.

Perhaps *Selected works* with this title leading. Vives is also represented in 112.68 and 112.196. *Language(s)*: Latin. Appraised at 4d in 1576.

112.89 osorius de gloria
Jeronimo Osorio da Fonseca, *Bishop*. *De gloria*. Continent: date indeterminable.

Conceivably Osorio's *Selected works* with *De gloria* leading. For other works by Osorio see 112.64 and 112.90. *Language(s)*: Latin. Appraised at 8d in 1576.

112.90 Idem de Justicia
Jeronimo Osorius da Fonseca, *Bishop*. *De justitia*. Continent: 1564-1574.

The work was dedicated to Cardinal Pole. *Language(s)*: Latin. Appraised at 8d in 1576.

112.91 Ethica melanctonis
Philipp Melanchthon. [*Aristotle–Ethica: commentary*]. Continent: date indeterminable.

Language(s): Latin. Appraised at 4d in 1576.

112.92 Bonfinius de virginitate
Antonius Bonfinius. *Symposion trimeron*. Edited by Joannes Leunclavius. Basle: ex officina Oporiniana, 1572.
Language(s): Latin. Appraised at 4d in 1576.

112.93 Agrippa de vanitate scientiarum
Henricus Cornelius Agrippa. *De incertitudine et vanitate scientiarum*. Continent: date indeterminable.
Another work by Agrippa is at 112.78. *Language(s)*: Latin. Appraised at 6d in 1576.

112.94 Aulus gelius
Aulus Gellius. *Noctes Atticae*. Continent: date indeterminable.
Language(s): Latin. Appraised at 4d in 1576.

112.95 Ringelbergii opera
Joachimus Fortius Ringelbergius. [*Works*]. Continent: 1531–1556.
Language(s): Greek Latin. Appraised at 8d in 1576.

112.96 Ethica Aristotelis
Aristotle. *Ethica*. Continent: date indeterminable.
Language(s): Latin (probable) Greek (perhaps). Appraised at 6d in 1576.

112.97 pascasius de alea
Pascasius Justus. *Alea, sive de curanda ludendi in pecuniam cupiditate*. Basle: per Joannem Oporinum, 1561.
Language(s): Latin. Appraised at 4d in 1576.

112.98 Sententie tullii
Marcus Tullius Cicero. [*Selections*]. Britain or Continent: date indeterminable.
STC 5318.3 and non-STC. The STC edition (1575) and others from 1556 on also contained selections from one or more other authors such as Demosthenes, Terence, and Erasmus. At least one edition (Cologne, 1558) advertised the contents as "in locos communes digestae." *Language(s)*: Latin Greek (perhaps). Appraised at 4d in 1576.

112.99 gordonius
Bernardus de Gordonio. Probably [*Practica, seu Lilium medicinae*]. Continent: date indeterminable.
Language(s): Latin. Appraised at 10d in 1576.

112.100 haddoni opera
Walter Haddon. *Lucubrationes passim collectae, et editae*. Edited by Thomas Hatcher. London: apud G. Seresium, 1567.
STC 12596. *Language(s)*: Latin. Appraised at 10d in 1576.

112.101 testamentum grecolatine
[*Bible–N.T.*]. Continent: date indeterminable.
Language(s): Greek Latin. Appraised at 14d in 1576.

112.102 fernelius
Joannes Fernelius. Unidentified. Continent: date indeterminable.
Beginning with this entry, the inventory is in a different hand, continuing through 112.209. Fernelius, physician to Henry II, wrote on medical and other scientific topics. *Language(s)*: Latin. Appraised at 6d in 1576.

112.103 pars 2a hypirii
Andreas Gerardus, *Hyperius*. Perhaps *Opusculorum theologicorum pars secunda*. Basle: ex officina Oporiniana, 1571.
This might, alternatively, be part, along with 112.18 and 112.104, of *Methodus theologiae sive loci communes*. *Language(s)*: Latin. Appraised at 8d in 1576.

112.104 hypirii loci communes
Andreas Gerardus, *Hyperius*. [*Methodus theologiae sive loci communes*]. Basle: Joannes Oporinus, 1567–1574.
See 112.18; the two might be parts of the same whole. See also the preceding. *Language(s)*: Latin. Appraised at 10d in 1576.

112.105 officii ciceronis
Marcus Tullius Cicero. *De officiis*. Continent (probable): date indeterminable.
Probably not an STC book, but see STC 5278 *et seq*. Often the leading title in Cicero's *Works* and other collections. *Language(s)*: Latin. Appraised at 4d in 1576.

112.106 machivell in itali
Niccolò Macchiavelli. Unidentified. Continent: date indeterminable.
One of Macchiavelli's political works, or the *Discorsi* on Livy, would be more appropriate to this collection than one of his dramas. *Language(s)*: Italian. Appraised at 4d in 1576.

112.107 guevara epistelles
Antonio de Guevara, *Bishop*. *The familiar epistles*. Translated by Edward Hellowes. London: (different houses) for Ralph Newbery, 1574–1575?
STC 12432 *et seq*. See 112.108. *Language(s)*: English. Appraised with one other at 2s in 1576.

112.108 golden epistelles by fentun
Sir Geoffrey Fenton. *Golden epistles, contayning varietie of discourse gathered as well out of the remaynder of Guevaraes workes, as other authors, Latine, French, and Italian*. London: H. Middelton for R. Newbery, 1575.

112.109 manucii epistole
Paolo Manuzio. [*Epistolae*]. Britain or Continent: date indeterminable.
STC 17286 *et seq.* and non-STC. *Language(s)*: Latin. Appraised at 6d in 1576.

112.110 policiani
Angelus Politianus (Angelo Ambrogini). Probably [*Epistolae*]. Continent: date indeterminable.
Fourth in a group of eleven entries, nine of which are explicitly called epistles. *Language(s)*: Latin. Appraised at 4d in 1576.

112.111 pliniii [sic] epistole
Pliny, *the Younger. Epistolae.* Continent: date indeterminable.
Also, many editions of Pliny's *Works* mentioned the epistles first on the title page. *Language(s)*: Latin. Appraised at 2d in 1576.

112.112 epistole ciceroni*
Marcus Tullius Cicero. Perhaps *Epistolae ad familiares.* Britain or Continent: date indeterminable.
STC 5295 *et seq.* and non-STC. A collection of selected epistles is also a possibility. *Language(s)*: Latin. Appraised at 6d in 1576.

112.113 longolius
Christophorus Longolius. [*Epistolae*]. Continent: date indeterminable. *Language(s)*: Latin. Appraised at 4d in 1576.

112.114 Sadoleti epistole
Jacobus Sadoletus. [*Epistolae*]. Continent: 1550–1575.
Two single letters were published separately in 1539, one addressed to Joannes Sturmius and the other to the City of Geneva, published with Calvin's reply. *Language(s)*: Latin. Appraised at 6d in 1576.

112.115 ascamii epistole
Roger Ascham. *Familiarium epistolarum libri tres.* Edited by Edward Grant. London: [H. Middleton,] imp. F. Coldocki, 1576.
STC 826. Also includes the editor's *Oratio de vita et obitu Rogeri Aschami. Language(s)*: Latin. Appraised at 6d in 1576.

112.116 epistole textoris
Joannes Ravisius (Textor). *Epistolae.* Britain or Continent: date indeterminable.
STC 20761.2 and non-STC. The STC edition (1574) was the latest in Tatham's lifetime. *Language(s)*: Latin. Appraised at 2d in 1576.

112.117 epistole cellii
Caelius Secundus Curio. *Selectarum epistolarum libri duo. Orationum liber unus*. Basle: per Joannem Oporinum, 1553.
Language(s): Latin. Appraised at 3d in 1576.

112.118 enchiridion hemingii
Niels Hemmingsen. *Enchiridion theologicum*. Continent: 1557-1568.
VD16 H1844-50. Another work by the same author is at 112.148. *Language(s)*: Latin. Appraised at 4d in 1576.

112.119 gortius de figuris
Joannes Garcaeus. *Tractatus brevis de erigendis figuris coeli*. Wittenberg: (different houses), 1556-1573.
VD16 G462-63. The book, published when Garcaeus was twenty-six, contains verses addressed to him by his Wittenberg teacher, Kaspar Peucer (see 112.82). See also 112.84. *Language(s)*: Latin. Appraised at 6d in 1576.

112.120 homeri iliada latine
Homer. *Iliad*. Continent: date indeterminable.
Collected *Works* also possible, with the other poems having separate title pages later in the volume. This is one of two copies (see 112.122). *Language(s)*: Latin. Appraised at 8d in 1576.

112.121 augustinus de herecibus
Augustine, *Saint. De haeresibus*. Edited with commentaries by Lambert Daneau. Geneva: Eustathius Vignon, 1576.
To the heresies attacked by Augustine the editor adds the Papist and Mohammedan "heresies." He also appended two tracts, one against "papistic tyranny" and his own *Arbor haereseon* (BN 5:425). *Language(s)*: Latin. Appraised at 8d in 1576.

112.122 homiri illias latine
Homer. *Iliad*. Continent: date indeterminable.
Another copy of 112.120 (probably a different edition: *illias* vs. *iliada*). Unlikely to be part of a two-volume set, since the other title page would presumably be for the *Odyssey*. See also 112.124. *Language(s)*: Latin. Appraised at 6d in 1576.

112.123 epitome adagiorum
Desiderius Erasmus. [*Adagia–Epitome*]. Continent: date indeterminable.
Language(s): Latin. Appraised at 4d in 1576.

112.124 homiri illias grece
Homer. *Iliad*. Continent: date indeterminable.
Perhaps *Works* with *Ilias* on the title page. For Latin translations see 112.120 and 112.122. *Language(s)*: Greek. Appraised at 6d in 1576.

112.125 horatius
Quintus Horatius Flaccus. Probably [*Works*]. Britain or Continent: date indeterminable.
STC 13784 and non-STC. *Language(s)*: Latin. Appraised at 3d in 1576.

112.126 virgilius
Publius Virgilius Maro. Probably [*Works*]. Britain or Continent: date indeterminable.
STC 24787 *et seq.* and non-STC. *Language(s)*: Latin. Appraised at 3d in 1576.

112.127 terentius
Publius Terentius, *Afer*. [*Works*]. Britain or Continent: date indeterminable.
STC 23885 *et seq.* and non-STC. *Language(s)*: Latin. Appraised at 4d in 1576.

112.128 plautus bis
Titus Maccius Plautus. *Comoediae*. Continent: date indeterminable.
The word *bis* was entered in copy B but then struck out, and omitted from copy C. This is the second Plautus entry (see 112.40). *Language(s)*: Latin. Appraised at 12d in 1576.

112.129 tragedii cenice
Lucius Annaeus Seneca. *Tragoediae*. Continent: date indeterminable.
See also 112.39. *Language(s)*: Latin. Appraised at 3d in 1576.

112.130 martial epigram
Marcus Valerius Martialis. *Epigrammata*. Continent: date indeterminable. *Language(s)*: Latin. Appraised at 3d in 1576.

112.131 ovid metamor
Publius Ovidius Naso. *Metamorphoses*. Continent (probable): date indeterminable.
Probably not an STC book, but see STC 18955 *et seq. Language(s)*: Latin (probable) English (perhaps). Appraised at 2d in 1576.

112.132 ovid de tristibus
Publius Ovidius Naso. *Tristia*. Britain or Continent: date indeterminable.
STC 18976.4 and non-STC. *Language(s)*: Latin. Appraised at 2d in 1576.

112.133 grammati linacri
Thomas Linacre. Probably *Rudimenta grammatices*. Translated by George Buchanan. Britain or Continent: 1525 (probable)–1559.
STC 15636 *et seq.* and non-STC. Originally written in English, but the

much-used school texts were in Buchanan's translation, most editions of which were published abroad. Linacre's *Progymnasmata grammatices* also would fit the manuscript description, but is less likely because this inventory contains other works entitled *Progymnasmata* and so describes them. The *Rudimenta* was also much more widely published. *Language(s)*: Latin. Appraised at 6d in 1576.

112.134 gram melankto

Philipp Melanchthon. Probably *Grammatica latina*. Continent: date indeterminable.

This earliest of Melanchthon's writings (1517) went through more than a hundred printings (Keen, 68–73). He followed it the next year with a Greek grammar which by his death in 1560 had seen thirty-six editions (Keen, 65–67), but the fact that the language is not specified suggests that the work referred to here is the Latin one. *Language(s)*: Latin. Appraised at 4d in 1576.

112.135 a commen gram [grammar]

Probably William Lily. Probably *Institutio compendiaria totius grammaticae*. Britain or Continent: 1540–1575.

STC 15610.5 *et seq*. *Language(s)*: Latin. Appraised at 3d in 1576.

112.136 collocum erasmi

Desiderius Erasmus. *Colloquia*. Britain or Continent: date indeterminable.

STC 10450.6 *et seq*. and non-STC. Other works by Erasmus are at 112.41, 112.123, 112.193–95, and 112.201. *Language(s)*: Latin. Appraised at 2d in 1576.

112.137 valla de lingua la.

Laurentius Valla. *Elegantiae*. Continent: date indeterminable.
Language(s): Latin. Appraised at 4d in 1576.

112.138 the Secund replye of cartwryght

Thomas Cartwright. *The second replie of Thomas Cartwright: agaynst maister Whitgiftes second answer*. Heidelberg: M. Schirat, 1575.

STC 4714. A reply to 112.34 above. Cartwright's first *Replye* (STC 4711–12), sold in two editions in April and June 1573, had been suppressed by royal proclamation (STC 8063), and he fled to Heidelberg, where he produced this rejoinder and worked with Walter Travers on 112.147. *Language(s)*: English. Appraised at 10d in 1576.

112.139 beroauldi opuscule

Philippus Beroaldus, *the Elder*. [*Selected works*]. Continent: date indeterminable.

Appraisal figure 6 at first (struck out). Titles vary: *Opuscula* or (later)

Varia opuscula. Works included vary from one edition to another. Individual works under a title beginning *Opusculum* had appeared as early as 1501 (*Aureliensis* 117.760 *et seq.*). *Language(s)*: Latin. Appraised at 4d in 1576.

112.140 suplitium valentini gentilis
Benedictus Aretius. *Valentini Gentilis justo capitis supplicio Bernae affecti brevis historia.* Geneva: ex officina Francisci Perrini, 1567.
Two editions. *Language(s)*: Latin. Appraised at 6d in 1576.

112.141 phylo Judeus
Philo, *Judaeus.* Unidentified. Continent: date indeterminable. *Language(s)*: Latin (probable). Appraised at 6d in 1576.

112.142 lombardi sententie
Peter Lombard. *Sententiarum libri IIII.* Continent: date indeterminable. *Language(s)*: Latin. Appraised at 12d in 1576.

112.143 a syck mans Sawve
Thomas Becon. *The sycke mannes salve.* London: J. Day, c. 1560 (probable)–1576.
STC 1756.5 *et seq. Language(s)*: English. Appraised at 8d in 1576.

112.144 doctor cawfylde agaynst martiall
James Calfhill. *An aunswere to the Treatise of the crosse.* London: H. Denham for L. Harryson, 1565.
STC 4368. *Language(s)*: English. Appraised at 4d in 1576.

112.145 homellie Judocii
Probably Jodocus Clichtoveus. [*Homiliae*]. Continent: 1534–1575.
Justus Judocus (also known as Jodocus, *Isenacensis*) is not known to have published homilies, nor is Jodocus Harchius nor Matthias Judex. Those of Jodocus Clichtoveus appeared in many competing editions, varying as to both title and selection of sermons included. There were other homilists with the forename Jodocus (Eichmann, for example), whose sermons, however, were less widely disseminated. *Language(s)*: Latin. Appraised at 4d in 1576.

112.146 lactantius
Lucius Coelius Lactantius. Probably [*Works*]. Continent: date indeterminable.
Language(s): Latin. Appraised at 10d in 1576.

112.147 ecclesiastica disciplina
Walter Travers. *Ecclesiastica disciplina.* Heidelberg: Michael Schirat, 1574.
False imprint ("Rupellae: excudebat Adamus de Monte"). *Language(s)*: Latin. Appraised at 4d in 1576.

112.148 pastor hemingii
Niels Hemmingsen. *Pastor, sive pastoris optimus vivendi agendique modus.* Continent: 1562–1574.

See 112.118 for another work by Hemmingsen. *Language(s)*: Latin. Appraised at 4d in 1576.

112.149 the shyp of Safttye
Edward Cradocke. *The shippe of assured safetie.* London: H. Bynneman for W. Norton, 1572.

STC 5952. *Language(s)*: English. Appraised at 6d in 1576.

112.150 compendium theologie
Unidentified. Continent: date indeterminable.

Most likely possibilities include Albertus Magnus, Hugo, *Argentinensis*, and Erasmus. *Language(s)*: Latin. Appraised at 4d in 1576.

112.151 de adoratione Imaginum
Probably Nicholas Sanders. *De typica et honoraria sacrarum imaginum adoratione libri duo.* Louvain: apud Joannem Foulerum, 1569.

Shaaber S20. A confutation of item 112.8. See 112.144 for a related controversy. *Language(s)*: Latin. Appraised at 4d in 1576.

112.152 flaminius in spalmo
Marco Antonio Flaminio. Probably [*Psalms: commentary and text*]. (*Bible– O.T.*). Continent: date indeterminable.

Could be his paraphrases of the Psalms. *Language(s)*: Latin. Appraised at 6d in 1576.

112.153 spalterium greco latine
[*Bible–O.T.–Psalms*]. Continent: date indeterminable.
Language(s): Greek Latin. Appraised at 4d in 1576.

112.154 gerson de immitatione christi
Thomas, *à Kempis. De imitatione Christi.* Continent: date indeterminable.

Falsely attributed to Joannes Gerson. *Language(s)*: Latin. Appraised at 4d in 1576.

112.155 status gallie
Pierre de La Place and Jean de Serres. *De statu religionis et reipublicae in regno Galliae.* Continent: date indeterminable.

Part 1 of the Latin version is a translation and abridgment by Serres of a 1565 vernacular history by Pierre de La Place. *Language(s)*: Latin. Appraised at 4d in 1576.

112.156 fabritii histore
Unidentified. Continent: date indeterminable.

Georgius Fabricius wrote historical works on Rome (*Roma. Antiquitatum libri duo*, 1540 *et seq.*) and Saxony (*Rerum Misnicarum libri septem*, 1569), but the word *historia* is not in those titles. He also wrote *De historia et meditatione mortis Christi*, published together with other titles in 1552, *Historiarum sacrarum e poetis veteribus christianis libri ii* (1566), and *Virorum illustrium seu historiae sacrae libri ix* (1564); but this manuscript entry is followed by several works of secular, not sacred, history. For the same reason Paul Fabricius, *Historia de Christo compescente tempestatem maris* (1560), seems unlikely. Yet another possibility is Franciscus Fabricius, *Marcoduranus, M. Tullii Ciceronis historia* (1564), a work of biography. *Language(s)*: Latin. Appraised at 4d in 1576.

112.157 Justinus

Trogus Pompeius and Justinus, *the Historian*. [*Epitomae in Trogi Pompeii historias*]. Britain or Continent: date indeterminable.

STC 24287 and non-STC. Only in Justin's abridgment has the monumental *Historiae Philippicae* of Trogus Pompeius survived. The one edition printed in England appeared in 1572. There were also English translations of Justin (STC 24290 *et seq.*). An alternative identification is the *Opera* of Justin, *Martyr*, but the low valuation points to a slighter volume, and this entry is surrounded by other histories. *Language(s)*: Latin. Appraised at 2d in 1576.

112.158 Valerius maxi

Valerius Maximus. *Facta et dicta memorabilia*. Continent: date indeterminable.

Language(s): Latin. Appraised at 2d in 1576.

112.159 Salustius

Caius Sallustius Crispus. Unidentified. Place unknown: stationer unknown, date indeterminable.

STC/non-STC status unknown. If not *Works*, perhaps only the *De bello Jugurthino* or *De conjuratione Catilinae*. *Language(s)*: Latin. Appraised at 2d in 1576.

112.160 bodinus

Jean Bodin, *Bishop*. Probably *Methodus ad facilem historiarum cognitionem*. Paris: apud Martinum Juvenem, 1566-1572.

Language(s): Latin. Appraised at 6d in 1576.

112.161 comminei cronicon

Philippe de Comines. [*Memoires*]. Continent: date indeterminable.

Earlier editions carried the title *Cronique et histoire*. A Latin translation by Joannes Philippson, *Sleidanus*, appeared as early as 1545. *Language(s)*: Latin. Appraised at 4d in 1576.

112.162 boemus

Joannes Boemus. [*Omnium gentium mores, leges et ritus*]. Britain or Continent: date indeterminable.

Probably not an STC book, but see STC 3196.5 *et seq*. Possibly in the partial English translation of 1554 or that of 1555. *Language(s)*: Latin (probable) English (perhaps). Appraised at 4d in 1576.

112.163 Vita plutarchi

Plutarch. *Vitae parallelae*. Continent: date indeterminable.

See the more expensive edition at 112.42. *Language(s)*: Latin Greek (perhaps). Appraised at 3d in 1576.

112.164 galeni pars

Galen. Unidentified. Continent: date indeterminable.

Almost certainly a fragment at the valuation. *Language(s)*: Latin. Appraised at 2d in 1576.

112.165 paracelsus

Paracelsus. Unidentified. Continent: date indeterminable.
Language(s): Latin. Appraised at 3d in 1576.

112.166 ficinus de Vita

Marsilio Ficino. [*De triplici vita*]. Continent: date indeterminable.
Language(s): Latin. Appraised at 3d in 1576.

112.167 caesars commentar*es

Caius Julius Caesar. *Commentarii*. Britain or Continent: date indeterminable.

STC 4335, 4337 and non-STC. This entry and the next five are damaged by a tear in the manuscript. There were many Latin editions of the *Commentarii* published on the Continent, of course, but the language of the entry suggests that this copy was in English. *Language(s)*: English (perhaps) Latin (perhaps). Appraised at 2d in 1576.

112.168 tunstallus arithmeti

Cuthbert Tunstall, *Bishop*. *De arte supputandi libri quattuor*. Britain or Continent: 1522–1551.

STC 24319 and non-STC. After Pynson's *editio princeps*, five more editions were published in France (Shaaber T155-59). See 112.167 note regarding manuscript damage. *Language(s)*: Latin. Appraised at 2d in 1576.

112.169 regiment Sanit*tis

[*Regimen sanitatis Salernitatum*]. Britain or Continent: date indeterminable.

STC 21596 *et seq*. and non-STC. See 112.167 note regarding manuscript damage. Six London editions are known (1528-1575) containing an English translation along with the Latin verse text and an English translation of the commentary. *Language(s)*: Latin English (perhaps). Appraised at 3d in 1576.

112.170 Biblia Hieronimi
The Bible. Continent: date indeterminable.

St. Jerome's Vulgate. Not in A version of inventory; inserted in B version, included in text of C. The valuation suggests a particularly fine copy. *Language(s)*: Latin. Appraised at 3s 4d in 1576.

112.171 pollidor Virgill
Polydorus Vergilius. Unidentified. Place unknown: stationer unknown, date indeterminable.

STC/non-STC status unknown. Several possibilities. *Language(s)*: Latin (probable) English (perhaps). Appraised at 4d in 1576.

112.172 epitome Rodolp*i
Rodolphus Agricola. *Epitome commentariorum dialecticae inventionis Rodolphi Agricolae*. Edited by Bartholomew Latomus. Continent: 1530-1575.

See 112.167 note regarding manuscript damage. *Language(s)*: Latin. Appraised at 3d in 1576.

112.173 xenophon de re puplica
Xenophon. *De re publica Lacedaemoniorum*. Continent: date indeterminable.

The last word of the entry is *pubplica* with the *b* struck out. Either the Greek edition (Paris, 1539) or the compiler was reading from the title page or a running head of one of the many Latin collected editions published in the sixteenth century. *Language(s)*: Greek (perhaps) Latin (perhaps). Appraised at 3d in 1576.

112.174 markcus aurelius
Perhaps Marcus Aurelius Antoninus. [*De vita sua*]. Continent: 1558-1568.

Antonio de Guevara's fictional biography, *The golden boke of Marcus Aurelius*, of which STC records thirteen editions before Tatham's death, is certainly a possibility. *Language(s)*: Latin Greek (perhaps). Appraised at 3d in 1576.

112.175 elyotes governor
Sir Thomas Elyot. *The boke named the governour*. London: (different houses), 1531-1565.

STC 7635 *et seq*. *Language(s)*: English. Appraised at 3d in 1576.

112.176 paradinus
Probably Guillaume Paradin. Unidentified. Continent: date indeterminable.

Paradin was best known for several works in French history. He also wrote, during Tatham's lifetime, *Anglicae descriptionis compendium* (1545), *Afflictae Britannicae religionis* (1555), *Le blason des danses* (1556), and *Historiarum memorabilium ex Genesi descriptio* (1558). The last two seem unlikely for this library, and at this value, so do works by the contemporary engraver Claude Paradin. *Language(s)*: Latin. Appraised at 2d in 1576.

112.177 omphalius
Jacobus Omphalius. Unidentified. Continent: date indeterminable.

As Omphalius wrote on both politics and rhetoric, the inventory entries preceding and following this one cannot help narrow the identification. *Language(s)*: Latin. Appraised at 3d in 1576.

112.178 phrasis manutii
Aldo Manuzio, *the Younger*. *Purae, elegantes et copiosae latinae linguae phrases*. Britain or Continent: date indeterminable.

STC 17278.8 and non-STC. There were at least nine Continental editions that Tatham could have owned (VD16 M791-98 and BL). Previously, Manuzio had produced a similar work in Italian and Latin (BN 105:519). Thomas Vautrollier obtained a ten-year patent for this work with an English translation; of his four editions, Tatham could have obtained only the first (1573). *Language(s)*: Latin English (perhaps). Appraised at 3d in 1576.

112.179 corderius
Mathurin Cordier. Unidentified. Continent: date indeterminable.

Probably either *De corrupti sermonis emendatione* or the more elementary handbook of correct diction, *Colloquiorum scholasticorum libri quatuor*. *Language(s)*: Latin. Appraised at 2d in 1576.

112.180 scorus de lingua latine
Antonius Schorus. Probably *Phrases linguae latinae*. Continent: date indeterminable.

Compiled, according to title page, for "the studious youth." Other works by Schorus which could fit this entry are *De ratione docendae discendaeque linguae Latinae et Graecae* (1544-75: commentaries on Cicero and Isocrates, with texts) and *Thesaurus verborum linguae Latinae Ciceronianus in usum . . . studiosae juventutis collectus . . . cum praefatione J. Sturmii*. *Language(s)*: Latin. Appraised at 4d in 1576.

112.181 silvii progimnasmata
Franciscus Sylvius, *of Amiens*. *In artem oratoriam progymnasmata*. Continent: date indeterminable.

Language(s): Latin. Appraised at 4d in 1576.

112.182 quintilianus
Marcus Fabius Quintilianus. Unidentified. Continent: date indeterminable.

Institutiones oratoriae more likely than the *Declamationes*, but the complete *Works* might be intended. *Language(s)*: Latin. Appraised at 8d in 1576.

112.183 apiani cosmogra
Peter Apian. *Cosmographia*. Continent: date indeterminable.
Language(s): Latin. Appraised at 4d in 1576.

112.184 melanctonis rethori
Philipp Melanchthon. [*Rhetorica*]. Continent: date indeterminable.
The entry could refer to any of three works with similar titles, whose numerous editions are listed by Keen, 50-54. For other works of Melanchthon owned by Tatham—all Aristotelian commentaries—see 112.91, 112.134, 112.207, and 112.217. *Language(s)*: Latin. Appraised at 4d in 1576.

112.185 brandolinus
Aurelius Brandolinus (Lippus). Probably *De ratione scribendi*. Britain or Continent: 1549-1573.
STC 3542 and non-STC. Also contained "libelli" on letter-writing by Vives, Erasmus, and others. The London edition was the most recent one. *Language(s)*: Latin. Appraised at 3d in 1576.

112.186 rethorica ciceronis
Marcus Tullius Cicero. [*Selected works–Rhetorica*]. Continent: date indeterminable.
Language(s): Latin. Appraised at 3d in 1576.

112.187 cicero ad herenium
Marcus Tullius Cicero (spurious). *Rhetorica ad Herennium*. Britain or Continent: date indeterminable.
STC 5323.5 and non-STC. *Language(s)*: Latin. Appraised at 4d in 1576.

112.188 athoninus
Aphthonius, *Sophista*. *Progymnasmata*. Britain or Continent: date indeterminable.
STC 700 *et seq.* and non-STC. Some editions included both the Greek text and a Latin translation. *Language(s)*: Latin (probable) Greek (perhaps). Appraised at 3d in 1576.

112.189 sturmius de periodis
Joannes Sturmius. *De periodis*. Strassburg: (different houses), 1550-1567.
The 1550 edition (Adams S1991, NUC 575:36) also contained his *De literarum ludis recte aperiendis* and the *De collocatione verborum* of Dionysus, *of Halicarnassus* in Greek; the 1567 edition also contained Sturmius, *Ad Bartholomaeum Siffertum epistola*, and commentary by Valentinus Erythraeus. Printers of the two editions were Wendelin Rihelius and Josias Rihelius, re-

spectively. Another work by Sturmius is at 112.192. *Language(s)*: Latin Greek (perhaps). Appraised at 3d in 1576.

112.190 hermogines

Hermogenes. [*Rhetorica*]. Continent: date indeterminable.

Either his popular *Ars rhetorica*, alone or with other texts, or some other collection of his rhetorical texts. Both were often accompanied by rhetorical texts by other authors. *Language(s)*: Greek (probable) Latin (probable). Appraised at 3d in 1576.

112.191 trapesuntius

Georgius Trapezuntius. Probably *Rhetorica*. Continent: date indeterminable.

This rather than his work on logic because of its placement in this section of the inventory; yet the appraisal is more in keeping with the *Dialectica*. *Language(s)*: Latin. Appraised at 3d in 1576.

112.192 sturminus in partitionibus

Joannes Sturmius. *In partitiones oratorias Ciceronis dialogi*. Continent: date indeterminable.

See also 112.189. *Language(s)*: Latin. Appraised at 3d in 1576.

112.193 erasmus de epistolis

Desiderius Erasmus. *De conscribendis epistolis*. Continent (probable): date indeterminable.

STC 10496 and non-STC. The 1521 *editio princeps* was published in Cambridge. Tatham had another edition of this work as a part of 112.185. See also notes on next entry. *Language(s)*: Latin. Appraised at 2d in 1576.

112.194 Idem de copie

Desiderius Erasmus. *De duplici copia verborum ac rerum*. Britain or Continent: date indeterminable.

STC 10471.4 *et seq.* and non-STC. Second of three rhetorical works by Erasmus in the collection; see also 112.41, 112.123, 112.136, and 112.201. *Language(s)*: Latin. Appraised at 3d in 1576.

112.195 Idem de pronuntiatione

Desiderius Erasmus. *De recta pronuntiatione* [and others]. Continent: 1528–1558.

Bezzel 1763–72. *Language(s)*: Greek Latin. Appraised at 1d in 1576.

112.196 Vivis rethorica

Joannes Lodovicus Vives. *De ratione dicendi. De consultatione praeceptiones.* Continent: 1533–1537.

For other works by Vives in this library, see 112.68, 112.88 and notes to 112.185. *Language(s)*: Latin. Appraised at 2d in 1576.

112.197 arisstotilis retho
Aristotle. *Rhetorica*. Continent: date indeterminable.
Language(s): Latin. Appraised at 2d in 1576.

112.198 organum aristotilis grece
Aristotle. *Organon*. Continent: date indeterminable.
Language(s): Greek. Appraised at 3d in 1576.

112.199 gorsii dialec
Jakób Górski. *Commentariorum artis dialecticae libri decem*. Leipzig: in officina Voegeliana, 1563 (probable).
VD16 G2673. *Language(s)*: Latin. Appraised at 4d in 1576.

112.200 organum latine
Aristotle. *Organon*. Continent: date indeterminable.
Language(s): Latin. Appraised at 2d in 1576.

112.201 encomium morie
Desiderius Erasmus. *Moriae encomium*. Continent: date indeterminable.
Language(s): Latin. Appraised at 4d in 1576.

112.202 perronie dialec
Joachim Perion. *De dialectica*. Continent: 1544–1555.
Language(s): Latin. Appraised at 3d in 1576.

112.203 rodulphi
Probably Caspar Rhodolphus. [*Dialectica*]. Continent: date indeterminable.
Conjecture is from context. Rodolphus Agricola's *De inventione dialectica* is certainly a possibility. Compare 112.172. *Language(s)*: Latin. Appraised at 2d in 1576.

112.204 valerii tabule
Cornelius Valerius. *Tabulae totius dialectices*. Continent: date indeterminable.
Language(s): Latin. Appraised at 2d in 1576.

112.205 Rami dialec
Pierre de La Ramée. [*Dialectica*]. Britain or Continent: 1543–1576.
STC 15241.7 *et seq.* and non-STC. *Language(s)*: Latin. Appraised at 2d in 1576.

112.206 viottus de demonstratione
Bartolomeo Viotti. *De demonstratione libri quinque*. Paris: apud Andream Wechelum, 1560.
Adams V842. *Language(s)*: Latin. Appraised at 2d in 1576.

112.207 dialectica melanctonis
Philipp Melanchthon. [*Dialectica*]. Continent: date indeterminable.
See 112.91, 112.134, 112.184, and 112.217 for other works by Melanchthon. *Language(s)*: Latin. Appraised at 2d in 1576.

112.208 erithrerius de periedis
Valentinus Erythraeus. *De grammaticorum figuris* [and others]. Strassburg: (different houses), 1549–1561.
Perhaps the compiler was reading from the running-head to the section *De periodis*, especially if the title page was missing. VD16 E3896-97. *Language(s)*: Latin. Appraised at 2d in 1576.

112.209 faleti orationis
Girolamo Falletti. *Orationes XII*. Venice: Aldus, 1558.
Language(s): Latin. Appraised at 4d in 1576.

112.210 orationes demost grec
Demosthenes. Probably [*Selected works–Orations*]. Continent: date indeterminable.
The valuation suggests a smaller collection. For a Latin edition of Demosthenes, see 112.218. *Language(s)*: Greek. Appraised at 1d in 1576.

112.211 aristot metaphys
Aristotle. *Metaphysica*. Continent: date indeterminable.
See also 112.22. *Language(s)*: Latin. Appraised at 2d in 1576.

112.212 Vico merca de animio
Franciscus Vicomercatus (Francesco Vimercati). [*Aristotle–De anima* (part)*: commentary and text*]. Continent: 1543–1574.
Aristotle's text is in Greek with a Latin translation by Vicomercatus. *Language(s)*: Greek Latin. Appraised at 2d in 1576.

112.213 problemata aristo
Aristotle (spurious). *Problemata*. Continent: date indeterminable.
Language(s): Latin. Appraised at 2d in 1576.

112.214 compendium philoso
Probably Franz Titelmann. [*Aristotle–Selected works–Philosophia naturalis: commentary*]. Continent: date indeterminable.
Language(s): Latin. Appraised at 1d in 1576.

112.215 lucanus
Marcus Annaeus Lucanus. *Pharsalia*. Continent: date indeterminable. *Language(s)*: Latin. Appraised at 2d in 1576.

112.216 bebelii facestii
Heinrich Bebel. *Facetiae*. Continent: 1540-1570.

All eleven of the editions published during this date range supplement Bebel's *Facetiae* with selections in a similar vein from other authors (varying by edition—see *Aureliensis* 115.357 *et seq.* for names). *Language(s)*: Latin. Appraised at 2d in 1576.

112.217 phisica melanctonis
Philipp Melanchthon. [*Aristotle–Physica: commentary*]. Continent: 1549-1575.

Melanchthon also published *Orationes* on physics in 1542 and 1550 (Keen, 170, 162). See 112.91 and 112.207 for other Aristotelian works by him in this collection. *Language(s)*: Latin. Appraised at 1d in 1576.

112.218 oracones demostini
Demosthenes. Probably [*Selected works–Orations*]. Continent: date indeterminable.

Probably not an STC book, but see STC 6577. With this entry, the first hand resumes writing. On the preceding line (in the hand of items 112.102-217) is the word *philippica*, struck out; this premature entry points to one of the Continental editions in which the *Philippicae* came first, rather than to the STC Latin edition. *Language(s)*: Latin. Appraised at 3d in 1576.

112.219 sambucus
Joannes Sambucus. Unidentified. Continent: date indeterminable.

More likely the *Epistolarum conscribendarum methodus* (1552) or *De imitatione Ciceroniana dialogi tres* (editions 1561 and 1563), both of which also included other works also, than the later, more expensive *Emblemata* or *Icones veterum*. *Language(s)*: Latin. Appraised at 2d in 1576.

112.220 nunnius
Unidentified. Continent: date indeterminable.

Possibilities include Nonius Marcellus, fourth-century author of *De compendiosa doctrina*; Pedro Nuñez or Nunes (Nonius), Portuguese mathematician; Pedro Juan Nuñez (Nunnesius), author of works on grammar and rhetoric (RRstc 215) and commentator on Aristotle and Cicero (perhaps the most likely possibility in this library); Petrus Nunnez de Avendano, author of *Dictionarium Hispanum vocum antiquarum*; Francisco Nuñez de Oria, medical writer and poet; Fernando Nuñez de Guzmán (Nonius, *Pintianus*), author of criticism on Seneca and other Roman writers (see PLRE 67.151). *Language(s)*: Latin. Appraised at 1d in 1576.

112.221 willikius

Jodocus Willich. Unidentified. Continent: date indeterminable.

He wrote on a wide variety of subjects including medicine, arithmetic, prosody, rhetoric (RRstc 304), dialectics (see PLRE 64.99), and cookery, and produced commentary on classical and biblical authors. *Language(s)*: Latin. Appraised at 4d in 1576.

112.222 multiple a great many of lytell bookes in parchment to the nomber of on [one] hundrethe

Unidentified. Place unknown: stationer unknown, date indeterminable.

STC/non-STC status unknown. Misread as "vii hundreth" by Ker (473). It may be conjectured that at least some of these are vernacular ephemera. *Language(s)*: Unknown. Appraised at 6s 8d in 1576.

PLRE Cumulative Catalogue

In the following lists, *entry* refers to a single entry made by a compiler of a manuscript book-list; *record* refers to a single record created from an *entry* by an editor. An *entry* may contain more than one *record*; conversely, a *record* may constitute only part of an *entry*. A *record* always represents at least one book but may represent more, including a volume set.

I. PLRE Database Totals

Book-lists: 142; Entries: 6,195; Records: 6,455
Number of Books Represented: More than 6,867
  (Seventy records of the 6,455 records specify two or more unidentified books for a determinable total of 482 books, adding a net 412 books to the record total. In addition, forty-one records contain an indeterminable number of books, identified in the database as *multiple*. Also, one book may possibly be traced to two owners of collections included in the PLRE database [see PLRE 52.14:1–2 and PLRE 57.3], and another may have been listed twice in one owner's list, once when purchased and later in his probate inventory [PLRE Ad5.5 and PLRE Ad5.21].)

II. Book-list Indices

A. Arrangement and Size of Each PLRE Unit
  Volume 1: PLRE 1–4   1,387 records
  Volume 2: PLRE 5–66   1,151 records
  Volume 3: PLRE 67–86   1,365 records
  Volume 4: PLRE 87–112   1,673 records
  APND Lists: PLRE Ad1–Ad30   879 records

B. Owners of Book-lists Arranged by Owners' Names
Owner and book-list information below is ordered in the following manner:

Name, degree(s). (Born–died) PLRE number. Profession. Social status. *Date* [of book-list, actual or *terminus ad quem*]: 1631. *Type* [of book-list]: inventory (probate). *Entries*: 25; *Records*: 29.

Allen, Richard, B.A. (c.1547–1569) PLRE 79. Scholar. Professional. *Date:* 1569. *Type:* inventory (probate). *Entries:* 97; *Records:* 98.

Allen, Thomas, B.A. (?–1561) PLRE 69. Scholar. Professional. *Date:* 1561. *Type:* inventory (probate). *Entries:* 34; *Records:* 35.

Anlaby (Aulaby), Edmund, M.A., B.Th. (?–1559) PLRE Ad5. Scholar. Professional. *Date:* 1533, 1559. *Type:* bookseller's accounts, inventory (probate). *Entries:* 28; *Records:* 31.

Atkinson, John, M.A. (?–1570) PLRE 83. Scholar. Professional. *Date:* 1570. *Type:* inventory (probate). *Entries:* 25. *Records:* 25.

Austin (given name unknown). (?–?) PLRE 98. Scholar (probable). Professional (probable). *Date:* 1572. *Type:* inventory. *Entries:* 20; *Records:* 20.

Balborough, William, D.U.L. (?–1514) PLRE 29. Scholar. Professional. *Date:* 1514. *Type:* inventory (probate). *Entries:* 25; *Records:* 29.

Balyn, John, B.A. (?–1513) PLRE 25. Scholar. Professional. *Date:* 1513. *Type:* inventory (probate). *Entries:* 18; *Records:* 18.

Barwyck, Stephen. (?–1547) PLRE Ad29. Butler, Scholar (student) (probable). Retainer, Professional (probable). *Date:* 1547. *Type:* inventory (probate). *Entries:* 35; *Records:* 36.

Batchelor, Robert. (1506–?) PLRE Ad6. Cleric, Scholar. Professional. *Date:* 1533. *Type:* bookseller's accounts. *Entries:* 8; *Records:* 10.

Battbrantes, William. (?–1572) PLRE 99. Scholar (student, probable). Professional. *Date:* 1572. *Type:* inventory (probate). *Entries:* 35; *Records:* 35

Beaumont, Edward, B.A. (1531–1552) PLRE 64. Scholar. Professional. *Date:* 1552. *Type:* inventory (probate). *Entries:* 117; *Records:* 118.

Beddow, John, M.A. (?–c.1577) PLRE 91. Scholar (schoolmaster). Professional. *Dates:* 1571 and 1577. *Type:* inventories. *Entries:* 40; *Records:* 41.

Bidnell, William, M.A. (?–1512) PLRE 23. Scholar. Professional. *Date:* 1512. *Type:* inventory (probate). *Entries:* 9; *Records:* 9.

Bill, Thomas, M.A. (?–1552) PLRE Ad7. Physician, Scholar. Professional. *Date:* 1532. *Type:* bookseller's accounts. *Entries:* 4; *Records:* 4.

Bisley (given name unknown), M.A. (perhaps), B.Th. (perhaps). (?–1543?) PLRE 60. Scholar. Professional. *Date:* 1543. *Type:* inventory (probate). *Entries:* 122; *Records:* 134.

Blomefield, Miles. (1525-1603) PLRE Ad2. Physician, Alchemist. Professional. *Date:* reconstruction. *Type:* reconstruction. *Entries:* 26; *Records:* 27.

Bonenfant, Thomas, M.A. (?-?) PLRE Ad8. Scholar. Professional. *Date:* 1533. *Type:* bookseller's accounts. *Entries:* 17; *Records:* 18.

Bowerman, John, M.A., B.C.L. (?-1507) PLRE 5. Scholar. Professional. *Date:* 1507. *Type:* will. *Entries:* 3; *Records:* 4.

Bradford, Ralph, M.A. (c.1502-?) PLRE Ad9. Scholar. Professional. *Date:* c.1527. *Type:* bookseller's accounts. *Entries:* 13; *Records:* 13.

Brewer, John, M.A. (?-1535) PLRE Ad10. Scholar. Professional. *Date:* 1533. *Type:* bookseller's accounts. *Entries:* 4; *Records:* 4.

Bromsby, John, B.Th. (?-?) PLRE Ad11. Scholar. Professional. *Date:* 1531. *Type:* bookseller's accounts. *Entries:* 4; *Records:* 5.

Brown, William, M.A. (?-1558) PLRE 67. Scholar. Professional. *Date:* 1558. *Type:* inventory (probate). *Entries:* 223; *Records:* 242.

Bryan, Robert, D.Cn.L. (?-1508) PLRE 11. Scholar. Professional. *Date:* 1508. *Type:* inventory (probate). *Entries:* 19; *Records:* 19.

Buckingham, Edward, B.Cn.L. (?-1568) PLRE Ad12. Scholar. Professional. *Date:* 1533. *Type:* bookseller's accounts. *Entries:* 3; *Records:* 3.

Burton, Edmund, M.A. (?-1529) PLRE 43. Scholar. Professional. *Date:* 1529. *Type:* inventory (probate). *Entries:* 42; *Records:* 46.

Bury, John, B.A. (probable). (?-1567) PLRE 74. Scholar. Professional. *Date:* 1567. *Type:* inventory (probate). *Entries:* 19; *Records:* 19.

Carter, John, B.C.L. (?-1509) PLRE 17. Scholar. Professional. *Date:* 1509. *Type:* inventory (probate). *Entries:* 3; *Records:* 5.

Cartwright, Thomas, M.A. (?-1532) PLRE 50. Scholar. Professional. *Date:* 1532. *Type:* inventory (probate) and will. *Entries:* 8; *Records:* 11.

Cauthorn, John, B.A. (?-?) PLRE Ad13. Scholar. Professional. *Date:* 1531. *Type:* bookseller's accounts. *Entries:* 12; *Records:* 12.

Chantry, William, B.A. (?-1507) PLRE 6. Scholar. Professional. *Date:* 1507. *Type:* will. *Entries:* 2; *Records:* 3.

Chastelain, George. (?-1513) PLRE 26. Stationer. Middle-class. *Date:* 1513. *Type:* inventory (probate). *Entries:* 1; *Records:* 1.

Cheke, Agnes. (?-1549) PLRE Ad30. Merchant (vintner). Middle class, Privileged person. *Date:* 1549. *Type:* inventory (probate) *Entries:* 3; *Records:* 4.

Chogan, William. (?-1537) PLRE 56. Scholar (student). Professional. *Date:* 1537. *Type:* will. *Entries:* 1; *Records:* 1.

Cliff, Richard, M.A. (?-1566) PLRE 73. Cleric (chaplain), Scholar. Professional. *Date:* 1566. *Type:* inventory (probate) and will. *Entries:* 261; *Records:* 261.

Coles, John, B.Th. (?-1529) PLRE 44. Scholar. Professional. *Date:* 1529. *Type:* inventory (probate). *Entries:* 5; *Records:* 5.

Collins, Robert. (?-?) PLRE 24. Scholar (student). Professional. *Date:* 1512. *Type:* receipt. *Entries:* 8; *Records:* 8.

Conner, John, B.Th. (c.1490–1569) PLRE 80. Cleric, Scholar. Professional. *Date:* 1569. *Type:* inventory (probate). *Entries:* 46; *Records:* 48.

Cox, Richard, D.Th. (1500–1581) PLRE 1. Cleric (bishop). Gentry. *Date:* 1581. *Type:* inventory. *Entries:* 196; *Records:* 208.

Dalaber, Anthony. (?–1562) PLRE 45. Scholar (student). Professional. *Date:* 1529. *Type:* inventory. *Entries:* 8; *Records:* 8.

Davy, William (perhaps), B.Cn.L. (?–1546) PLRE Ad14. Scholar. Professional. *Date:* 1533. *Type:* bookseller's accounts. *Entries:* 9; *Records:* 9.

Day, Thomas, B.C.L. (?–1570) PLRE 84. Cleric, Scholar. Professional. *Date:* 1570. *Type:* inventory (probate). *Entries:* 137; *Records:* 149.

Deegen, Peter. (?–1527) PLRE 37. Scholar (student). Professional. *Date:* 1527. *Type:* will. *Entries:* 5; *Records:* 5.

Derbyshire, William. (?–1551) PLRE 61. Scholar (student). Professional. *Date:* 1551. *Type:* inventory (probate). *Entries:* 11; *Records:* 23.

Dering, Sir Edward. (1598–1644) PLRE 4. Member of Parliament. Gentry. *Date:* 1628 and c.1642. *Type:* account book, catalogue, and reconstruction. *Entries:* 631; *Records:* 676.

Dewer, William, M.A. (probable). (?–1514) PLRE 30. Scholar. Professional. *Date:* 1514. *Type:* inventory (probate). *Entries:* 6; *Records:* 10.

Dickinson, Thomas (probable), B.A. (?–1558) PLRE Ad15. Scholar. Professional. *Date:* 1533. *Type:* bookseller's accounts. *Entries:* 7; *Records:* 8.

Digby, George and Simon. (?–?) PLRE 81. Scholars (students). Professional. *Date:* 1569. *Type:* inventory. *Entries:* 47; *Records:* 48.

Digby, Simon (see George Digby).

Dunnet, John. (?–1570) PLRE 85. Scholar (student). Professional. *Date:* 1570. *Type:* inventory (probate). *Entries:* 37; *Records:* 37.

Dyllam, Walter. (?–?) PLRE 106. Scholar (student). Professional. *Date:* 1575. *Type:* inventory. *Entries:* 1; *Records:* 3.

Froster, Roger. (?–1514) PLRE 31. Scholar (student). Professional. *Date:* 1514. *Type:* inventory (probate). *Entries:* 1; *Records:* 1.

Gilbert, John. (?–?) PLRE Ad16. Scholar (student). Professional. *Date:* 1528. *Type:* bookseller's accounts. *Entries:* 2; *Records:* 2.

Gilbert, Nicholas. (see Hilbert, Nicholas).

Gofton, William, B.C.L. (?–1507) PLRE 7. Scholar. Professional. *Date:* 1507. *Type:* inventory (probate). *Entries:* 11; *Records:* 12.

Goldsmith, Francis. (?–?) PLRE Ad17. Scholar (student) (probable). Professional (probable). *Date:* 1533. *Type:* bookseller's accounts. *Entries:* 1; *Records:* 1.

Griffin, Roger, B.A. (?–1510) PLRE 19. Scholar. Professional. *Date:* 1510. *Type:* inventory (probate). *Entries:* 2; *Records:* 2.

Griffith, Thomas, M.A., B.M. (perhaps). (?–1562) PLRE 70. Scholar, Physician (perhaps). Professional. *Date:* 1562. *Type:* inventory (probate). *Entries:* 92; *Records:* 97.

Gryce, William, D.Th. (?-1528) PLRE 41. Scholar. Professional. *Date:* 1528. *Type:* inventory (probate). *Entries:* 15; *Records:* 15.

Hamlyn, William, M.A. (?-1534) PLRE 51. Scholar. Professional. *Date:* 1534. *Type:* inventory (probate). *Entries:* 10; *Records:* 15.

Hart, Robert, M.A. (?-1571) PLRE 92. Scholar. Professional. *Date:* 1571. *Type:* inventory (probate). *Entries:* 135; *Records:* 137.

Hartburn, John, M.A. (?-1513) PLRE 27. Scholar. Professional. *Date:* 1513. *Type:* inventory (probate). *Entries:* 2; *Records:* 4.

Harwood, Thomas, B.A., D.M. (?-?) PLRE Ad18. Scholar. Professional. *Date:* 1530. *Type:* bookseller's accounts. *Entries:* 14; *Records:* 14.

Hawarden, Robert, M.A. (?-1527) PLRE 38. Scholar. Professional. *Date:* 1527. *Type:* inventory (probate). *Entries:* 6; *Records:* 6.

Heywood, John, B.A. (?-1514) PLRE 32. Scholar. Professional. *Date:* 1514. *Type:* inventory (probate). *Entries:* 13; *Records:* 14.

Hilbert, John. (see Gilbert, John)

Hilbert, Nicholas. (c.1509-1561) PLRE Ad19. Scholar (student). Professional. *Date:* 1528. *Type:* bookseller's accounts. *Entries:* 1; *Records:* 1.

Hodges, Thomas, B.A. (?-1539) PLRE 58. Scholar. Professional. *Date:* 1539. *Type:* inventory (probate). *Entries:* 28; *Records:* 33.

Hogan, Matthias. (?-1508) PLRE 12. Scholar (student). Professional. *Date:* 1508. *Type:* inventory (probate). *Entries:* 2; *Records:* 2.

Hooper, Robert, M.A. (?-c.1571) PLRE 93. Scholar. Professional. *Date:* 1571. *Type:* inventory (probate). *Entries:* 77; *Records:* 77.

Hoppe, Edward, M.A. (?-1538) PLRE 57. Scholar. Professional. *Date:* 1538. *Type:* will. *Entries:* 17; *Records:* 19.

Hornby, Nicholas, B.A., M.A. (perhaps). (?-?) PLRE Ad20. Scholar. Professional. *Date:* c.1532. *Type:* bookseller's accounts. *Entries:* 4; *Records:* 4.

Horsley, Thomas. (?-?) PLRE Ad21. Scholar. Professional. *Date:* 1533. *Type:* bookseller's accounts. *Entries:* 4; *Records:* 4.

Horsman, Leonard, M.A. (?-1551) PLRE Ad22. Scholar. Professional. *Date:* 1531. *Type:* bookseller's account. *Entries:* 24; *Records:* 24.

Horsman, Ralph. (?-?) PLRE Ad23. Scholar (student). Professional. *Date:* 1531. *Type:* bookseller's accounts. *Entries:* 2; *Records:* 2.

Hunt, Robert, D.C.L., D.Th. (c.1499-1536) PLRE 53. Scholar. Professional. *Date:* 1536. *Type:* inventory (probate). *Entries:* 2; *Records:* 5.

Hurde, William. (?-1551) PLRE 62. Scholar (student). Professional. *Date:* 1551. *Type:* inventory (probate). *Entries:* 20; *Records:* 21.

Hutchinson, Henry, B.A. (1550-1573) PLRE 103. Scholar. Professional. *Date:* 1573. *Type:* inventory (probate). *Entries:* 99; *Records:* 99.

Jackson, Lionel, M.A. (?-1514) PLRE 33. Scholar. Professional. *Date:* 1514. *Type:* inventory (probate) and will. *Entries:* 32; *Records:* 33.

Jewel, John, D.Th. (1522-1571) PLRE Ad1. Cleric (bishop). Professional. *Date:* reconstruction. *Type:* reconstruction. *Entries:* 74; *Records:* 74.

Johnson, James. (?–1568) PLRE 77. Cleric (chaplain). Professional. *Date:* 1568. *Type:* inventory (probate). *Entries:* 4; *Records:* 4.

Johnson, Philip, B.Th. (?–1576) PLRE 110. Scholar. Professional. *Date:* 1576. *Type:* inventory (probate). *Entries:* 270; *Records:* 274.

Jones, Lewis, B.A. (?–1571) PLRE 94. Scholar. Professional. Date: 1571. Type: inventory (probate). Entries: 41; Records: 41.

Jones, Robert. (?–1567) PLRE 75. Sexton. Professional. *Date:* 1567. *Type:* inventory (probate). *Entries:* 23; *Records:* 27.

Kettelby, William, M.A. (?–c.1572) PLRE 104. Scholar. Professional. *Date:* 1573. *Type:* inventory (probate). *Entries:* 93; *Records:* 96.

Kitley, John, M.A. (?–1531) PLRE 49. Scholar. Professional. *Date:* 1531. *Type:* inventory (probate). *Entries:* 1; *Records:* 2.

Kitson, John, M.A. (?–1536) PLRE 54. Scholar. Professional. *Date:* 1536. *Type:* will. *Entries:* 1; *Records:* 1.

Kyffen, John, B.Cn.L. (?–1514) PLRE 34. Scholar. Professional. *Date:* 1514. *Type:* inventory (probate). *Entries:* 22; *Records:* 24.

Lacy, Dunstan, M.A. (?–1534) PLRE 52. Scholar. Professional. *Date:* 1534. *Type:* will. *Entries:* 27; *Records:* 29.

Lanham, Richard, B.A. (?–?) PLRE 105. Scholar. Professional. *Date:* 1573. *Type:* inventory. *Entries:* 4; *Records:* 4.

Lilbourn, William, M.A. (?–1514) PLRE 35. Scholar. Professional. *Date:* 1514. *Type:* inventory (probate). *Entries:* 9; *Records:* 10.

Lisle (given name unknown). (?–?) PLRE 86. Scholar (student). Professional. *Date:* 1570. *Type:* inventory. *Entries:* 11; *Records:* 11.

Llewellyn, David ap. (?–?) PLRE Ad24. Cleric (friar). Professional. *Date:* 1533. *Type:* bookseller's accounts. *Entries:* 7; *Records:* 7.

Lombard, Nicholas, M.A. (?–1575) PLRE 107. Scholar. Professional. *Date:* 1575. *Type:* inventory (probate) and will. *Entries:* 131; *Records:* 132.

Ludby, Richard. (?–1567) PLRE 76. Cleric. Professional. *Date:* 1567. *Type:* inventory (probate). *Entries:* 25; *Records:* 25.

Lye, Richard. (?–1575) PLRE 108. Manciple. Professional, Privileged person. Date: 1575. Type: inventory (probate). Entries: 94; Records: 95

Mason, Roger, B.Cn.L. (?–1513) PLRE 28. Scholar. Professional. *Date:* 1513. *Type:* inventory (probate). *Entries:* 1; *Records:* 1.

Maudesley, Thomas, B.A. (?–1571) PLRE 95. Scholar (student). Professional. *Date:* 1571. *Type:* inventory (probate). *Entries:* 17; *Records:* 17.

Merven, George, B.A. (?–1529) PLRE 46. Scholar. Professional. *Date:* 1529. *Type:* inventory (probate). *Entries:* 5; *Records:* 5.

Mitchell, John (?–1572) PLRE 100. Servant. Retainer, Privileged person. *Date:* 1572. *Type:* inventory (probate). *Entries:* 11; *Records:* 11.

Morcote, John, M.A. (?–1508) PLRE 13. Scholar. Professional. *Date:* 1508. *Type:* inventory (probate). *Entries:* 75; *Records:* 80.

Morgan, Thomas (?-?) PLRE 87. Scholar (student). Professional. *Date:* 1570. *Type:* inventory. *Entries:* 4; *Records:* 4.

Mychegood, Robert. (?-1508) PLRE 14. Cleric (probable). Professional. *Date:* 1509. *Type:* inventory (probate). *Entries:* 8; *Records:* 8.

Napper, William, B.A. (c.1544–1569) PLRE 82. Scholar. Professional. *Date:* 1569. *Type:* inventory (probate). *Entries:* 118; *Records:* 118.

Neale, Thomas. (1553–1572) PLRE 101. Scholar (student). Professional. *Date:* 1572. *Type:* inventory (probate). *Entries:* 6; *Records:* 6.

Pannell, William, M.A. (?-1537) PLRE Ad25. Scholar. Professional. *Date:* 1533. *Type:* bookseller's accounts. *Entries:* 14; *Records:* 15.

Pantry, John, M.A., D.Th. (?-1541) PLRE 59. Scholar. Professional. *Date:* 1541. *Type:* will and reconstruction. *Entries:* 3; *Records:* 3.

Peerpoynt, William. (?-?) PLRE Ad26. Scholar (student). Professional. *Date:* 1531. *Type:* bookseller's accounts. *Entries:* 6; *Records:* 6.

Petcher, Robert, M.A. (?-1507) PLRE 8. Scholar. Professional. *Date:* 1507. *Type:* will. *Entries:* 1; *Records:* 2.

Powell, James, M.A. (?-1575) PLRE 109. Scholar. Professional. *Date:* 1575. *Type:* inventory (probate). *Entries:* 42; *Records:* 42.

Price, John, B.Cn.L., B.C.L. (?-1554) PLRE 66. Scholar. Professional. *Date:* 1554. *Type:* inventory (probate). *Entries:* 17; *Records:* 25.

Purfrey, Anthony, B.C.L. (?-1527) PLRE 39. Scholar. Professional. *Date:* 1527. *Type:* inventory (probate). *Entries:* 7; *Records:* 7.

Purviar, Robert, M.A. (?-1536) PLRE 55. Scholar. Professional. *Date:* 1536. *Type:* will and reconstruction. *Entries:* 7; *Records:* 7.

Quarrendon, Thomas, B.C.L. (?-c.1507) PLRE 9. Scholar. Professional. *Date:* 1507. *Type:* inventory (probate). *Entries:* 14; *Records:* 15.

Rawson, Nicholas, B.Th. (?-1511) PLRE 20. Scholar. Professional. *Date:* 1511. *Type:* inventory (probate). *Entries:* 6; *Records:* 6.

Reynolds, Jerome, M.A., B.M. (perhaps). (?-1571) PLRE 96. Scholar, Physician. Professional. *Date:* 1571. *Type:* inventory (probate). *Entries:* 108; *Records:* 108

Reynolds, John, M.A. (?-1571). PLRE 97. Scholar. Professional. *Date:* 1571. *Type:* inventory (probate). *Entries:* 59; *Records:* 59.

Ringstead, Henry. (?-1561) PLRE Ad27. Appraiser. Privileged person. *Date:* 1533. *Type:* bookseller's acounts. *Entries:* 1; *Records:* 1.

Robinson, John. (?-1508) PLRE 15. Manciple. Professional, Privileged person. *Date:* 1508. *Type:* inventory (probate). *Entries:* 2; *Records:* 2.

Robinson, John, M.A. (?-1511) PLRE 21. Scholar. Professional. *Date:* 1511. *Type:* inventory (probate). *Entries:* 6; *Records:* 6.

Rothley, John, B.Cn.L., B.C.L. (?-1511) PLRE 22. Scholar. Professional. *Date:* 1507. *Type:* inventory. *Entries:* 23; *Records:* 24.

Roxburgh, John, M.A. (?-1509) PLRE 18. Scholar. Professional. *Date:* 1509. *Type:* inventory (probate). *Entries:* 1; *Records:* 1.

Shoesmith, John. (?–1568) PLRE 78. Profession unknown. Privileged person (probable). *Date:* 1568. *Type:* inventory (probate). *Entries:* 11; *Records:* 11.

Sibthorpe, Henry. (?–c.1664) **(and Lady Anne Southwell)** PLRE Ad3. Soldier, Statesman. Gentry. *Date:* c.1640, c.1650. *Type:* inventory. *Entries:* 110; *Records:* 110.

Simons, Thomas, M.A., B.M. (?–1553) PLRE 65. Scholar. Professional. *Date:* 1553. *Type:* inventory (probate). *Entries:* 131; *Records:* 143.

Slatter, Richard, M.A. (?–?) PLRE 111. Scholar. Professional. *Date:* 1576. *Type:* inventory. *Entries:* 12; *Records:* 12.

Smallwood, William, M.A. (?–?) PLRE 102. Scholar. Professional. *Date:* 1572. *Type:* inventory. *Entries:* 17; *Records:* 17.

Southwell, Lady Anne. (?–1636) (see Henry Sibthorpe).

Stanhope, Sir Edward, D.U.L. (c.1546–1608) PLRE 2. Lawyer. Nobility. *Date:* c.1612. *Type:* will and reconstruction. *Entries:* 161; *Records:* 207.

Stocker, William, M.A. (?–?) PLRE 88. Scholar. Professional. *Date:* c.1570. *Type:* inventory. *Entries:* 23; *Records:* 23.

Stonely, Richard. (c.1520–1600) PLRE Ad4. Court official (Teller of the Exchequer). Gentry. *Date:* 1597. *Type:* inventory against debt. *Entries:* 413; *Records:* 415.

Sykes, Nicholas. (?–1562) PLRE 71. Butler. Retainer, Privileged person. *Date:* 1562. *Type:* inventory (probate). *Entries:* 42; *Records:* 42.

Talley, Abbot of. (?–?) PLRE 42. Cleric (monk). Professional. *Date:* 1528. *Type:* inventory. *Entries:* 2; *Records:* 3.

Tatham, John, M.A. (?–1576) PLRE 112. Scholar. Professional. *Date:* 1576. *Type:* inventory (probate). *Entries:* 222; *Records:* 222.

Thixtell, John, B.Th. (?–1541) PLRE Ad28. Scholar. Professional. *Date:* 1528. *Type:* bookseller's accounts. *Entries:* 14; *Records:* 15.

Thomson, Thomas, M.A. (?–1514) PLRE 36. Scholar. Professional. *Date:* 1514. *Type:* will. *Entries:* 14; *Records:* 17.

Thomson, William, M.A. (?–1507) PLRE 10. Scholar. Professional. *Date:* 1507. *Type:* inventory (probate). *Entries:* 30; *Records:* 30.

Thornbury, Thomas. (?–1570) PLRE 89. Scholar (student, perhaps). Professional. *Date:* 1570. *Type:* inventory (probate). *Entries:* 5; *Records:* 5.

Tichborne (given name unknown), B.C.L. (probable) (?–?) PLRE 90. Scholar. Professional. *Date:* 1570. *Type:* inventory. *Entries:* 93; *Records:* 93.

Tolley, David, M.A., B.M. (c.1506–1558) PLRE 68. Physician. Professional. *Date:* 1558. *Type:* inventory (probate). *Entries:* 50; *Records:* 50.

Townrow, Henry, B.A. (?–1565) PLRE 72. Scholar. Professional. *Date:* 1565. *Type:* inventory (probate). *Entries:* 18; *Records:* 18.

Townshend, Sir Roger. (1596–1636) PLRE 3. Member of Parliament. Gentry. *Date:* c.1625. *Type:* inventory. *Entries:* 286; *Records:* 296.

Upton, William, M.A., B.Th. (perhaps). (?–1527) PLRE 40. Scholar. Professional. *Date:* 1527. *Type:* will. *Entries:* 1; *Records:* 1.

Wicking, John. (?-1551) PLRE 63. Almsman. Retainer. *Date:* 1551. *Type:* inventory (probate) and will. *Entries:* 1; *Records:* 1.

Wood, Richard, M.A. (?-1508) PLRE 16. Scholar. Professional. *Date:* 1508. *Type:* inventory (probate). *Entries:* 13; *Records:* 13.

Woodruff, William, M.A. (?-?) PLRE 47. Scholar. Professional. *Date:* 1529. *Type:* inventory. *Entries:* 35; *Records:* 35.

Yardley, William, B.Cn.L., B.C.L. (?-1530) PLRE 48. Scholar. Professional. *Date:* 1530. *Type:* inventory (probate). *Entries:* 11; *Records:* 11.

C. Owners of Book-lists According to PLRE Number

1. LISTS IN PLRE VOLUMES

PLRE 1: Cox, Richard, D.Th.
PLRE 2: Stanhope, Sir Edward, D.U.L.
PLRE 3: Townshend, Sir Roger
PLRE 4: Dering, Sir Edward
PLRE 5: Bowerman, John, M.A., B.C.L.
PLRE 6: Chantry, William, B.A.
PLRE 7: Gofton, William, B.C.L.
PLRE 8: Petcher, Robert, M.A.
PLRE 9: Quarrendon, Thomas, B.C.L.
PLRE 10: Thomson, William, M.A.
PLRE 11: Bryan, Robert, D.Cn.L.
PLRE 12: Hogan, Matthias
PLRE 13: Morcote, John, M.A.
PLRE 14: Mychegood, Robert
PLRE 15: Robinson, John
PLRE 16: Wood, Richard, M.A.
PLRE 17: Carter, John, B.C.L.
PLRE 18: Roxburgh, John, M.A.
PLRE 19: Griffin, Roger, B.A.
PLRE 20: Rawson, Nicholas, B.Th.
PLRE 21: Robinson, John, M.A.
PLRE 22: Rothley, John, B.Cn.L., B.C.L.
PLRE 23: Bidnell, William, M.A.
PLRE 24: Collins, Robert
PLRE 25: Balyn, John, B.A.
PLRE 26: Chastelain, George
PLRE 27: Hartburn, John, M.A.
PLRE 28: Mason, Roger, B.Cn.L.
PLRE 29: Balborough, William, D.U.L.
PLRE 30: Dewer, William, M.A. (probable)
PLRE 31: Froster, Roger
PLRE 32: Heywood, John, B.A.
PLRE 33: Jackson, Lionel, M.A.
PLRE 34: Kyffen, John, B.Cn.L.

PLRE 35: Lilbourn, William, M.A.
PLRE 36: Thomson, Thomas, M.A.
PLRE 37: Deegen, Peter
PLRE 38: Hawarden, Robert, M.A.
PLRE 39: Purfrey, Anthony, B.C.L.
PLRE 40: Upton, William (perhaps), M.A., B.Th.
PLRE 41: Gryce, William, D.Th.
PLRE 42: Talley, Abbot of
PLRE 43: Burton, Edmund, M.A.
PLRE 44: Coles, John, B.Th.
PLRE 45: Dalaber, Anthony
PLRE 46: Merven, George, B.A.
PLRE 47: Woodruff, William, M.A.
PLRE 48: Yardley, William, B.Cn.L., B.C.L.
PLRE 49: Kitley, John, M.A.
PLRE 50: Cartwright, Thomas, M.A.
PLRE 51: Hamlyn, William, M.A.
PLRE 52: Lacy, Dunstan, M.A.
PLRE 53: Hunt, Robert, D.C.L., D.Th.
PLRE 54: Kitson, John, M.A.
PLRE 55: Purviar, Robert, M.A.
PLRE 56: Chogan, William
PLRE 57: Hoppe, Edward, M.A.
PLRE 58: Hodges, Thomas, B.A.
PLRE 59: Pantry, John, M.A., D.Th.
PLRE 60: Bisley, M.A. (perhaps), B.Th. (perhaps)
PLRE 61: Derbyshire, William
PLRE 62: Hurde, William
PLRE 63: Wicking, John
PLRE 64: Beaumont, Edward, B.A.
PLRE 65: Simons, Thomas, M.A., B.M.
PLRE 66: Price, John, B.Cn.L., B.C.L.
PLRE 67: Brown, William, M.A.
PLRE 68: Tolley, David, M.A., B.M.
PLRE 69: Allen, Thomas, B.A.
PLRE 70: Griffith, Thomas, M.A., B.M. (perhaps)
PLRE 71: Sykes, Nicholas
PLRE 72: Townrow, Henry, B.A.
PLRE 73: Cliff, Richard, M.A.
PLRE 74: Bury, John, B.A. (probable)
PLRE 75: Jones, Robert
PLRE 76: Ludby, Richard
PLRE 77: Johnson, James
PLRE 78: Shoesmith, John
PLRE 79: Allen, Richard, B.A.
PLRE 80: Conner, John, B.Th.
PLRE 81: Digby, George and Simon
PLRE 82: Napper, William, B.A.

PLRE 83: Atkinson, John, M.A.
PLRE 84: Day, Thomas, B.C.L.
PLRE 85: Dunnet, John
PLRE 86: Lisle
PLRE 87: Morgan, Thomas
PLRE 88: Stocker, William, M.A.
PLRE 89: Thornbury, Thomas
PLRE 90: Tichborne, B.C.L. (probable)
PLRE 91: Beddow, John, M.A.
PLRE 92: Hart, Robert, M.A.
PLRE 93: Hooper, Robert, M.A.
PLRE 94: Jones, Lewis, B.A.
PLRE 95: Maudesley, Thomas, B.A.
PLRE 96: Reynolds, Jerome, B.A., B.M. (perhaps)
PLRE 97: Reynolds, John, M.A.
PLRE 98: Austin
PLRE 99: Battbrantes, William
PLRE 100: Mitchell, John
PLRE 101: Neale, Thomas
PLRE 102: Smallwood, Thomas, M.A.
PLRE 103: Hutchinson, Henry, B.A.
PLRE 104: Kettelby, William, M.A.
PLRE 105: Lanham, Richard, B.A.
PLRE 106: Dyllam, Walter
PLRE 107: Lombard, Nicholas, M.A.
PLRE 108: Lye, Richard
PLRE 109: Powell, James, M.A.
PLRE 110: Johnson, Philip, B.Th.
PLRE 111: Slatter, Richard, M.A.
PLRE 112: Tatham, John, M.A.

2. APND LISTS

[The source of each book-list follows the name of the owner. In the case of groups of lists from one source, the reference may precede the group.]

PLRE Ad1: Jewel, John, Bishop, D.Th.
(Neil Ker, "The Library of John Jewel." *Bodleian Library Record* [1977] 9:256-65.)
PLRE Ad2: Blomefield, Miles.
(Donald Baker and J. L. Murphy, "The Books of Myles Blomefylde." *The Library*, 5th ser. [1976] 31:374-85; John C. Coldewey, "Myles Blomefylde's Library: Another Book." *English Language Notes* [1977] 14:249-50.)
PLRE Ad3: Sibthorpe, Captain Henry (and Lady Anne Southwell).
(Sister Jean Carmel Cavanaugh, S. L., "The Library of Lady Southwell and Captain Sibthorpe." *Studies in Bibliography* [1967] 20:243-54).
PLRE Ad4: Stonely, Richard.
(Leslie Hotson, "The Library of Elizabeth's Embezzling Teller." *Studies in Bibliography* [1949] 2:49-61).

APND lists PLRE Ad5–Ad28 are taken from: Elisabeth Leedham-Green, D. E. Rhodes, and F. H. Stubbings. *Garrett Godfrey's Accounts c. 1527–1533*. Cambridge Bibliographical Society, Monograph no. 12. Cambridge: Cambridge University Library, 1992. [*Note:* Degrees assigned are senior degrees that had been earned when books were purchased.]

PLRE Ad5: Anlaby (Aulaby), Edmund (some entries drawn from BCI 1:244–45), M.A. (1533), B.Th. (1559).
PLRE Ad6: Batchelor, Robert.
PLRE Ad7: Bill, Thomas, M.A.
PLRE Ad8: Bonenfant, Thomas, M.A.
PLRE Ad9: Bradford, Ralph, M.A.
PLRE Ad10: Brewer, John, M.A.
PLRE Ad11: Bromsby, John, B.Th.
PLRE Ad12: Buckingham, Edward, B.Cn.L.
PLRE Ad13: Cauthorn, John, B.A.
PLRE Ad14: Davy, William (perhaps), B.A.
PLRE Ad15: Dickinson, Thomas (probable), B.A.
PLRE Ad16: Gilbert, John.
PLRE Ad17: Goldsmith, Francis.
PLRE Ad18: Harwood, Thomas, B.A., D.M.
PLRE Ad19: Hilbert, Nicholas.
PLRE Ad20: Hornby, Nicholas, M.A.
PLRE Ad21: Horsley, Thomas.
PLRE Ad22: Horsman, Leonard, M.A.
PLRE Ad23: Horsman, Ralph.
PLRE Ad24: Llewellyn, David ap.
PLRE Ad25: Pannell, William, M.A.
PLRE Ad26: Peerpoynt, William.
PLRE Ad27: Ringstead, Henry.
PLRE Ad28: Thixtell, John, B.Th.
PLRE Ad29: Barwyck, Stephen. (BCI 1:93–94)
PLRE Ad30: Cheke, Agnes. (BCI 1:101–2)

D. Dates of Book-lists (actual or *terminus ad quem*), with PLRE Number

1507:	PLRE 5, 6, 7, 8, 9, 10, 22
1508:	PLRE 11, 12, 13, 15, 16
1509:	PLRE 14, 17, 18
1510:	PLRE 19
1511:	PLRE 20, 21
1512:	PLRE 23, 24
1513:	PLRE 25, 26, 27, 28
1514:	PLRE 29, 30, 31, 32, 33, 34, 35, 36
1527:	PLRE 37, 38, 39
c.1527:	PLRE Ad9
1528:	PLRE 40, 41, 42, Ad19, Ad28
1529:	PLRE 43, 44, 45, 46, 47
1530:	PLRE 48, Ad18
1531:	PLRE 49, Ad11, Ad13, Ad22, Ad23, Ad26
1532:	PLRE 50, Ad7
c.1532:	PLRE Ad20
1533:	PLRE Ad5 (part), Ad6, Ad8, Ad10, Ad12, Ad14, Ad15, Ad16, Ad17, Ad21, Ad24, Ad25, Ad27
1534:	PLRE 51, 52
1536:	PLRE 53, 54, 55
1537:	PLRE 56
1538:	PLRE 57
1539:	PLRE 58
1541:	PLRE 59
1543:	PLRE 60
1547:	PLRE Ad29
1549:	PLRE Ad30
1551:	PLRE 61, 62, 63
1552:	PLRE 64
1553:	PLRE 65
1554:	PLRE 66
1558:	PLRE 67, 68
1559:	PLRE Ad5 (part)
1561:	PLRE 69
1562:	PLRE 70, 71
1565:	PLRE 72
1566:	PLRE 73
1567:	PLRE 74, 75, 76
1568:	PLRE 77, 78
1569:	PLRE 79, 80, 81, 82, 90 (part)
1570:	PLRE 83, 84, 85, 86, 87, 88, 89, 90
1571:	PLRE 91, 92, 93, 94, 95, 96, 97
1572:	PLRE 98, 99, 100, 101, 102
1573:	PLRE 103, 104, 105
1575:	PLRE 106, 107, 108, 109

1576:   PLRE 110, 111, 112
1577:   PLRE 91 (part)
1581:   PLRE 1
1597:   PLRE Ad4
c.1612:   PLRE 2
c.1625:   PLRE 3
1628:   PLRE 4 (part)
c.1640:   PLRE Ad3 (part)
c.1642:   PLRE 4 (part)
c.1650:   PLRE Ad3 (part)
No date (reconstruction):
             PLRE 2 (part), 4 (part), 55 (part), 59 (part), Ad1, Ad2

III. Summaries and Concordances

A. Manuscript Types

1. RECORD TOTALS FROM EACH MANUSCRIPT TYPE

Account book:	177
Bookseller's accounts:	188
Catalogue:	496
Inventory:	960
Inventory (against debt):	415
Inventory (probate):	3,754
Inventory (probate) and Will:	86
Memorial book (benefaction):	200
Receipt:	8
Will:	58
No manuscript (reconstruction):	114

2. NUMBER OF MANUSCRIPT TYPES PROVIDING BOOK-LISTS
(Some lists derive from more than one manuscript type.)

Account book:	1
Bookseller's accounts:	23
Catalogue:	1
Inventory:	17
Inventory (against debt):	1
Inventory (probate):	78
Inventory (probate) and Will:	7
Memorial book (benefaction):	1
Receipt:	1
Will:	16
No manuscript (reconstruction):	4

3. MANUSCRIPT TYPES ACCORDING TO PLRE NUMBERS
(Some lists derive from more than one manuscript type.)

Account book: PLRE 4 (part)
Bookseller's accounts: PLRE Ad5 (part), Ad6, Ad7, Ad8, Ad9, Ad10, Ad11, Ad12, Ad13, Ad14, Ad15, Ad16, Ad17, Ad18, Ad19, Ad20, Ad21, Ad22, Ad23, Ad24, Ad25, Ad26, Ad27, Ad28
Catalogue: PLRE 4 (part)
Inventory: PLRE 1, 3, 22, 42, 45, 47, 81, 86, 87, 88, 90, 91, 98, 102, 105, 106, 111, Ad3
Inventory (against debt): PLRE Ad4
Inventory (probate): PLRE 7, 9, 10, 11, 12, 13 (part), 14, 15, 16, 17, 18, 19, 20, 21, 23, 25, 26, 27, 28, 29, 30 (part), 31, 32, 34, 35, 36 (part), 38, 39, 41, 43, 44, 46, 48, 49, 51, 53, 57 (part), 58, 60, 61, 62, 64 (part), 65, 66, 67, 68, 69, 70, 71, 72, 73 (part), 74, 75, 76, 77, 78, 79, 80, 82, 83, 84, 85, 89, 92, 93, 94, 95, 96, 97, 99, 100, 101, 103, 104, 107 (part), 108, 109, 110, 112, Ad5 (part), Ad30
Inventory (probate) and Will: PLRE 33 (part), 50, 52 (part), 57, 63, 64 (part), 107 (part)
Memorial book (benefaction): PLRE 2 (part)
Receipt: PLRE 24
Will: PLRE 5, 6, 8, 13 (part), 30 (part), 33 (part), 36 (part), 37, 40, 52 (part), 54, 55 (part), 56, 57 (part), 59 (part), 73 (part)
No manuscript (reconstruction): (See also Account book, Catalogue, Memorial book, and Will) PLRE 2 (part), 4 (part), 55 (part), 59 (part), Ad1, Ad2

B. Renaissance Locations of Book-lists

1. RECORD TOTALS FOR EACH LOCATION

Cambridgeshire, Cambridge:	459
Downham:	187
Fenstanton:	21
Kent, Surrenden:	673
London:	415
Middlesex, Acton:	110
Norfolk:	296
Northamptonshire, Brackley:	2
Oxfordshire, Oxford:	4,184
No Renaissance location (reconstruction):	114

2. PLRE NUMBERS OF LISTS IN EACH LOCATION

Cambridgeshire, Cambridge: PLRE 2, Ad5, Ad6, Ad7, Ad8, Ad9, Ad10, Ad11, Ad12, Ad13, Ad14, Ad15, Ad16, Ad17, Ad18, Ad19, Ad20, Ad21, Ad22, Ad23, Ad24, Ad25, Ad26, Ad27, Ad28, Ad29, Ad30
  Downham: PLRE 1 (part)
  Fenstanton: PLRE 1 (part)
Kent, Surrenden: PLRE 4
London: PLRE Ad4
Middlesex, Acton: PLRE Ad3
Norfolk: PLRE 3
Northamptonshire, Brackley: PLRE 91 (part)
Oxfordshire, Oxford: PLRE 5, 6, 7, 8, 9, 10, 11, 12, 13, 14, 15, 16, 17, 18, 19, 20, 21, 22, 23, 24, 25, 26, 27, 28, 29, 30, 31, 32, 33, 34, 35, 36, 37, 38, 39, 40, 41, 42, 43, 44, 45, 46, 47, 48, 49, 50, 51, 52, 53, 54, 55, 56, 57, 58, 59, 60, 61, 62, 63, 64, 65, 66, 67, 68, 69, 70, 71, 72, 73, 74, 75, 76, 77, 78, 79, 80, 81, 82, 83, 84, 85, 86, 87, 88, 89, 90, 91 (part), 92, 93, 94, 95, 96, 97, 98, 99, 100, 101, 102, 103, 104, 105, 106, 107, 108, 109, 110, 111, 112
No Renaissance location (reconstruction): PLRE 2 (part), 4 (part), 55 (part), 59 (part), Ad1, Ad2

C. Professions of Owners

1. TOTALS OF PROFESSIONS REPRESENTED

Alchemist (see Physician)	
Almsman:	1
Appraiser:	1
Butler:	2
Cleric:	1
Cleric (probable):	1
Cleric (bishop):	1
Cleric (chaplain):	2
Cleric (friar):	1
Cleric (monk):	1
Cleric, Scholar:	3
Court Official:	1
Lawyer:	1
Manciple:	2
Merchant (vintner):	1
Member of Parliament:	2
Physician:	1
Physician, Alchemist:	1

Physician, Scholar:	2
Physician (perhaps), Scholar:	1
Scholar:	71
(see also Cleric, Physician, Schoolmaster)	
Scholar (student):	17
Schoolmaster, Scholar:	1
Servant:	1
Sexton:	1
Soldier, Statesman:	1
Statesman (see Soldier)	
Stationer:	1
Unknown:	1

2. NUMBER OF RECORDS LISTED FOR EACH PROFESSION

Alchemist (see Physician)	
Almsman:	1
Appraiser:	1
Butler:	78
Cleric:	25
Cleric (probable):	8
Cleric (bishop):	282
Cleric (chaplain):	265
Cleric (friar):	7
Cleric (monk):	3
Cleric, Scholar:	207
Court Official:	415
Lawyer:	207
Manciple:	97
Merchant (vintner):	4
Member of Parliament:	972
Physician:	50
Physician, Alchemist:	27
Physician, Scholar:	112
Physician (perhaps), Scholar:	97
Scholar:	3,132
(see also Cleric, Physician, Schoolmaster)	
Scholar (student):	267
Schoolmaster, Scholar:	41
Servant:	11
Sexton:	27
Soldier, Statesman:	110
Statesman (see Soldier)	
Stationer:	1
Unknown:	11

3. BOOK-LISTS BY PROFESSIONS, WITH PLRE NUMBERS

Alchemist (see Physician)
Almsman: PLRE 63
Appraiser: PLRE Ad27
Butler: PLRE 71, Ad29
Cleric: PLRE 76
Cleric (probable): PLRE 14
Cleric (bishop): PLRE 1, Ad1
Cleric (chaplain): PLRE 73, 77
Cleric (friar): PLRE Ad24
Cleric (monk): PLRE 42
Cleric, Scholar: PLRE 80, 84, Ad6
Court Official: PLRE Ad4
Lawyer: PLRE 2
Manciple: PLRE 15, 108
Member of Parliament: PLRE 3, 4
Merchant (vintner): PLRE Ad30
Physician: PLRE 50
Physician, Alchemist: PLRE Ad2
Physician, Scholar: PLRE 96, Ad7
Physician (perhaps), Scholar: PLRE 70
Scholar (see also Cleric, Physician, Schoolmaster): PLRE 5, 6, 7, 8, 9, 10, 11, 13, 16, 17, 18, 19, 20, 21, 22, 23, 25, 27, 28, 29, 30, 32, 33, 34, 35, 36, 38, 39, 40, 41, 43, 44, 46, 47, 48, 49, 50, 51, 52, 53, 54, 55, 57, 58, 59, 60, 64, 65, 66, 67, 69, 72, 74, 79, 82, 83, 88, 90, 92, 93, 94, 97, 102, 103, 104, 105, 107, 109, 110, 111, 112, Ad5, Ad8, Ad9, Ad10, Ad11, Ad12, Ad13, Ad14, Ad15, Ad18, Ad20, Ad21, Ad22, Ad23, Ad25, Ad28
Scholar (student): PLRE 12, 24, 31, 37, 45, 56, 61, 62, 83, 85, 86, 87, 89, 95, 98, 99, 101, 106, Ad16, Ad17, Ad19, Ad26
Schoolmaster, Scholar: PLRE 91
Servant: PLRE 100
Sexton: PLRE 75
Soldier, Statesman: PLRE Ad3
Statesman (see Soldier)
Stationer: PLRE 26
Unknown: PLRE 78

D. Social Status of Owners

1. TOTAL OF RECORDS IN PLRE DATABASE

Gentry:	1,705
Middle class:	5
Nobility:	207
Privileged person (with others):	200
Privileged person (probable):	11
Professional:	4,474
Retainer:	90

2. BOOK-LISTS BY SOCIAL STATUS, WITH PLRE NUMBERS

Gentry: PLRE 1, 3, 4, Ad3, Ad4
Middle class: PLRE 26, Ad30
Nobility: PLRE 2
Privileged person (sometimes with others): PLRE 71, 100, 108, Ad27, Ad30
Privileged person (probable): PLRE 78
Professional: PLRE 5, 6, 7, 8, 9, 10, 11, 12, 13, 14, 15, 16, 17, 18, 19, 20, 21, 22, 23, 24, 25, 27, 28, 29, 30, 31, 32, 33, 34, 35, 36, 37, 38, 39, 40, 41, 42, 43, 44, 45, 46, 47, 48, 49, 50, 51, 52, 53, 54, 55, 56, 57, 58, 59, 60, 61, 62, 67, 68, 69, 70, 72, 73, 74, 75, 76, 77, 79, 80, 81, 82, 83, 84, 85, 86, 87, 88, 89, 90, 91, 92, 93, 94, 95, 96, 97, 98, 99, 101, 102, 103, 104, 105, 106, 107, 109, 110, 111, 112, Ad1, Ad2, Ad5, Ad6, Ad7, Ad8, Ad9, Ad10, Ad11, Ad12, Ad13, Ad14, Ad15, Ad16, Ad17, Ad18, Ad19, Ad20, Ad21, Ad22, Ad23, Ad24, Ad25, Ad26, Ad28
Retainer: PLRE 63, 71, 100, Ad29

APND Lists in Preparation (Selected)

Betts, John
  Source: Alain Wijffels, *Late Sixteenth-Century Lists of Law Books at Merton College.* Cambridge: LP Publications, 1992.

Bludder, Sir Thomas
  Source: John L. Lievsay and Richard B. Davis, "A Cavalier Library—1643." *Studies in Bibliography* (1954), 6:142-60.

Goodborne, John
  Source: R.G. Marsden, "A Virginian Minister's Library, 1635," *American Historical Review* (1906), 11:328-32.

Harding, Thomas
  Source: Christian Coppens, *Reading in Exile.* Cambridge: LP Publications, 1993.

Jonson, Ben
  Source: David McPherson, "Ben Jonson's Library and Marginalia: An Annotated Catalogue." *Studies in Philology* (1974) 71:23-106 [*Texts and Studies*].

Leech, John
  Source: Alain Wijffels, *Late Sixteenth-Century Lists of Law Books at Merton College.* Cambridge: LP Publications, 1992.

Shaw, Peter
  Source: David Pearson, "The Books of Peter Shaw in Trinity College, Cambridge." *Transactions of the Cambridge Bibliographical Society* (1986) 9:76-89.

Additions and Corrections

PLRE 1.49	*For:*	Unidentified
	Read:	Unidentified *(Corpus juris civilis)*
PLRE 1.168	*For:*	Basle: ex officiana Oporiniana, 1563–1575
	Read:	Continent: 1558–1575
PLRE 43.7	*For:*	*Language(s):* Latin
	Read:	*Language(s):* Greek Latin
PLRE 60.37	*For:*	*Language(s):* Greek Latin
	Read:	*Language(s):* Latin
PLRE 60.74	*For:*	*Language(s):* Latin
	Read:	*Language(s):* Greek Latin
PLRE 60.83	*Add to Annotation:* Aphthonius's *Progymnasmata* is also a good possibility. [Source: Charles Huttar, Hope College]	
PLRE 67.90	*For:*	*Language(s):* Latin.
	Read:	*Institutiones oratoriae* more likely than the *Declamationes*, but the complete works might be intended. *Language(s):* Latin.
PLRE 67.215:3	*For:*	*Language(s):* Greek
	Read:	*Language(s):* Greek Latin
PLRE 71.15	*For:*	*Language(s):* Latin
	Read:	*Language(s):* Latin (probable) English (perhaps)
PLRE 73.203	*For:*	*Language(s):* Latin
	Read:	*Language(s):* Latin Greek (perhaps)
PLRE 73.250	*For:*	*Language(s):* Latin (probable)
	Read:	*Language(s):* Latin (probable) English (perhaps)

PLRE 73.256   *For:* 1504–1566
               Read: 1498–1566

PLRE 74.13   *For:* STC 19138.5 and non-STC
               Read: Probably not an STC book, but see STC 19148 *et seq.*

PLRE 78.5   *For:* STC 1756.5
               Read: STC 1756.5 *et seq.*

PLRE 78.10   *Add to Annotation:*
               Bernardino Ochino, *A tragoedie or dialoge of the uniuste primacie of the bishop of Rome* (STC 18770) is another possibility.

PLRE 79.57   *For:* 1559–1568
               Read: 1557–1568

PLRE 82.78   *For: Language(s):* Greek Latin (probable)
               Read: Language(s): Latin (probable) Greek (perhaps)

PLRE 82.109   *For: Language(s):* Latin Greek (probable)
               Read: Language(s): Latin (probable) Greek (perhaps)

PLRE 83.11   *For:* Hermannus Schottenius, *Hessus*
               Read: Hermannus Schottenius, *Hessus* and Desiderius Erasmus

               For: 1533–1556
               Read: 1525–1560

PLRE 84.17   *For:* [*Decretales: commentary*]
               Read: [*Decretales–Liber Sextus: commentary*]

PLRE 85.2   *For:* Unidentified
               Read: Probably [*Observationes*]
               Delete all of the Annotation preceding Language(s).

ADDRESSES FOR REQUESTING DATA
OR FOR SENDING CORRECTIONS

R. J. Fehrenbach
Department of English
College of William and Mary
Williamsburg, VA 23187-8795 USA

E. S. Leedham-Green
University Archives
University Library, West Road
Cambridge CB3 9DR UK

Index I
Authors and Works

The words *perhaps* and *probable* indicate degrees of doubt about an identification. Names and titles appear in accordance with the methodology described in the introduction to this volume. A search of the database, available upon request, will provide more detailed information, including cross-referencing, than can be offered here.

Abdias, *Bishop of Babylon. De historia certaminis apostolici*: 110.80
Abulcasis. *Methodus medendi*: 96.41
Academia Veneta (probable). *Unidentified*: 107.52
Acciaiolus, Donatus. *Aristotle–Ethica: commentary*: 92.15
Acta Concilii Tridentini (probable): 110.214
Actuarius, Joannes. *De urinis*: 96.101
Aegidius, *Corboliensis. De urinis*: 104.64
Aepinus, Joannes. *In evangelium ascensionis Domini enarratio*: 93.77
Aeschines. *Selected works–Orations*: 92.60
Aesop. *Fabulae*: 110.170; 110.203
Agricola, Rodolphus. *De inventione dialectica*: 92.79; 93.62; 98.10; (probable): 103.43; 104.44; *Epitome commentariorum dialecticae inventionis Rodolphi Agricolae*: 112.172
Agrippa, Henricus Cornelius. *De incertitudine et vanitate scientiarum*: 97.49; 107.115; 112.93; *De occulta philosophia*: 94.16; 112.78; *In artem brevem Raymundi Lullii*: 92.54; *Unidentified*: 93.70
Albertus Magnus. *Unidentified*: 112.44
Albertus Magnus (probable). *Unidentified*: 107.13
Albertus, *de Padua. Gospels (liturgical): commentary and text*: 96.77
Albertus, *de Saxonia. Aristotle–De caelo: commentary*: 92.78
Alchabitius. *Unidentified*: 104.16
Alciati, Andrea. *Ad rescripta principum commentarii*: 90.60
Alcuin (perhaps). *Unidentified*: 110.253
Alexander, *Anglus. Destructorium viciorum*: 93.28; 93.30; 107.14; 110.154
Alexander, *Aphrodisiensis. Aristotle–De anima: commentary*: 107.39; *Aristotle–Sophistici elenchi: commentary*:

107.53:1; *Aristotle–Topica: commentary*: 107.53:2
Alger, *Monk of Cluny. De veritate corporis et sanguinis dominici in Eucharistia* [and others]: 110.265
Alonso, *of Madrid. Libellus aureus de vera Deo apte inserviendi methodo. Speculum illustrium personarum*: 90.84
Alphabetum hebraicum (part) (probable): 96.106
Althamer, Andreas. *Conciliatio locorum scripturae*: 93.68
Althamer, Andreas (probable). *Conciliatio locorum scripturae* (probable): 110.257
Ambrose, *Saint. Works*: 112.13; (probable): 107.126
Ammonius, *Hermiae. Porphyrius, of Tyre–Isagoge: commentary*: 92.101; 108.36
Anonymous. (also listed under individual titles): 93.52; 100.7; 103.59; 103.62; 103.83
Anthologia graeca (probable): 110.217
Antoninus, *Archbishop of Florence. Summa theologica* (part): 90.5; 90.59
Aphthonius, *Sophista. Progymnasmata*: 109.9; 110.242; 112.188; (probable): 108.75
Apian, Peter. *Cosmographia*: 103.16; 104.11; 112.183
Apollonius, *Rhodius* (probable). *Argonautica* (probable): 104.40:2
Appian, *of Alexandria. Historia Romana*: 92.52
Apuleius, Lucius. *Metamorphoses*: 103.73
Aquinas, Thomas, *Saint. Aristotle–Ethica: commentary*: 93.16; *Aristotle–Politica: commentary*: 112.26; *Epistles–Paul: commentary*: 110.10; *Gospels: commentary*: 110.32; *Sentences: commentary*: 97.8; 110.145; *Summa contra gentiles*: 93.66; *Summa theologica–Part II (1)*: 96.45; *Unidentified*: 93.20
Arboreus, Joannes. *Commentarii in quatuor Domini Evangelistas*: 96.21; *Theosophia*: 96.29
Aretius, Benedictus. *Examen theologicum*: 103.54; 110.69; *Valentini Gentilis justo capitis supplicio Bernae affecti brevis historia*: 112.140

Aristophanes. *Plutus*: 92.93; *Works*: 103.10
Aristotle. *De anima–Epitome*: 103.81; *Ethica*: 92.134; 94.28; 95.13; 98.1; 99.13; 103.46; 107.114; 108.55; 110.227; 112.96; *Flores illustriores Aristotelis* (probable): 112.83; *Historia animalium*: 104.3; *Librorum Aristotelis compendium*: 107.112; *Magna moralia*: 107.42; *Metaphysica*: 112.211; *Organon*: 92.69; 93.15; 93.50; 94.12; 95.17; 104.34; 108.26; 108.50; 112.198; 112.200; *Parva naturalia*: 93.7; 94.2; 95.6; 97.56; 108.51; 109.4; 111.11; 112.28; 112.29; *Politica*: 92.71; 97.52; 107.117; 108.54; 110.52; 112.69; *Rhetorica*: 112.197; *Selected works–Natural history* (probable): 98.20; *Selected works–Philosophia naturalis*: 96.20; *Unidentified*: 92.4; *Works*: 110.3; *Works* (part): 112.22
Aristotle (probable): *Selected works* (probable): 108.24
Aristotle (spurious). *Meteorologica*: 110.162; *Problemata*: 92.23; 110.231; 112.213
Arnaldus, *de Villa Nova. Works*: 104.12
Ars notariatus sive tabellionum libri 2: 90.69
Ascham, Roger. *Familiarium epistolarum libri tres*: 112.115; *scholemaster or plaine and perfite way of teachyng children, the Latin tong, The*: 110.159
Astesanus de Ast. *Summa de casibus conscientiae* (probable): 102.9
Augustine, *Saint. De civitate Dei*: 96.3; *De haeresibus*: 112.121; *De natura et gratia*: 90.26; *Epistolae*: 110.144; *Omnium operum epitome*: 110.51; *Opus quaestionum*: 93.25; *Psalms: commentary*: 96.34; 107.4; 107.9; 110.152; *Quaestiones evangeliorum*: 110.149; *Selected works–Opuscula*: 107.111; *Sermones ad heremitas*: 110.11; *Soliloquia*: 99.27; *Unidentified*: 88.8; 96.108; 112.21; *Works* (part): 96.9
Augustine, *Saint* (perhaps). *Unidentified*: 108.70:2
Augustine, *Saint* (spurious). *Meditationes*: 110.113
Aurelius Antoninus, Marcus (probable).

De vita sua (probable): 109.32
Aurelius Antoninus, Marcus (perhaps). *De vita sua* (perhaps): 112.174
Ausonius, Decimus Magnus. *Works*: 103.40
Autpertus, Ambrosius. *In Apocalypsim libri decem*: 107.10

Bairo, Pietro. *De medendis humani corporis malis enchiridion*: 96.83
Balduinus, Franciscus. *Commentarii in libros quatuor Institutionum juris civilis*: 90.93
Barletta, Gabriel. *Sermones*: 108.8
Bartolus, *de Saxoferrato. Digestum novum* (part 1): commentary: 88.6
Bartolus, *de Saxoferrato* (probable). *Codex*: commentary (part): 88.14
Basil, Saint, the Great. *Opus argutum De spiritu sancto*: 110.235; *Works*: 96.31; 96.35
Beaucaire de Peguillon, François, *Bishop of Metz*. *Unidentified*: 97.48
Bebel, Heinrich. *Facetiae*: 112.216
Beccadelli, Lodovico. *Vita Reginaldi Poli, Cardinalis*: 92.27
Becon, Thomas. *relikes of Rome, concernynge church ware and matters of religion, The*: 103.88
Becon, Thomas. *sycke mannes salve, The*: 112.143
Beda, Natalis (probable). *Annotationum in Jacobum Fabrum Stapulensem libri duo* (probable): 93.31
Beda, *the Venerable*. *Works* (part): 96.16
Bembo, Pietro. *Epistolae*: 92.112
Benedictus, Alexander. *Anatomice sive historia corporis humani*: 107.88
Bernard, John. *Oratio pia, religiosa, et solatii plena, de vera animi tranquillitate*: 103.17
Bernard, *Saint*. *Works*: 97.2; 110.19
Bernard, *Saint* (probable). *Works* (probable): 107.125
Bernardi, Gulielmus, *Franciscanus*. *De sacrarum literarum communicatione*: 96.74
Bernardinus, *of Siena, Saint*. *Unidentified*: 110.201
Bernardus, *de Lutzenburgo*. *Catalogus hereticorum*: 96.107

Beroaldus, Philippus, *the Elder*. *Apuleius–Metamorphoses*: commentary and text: 92.75; *Cicero–Philippicae*: commentary: 92.57; *Selected works*: 112.139
Beroius, Augustinus (perhaps). *Unidentified*: 90.17
Berthorius, Petrus. *Liber Bibliae moralis*: 102.10; *Unidentified*: 93.32
Bertrandus, *de Turre*. *Sermones*: 110.160; 110.178
Bèze, Théodore de. *Epistolarum theologicarum liber unus*: 110.74; *Quaestionum et responsionum christianarum libellus*: 103.53; 110.128
Bèze, Théodore de (probable). *Confessio christianae fidei* (probable): 110.248
Bible, The: 92.1; 93.1; 96.6; 96.7; 97.1; 103.15; 104.76; 107.92; 109.14; 110.23; 110.53; 110.103; 111.1; 112.1; 112.2; 112.170; (probable): 110.139; *Selections*: 108.77
Old Testament: 103.68; 107.24
Chronicles: 110.26
Genesis: 110.14
Joel, Malachi: 92.102
Kings: 110.21
Leviticus: 93.26; 96.47
Micah: 96.66
Minor prophets: 96.38; 110.33
Proverbs: 110.218
Psalms: 90.40; 93.54; 96.39; 99.1; 107.19; 107.93; 108.90; 109.25; 110.49; 110.56; 110.106; 110.185; 110.262; 112.152; 112.153
New Testament: 92.21; 93.57; 94.23; 94.31; 96.25; 96.99; 98.9; 103.14; 103.41; 104.85; 107.6; 107.27; 107.37; 109.35; 110.68; 110.90; 111.2; 111.5; 112.61; 112.101
Acts: 110.15
Epistles: 91.27; 96.30; 96.46; 96.72; 96.82; 99.9; 99.21; 110.47
Epistles–Paul: 96.81; 97.27; 110.193
Epistles–Corinthians: 110.13
Epistles–Romans: 96.88; 110.38
Epistles–Timothy 1 and 2: 107.101
Gospels: 93.43; 96.14; 96.27; 97.34; 99.12
Gospels (liturgical): 96.77; 107.69
Gospels and Epistles: 107.22; 107.58; 107.66

Gospels and Epistles (liturgical): 107.71; 110.98; 110.143
Gospels–John: 110.5
Gospels–Luke: 110.9
Gospels–Mark: 110.29
Gospels–Matthew: 96.50; 110.157
Revelation: 107.10
Bibliander, Theodore. Unidentified: 107.75
Biblical concordance (unidentified): 96.52; 97.20; 107.128; 110.243 (see also 93.37)
Biel, Gabriel. Unidentified: 96.44
Boccaccio, Giovanni. Unidentified: 110.146
Bodeus, Stephanus. In quatuor institutionum imperialium libros commentarii: 90.80
Bodin, Jean, Bishop. Methodus ad facilem historiarum cognitionem (probable): 112.160
Bodius, Herman, pseudonym. Unio dissidentium: 107.103
Boemus, Joannes. Omnium gentium mores, leges et ritus: 110.213; 112.162
Boethius, Anicius M.T.S. Arithmetica: 112.43; De consolatione philosophiae: 90.53; (perhaps): 110.148
Bonatus, Guido. Decem tractatus astronomiae: 112.38
Bonfinius, Antonius. Symposion de virginitate et pudicitia conjugali [Symposion trimeron]: 107.106; Symposion trimeron: 112.92
Boniface VIII, Pope. Sextus liber Decretalium: 90.46; 90.75; 96.12; 102.6; 112.60
book of precedents, A: 103.59
Boulenger, Pierre. Institutionum christianarum libri octo: 110.71
Bradford, John, Prebendary of St. Paul's. Two notable sermons, . . . the one of repentance, and the other of the Lordes supper: 112.63
Brandolinus, Aurelius. De ratione scribendi: 92.43; 108.2; 110.223; (probable): 108.3; 112.185
Brandolinus, Raphael (probable). Unidentified: 107.72
Brant, Sebastian. Stultifera navis: 108.58
Brasavola, Antonio, Musa. Unidentified: 100.10

Bricot, Thomas. Aristotle–Physica: commentary: 88.18; 93.51; Textus abbreviatus totius logices Aristotelis: 103.4
Bridges, John, Bishop (probable). supremacie of christian princes, The (probable): 110.60
Brunfels, Otto. Herbarium: 96.15
Bruno, Carthusian, Saint. Works: 97.3
Brunus, Conrad. Unidentified: 110.17
Brusonius, Lucius Domitius. Facetiarum exemplorumque libri VII: 108.49; 110.188
Bucchinger, Michael. Tyrocinium. De sacro altaris mysterio: 93.58
Bucer, Martin. Psalms: commentary and text: 110.49
Bucer, Martin (perhaps). Psalms: commentary and text: 107.19
Budaeus, Gulielmus. Commentarii linguae graecae: 110.8
Bullinger, Heinrich. De fine seculi et juditio venturo Domini nostri Jesu Christi: 91.17; Epistles–commentary and text: 96.46; Institutio eorum qui propter Dominum nostrum Jesum Christum de fide examinantur (probable): 104.43; Orthodoxa Tigurinae ecclesiae ministrorum confessio: 96.19; Revelation: commentary: 110.41; Sermonum decades: 112.3
Bullinger, Heinrich (probable). Unidentified: 107.131
Bunderius, Joannes. Compendium concertationis: 96.63; 99.18
Bunel, Pierre. Epistolae: 104.47
Buridanus, Joannes. Aristotle–Ethica: commentary: 92.73; 111.9; Aristotle–Unidentified: commentary (probable): 95.2
Burley, Walter. Aristotle–Ethica: commentary: 93.10; Aristotle–Physica: commentary: 92.77; Aristotle–Unidentified: commentary (probable): 95.5

Caesar, Caius Julius. Commentarii: 92.65; 103.29; 108.72; 109.27; 112.67
Caesarius, Joannes, Juliacensis. Dialectica: 90.25; 92.128:A; 94.39; 104.14:A
Calepino, Ambrogio. Dictionarium: 88.9; 88.11; 91.40:A; 93.47; 102.12; 112.33

Calepino, Ambrogio (probable). *Dictionarium* (probable): 92.132:1
Calepino, Ambrogio (perhaps). *Dictionarium* (perhaps): 108.47
Calfhill, James. *aunswere to the Treatise of the crosse, An*: 103.87; 112.144
Calvin, Jean. *Catechism*: 103.69; *Epistles–Paul: commentary*: 110.44; *Genesis: commentary*: 110.36; *Harmonia*: 110.43; *In viginti prima Ezechielis prophetae capita praelectiones*: 110.57; *Institutio Christianae religionis*: 90.4; 97.12; 107.129; 110.46; 111.3; 112.7; *institution of christian religion, The*: 103.6; *Isaiah: commentary*: 110.39; *Joshua: commentary*: 110.101; *Psalms: commentary and text*: 110.56; *Unidentified*: 110.45
Calvus, Marcus Fabius (perhaps). *Unidentified*: 104.66
Camers, Joannes. *Prima (secunda) pars Pliniani indicis*: 100.5
Campensis, Joannes. *Grammatica hebraica*: 110.96; *Psalms: paraphrase*: 107.93
Canisius, Petrus, Saint. *Authoritates sacrae scripturae* (perhaps): 112.6
Capreolus, Joannes (probable). *Commentaria in IV libros Sententiarum, seu libri IV defensionum theologiae Thomae Aquinatis* (probable): 93.49
Cardano, Girolamo. *Contradicentes medici*: 96.69; *De rerum varietate*: 107.122; 112.80; *De subtilitate*: 107.121; 112.81; *In Cl. Ptolemaei de astrorum judiciis*: 112.79
Carion, Johann. *Chronica*: 97.22; 104.72; 110.107
Carpentarius, Jacobus. *Aristotle–Physica: commentary and text*: 112.77
Carranza, Bartolome, *Archbishop*. *Summa conciliorum*: 110.91
Cartwright, Thomas. *second replie of Thomas Cartwright: agaynst maister Whitgiftes second answer, The*: 112.138
Cassander, Georgius. *De baptismo infantium*: 93.61
Castalio, Sebastian. *Dialogorum sacrorum libri quatuor*: 92.55
Castellensis, Hadrianus, *Cardinal*. *De vera philosophia*: 110.256
Castiglione, Baldassare, *Count*. *courtyer, The*: 112.65

Castro, Alfonso de. *Adversus omnes haereses*: 96.1; 97.29
Catechismus ex decreto Concilii Tridentini (perhaps): 108.64
Catena patrum in acta et epistolas: 96.33
Cato, Dionysius. *Disticha*: 99.14
Celaya, Joannes de. *Unidentified*: 107.110
Celsus, Aulus Cornelius. *De re medica*: 104.92
Ceporinus, Jacobus. *Compendium grammaticae graecae*: 92.59; 92.84; 92.91; 101.3; 103.51; 110.220
Ceporinus, Jacobus (probable). *Compendium grammaticae graecae* (probable): 108.71
Cevallerius, Antonius Rodolphus. *Rudimenta hebraicae linguae* (perhaps): 110.59
Chalmeteus, Antonius. *Enchiridion chirurgicum*: 100.2
Champier, Symphorien. *Practica in medicina*: 104.18
Cheke, Sir John. *De pronuntiatione graecae*: 92.33
Chemnitius, Martinus. *Examen concilii Tridentini*: 110.27
Chromatius, Saint, *Bishop of Aquileia*. *In v and vi caput Matthaei dissertatio*: 96.102
Chytraeus, David. *De lectione historiarum*: 110.116; *Dispositiones epistolarum*: 107.99; 110.102; *Exodus: commentary*: 110.133; *Genesis: commentary*: 107.57; 110.119; *In Numeros enarratio*: 110.117; *Leviticus: commentary*: 110.114; *Luke: commentary* [probably a ghost]: 107.45; *Regulae vitae*: 107.105; *Unidentified*: 110.205
Cicero, Marcus Tullius. *De finibus*: 99.22; *De natura Deorum*: 90.13; *De officiis*: 91.13; 91.14; 98.4; 99.25; 109.7; 110.30; 110.228; 112.105; (probable): 108.79; *De oratore*: 90.45; 99.23; *Epistolae ad Atticum*: 98.13; 110.110; *Epistolae ad familiares*: 92.12; (perhaps): 112.112; *Epistolae–Selections*: 108.33; *Philippicae*: 94.13; *Quaestiones Tusculanae*: 92.119; 110.195; *Selected works–Epistolae*: 89.5; 91.7; 94.7; 94.22; 104.50; 108.31;

109.39; 110.268; (probable): 107.120; (perhaps): 91.5; *Selected works–Orations*: 91.35; 95.1; 98.14; 101.2; 107.36; 109.18; 110.109:2; 110.130; 110.196; 112.45; *Selected works–Philsophica*: 90.90; 97.55; 98.6; 101.1; 110.109:1; *Selected works–Rhetorica*: 91.12; 112.186; (probable): 95.8; *Selections*: 94.33; 110.229; 112.98; *Unidentified*: 107.1; 108.46; 110.108; *Works*: 92.11; 104.35; 112.37; *Works* (part) (perhaps): 103.42
Cicero, Marcus Tullius (spurious). *Rhetorica ad Herennium*: 94.26; 110.183; 112.187
Clarorum virorum epistolae (probable): 97.54
Clavasio, Angelus de. *Summa Angelica*: 90.6; 110.194
Clement I, Saint, Pope. *De rebus gestis, peregrinationibus atque concionibus Petri*: 90.56
Clenardus, Nicolaus. *Institutiones ac meditationes in graecam linguam, cum scholiis et praxi P. Antesignani*: 90.10; 92.82; 92.85; 94.27; 103.18; 107.63; 109.20
Clichtoveus, Jodocus. *Homiliae*: 110.204
Clichtoveus, Jodocus (probable). *Homiliae*: 112.145
Clingius, Conradus (perhaps). *Loci communes theologici* (perhaps): 97.14
Cochlaeus, Joannes. *Consyderatio de futuro concordiae in religione tractatu*: 93.56; *Defensio caeremoniarum ecclesiae adversus errores et calumnias trium librorum Ambrosii Moibani*: 96.64; *Unidentified*: 110.141
Comines, Philippe de. *Memoires*: 112.161; *Unidentified*: 107.30
Commentaria in Isagogen Porphyrii et in omnes libros Aristotelis de dialectica: 95.4
Contarini, Gasparo. *Unidentified*: 92.117
Cooper, Thomas, *Bishop*. *Thesaurus linguae Romanae et Britannicae*: 91.2; 103.3
Concordantiae majores biblie: 93.37
Cordier, Mathurin. *De corrupti sermonis emendatione*: 107.119; *Unidentified*: 112.179

Cordus, Valerius. *Dispensatorium*: 104.58
Cornax, Matthias. *Medicae consultationis apud aegrotos enchiridion*: 104.79
Corpus juris canonici: 88.1; 88.3; 90.16; 90.29; 90.43; 90.73; 90.81; 96.13; 102.1; 102.2; 102.4; 102.5; 102.8; 102.13; 102.14; 112.48; 112.59
Clementinae: 88.2
Liber Extra (probable): 102.7
Liber Sextus: 90.46; 90.75; 96.12; 102.6; 112.51; 112.60
Corpus juris civilis: 88.6; 88.13; 88.15; 90.1; 90.2; 90.7; 90.8; 90.20; 90.24; 90.30; 90.32; 90.33; 90.37; 90.49; 90.50; 90.51; 90.52; 90.54; 90.64; 90.68; 90.85; 92.95; 109.23; 110.89; 112.47; 112.57
Corvinus, Antonius. *Postilla*: 96.89; 107.58; *Unidentified*: 93.63
Covarruvias a Leyva, Diego, *Bishop of Segovia*. *Decretales–Epitome* (probable): 112.52
Councils of the Church: 110.67
Councils–Trent: 110.214
Cradocke, Edward. *shippe of assured safetie, The*: 112.149
Cranmer, Thomas, *Archbishop*. *answer of ... Thomas archebyshop of Canterburye, unto a crafty cavillation by S. Gardiner, An*: 103.11; *Reformatio legum ecclesiasticarum*: 112.54
Cromer, Martin, *Bishop*. *Unidentified*: 110.54
Crusius, Martin. *Grammatica graeca, cum latina congruens*: 104.38
Curio, Caelius Secundus. *Aristotle–Topica: commentary*: 97.45; *Cicero–De partitione oratoria: commentary* [and others]: 97.23; *De bello Melitensi historia nova*: 110.259; *Pro vera et antiquae ecclesiae Christi autoritate, in Antonium Florebellum Mutinensem, oratio*: 103.55; *Selectarum epistolarum libri duo. Orationum liber unus*: 104.48; 112.117
Curio, Caelius Secundus (perhaps). *Cicero–De partitione oratoriae: commentary* [and others]: 108.67; *Unidentified*: 107.46
Curio, Jacobus. *Hippocratis ... de naturae temporum anni, et aeris irregulari-*

um constitutionum propriis, hominisque omnium aetatum morbis, theoria: 104.19
Curtius Rufus, Quintus. *De rebus gestis Alexandri Magni*: 91.20; 92.58; 97.40
Cusa, Nicolaus de. *Unidentified*: 93.35
Cyprian, Saint. *Works*: 96.10; 97.5; 107.33; 110.31
Cyprian, Saint (probable). *Unidentified*: 108.70:1
Cyril, *of Alexandria, Saint. Works*: 96.24
Cyril, *of Jerusalem, Saint. Catechesis*: 108.86

Dedicus, Joannes. *Questiones moralissime super libros ethicorum*: 93.75
Demosthenes. *Adversus Leptinem*: 92.92; *De falsa legatione*: 104.52; *Graecorum oratorum principis, Olynthiacae orationes tres, et Philippicae quatuor*: 103.26; *Olynthiacae orationes tres*: 103.45; *Selected works–Epistolae*: 104.91; *Selected works–Orations*: 90.66; 103.89; (probable): 112.210; 112.218; *Selected works* (probable): 105.3; *Unidentified*: 99.32; 104.84
Denyse, Nicolaus. *Resolutio theologorum*: 93.24
Despautère, Jean. *Grammatica*: 108.52; *Unidentified*: 91.25; 109.6
Dinus de Mugello. *De regulis juris*: 112.51
Dictionaries (unidentified): 92.2; 98.2; 103.7; 106.1:1; 106.1:2; 107.16; 112.32
Diogenes Laertius. *De vita et moribus philosophorum*: 92.50; 103.35
Diogenes Laertius (perhaps). *De vita et moribus philosophorum* (perhaps): 108.84
Dionysius Areopagita. *Works*: 110.76
Dionysius, *Carthusianus. Gospels: commentary*: 96.28; 102.17; *Works* (perhaps): 93.19
Dionysius, *of Halicarnassus. Antiquitates sive origines Romanae*: 110.105
Dioscorides. *De medica materia*: 104.57
Dorn, Gerard. *Chymisticum artificum naturae, theoricum et practicum*: 107.55
Dorotheus, *Archimandrite of Palestine, Saint* (perhaps). *Sermones* (perhaps): 93.67

Dryander, Joannes. *Anatomia capitas humani*: 96.105
Duarenus, Franciscus. *Unidentified*: 112.58
Dubois, Jacques. *De febribus commentarius ex libris aliquot Hippocratis et Galeni*: 104.82; *De medicamentorum simplicium delectu*: 104.54
Ducherius, Gilbertus. *Epigrammata* (probable): 108.41; *Aristotle–Metaphysica: commentary*: 93.9; 109.1; *Aristotle–Sophistici elenchi: commentary*: 112.25; *Flores totius sacre teologie*: 93.40; *Sentences I: commentary*: 88.20; *Sentences: commentary*: 96.43; (probable): 96.97; *Sentences: commentary* (part): 107.11; *Unidentified*: 88.19; 110.182
Dunus, Thaddeus. *Unidentified*: 104.61
Durandus, Gulielmus I, *Bishop of Mende. Rationale divinorum officiorum*: 93.42

Eckius, Joannes. *De sacrificio missae contra Lutheranos*: 110.136; *Enchiridion locorum communium adversus Lutheranos*: 92.24; 110.245
Eckius, Joannes. *Homiliae*: 108.1; 110.184; 110.206; *Unidentified*: 110.142
Eder, Georg. *Unidentified*: 110.12
Elyot, Sir Thomas. *boke named the governour, The*: 112.175; *dictionary of syr Thomas Eliot, The*: 104.1; 110.147
En lector, librum damus vere areum; planeo scholasticum, quo continentur haec Pythagorae carmina aurea. Phocylidae poema admonitorium. Theognidis gnomologia. Coluthi Helenae raptus. Tryphiodori de Troiae excidio: 90.58
Eobanus, Helius, *Hessus. De tuenda bona valetudine*: 92.29
Epigrammata graeca: 110.238
Epiphanius, *Bishop of Constantia. Works*: 110.65
Erasmus, Desiderius: *Adagia*: 99.8; 108.4; 110.6; 112.41; *Adagia–Epitome*: 112.123; *Apophthegmata*: 92.62; 93.59; 94.24; 108.53; 108.91; 109.19; *Colloquia*: 87.2; 90.19; 91.19; 92.106; 94.40; 95.14; 95.15; 103.64; 112.136;

Colloquia–Epitome: 89.2; *Concionalis interpretatio, plena pietatis, in Psalmum LXXXV*: 90.67; *De conscribendis epistolis*: 112.193; *De duplici copia verborum ac rerum*: 87.1; 94.8; 94.10; 101.4; 110.264; 112.194; *De misericordia Domini*: 103.75; *De praeparatione ad mortem*: 104.83; *De recta pronuntiatione* [and others]: 91.30; 112.195; *Ecclesiastes, sive de ratione concionandi*: 108.7; *Enchiridion militis Christiani*: 91.21; 99.10; *Epicureus*: 108.20; *Epistles–Paul: paraphrase*: 96.81; *Epistles: paraphrase*: 96.30; 96.72; *Epistolae*: 94.34; 107.43; *Explanatio symboli apostolorum*: 108.27; *Lingua*: 94.20; *Moriae encomium*: 92.61; 112.201; *New Testament: commentary*: 96.22; 110.37; 111.5; *Precationes*: 108.30; 109.40; *Unidentified*: 91.31; 96.99; 107.29; 107.38; 108.39

Erasmus, Desiderius (probable). *De duplici copia verborum ac rerum* (probable): 92.127; 108.82; *Methodus: Ratio verae theologiae* (probable): 96.103

Erythraeus, Valentinus. *De grammaticorum figuris* [and others]: 112.208; *In orationem M.T.C. pro lege Manilia de Pompeii laudibus annotationes*: 99.30; *Tabulae in Ciceronem et Sturmium*: 97.19; *Unidentified*: 92.121

Estienne, Charles. *Dictionarium historicum ac poeticum*: 90.70

Estienne, Robert, *the Elder* (probable). *Dictionariolum puerorum, tribus linguis Latina, Anglica et Gallica conscriptum*: 109.16

Eusebius, *Pamphili, Bishop. Historia ecclesiastica*: 96.53; 110.1

Eusebius, *Pamphili, Bishop* (probable). *Unidentified*: 107.20

Evans, Lewis. *shorte treatyse of the mysterie of the euchariste, A*: 103.98

Everardus, Nicolaus, *of Middelburg. Consilia sive responsa*: 90.61

Faber, Jacobus, *Stapulensis. Aristotle–Ethica: commentary*: 92.19; 108.62; *Aristotle–Physica: commentary and paraphrase*: 97.33; 112.86; *Aristotle–Selected works–Logica: commentary*: 93.11; 107.8; *Aristotle–Selected works–Philosophia naturalis: paraphrase*: 100.3; *Aristotle–Unidentified: paraphrase*: 96.23; *Gospels: commentary and text*: 96.14; *Unidentified*: 93.73; 112.20

Falletti, Girolamo. *Orationes XII*: 112.209

Fallopius, Gabriel. *Observationes anatomicae* (probable): 104.21

Fenton, Sir Geoffrey. *A forme of christian pollicie*: 112.71; *Golden epistles, contayning varietie of discourse gathered as well out of the remaynder of Guevaraes workes, as other authors, Latine, French, and Italian*: 112.108

Fernelius, Joannes. *Therapeutices universalis seu medendi rationis libri septem* (probable): 104.5; *Unidentified*: 100.6; 112.102

Ferrerio, Giovanni, *Piemontese. Academica de animorum immortalitate enarratio*: 112.76

Ferus, Joannes. *Postilla*: 103.32; *Gospels and Epistles (liturgical): commentary*: 103.13

Ferus, Joannes (probable). *Postilla* (probable): 110.104

Ficino, Marsilio. *De triplici vita*: 110.230; 112.166; *Unidentified*: 100.4

Finé, Oronce. *De mundi sphaera*: 103.21; 104.33

Fisher, John, *Saint and Cardinal. Assertionis Lutheranae confutatio*: 90.28; (probable): 96.94; *De veritate corporis et sanguinis Christi in eucharistia*: 96.85; 97.4

Flacius, Matthias, *Illyricus. Clavis scripturae*: 110.18; *De sectis, dissensionibus, scriptorum et doctorum pontificiorum liber* (perhaps): 110.20

Flacius, Matthias, *Illyricus* (probable). *Unidentified*: 91.26

Flaminio, Marco Antonio. *Psalms: commentary and text* (probable): 112.152; *Psalms: paraphrase*: 90.40

Floccus, Andreas Dominicus. *De magistratibus sacerdotiisque Romanorum*: 92.35; (probable): 90.38; *Unidentified*: 110.263

Flores Bibliae: 108.77

Flores poetarum: 90.65

Florus, Lucius Annaeus. *Epitomae de Tito Livio bellorum omnium annorum*: 104.39; 110.221; (probable): 92.56
Fox Morzillo, Sebastiano. *De naturae philosophia, seu de Platonis et Aristotelis consensione*: 97.35; 112.85; *De regni regisque institutione*: 112.67
Foxe, John, the Martyrologist. *first (second) volume of the ecclesiasticall history contaynyng the Actes and monumentes of the church, The*: 103.2; *Syllogisticon hoc est: argumenta, . . . de re et materia sacramenti eucharistici*: 108.15
Francis I, King of France. *Exemplaria literarum quibus Rex Franciscus ad adversariorum maledictis defenditur*: 93.45
Fuchs, Leonard. *De componendorum medicamentorum ratione*: 104.25; 107.34; *De medendi methodo*: 104.6; 107.51; *Institutiones medicinae*: 104.4; *Methodus seu ratio compendiaria perveniendi ad medicinam*: 100.1
Fulgentius, Bishop of Ruspa. *Works*: 110.73
Fulgosus, Baptista (probable). *Facta dictaque memorabilia* (probable): 97.15
Fumus, Bartholomaeus. *Summa, sive aurea armilla*: 99.3
Funck, Johann. *Chronologia*: 110.16

Gagneius, Joannes. *Epitome paraphrastica in epistolam ad Romanos*: 96.88
Gaietanus, de Thienis. *Unidentified*: 88.17
Galatino, Pietro. *Opus de arcanis catholicae veritatis*: 96.42
Galen. *Ars medica*: 104.26; *De alimentorum facultatibus*: 96.60; 104.32; *De anatomicis administrationibus*: 104.30; *De compositione medicamentorum secundum locos*: 104.31; *De constitutione artis medicae*: 104.22; *De curandi ratione per venae sectionem*: 104.15; *De Hippocratis et Platonis decretis*: 104.28; *De locis affectis*: 96.61; *De morborum et symptomatum differentiis et causis libri sex*: 104.73; *De naturalibus facultatibus*: 104.86; *De sanitate tuenda*: 96.49; 108.14; *De simplicium medicamentorum facultatibus*: 104.59; *De symptomatum differentiis. De symptomatum causis*: 96.55; *De usu partium*: 104.27; *Methodus medendi*: 104.24; *Unidentified*: 104.23; 112.164; *Works*: 96.40
Galen (probable). *Ad Glauconem* (probable): 104.70
Galen (ascribed). *De prognostica de decubitu infirmorum*: 104.90
Gambellionibus, Angelus de, Aretinus. *De maleficiis* (perhaps): 94.17
Garcaeus, Joannes. *Meteorologia*: 112.84; *Tractatus brevis de erigendis figuris coeli*: 112.119
Gardiner, Stephen, Bishop. *Ad Martinum Bucerum*: 92.103; *Confutatio cavillationum quibus eucharistiae sacramentum ab impiis Capernaitis impeti solet*: 96.62; *Unidentified*: 110.78
Garetius, Joannes. *Sacrificii missae ex Sanctis Patribus assertio*: 110.111
Gasser, Achilles. *Historiarum et chronicorum mundi epitome*: 107.95
Gellius, Aulus. *Noctes Atticae*: 91.36; 97.6; 107.91; 112.94
Gemma, Reiner, Frisius. *Arithmeticae practicae methodus facilis*: 98.16; 103.77; *Unidentified*: 110.127
Gentile da Foligno. *De febribus*: 96.17
Gerardus, Andreas, Hyperius. *De sacrae scripturae lectione*: 110.244; *De theologo, sive De ratione studii theologici*: 97.25; 110.85; 112.19; (probable): 107.65; *Methodus theologiae sive loci communes*: 107.127; 110.61; 112.18; 112.104; *Opuscula theologica*: 107.64; 110.70; *Opusculorum theologicorum pars secunda* (perhaps): 112.103; *Topica theologica*: 107.47; 110.247:1; *Unidentified*: 97.41; 110.237
Gerson, Joannes. *Unidentified*: 107.12
Gerson, Joannes (perhaps). *Works* (part) (perhaps): 93.21
Gesner, Conrad. *Onomasticon*: 91.40:B
Gibault, Hector. *Galen–De differentiis febrium: commentary and text*: 104.55
Gilles, Peter. *Unidentified*: 88.7
Giovio, Paolo, Bishop. *Unidentified*: 107.77
godly and necessarye admonition of the decrees and canons of the counsel of Trent, A: 103.83
Goodman, Christopher. *How superior*

powers oght to be obeyd of their subjects: and wherin they may lawfully be disobeyed: 103.94
Gordonio, Bernardus de. *Practica, seu Lilium medicinae*: 104.8; (probable): 112.99; *Tractatus de conservatione vitae humanae*: 104.74
Górski, Jakób. *Commentariorum artis dialecticae libri decem*: 112.199
Grapaldus, Franciscus Marius. *De partibus aedium*: 96.57
Gratianus, *the Canonist. Decretum*: 96.13; 102.8; 102.13; 112.48; *Decretum* (part): 90.43
Gregory I, Saint, Pope. *Homiliae super Evangeliis*: 110.163
Gregory I, Saint, Pope (probable). *Works* (part): 112.10
Gregory IX, Pope. *Decretales*: 90.73; 102.4; 102.14; 112.59; *Decretales* (part): 90.16; 90.29; 90.81
grete herball, The: 100.7
Grimald, Nicholas. *Unidentified*: 99.33
Groepper, Johann. *Antididagma seu Christianae et Catholicae religionis propugnatio*: 96.70
Groepper, Johann (probable). *Antididagma seu Christianae et Catholicae religionis propugnatio* (probable): 110.247:2
Grynaeus, Simon. *De utilitate legendae historiae*: 108.28
Guerricus, *Abbot of Igny* (perhaps). *Sermones* (perhaps): 93.53
Guevara, Antonio de, Bishop. *familiar epistles, The*: 112.107
Guido (probable). *Casus longi super Institutis*: 112.53
Guillon, René. *De generibus carminum graecorum*: 98.19
Gulielmus, de Conchis. *Dialogus de substantiis physiciis*: 97.38
Guntherus, Petrus. *De arte rhetorica libri duo*: 92.122

Habermann, Johann. *Grammatica hebraica*: 107.59
Haddon, Walter. *Lucubrationes passim collectae, et editae*: 112.100
Haly, *Filius Abenragel. De judiciis astrorum*: 97.30

Hamelmann, Hermann. *De traditionibus apostolicis*: 110.50
Hanapus, Nicolaus. *Exempla sacrae scripturae*: 107.92
Harmenopoulos, Constantine. *Procheiron, sive Epitome juris civilis*: 90.74
Haymo, *Bishop of Halberstadt. Epistles–Paul: commentary*: 110.215
Helmesius, Heinrich. *Homiliae*: 110.97
Hemmingsen, Niels. *Catechismi quaestiones concinnatae*: 110.121; *Commentaria in omnes epistolas Apostolorum, Pauli, Petri, Judae, Johannis, Jacobi, et in eam quae ad Hebraeos inscribitur* (probable): 110.47; *De lege naturae apodictica methodus*: 107.87; *Enchiridion theologicum*: 110.93; 112.118; *Gospels (liturgical): commentary*: 107.67; *Pastor, sive pastoris optimus vivendi agendique modus*: 112.148; *Unidentified*: 110.224
Herburt, Jan. *Chronica sive historiae Polonicae descriptio*: 107.116
Herdesianus, Christoph. *Unidentified*: 107.124
Hermogenes. *Ars rhetorica*: 92.39; *Rhetorica*: 112.190
Herodian. *Historiae*: 90.71; 97.39; 109.22
Herolt, Joannes. *Sermones discipuli*: 112.11
Heshusius, Tilemannus, Bishop. *Sexcenti errores pleni blasphemiis in Deum*: 110.125
Hessels, Joannes (perhaps). *De officio pii et christianae pacis vere amantis viri* (perhaps): 97.37
Hesychius, *of Jerusalem. In Leviticum libri septem*: 93.26; 96.47
Hierocles, *of Alexandria. Pythagoras–Carmina aurea: commentary and text*: 107.90
Hippocrates. *Aphorismi*: 104.60; *Works*: 96.18; 104.17
Hoffmeister, Johann. *Judicium de articulis Confessionis fidei anno (1530) Augustae exhibitis* (probable): 110.250
Hoffmeister, Johann (probable). *Gospels (liturgical): commentary*: 96.95; *Loci communes rerum theologicarum* (probable): 96.71
Holcot, Robert. *Proverbs: commentary*: 110.173

INDEX I: AUTHORS AND WORKS 327

Holywood, John. *Sphaera mundi*: 109.41; 110.123; *Unidentified*: 92.31; 110.132

Homer. *Iliad*: 98.5; 103.30; 107.35; 110.255; 112.120; 112.122; 112.124; *Works* (perhaps): 103.67

Honterus, Joannes. *Rudimenta cosmographica*: 103.95

Honterus, Joannes (probable). *Rudimenta cosmographica* (probable): 92.32

Hopper, Joachim. *Ad Justinianum de obligationibus peithanon*: 90.37; *Dispositio in libros pandectarum*: 90.68; *Institutiones imperiales*: 110.89; 112.57

Horatius Flaccus, Quintus. *Sermones sive Satirae*: 91.22; *Works*: 103.38; (probable): 91.9; 91.29; 92.64; 94.4; 109.17; 112.125; (perhaps): 90.31

Hotman, François. *De furoribus Gallicis*: 110.240

Hugo, *de Sancto Victore* (perhaps). *Unidentified*: 110.161

Huloet, Richard. *Abcedarium Anglico Latinum, pro tyrunculis*: 91.34

Humphrey, Laurence. *Joannis Juelli Angli, episcopi Sarisburiensis vita et mors, eiusque; verae doctrinae defensio*: 110.137; *Optimates, sive de nobilitate*: 104.51:A

Hunnaeus, Augustinus. *Dialectica, seu generalis logices praecepta*: 95.11

Hutten, Ulrich von. *Epigrammata*: 108.11

Ignatius, *Saint, Bishop of Antioch. Epistolae*: 99.16

Irenaeus, *Saint. Adversus haereses*: 110.92

Irenaeus, *Saint* (probable). *Unidentified*: 107.31

Isaac, Joannes, *Levita. Grammatica hebraea*: 107.50

Isidore, *Saint, Bishop of Seville. De summo bono*: 92.81; *Etymologiae*: 102.11

Isocrates. *Ad Demonicum*: 108.19; *Archidamus*: 104.53; *Oratio ad Nicoclem*: 104.45; *Selected works—Orations*: 108.17; *Works*: 92.14; (probable): 110.82

Jammetius Textor, Franciscus. *Commentarius in XLIIII leges*: 90.72

Janduno, Joannes de. *Aristotle–Physica: commentary*: 93.12

Javellus, Chrysostomus. *Unidentified*: 104.77

Jerome, *Saint. Epistolae*: 93.41; 96.8; 107.7; *Unidentified*: 107.2; *Vitae patrum*: 93.22

Jewel, John, *Bishop. apologie, or aunswer in defence of the Church of England, An*: 103.20; (perhaps): 110.40; *defence of the Apologie of the Churche of Englande, A*: 103.12; *replie unto M. Hardinges answeare, A*: 112.8; (probable): 95.3; *Unidentified*: 110.270

Joannes, *Canonicus. Aristotle–Physica: commentary*: 88.10; 107.108; 112.24 112.30

John, *Chrysostom, Saint. Acts: commentary*: 96.80; *De orando Deum*: 90.87; *Homiliae*: 92.100; *Mark, Luke: commentary*: 96.79; *Unidentified*: 96.67; 107.5; *Works*: 96.4; 110.4; 110.140

John, *of Damascus, Saint. De fide orthodoxa*: 92.76; *Theologia*: 110.168; *Works*: 96.32

Joliffe, Henry. *Responsio ad articulos Joannis Hoperi*: 110.211

Josephus, Flavius. *Antiquitates Judaicae*: 93.46; *Works*: 97.21; 110.35

Joubert, Laurent. *Medicinae practicae priores libri tres* (perhaps): 104.7

Joye, George (perhaps). *unite and scisme of the olde chirche, The* (perhaps): 103.92

Justinian I. *Codex*: 88.13; 90.30; 90.33; *Digesta*: 90.8; 90.64; *Digesta* (part): 90.7; 90.20; 90.49; 90.50; 90.51; 90.52; *Digestum novum*: 90.2; *Institutiones*: 90.1; 90.54; 90.85; 109.23; *Novellae constitutiones*: 88.15; 90.32; *Unidentified*: 112.47

Justinian I (probable). *Institutiones* (probable): 92.95

Justinus, *the Historian* (see Trogus Pompeius)

Justinus, *Martyr. Works*: 110.75; *Works* (part) (perhaps): 108.68

Justus, Pascasius. *Alea, sive de curanda ludendi in pecuniam cupiditate*: 112.97

Juvenalis, Guido. *Interpretatio in Laurentii Vallae Elegantias latinae linguae* (perhaps): 92.109

Katzschius, Joannes. *De gubernanda sanitate*: 104.81

Kimchi, David. *Joel et Malachias cum commentario*: 92.102

La Place, Pierre de. *De statu religionis et reipublicae in regno Galliae*: 112.155
La Ramée, Pierre de. *Aristotelicae animadversiones*: 103.50; *Dialectica*: 112.205
Lactantius, Lucius Coelius. *Unidentified*: 92.51; *Works* (probable): 91.15; 97.24; 103.61; 112.146
Lancelotto, Giovanni Paolo. *Institutiones juris canonici* (probable): 112.56
Lancelotto, Giovanni Paolo (probable). *Institutiones juris canonici*: 109.26
Lancelotto, Giovanni Paolo (perhaps). *Institutiones juris canonici* (perhaps): 90.76
Langdaile, Alban. *Catholica confutatio impiae cuiusdam determinationis N. Ridlei*: 96.59
Lanquet, Thomas. *epitome of cronicles, An*: 112.73
Latimer, Hugh, *Bishop. Sermons*: 112.62
Lavater, Ludwig. *De spectris*: 110.120; *In libros Paralipomenon sive Chronicorum commentarius*: 110.26; *Joshua: commentary*: 110.55; *Unidentified*: 110.25
Lee, Edward, *Archbishop of York. Apologia contra quorundum calumnias* [and others]: 96.54
Leo I, *Emperor of the East*, and others. *Constitutiones novellae*: 90.24
Lever, Thomas. *sermon preached at Pauls crosse, the .xiiii. day of December, ... M.D.L., A*: 103.84
Lily, William. *De octo partium orationis constructione*: 91.37; *Institutio compendiaria totius grammaticae*: 92.115
Lily, William (probable). *Institutio compendiaria totius grammaticae* (probable): 112.135
Linacre, Thomas. *Rudimenta grammatices*: 92.63; (probable): 91.32; 110.236; 112.133
Lindanus, Willelmus, *Bishop. Panoplia evangelica*: 110.22
Littleton, Sir Thomas. *Tenures*: 107.32
Liturgies—Church of England
 Book of Common Prayer: 102.16; (with Geneva Psalms, perhaps) 108.88

Liturgies—Latin Rite
 Hours and Primers—Salisbury and Reformed: 87.4
Livius, Titus. *Historiae Romanae decades*: 97.11; *Historiae Romanae decades—Selected works*: 94.1; 107.89
Lizet, Pierre. *Unidentified*: 97.47
Longolius, Christophorus. *Epistolae*: 107.26; 108.59; 110.189; 112.113; *Unidentified*: 92.113
Lorich, Gerhard. *De missa publica proroganda*: 96.91
Louvain University: *Commentaria in Isagogen Porphyrii et in omnes libros Aristotelis de dialectica*: 95.4
Lucanus, Marcus Annaeus. *Pharsalia*: 107.85; 112.215
Lucian, *of Samosata. Deorum dialogi*: 92.97; *Dialogues—Selected*: 97.57; 101.5; 103.58; (probable): 87.3; 104.49; *Unidentified*: 93.8; *Works* (probable): 110.252
Ludolphus, *de Saxonia. Vita Jesu Christi*: 93.23; 93.36; 110.151; 112.9
Ludolphus, *de Saxonia* (probable). *Unidentified*: 93.38; *Vita Jesu Christi* (probable): 93.4
Luis, *de Granada. Unidentified*: 110.226
Lull, Ramón. *De secretis naturae* (perhaps): 92.26; *Testamentum artem chymicam complectens*: 92.25; *Unidentified*: 107.113
Luther, Martin. *Galatians: commentary*: 110.72; *Postilla*: 96.11; *Unidentified*: 110.158; *Works* (part): 111.7
Lychetus, Franciscus. *Duns, Scotus—Sentences: commentary* (probable): 93.39
Lycosthenes, Conrad. *Apophthegmata*: 95.12; 110.174; 112.17; *Similium loci communes*: 110.192:A
Lyndewode, William, *Bishop. Constitutiones provinciales*: 112.50
Lyra, Nicolaus de. *Postilla*: 97.16; *Postilla* (part) (probable): 109.12

Macchiavelli, Niccolò. *Unidentified*: 112.106
Macrobius, Ambrosius Aurelius Theodosius. *In somnium Scipionis. Saturnalia*: 92.116
Macropedius, Georgius. *Graecarum*

INDEX I: AUTHORS AND WORKS 329

institutionum rudimenta: 92.90; *Methodus de conscribendis epistolis*: 108.18; 108.81
Magistris, Joannes de. *Unidentified*: 93.18
Mainardi, Agostino. *anatomi, that is to say a parting in peeces of the mass, An*: 103.37
Maino, Jason de. *Unidentified*: 96.36
Major, Joannes. *Ethica Aristotelis peripateticorum principis cum Joannis Majoris commentariis*: 92.20
Manlius, Joannes. *Locorum communium collectanea*: 107.68
Manuscript(s), including (probable) and (perhaps): 90.27; 90.55; 90.77; 92.38; 93.3; 94.41; 97.13:1-3; 100.11; 103.99; 104.87:1-3; 110.269:1-2; 111.10
Manuzio, Aldo, *the Younger*. *Purae, elegantes et copiosae latinae linguae phrases*: 112.178
Manuzio, Paolo: *Epistolae*: 92.80; 109.24; 110.190; 112.109
Martialis, Marcus Valerius. *Epigrammata*: 91.11; 112.130
Marulic, Marko (probable). *Unidentified*: 110.241
Matthisius, Gerardus. *Aristotle–Selected works–Philosophia naturalis–Epitome: commentary*: 107.40; *Aristotle–Unidentified: commentary*: 107.25; 107.41
Maurus Rabanus. *De sacramento eucharistae*: 96.56
Meier, Georg, *Professor at Wittenberg. Enarratio epistolae ad Hebraeos*: 107.97; 110.83
Mela, Pomponius. *De situ orbis*: 94.25; 103.78
Melanchthon, Philipp. *Aristotle–Ethica: commentary*: 94.32; 112.91; *Aristotle–Physica: commentary*: 112.217; *Dialectica*: 112.207; *Examen eorum qui audiuntur ante ritum publicae ordinationis*: 107.98; *Gospels (liturgical): commentary and text*: 107.69; *Grammatica latina* (probable): 112.134; *Loci communes theologici*: 103.56; 110.77; *Proverbs: commentary*: 103.52; *Rhetorica*: 112.184; *Unidentified*: 107.104
Mena, Ferdinandus de, *Physician*. *Methodus febrium omnium*: 104.29
Mesue, Joannes. *De re medica*: 96.37; *Unidentified*: 104.67
Micyllus, Jacobus, *pseudonym*. *Arithmetica logistica*: 103.57
Molitoris, Ulricus. *De lamiis et pythonicis mulieribus*: 97.59
Montanus, Joannes Baptista. *Consultationes medicinales*: 96.100; 104.2
Montanus, Joannes Baptista (probable). *Unidentified*: 104.10
Muenster, Sebastian. *Grammatica hebraica*: 103.34; 110.99; *Unidentified*: 110.95
Murmellius, Joannes. *Aristotle–Categoriae: commentary*: 92.128:B
Murmellius, Joannes (probable). *Aristotle–Categoriae: commentary* (probable): 104.14:B
Musculus, Andreas. *Loci communes sacri*: 110.2
Musculus, Wolfgang. *Loci communes*: 110.62
Musculus, Wolfgang (probable). *Loci communes*: 107.130; 112.5
Mynsinger, Joachim. *Unidentified*: 109.37

Nannus, Dominicus, *Mirabellius*. *Polyanthea*: 110.28
Nannus, Dominicus, *Mirabellius* (perhaps). *Polyanthea* (perhaps): 108.48
Natura brevium: 90.35
Nemesius, *Bishop*. *De natura hominis*: 90.89
Nicephorus Callistus. *Ecclesiastica historia*: 110.166; (probable): 110.191
Nicolaus, *de Blony*. *Sermones*: 93.34
Niphus, Augustinus. *Aristotle–De interpretatione: commentary*: 107.17; *Aristotle–Topica: commentary*: 95.7; 107.18; *Unidentified*: 99.34
Nizolius, Marius. *Observationes* (probable): 112.35
Northbrooke, John. *Spiritus est.... A breefe and pithy summe of the christian faith* (probable): 110.124
Novellus, Jacobus. *Practica et theorica causarum criminalium*: 90.62
Nowell, Alexander. *Catechismus, sive prima institutio, disciplináque pieta-*

tis christianae: 103.22; *Catechismus*: 110.138; *Unidentified*: 103.25

Ochino, Bernardino. *Dialogi*: 107.56

Oecolampadius, Joannes. *Graecae literaturae dragmata*: 90.79

Olde, John (attributed). *short description of Antichrist unto the nobilitie of Englande, A*: 103.93

Oldendorp, Johann. *Actionum forensium progymnasmata*: 90.78

Omphalius, Jacobus. *De elocutionis imitatione ac apparatu*: 92.40; 108.80; *Unidentified*: 112.177

Optatus, Saint. *De schismate Donatistarum*: 110.216

Orbellis, Nicolaus de. *Cursus librorum philosophiae naturalis*: 103.33; *Unidentified*: 99.15

Origen. *Works*: 112.12; *Works* (part): 111.6

Orosius, Paulus. *Historiae adversus paganos* (probable): 96.76

Osiander, Andreas, the Elder. *Conjecturae de ultimis temporibus*: 103.79

Osorio da Fonseca, Jeronimo, Bishop. *De gloria*: 92.7; 110.186; 112.89; *De justitia*: 92.9; 108.63; 110.66; 112.90; *De nobilitate civili libri II. De nobilitate christiana libri III.*: 92.8; *De regis institutione et disciplina*: 110.79; 112.64; *Epistola ad Elisabetam, Angliae Reginam*: 110.135; *In Gualterum Haddonum magistrum libellorum supplicum libri tres*: 92.130; *Unidentified*: 109.21

Ovidius Naso, Publius. *Ars amatoria*: 108.89; *De ponto*: 104.37; *Fasti*: 108.23; *Heroides*: 94.18; *Metamorphoses*: 94.3; 94.15; 95.10; 103.39; 110.219; 112.131; *Tristia*: 90.48; 103.28; 112.132; *Works*: 92.47; 93.48

Pagninus, Sanctes. *Thesauri linguae sanctae epitome*: 110.94

Palingenius, Marcellus. *Zodiacus vitae*: 92.129; 103.63; 105.1

Palingenius, Marcellus (probable). *Zodiacus vitae* (probable): 108.65; 110.175

Palladinus, Jacobus, *de Theramo. Consolatio peccatorum, seu Processus Belial*: 96.2

Pantaleon, Heinrich. *Chronographia ec-*

clesiae christianae: 112.15

Papa, Guido. *Consilia*: 90.12

Paracelsus. *De gradibus*: 104.78; *Unidentified*: 112.165

Paradin, Guillaume (probable). *Unidentified*: 112.176

Paratus (perhaps). *Sermones*: 112.16

Pastregicus, Gulielmus. *De originibus rerum libellus*: 91.28

Paulii, Simon, the Elder. *Methodi aliquot locorum doctrinae ecclesiae Dei*: 110.87; *Postilla*: 107.66

Paulus, Aegineta. *Pharmaca simplicia*: 92.99

Paulus, de Sancta Maria. *Scrutinium scripturarum*: 88.22

Paulus, Venetus. *Aristotle–Analytica posteriora: commentary*: 107.107; *Unidentified*: 93.14; 112.23

Pavinis, Joannes Franciscus de. *Baculus pastoralis*: 96.73

Paynell, Thomas. *piththy [sic] and moost notable sayinges of al Scripture, The*: 103.36; 108.37

Pelbartus, de Themeswar. *Aureum sacrae theologiae rosarium*: 93.33

Peletier, Jacques. *De peste compendium*: 104.80

Pepin, Guillaume. *Sermones*: 110.172

Perez de Ayala, Martin, Archbishop of Valentia. *De divinis apostolicis, atque ecclesiasticis traditionibus*: 97.42

Perion, Joachim. *De dialectica*: 92.18; 107.80; 112.202; *De sanctorum virorum, qui Patriarchae ab Ecclesia appellantur, rebus gestis ac vitis*: 110.129; *Unidentified*: 110.246

Perottus, Nicolaus. *Cornucopia*: 92.132:2; 112.36

Perottus, Nicolaus (probable). *Cornucopia*: 91.1; 109.15

Peter Lombard. *Epistles–Paul: commentary and text*: 111.2; *Sententiarum libri IIII*: 92.22; 93.29; 93.74; 96.86; 96.98; 97.43; 110.155; 112.142

Petrus, Comestor. *Historia scholastica*: 96.78; 110.198

Petrus, de Abano. *Aristotle (spurious)–Problemata: commentary and text*: 93.17; *Unidentified*: 93.13

Peucer, Kaspar. *Commentarius de praec*

ipuis divinationum generibus: 107.96; 112.82
Philippson, Joannes, *Sleidanus*. Unidentified: 110.64; 110.112
Philo, Judaeus. *De mundo*: 103.24; *De nobilitate*: 104.51:B; 108.57; Unidentified: 110.84; 112.141
Philostratus. *De vita Apollonii Tyanei*: 104.41
Pighius, Albertus. *Controversiarum praecipuarum in comitiis Ratisponensibus tractatarum, explicatio*: 96.92; Unidentified: 93.60
Pilkington, James, Bishop. *burnynge of Paules church in London in 1561, The*: 103.91
Platina, Bartolomeo. *Historia de vitis pontificum*: 110.169
Plato. *Gemmae, sive illustriores sententiae*: 103.70
Plautus, Titus Maccius. *Comoediae*: 90.42; 112.40; 112.128; Unidentified: 92.53
Pliny, the Elder. *Historia naturalis*: 92.74; 103.19
Pliny, the Elder (probable). *Historia naturalis* (probable): 108.69
Pliny, the Younger. *Epistolae*: 93.76; 112.111
Plutarch. *Selected works*: 90.41; *Vitae parallelae*: 92.34; 112.42; 112.163; *Vitae parallelae–Epitome*: 90.14; 91.39; 108.87; 109.30; 110.176
Plutarch (spurious). *Peri paidon agoges (De educatione puerorum)*: 92.88
Politianus, Angelus. *Epistolae* (probable): 112.110; *Miscellaneorum centuria una*: 107.83; *Works*: 91.8
Pontanus, Joannes Jovianus. *De rebus coelestibus libri XIV*: 103.23
Porphyrius, *of Tyre. Isagoge*: 94.11; 95.9
Postillae majores: 97.31; 107.22; 110.143
Prayers (unidentified): 99.5
Preces privatae: 103.62
Primasius, *Bishop of Adrumetum*. Unidentified: 108.73
Proclus, Diadochus. *Sphaera*: 92.118

Quinquarboreus, Joannes. *De re grammatica Hebraeorum opus*: 107.49
Quintilianus, Marcus Fabius. *Institutiones oratoriae*: 92.16; 110.210; Unidentified: 97.36; 112.182; *Works*: 97.7; (probable): 99.19

Ratramnus, *Monachus. De corpore et sanguine Domini*: 90.57
Ravennas, Petrus. Unidentified: 90.36
Raverinus, Pantaleon Barteleone. *De ratione quantitatis syllabariae liber*: 92.94; 103.65; 107.48
Ravesteyn, Jodocus. *Confessionis ... a ministris, qui in ecclesiam Antwerpiensem ... confutatio*: 97.53
Ravisius, Joannes. *Dialogi. Epigrammata*: 98.3; 105.2; *Epistolae*: 112.116; *Epitheta–Epitome*: 107.44; *Officina*: 91.18; 91.24
Record, Robert. *ground of artes teachyng the worke and practise of arithmetike, The*: 92.30
Regimen sanitatis Salernitatum: 92.98; 104.9; 112.169
Regius, Hieronymus. *Linguae latinae commentarii tres*: 92.110; 92.123
Reisch, Gregor. *Margarita philosophica*: 92.5
Resendius, Lucius Andreas. *Sententia et exempla ex probatissimis quibusque scriptoris collecta*: 98.17; 99.6; 110.222
Rhodolphus, Caspar (probable). *Dialectica* (probable): 112.203
Riccius, Bartholomaeus. *De imitatione libri tres*: 92.36
Ringelbergius, Joachimus Fortius. *Works*: 92.17; 112.95
Rivius, Joannes. *Castigationes plurimorum ex Terentio locorum*: 89.4
Rodericus Sanctius. *Speculum vite humane*: 88.23
Rolandinus, *de Passageriis. Flores ultimarum voluntatum*: 90.63
Rondelet, Guillaume. Unidentified: 104.56
Roscius, Lucius Vitruvius. *De commoda ac perfecta elocutione*: 107.84; Unidentified: 107.123
Royardus, Joannes. *Homiliae*: 110.100
Ruland, Martin, *the Elder. De phlebotomia*: 104.72; *Medicina practica*: 104.68
Rupert, *of Deutz. De divinis officiis*: 110.225; *Minor prophets: commentary and text*: 96.38

Sabellicus, Marcus Antonius. *Enneades–Posterior pars*: 90.9
Sadoletus, Jacobus. *Epistolae*: 112.114
Saint German, Christopher. *treatise concernynge the division betwene the spirytualtie and the temporaltie, A*: 103.90
Sallustius Crispus, Caius. *Unidentified*: 92.44; 99.4; 104.40:1; 108.6; 108.12; 109.42; 110.251:2; 112.159; *Works*: 92.72; (probable): 94.35
Sambucus, Joannes. *Unidentified*: 112.219
Sampson, Richard, *Bishop*. *Psalms: commentary*: 93.6
Sancto Geminiano, Dominicus à. *Decretales–Liber Sextus: commentary*: 102.5; *Decretales: commentary*: 88.3
Sancto Georgio, Joannes Antonius de. *Decretum: commentary*: 88.5
Sandeo, Felino Maria. *Decretales: commentary* (probable): 102.7
Sanders, Nicholas (probable). *De typica et honoraria sacrarum imaginum adoratione libri duo* (probable): 112.151
Sarcerius, Erasmus. *Dialectica*: 92.126; *Matthew: commentary*: 96.96
Saxo, *Grammaticus. Gesta Danorum*: 103.5
Schade, Petrus, *Mosellanus. Tabulae de schematibus et tropis* [and others]: 103.82
Schorus, Antonius. *Phrases linguae latinae* (probable): 112.180
Schorus, Antonius (perhaps). *Unidentified*: 110.254
Schottenius, Hermannus, *Hessus. Confabulationes tyronum literariorum ad amussim Colloquiorum Erasmi*: 108.22
Selneccer, Nicolaus. *Responsio vera et christiana ad Theo: Bezae defensionem et censuram*: 107.100
Seneca, Lucius Annaeus. *Selections–Flores selecti*: 92.108; 99.29; 107.81; *Tragoediae*: 92.45; 103.48; 112.129; *Unidentified*: 112.39; *Works* (perhaps): 93.2; 99.20
Sermons (unidentified): 110.153; 110.164; 110.179; 110.197
Sermones dormi secure: 93.52
Seton, John. *Dialectica*: 110.249
Severus, Sulpicius. *Sacrae historia*: 103.72

Silius Italicus. *De bello punico*: 99.7; 108.56
Silvae morales: 91.4
Slotanus, Joannes. *Unidentified*: 96.58
Smith, Richard, *Dean*. *Unidentified*: 110.266
Snoy, Raynerius, *Goudanus. Psalms: paraphrase and text*: 110.106
Socinus, Bartholomaeus (probable). *Regulae et fallentiae juris* (probable): 90.11
Soto, Petrus de. *Unidentified*: 93.65
Spangenberg, Johann. *Gospels and Epistles (liturgical): commentary and text*: 107.71; 110.98; *sum of divinitie drawen out of the holy scripture, The*: 103.96
Sprenger, Jacob. *Malleus maleficarum*: 91.3; 109.8;
Stadius, Joannes. *Ephemerides*: 94.19
Staphylus, Fridericus. *Absoluta responsio in defensionem Apologiae*: 97.26; *Apologia*: 107.28
Stobaeus, Joannes. *Sententiae* (probable): 93.64
Strabo. *Geographia*: 92.46; 97.18; 103.8
Strebaeus, Jacobus Ludovicus. *Unidentified*: 92.135
Sturmius, Joannes. *De periodis*: 99.31; 112.189; *Dialectica*: 109.31; *In partitiones oratorias Ciceronis dialogi*: 112.192; (probable): 110.233
Suetonius Tranquillus, Caius. *De vita Caesarum*: 90.34; 92.49; 103.1; (probable): 99.17
Sulpitius, Joannes. *Grammatica*: 92.107
Surius, Laurentius. *Commentaria brevis rerum in orbe gestarum*: 92.42; 110.118
Susenbrotus, Joannes. *Epitome troporum ac schematum*: 92.83
Sylvius, Franciscus, *of Amiens. Cicero–Pro Ligario: commentary and text*: 92.89; *Commentarii in treis orationes Ciceronis*: 103.80; *In artem oratoriam progymnasmata*: 112.181
Symmachus, Quintus Aurelius (perhaps). *Epistolae* (perhaps): 112.66

Tacitus, Publius Cornelius. *Unidentified*: 90.47; 92.124
Talaeus, Aldomarus. *Rhetorica*: 103.60

Tapper, Ruard (probable). *Declaratio articulorum adversus nostri temporis haereses* (probable): 97.50

Tartaretus, Petrus. *Aristotle–Ethica: commentary*: 108.34

Tauler, Johann. *Exercitia super vita et passione Jesu Christi*: 108.66

Tavernerius, Joannes. *De veritate corporis et sanguinis Christi in sacramento altaris*: 93.69; (perhaps): 96.104

Terentius, Publius, *Afer. Works*: 91.6; 92.48; 92.105; 97.10; 108.40; 108.42; 108.78; 110.267; 112.127; (probable): 105.4; 109.11; *Unidentified*: 108.43

Themistius. *Aristotle–Unidentified: paraphrase*: 112.74; 112.75

Theodorus, *Gaza. Institutiones grammaticae* (probable): 89.3

Theodorus, *Metochita. In Aristotelis universam naturalem philosophiam paraphrasis*: 92.3

Theodosius II, *Emperor of the East. Codex Theodosianus*: 99.2

Theophilus, *Protospatharius. De urinis*: 104.88; *Galen–De usu partium–Epitome*: 104.69

Theophrastus. *Metaphysica*: 96.48; 107.3

Theophylact, *Archbishop of Achrida. Epistles–Paul: commentary and text*: 97.27; 99.9; 110.193; *Gospels: commentary and text*: 96.27; 97.34; 99.12

Thomas, à Kempis. *De imitatione Christi*: 104.63; 112.154

Thomas, *Hibernicus. Flores omnium fere doctorum*: 90.44; 107.94; 109.10

Titelmann, Franz. *Aristotle–Selected works–Philosophia naturalis: commentary*: 94.36; 107.79; *Dialectica*: 92.86; 98.7; *Epistles: commentary and text*: 96.82; (probable): 91.27; *Paraphrastica elucidatio in Evangelium secundum Matthaeum*: 110.157; *Psalms: commentary and text*: 96.39; 110.262; *Unidentified*: 94.5

Titelmann, Franz (probable). *Aristotle–Selected works–Philosophia naturalis: commentary* (probable): 112.214; *Epistles: commentary and text*: 99.21; *Psalms: commentary and text*: 99.1; *Tractatus de expositione mysteriorum missae* [and others] (probable): 96.75

Torrentinus, Hermann (probable). *Elucidarius carminum* (probable): 110.180

Toxites, Michael. *Cicero (spurious)–Rhetorica ad Herennium: commentary and text*: 92.10; 108.61

Trapezuntius, Georgius. *Rhetorica*: 92.6; (probable): 112.191

Travers, Walter. *Ecclesiastica disciplina*: 112.147

Travers, Walter (perhaps). *Ecclesiastica disciplina* (perhaps): 110.126

Triverius, Hieremias. *De temporibus morborum et opportunitate auxiliorum*: 104.89

Trogus Pompeius and Justinus, the *Historian. Epitomae in Trogi Pompeii historias*: 92.67; 103.66; 108.25; 108.74; 108.85; 109.34; 110.200; 112.157

Tudeschis, Nicolaus. *Consilia*: 102.3; *Decretales: commentary*: 102.1; 102.2

Tudeschis, Nicolaus (probable). *Unidentified*: 109.2

Tunstall, Cuthbert, Bishop. *De arte supputandi libri quattuor*: 92.70; 112.168; *Unidentified*: 97.46

Turner, William. *new boke of the natures of all wines commonlye used in England, A* (perhaps): 100.8

Tuscus, Vivianus (probable). *Unidentified*: 112.46

Tyndale, William. *exposicion uppon the. v.vi.vii. chapters of Mathew, An*: 103.85

Ulstadius, Philippus. *Coelum philosophorum*: 100.9

Unidentified author: *Aristotle–De caelo: commentary*: 88.21; *Aristotle–Metaphysica: commentary*: 111.12; *Aristotle–Physica: commentary*: 88.12; 88.16; 107.109; 112.31; *Aristotle–Unidentified: commentary*: 92.68; *Cicero–Selected works–Orations: commentary*: 92.120; *Clementines: commentary*: 88.2; *Corpus juris civilis: commentary*: 112.55; *Epistle 2–Paul: commentary*: 103.47; *Revelation: commentary*: 110.134; *Sentences: commentary*: 110.208

Unidentified author and work: 88.4; 90.3; 90.15; 90.18; 90.21; 90.22; 90.23; 90.27; 90.39; 90.55; 90.77;

90.82; 90.83; 90.86; 90.88; 90.91; 90.92:1-6; 91.23; 91.38; 92.2; 92.28; 92.38; 92.41; 92.96; 92.104; 92.111; 92.125; 92.133; 93.3; 93.5; 93.44; 93.71; 94.6; 94.21; 94.29; 94.30:1-2; 94.41; 96.26; 96.51; 96.52; 96.68; 96.84; 96.87; 96.90; 96.93; 97.9; 97.13:1-3; 97.20; 97.44; 97.51; 97.58:1-2; 98.2; 98.18; 99.5; 99.11; 99.26; 99.28; 99.35:1-4; 100.11; 101.6:1-4; 103.7; 103.74; 103.97; 103.99; 104.36; 104.46; 104.62; 104.71; 104.75; 104.87:1-3; 104.93; 106.1:1; 106.1:2; 106.1:3-15; 107.15; 107.16; 107.21; 107.60; 107.74; 107.76; 107.86; 107.118; 107.128; 108.10; 108.21; 108.29; 108.35; 108.44; 108.45; 108.60; 108.76; 108.83; 108.92; 108.93:1-5; 108.94:1-5; 109.13; 109.28; 109.29; 109.33; 110.7; 110.24; 110.42; 110.63; 110.81; 110.86; 110.88; 110.115; 110.122; 110.131; 110.150; 110.153; 110.156; 110.164; 110.165; 110.171; 110.179; 110.181; 110.197; 110.199; 110.207; 110.209; 110.212; 110.232; 110.234; 110.239; 110.243; 110.251:1; 110.258; 110.260; 110.269:1-2; 111.4; 111.8; 111.10; 112.14; 112.32; 112.49:1-3; 112.70; 112.150; 112.156; 112.220; 112.222

Valerius Maximus. *Facta et dicta memorabilia*: 91.10; 92.87; 93.72; 103.49; 108.9; 109.36; 112.158;
Valerius, Cornelius. *De sphaera*: 103.76; *Grammaticum institutionum libri IIII*: 92.114; *In universam bene dicendi rationem tabula*: 94.37; 98.8; *Physicae, seu de naturae philosophiae institutio*: 98.15; *Tabulae totius dialectices*: 92.131; 108.32; 112.204; *Unidentified*: 94.38
Valla, Laurentius. *Elegantiae*: 92.66; 103.44; 107.82; 112.137; *Unidentified*: 97.28; 108.38
Vega, Christophorus de. *Unidentified*: 104.13
Velcurio, Joannes. *Aristotle–Physica*: *commentary*: 97.32; 109.38; 110.167; (probable): 112.87; *Unidentified*: 107.78
Ventura, Laurentius. *De ratione conficiendi lapidis philosophici* [and others]: 104.20
Vergilius, Polydorus. *De inventoribus rebus*: 110.177; *Unidentified*: 103.9; 109.5; 112.171
Vermigli, Pietro Martire. *discourse or traictise of Petur Martyr Vermill a Florentine, wherin he declared his judgemente concernynge the sacrament of the Lordes supper, A*: 103.27; *In primum librum Mosis, qui vulgo Genesis dicitur, commentarii*: 110.14; *Judges: commentary*: 107.54; *Kings: commentary and text*: 110.21; *Loci communes*: 112.4; *Romans: commentary*: 110.34; *Samuel: commentary*: 110.48
Veron, Jean. *stronge battery against the idolatrous invocation of the dead saintes, made dialoguewise, A*: 103.86
Vesalius, Andreas. *Epistola, rationem modumque propinandi radicis Chynae decocti pertractans*: 108.16
Vicomercatus, Franciscus. *Aristotle–De anima* (part): *commentary and text*: 112.212
Victoriis, Leonellus de. *Practica medicinalis*: 104.65
Victorius, Petrus, *the Elder*. *Castigationes in M. T. Ciceronis Epistolas*: 98.12
Vincentius, *Bellovacensis*. *Speculum major* (part): 102.15
Viotti, Bartolomeo. *De demonstratione libri quinque*: 112.206
Viperano, Giovanni Antonio. *De rege, et regno liber. De historia scribenda liber*: 112.72
Virgilius Maro, Publius. *Georgics*: 91.16; *Works*: 98.11; (probable): 91.33; 94.9; 94.14; 103.31; 108.5; 112.126; (perhaps): 92.13
Vives, Joannes Lodovicus. *De officio mariti*: 112.88; *De ratione dicendi. De consultatione praeceptiones*: 112.196; *dialogues, Les*: 103.71; *Unidentified*: 108.13; 112.68
Vives, Joannes Lodovicus (probable). *Familiarium colloquiorum formulae, sive linguae latinae exercitatio* (probable): 92.37
Voragine, Jacobus de. *Legenda aurea* (probable): 93.27; *Sermones*: 110.202

Walther, Georg. *Regulae vitae christianae*: 107.70

Walther, Rudolph. *Acts: commentary and text*: 110.15; *De syllabarum et carminum libri duo*: 110.261; *In priorem (posteriorem) D. Pauli ad Corinthios epistolam homiliae*: 110.13; *John: commentary and text*: 110.5; *Luke: commentary and text*: 110.9; *Mark: commentary and text*: 110.29; *Minor prophets: commentary and text*: 110.33; *Romans: commentary and text*: 110.38

Westheimer, Bartholomaeus. *Conciliatio sacrae scripturae et patrum*: 107.62; 110.58; *Phrases seu modi loquendi divinae scripturae*: 99.24

White, John, Bishop. *Diacosiomartyrion*: 96.65

Whitgift, John, Archbishop. *defense of the aunswere to the Admonition, against the Replie, The*: 112.34

Wigand, Johann. *Bible* (part): *commentary*: 107.61; *Danielis prophetae explicatio brevis*: 107.73; *De imagine Dei in homine, et de larva Satanae*: 107.102; *Syntagma, seu corpus doctrinae veri et omnipotentis Dei, ex veteri Testamento tantum*: 97.17; 107.23

Wildenbergius, Hieronymus. *Aristotle–Unidentified: commentary* (probable): 95.16; *Totius philosophiae humanae digestio* (perhaps): 110.187

Wildenbergius, Hieronymus (perhaps). *Aristotle–Selected works–Philosophia naturalis: epitome* (perhaps): 93.55

William, of Occam. *Aristotle–Physica: commentary*: 112.27

Willich, Jodocus. *Commentaria in utramque ad Timotheum Pauli epistolam*: 107.101; *Unidentified*: 112.221

Withals, John. *shorte dictionarie for yonge begynners, A* (probable): 89.1

Witzell, Georg. *Postilla*: 96.5

Xenophon. *De re publica Lacedaemoniorum*: 112.173

Zerbus, Gabriel. *Unidentified*: 109.3

Zwinger, Theodor. *Similitudinem methodo*: 110.192:B

Index II
Editors and Compilers

Accursius, Gulielmus (attributed): 112.53
Antesignanus, Petrus: 103.18
Arias Montano, Benito: 110.103

Badius, Jodocus, *Ascensius*: 91.4; 92.72
Benedictus, Brixianus (probable): 108.8
Bernard, Thomas: 103.17
Beroaldus, Philippus, *the Elder*: 103.1
Bèze, Théodore de: 107.27; 110.57
Bing, Thomas: 103.26
Biondo, Michael Angelo: 91.28
Bouchereau, Jacques (probable): 112.83
Brunfels, Otto: 92.99
Budé, Jean: 110.57

Caversinus, Bartholomaeus: 108.20
Clichtoveus, Jodocus: 100.3
Curio, Caelius Augustinus: 92.33

Daneau, Lambert: 112.121
Draconites, Johann: 96.66
Du Chesne, Léger (perhaps): 108.46

Erasmus, Desiderius: 110.90
Erasmus, Desiderius (probable): 107.81
Estienne, Robert, *the Elder*: 107.24

Foxe, John, *the Martyrologist*: 112.54
Froben, Johann (perhaps): 93.5

Gagneius, Joannes: 93.53
Grant, Edward: 112.115

Hatcher, Thomas: 112.100

Latomus, Bartholomew: 112.172
Leunclavius, Joannes: 107.106; 112.92
Liburnio, Niccolò: 103.70
Lonicer, Joannes: 107.112
Lycosthenes, Conrad (Wolffhart): 110.188
Lyra, Nicolaus de: 93.43; 96.6; 107.6

Massonius, Robert: 112.4
Muenster, Sebastian: 92.102

Neander, Michael, *of Sorau*: 90.58

Oecumenius, *Bishop of Tricca*: 96.33

Pagninus, Sanctes: 110.53
Perion, Joachim: 112.28

Reuchlin, Johann (probable): 97.54

INDEX II: EDITORS AND COMPILERS

Sampson, Thomas, *Dean of Christ Church*: 112.63
Sichardus, Joannes: 96.47
Simler, Josias: 104.43
Soter, Joannes: 110.238

Theodorus, *Gaza*: 98.20

Thomas, Hibernicus: 108.77
Tyber, Darius (probable): 91.39

Varagius, Philippus: 93.40
Vietor, Hieronymus: 110.70

Wolfius, Hieronymus: 110.30

Index III
Translators

Agylaeus, Henricus: 90.24
Argyropoulos, Joannes: 92.20; 112.29

Bèze, Théodore de: 107.27
Buchanan, George: 112.133
Buchanan, George (probable): 91.32; 92.63; 110.236

Carr, Nicholas: 103.26
Castalio, Sebastian: 112.1
Caversinus, Bartholomaeus: 108.20

Dubois, Jacques: 96.37
Dudith, Andreas, *Bishop*: 92.27

Erasmus, Desiderius: 96.80; 110.235

Hellowes, Edward: 112.107
Hentensius, Joannes: 90.84
Hoby, Sir Thomas: 112.65
Hutten, Robert: 103.96

Lambinus, Dionysius: 107.114
Laurentianus, Laurentius: 104.55
Linacre, Thomas: 104.24

Neander, Michael, *of Sorau*: 90.58
Niphus, Augustine: 107.18
Norton, Thomas: 103.6

Pagninus, Sanctes: 97.1; 110.53
Parker, Matthew, *Archbishop* (perhaps): 103.83
Perion, Joachim: 90.56; 107.41; 112.28

Udall, Nicholas: 103.27

Valla, Laurentius: 107.35
Veron, Jean (probable): 109.16
Vicomercatus, Franciscus: 112.212

Walther, Rudolph: 96.19

Index IV
Stationers
(Publishers, Printers, Booksellers)

The stationers' names in the annotated book-lists are drawn either from imprints and colophons, which offer the names in a variety of forms, or from bibliographical sources, none of which consistently agrees with another on those forms. For indexing purposes and for searching the database, PLRE has, therefore, constructed a uniform stationers' names list. English stationers' names, with a few exceptions, are derived from the STC, Volume 3; the forms of Continental names derive from a number of sources, including the STC, but most especially Adams. Accordingly, the names below do not always duplicate forms that appear in the annotated book-lists.

Alantsee, Leonard and Luca: 100.5
Awdely, John: 112.63

Badius, Jodocus, *Ascensius*: 92.20; 97.3; 103.80; 104.52
Bascarinis, Nicolaus de: 91.28
Berthelet, Thomas: 91.2; 104.1; 110.147
Birckman, Arnold: 93.61
Birckman, Arnold, Heirs of: 90.61
Birckman, Arnold, Heirs of (probable): 94.19
Birckman, Johann: 92.25
Brubach, Petrus: 93.77
Bryling, Nicolaus: 92.3
Buon, Gabriel: 112.77

Bynneman, Henry: 112.34; 112.149
Bynneman, Henry (probable): 110.60

Calenius, Gervinus: 97.26; 110.89; 112.57
Caly, Robert: 96.65
Cawood, John (perhaps): 108.88
Cervicornus, Eucharius: 96.105; 107.10
Cock, Simon: 110.157
Coldock, Francis: 112.115
Corvinus, Georg: 104.19; 110.125
Cratander, Andreas: 93.26; 96.47
Crato, Johann: 96.66; 107.57; 107.70; 110.117; 110.119; 110.133
Crespin, Jean: 103.94; 110.39

Day, John 1: 103.2; 103.83; 103.88; 108.15; 110.137; 110.159; 112.54; 112.143
Denham, Henry: 103.26; 103.87; 112.144
Denham, Henry (probable): 103.3
Desboys, Guillaume: 110.71
Dupuys, Jacques: 90.93

Egenolph, Christian: 107.112
Egenolph, Christian, Heirs of: 104.81
Episcopius, Eusebius: 110.192:A; 110.192:B
Episcopius, Eusebius (probable): 110.18
Episcopius, Nicolaus 2: 92.33
Episcopius, Nicolaus, Heirs of: 110.192:A; 110.192:B
Erve, Egidius van der: 103.93

Ferrariis, Joannes Jacobus de: 93.40
Feyerabend, Sigismund: 104.19
Fouler, Joannes (probable): 112.151
Franco, Bartholomaeus (perhaps): 112.18; 112.104
Froben, Hieronymus: 90.67
Froben, Johann (probable): 93.5
Froschouer, Christoph: 96.46; 104.43; 107.54; 110.5; 110.9; 110.13; 110.14; 110.21; 110.26; 110.33; 110.38; 110.48; 112.3

Gallus, Wigand, Heirs of: 104.19
Gaultherot, Vivant: 96.74
Gregorius, Joannes: 104.7
Gryphius, Joannes: 92.9
Gryphius, Sebastian: 108.41
Guerra, Domenico: 92.27
Guerra, Giovanni Battista: 92.27
Gymnicus, Joannes 1: 110.149

Hacket, Thomas: 103.86
Harrison, Luke: 103.87; 112.144
Harrison, Richard: 103.6
Hervagius, Joannes: 90.67; 110.65
Hittorp, Godefridus: 107.10
Huttich, Gunther: 107.73

Jugge, Richard (perhaps): 108.88
Juvenis, Martin: 112.160

Kingston, John: 110.124; 112.4

Köpfel, Wolfgang, Heirs of (probable): 103.37

Le Preux, Franciscus: 110.69
Lufft, Joannes: 107.97; 110. 83

Manutius, Paulus: 112.209
Middleton, Henry: 112.71; 112.108; 112.115
Mierdman, Steven: 91.34
Mylius, Christian 1: 99.30
Mylius, Crato: 107.101

Newbery, Ralph: 112.71; 112.107; 112.108
Nivelle, Sebastian: 90.80; 110.71
Norton, William: 112.149

Oporinus, Joannes: 90.58; 91.17; 92.10; 97.23; 103.57; 104.51:A; 104.79; 104.80; 107.65; 107.127; 108.61; 110.61; 110.244; 110.259; 112.18; 112.97; 112.104; 112.117
Oporinus, Joannes (probable): 103.55; 110.18
Oporinus, House of: 107.64; 107.106; 107.116; 110.70; 112.92; 112.103

Parvus, Audoenus: 90.72
Parvus, Joannes: 92.20
Perna, Petrus: 104.20
Perrin, François: 110.57; 112.140
Petreius, Joannes: 103.79
Petri, Adam: 96.102
Petri, Henricus: 92.102; 96.41
Plantin, Christopher: 104.29; 110.94; 110.103; 110.211; 112.72
Prevost, Benedictus: 103.70
Purfoot, Thomas 1: 103.98

Quecus, Paul (probable): 110.18
Quentel, Joannes: 96.56
Quentel, Joannes, Heirs of: 97.26; 110.89; 112.57

Rhamba, Johannes: 104.74
Richard, Thomas: 92.90
Riddell, William: 91.34
Rihelius, Josias: 97.38; 104.68; 104.72
Roigny, Jean: 96.21; 110.187
Rotarius, Martin: 90.37
Rouille, Guillaume: 104.55

Rouille, Guillaume (perhaps): 108.47
Ruremunde, Christoffel, Widow of (probable): 103.92

Sassenus, Servatius 1: 90.61
Sassenus, Servatius (probable): 95.4
Schirat, Michael: 110.126; 112.138; 112.147
Schneider, Andreas: 110.47
Schoeffer, Ivo (probable): 96.91
Schwertel, Johann: 112.84
Scolar, John: 93.75
Scotus, Octavianus (probable): 93.49
Seres, William 1: 100.8; 103.17; 103.62; 103.91; 112.65; 112.100
Silvius, Gulielmus: 108.20
Singrenius, Joannes: 100.5
Stagnino, Bernardino: 112.22
Steelsius, Joannes: 110.157
Stephanus, Henricus 2: 107.27; 110.168
Stephanus, Robertus 1: 93.45; 107.24
Sutton, Henry: 103.86

Torrentinus, Laurentius: 92.7
Tortis, Baptista de: 90.2
Toy, Humphrey: 112.34
Toy, Humphrey (probable): 110.60

Trechsel, Johann: 91.4

Udall, Nicholas: 103.27

Vascosanus, Michael: 96.59; 96.88; 112.76
Vietor, Hieronymus: 100.5
Vignon, Eustathius: 110.74; 112.121
Voegelin, Ernest: 104.74
Voegelin, House of: 110.47; 110.53; 112.199

Wechel, Andreas: 112.206
Weissenhorn, Alexander: 93.56; 96.64
Whitchurche, Edward: 103.27
Wight, John: 112.63
Williamson, William: 110.124
Winter, Robert: 98.12; 107.84
Wolfe, Reyner: 92.30; 103.11; 103.20; 103.22
Wolfe, Reyner (probable): 109.16
Wolfe, Reyner (perhaps): 110.40
Wykes, Henry: 91.2; 95.3; 103.12; 112.8

Zangrius, Petrus, Tiletanus: 90.84
Zassenus, Servatius: 104.89
Ziletus, Jacobus: 92.9

Index V
Places of Publication

Antwerp: 103.76; 104.29; 108.20; 110.94; 110.103; 110.157; 110.211; 112.67; 112.72;
Antwerp: (probable): 103.92

Basle: 90.58; 90.67; 91.17; 91.40:A; 91.40:B; 92.3; 92.10; 92.33; 92.102; 93.26; 96.24; 96.41; 96.47; 96.102; 98.12; 103.33; 103.55; 103.57;104.20; 104.38; 104.48; 104.51:A; 104.51:B; 104.79; 104.80; 107.64; 107.65; 107.84; 107.106; 107.116; 107.127; 108.61; 110.18; 110.41; 110.61; 110.65; 110.70; 110.192:A; 110.192:B; 110.244; 110.259; 112.1; 112.15; 112.18; 112.92; 112.97; 112.103; 112.104; 112.117
Basle (probable): 93.5
Britain: 87.4; 100.7; 102.16; 103.84
Britain (probable): 103.47
Britain or Continent: 87.1; 87.2; 87.3; 89.2; 90.19; 91.6; 91.19; 91.32; 91.33; 92.13; 92.24; 92.48; 92.55; 92.63; 92.70; 92.83; 92.98; 92.105; 92.106; 92.107; 92.115; 92.118; 92.127; 92.129; 92.132:1; 92.134; 93.1; 93.27; 93.57; 94.8; 94.9; 94.10; 94.13; 94.14; 94.23; 94.31; 94.35; 94.40; 95.13; 95.14; 95.15; 96.55; 97.10; 97.57; 98.1; 98.11; 99.13; 99.14; 101.4; 103.15; 103.31; 103.46; 103.53; 103.63; 103.64; 103.66; 103.68; 103.82; 103.85; 104.9; 104.49; 104.73; 104.76; 104.86; 105.1; 105.3; 105.4; 107.32; 107.93; 108.2; 108.3; 108.5; 108.23; 108.25; 108.40; 108.42; 108.65; 108.74; 108.75; 108.78; 108.82; 108.85; 109.9; 109.11; 109.14; 109.17; 109.24; 109.25; 109.34; 109.35; 110.128; 110.175; 110.183; 110.190; 110.200; 110.223; 110.229; 110.236; 110.240; 110.242; 110.245; 110.248; 110.261; 110.264; 110.267; 111.1; 112.2; 112.7; 112.11; 112.24; 112.30; 112.50; 112.61; 112.98; 112.109; 112.112; 112.116; 112.125; 112.126; 112.127; 112.132; 112.133; 112.135; 112.136; 112.157; 112.162; 112.167; 112.168; 112.169; 112.178; 112.185; 112.187; 112.188; 112.194; 112.205

Cologne: 90.68; 92.25; 93.61; 94.19; 96.56; 96.85; 97.4; 97.26; 107.10; 107.40; 107.41; 110.89; 110.149; 110.225; 112.57

INDEX V: PLACES OF PUBLICATION 343

Continent: 88.1; 88.2; 88.3; 88.5; 88.6; 88.7; 88.8; 88.9; 88.10; 88.11; 88.12; 88.13; 88.14; 88.15; 88.16; 88.17; 88.18; 88.19; 88.20; 88.21; 88.22; 88.23; 89.3; 89.4; 89.5; 90.1; 90.3; 90.4; 90.5; 90.6; 90.7; 90.8; 90.9; 90.10; 90.11; 90.12; 90.13; 90.14; 90.16; 90.17; 90.20; 90.24; 90.25; 90.26; 90.28; 90.29; 90.30; 90.31; 90.32; 90.33; 90.34; 90.36; 90.38; 90.39; 90.40; 90.41; 90.42; 90.43; 90.44; 90.45; 90.46; 90.47; 90.48; 90.49; 90.50; 90.51; 90.52; 90.53; 90.54; 90.57; 90.59; 90.60; 90.62; 90.63; 90.64; 90.65; 90.66; 90.69; 90.70; 90.71; 90.73; 90.74; 90.75; 90.76; 90.78; 90.79; 90.81; 90.85; 90.86; 90.87; 90.89; 90.90; 91.1; 91.3; 91.5; 91.7; 91.8; 91.9; 91.10; 91.11; 91.12; 91.14; 91.15; 91.16; 91.18; 91.20; 91.22; 91.24; 91.26; 91.27; 91.29; 91.30; 91.31; 91.35; 91.36; 91.37; 91.39; 92.1; 92.2; 92.4; 92.5; 92.6; 92.8; 92.11; 92.12; 92.14; 92.15; 92.16; 92.18; 92.19; 92.21; 92.22; 92.23; 92.26; 92.29; 92.31; 92.32; 92.34; 92.35; 92.36; 92.37; 92.39; 92.40; 92.42; 92.43; 92.45; 92.46; 92.47; 92.49; 92.50; 92.52; 92.53; 92.54; 92.56; 92.57; 92.58; 92.59; 92.60; 92.61; 92.62; 92.64; 92.65; 92.66; 92.67; 92.68; 92.69; 92.71; 92.72; 92.73; 92.74; 92.75; 92.76; 92.77; 92.78; 92.79; 92.80; 92.81; 92.82; 92.84; 92.85; 92.86; 92.87; 92.88; 92.89; 92.91; 92.92; 92.93; 92.95; 92.96; 92.97; 92.99; 92.100; 92.101; 92.103; 92.108; 92.109; 92.112; 92.113; 92.114; 92.116; 92.117; 92.119; 92.120; 92.121; 92.122; 92.124; 92.126; 92.128:A; 92.128:B; 92.130; 92.131; 92.132:2; 92.135; 93.2; 93.4; 93.7; 93.11; 93.12; 93.13; 93.14; 93.15; 93.16; 93.17; 93.18; 93.19; 93.20; 93.21; 93.22; 93.23; 93.24; 93.25; 93.28; 93.29; 93.30; 93.31; 93.32; 93.33; 93.34; 93.35; 93.36; 93.37; 93.38; 93.39; 93.41; 93.42; 93.43; 93.44; 93.46; 93.47; 93.48; 93.50; 93.51; 93.52; 93.53; 93.54; 93.55; 93.59; 93.60; 93.62; 93.64; 93.65; 93.66; 93.68; 93.71; 93.72; 93.73; 93.74; 93.76; 94.1; 94.2; 94.3; 94.5; 94.11; 94.12; 94.16; 94.17; 94.20; 94.24; 94.25; 94.26; 94.27; 94.28; 94.32; 94.33; 94.34; 94.36; 94.37; 94.39; 95.1; 95.2; 95.6; 95.7; 95.8; 95.9; 95.10; 95.11; 95.12; 95.16; 95.17; 96.1; 96.2; 96.3; 96.4; 96.5; 96.6; 96.7; 96.8; 96.9; 96.10; 96.11; 96.12; 96.13; 96.14; 96.15; 96.16; 96.17; 96.18; 96.19; 96.20; 96.22; 96.23; 96.25; 96.27; 96.28; 96.30; 96.31; 96.32; 96.33; 96.34; 96.35; 96.36; 96.37; 96.38; 96.39; 96.40; 96.42; 96.43; 96.44; 96.45; 96.48; 96.49; 96.50; 96.52; 96.53; 96.54; 96.57; 96.58; 96.61; 96.62; 96.63; 96.69; 96.70; 96.71; 96.72; 96.75; 96.76; 96.77; 96.78; 96.79; 96.80; 96.81; 96.82; 96.83; 96.86; 96.89; 96.92; 96.94; 96.95; 96.96; 96.97; 96.98; 96.99; 96.100; 96.101; 96.103; 96.106; 96.107; 96.108; 97.1; 97.2; 97.5; 97.6; 97.7; 97.8; 97.9; 97.11; 97.12; 97.14; 97.15; 97.16; 97.17; 97.18; 97.19; 97.20; 97.21; 97.22; 97.23; 97.24; 97.25; 97.27; 97.28; 97.29; 97.30; 97.31; 97.32; 97.33; 97.34; 97.35; 97.36; 97.37; 97.39; 97.40; 97.41; 97.42; 97.43; 97.45; 97.47; 97.48; 97.49; 97.52; 97.53; 97.54; 97.55; 97.56; 97.59; 98.3; 98.4; 98.5; 98.6; 98.7; 98.8; 98.9; 98.10; 98.13; 98.14; 98.15; 98.16; 98.17; 98.19; 98.20; 99.1; 99.2; 99.3; 99.6; 99.7; 99.8; 99.9; 99.10; 99.11; 99.12; 99.15; 99.16; 99.17; 99.18; 99.19; 99.20; 99.21; 99.22; 99.23; 99.24; 99.25; 99.26; 99.27; 99.28; 99.29; 99.32; 99.33; 100.1; 100.2; 100.3; 100.4; 100.6; 100.9; 100.10; 101.1; 101.2; 101.3; 101.5; 102.1; 102.2; 102.3; 102.4; 102.5; 102.6; 102.7; 102.8; 102.9; 102.10; 102.11; 102.12; 102.13; 102.14; 102.15; 102.17; 103.1; 103.4; 103.5; 103.7; 103.8; 103.10; 103.13; 103.16; 103.18; 103.19; 103.23; 103.24; 103.28; 103.29; 103.30; 103.32; 103.34; 103.35; 103.38; 103.39; 103.40; 103.41; 103.42; 103.43;

103.44; 103.45; 103.48; 103.49; 103.50; 103.51; 103.52; 103.54; 103.56; 103.58; 103.60; 103.67; 103.71; 103.72; 103.73; 103.77; 103.78; 103.81; 103.89; 103.95; 104.2; 104.3; 104.4; 104.5; 104.6; 104.8; 104.10; 104.11; 104.12; 104.13; 104.14:A; 104.14:B; 104.15; 104.16; 104.17; 104.18; 104.21; 104.22; 104.23; 104.24; 104.25; 104.26; 104.27; 104.28; 104.30; 104.31; 104.32; 104.34; 104.35; 104.36; 104.37; 104.39; 104.40:2; 104.41; 104.42; 104.44; 104.45; 104.47; 104.50; 104.54; 104.56; 104.57; 104.58; 104.59; 104.61; 104.63; 104.64; 104.65; 104.66; 104.67; 104.69; 104.70; 104.71; 104.77; 104.78; 104.82; 104.83; 104.85; 104.88; 104.90; 104.91; 104.92; 105.2; 106.1:2; 107.2; 107.3; 107.4; 107.5; 107.6; 107.7; 107.8; 107.9; 107.11; 107.12; 107.14; 107.17; 107.18; 107.19; 107.20; 107.21; 107.22; 107.23; 107.25; 107.26; 107.28; 107.30; 107.31; 107.34; 107.35; 107.36; 107.37; 107.39; 107.42; 107.43; 107.44; 107.45; 107.47; 107.50; 107.51; 107.53:1; 107.53:2; 107.56; 107.58; 107.61; 107.63; 107.66; 107.68; 107.69; 107.71; 107.72; 107.74; 107.75; 107.76; 107.77; 107.78; 107.79; 107.80; 107.81; 107.82; 107.83; 107.85; 107.86; 107.88; 107.89; 107.90; 107.91; 107.92; 107.94; 107.95; 107.98; 107.103; 107.104; 107.105; 107.107; 107.108; 107.110; 107.111; 107.113; 107.114; 107.115; 107.117; 107.118; 107.119; 107.120; 107.121; 107.122; 107.123; 107.124; 107.125; 107.126; 107.128; 107.129; 107.130; 108.1; 108.7; 108.8; 108.9; 108.11; 108.14; 108.16; 108.17; 108.18; 108.19; 108.22; 108.24; 108.26; 108.27; 108.28; 108.30; 108.31; 108.32; 108.33; 108.34; 108.35; 108.36; 108.38; 108.45; 108.46; 108.48; 108.49; 108.50; 108.51; 108.52; 108.53; 108.54; 108.55; 108.56; 108.57; 108.59; 108.62; 108.63; 108.64; 108.66; 108.67; 108.68; 108.69; 108.70:1; 108.71; 108.72; 108.73; 108.77; 108.79; 108.80; 108.81; 108.84; 108.86; 108.87; 108.89; 108.90; 108.91; 109.2; 109.3; 109.4; 109.7; 109.8; 109.10; 109.12; 109.15; 109.18; 109.20; 109.21; 109.22; 109.23; 109.26; 109.27; 109.30; 109.31; 109.32; 109.36; 109.37; 109.38; 109.40; 109.41; 110.1; 110.2; 110.3; 110.4; 110.6; 110.8; 110.10; 110.11; 110.12; 110.15; 110.16; 110.17; 110.19; 110.20; 110.22; 110.23; 110.24; 110.25; 110.28; 110.29; 110.30; 110.31; 110.32; 110.34; 110.35; 110.36; 110.37; 110.49; 110.50; 110.51; 110.52; 110.53; 110.55; 110.58; 110.59; 110.62; 110.63; 110.66; 110.67; 110.68; 110.72; 110.73; 110.75; 110.76; 110.77; 110.79; 110.80; 110.82; 110.84; 110.85; 110.87; 110.90; 110.91; 110.92; 110.93; 110.95; 110.96; 110.97; 110.98; 110.99; 110.100; 110.104; 110.105; 110.106; 110.107; 110.109:1; 110.109:2; 110.110; 110.111; 110.113; 110.116; 110.118; 110.121; 110.123; 110.127; 110.129; 110.130; 110.132; 110.134; 110.135; 110.136; 110.139; 110.140; 110.141; 110.143; 110.144; 110.145; 110.151; 110.152; 110.153; 110.154; 110.155; 110.162; 110.163; 110.164; 110.165; 110.166; 110.167; 110.169; 110.170; 110.172; 110.174; 110.176; 110.177; 110.178; 110.179; 110.180; 110.182; 110.184; 110.185; 110.186; 110.188; 110.189; 110.191; 110.193; 110.194; 110.195; 110.196; 110.197; 110.198; 110.202; 110.203; 110.204; 110.205; 110.206; 110.208; 110.210; 110.213; 110.214; 110.215; 110.216; 110.217; 110.219; 110.220; 110.221; 110.222; 110.224; 110.226; 110.227; 110.228; 110.230; 110.231; 110.233; 110.235; 110.238; 110.241; 110.243; 110.246; 110.247:1; 110.247:2; 110.250; 110.252; 110.254; 110.255; 110.256; 110.257; 110.262; 110.263; 110.265;

INDEX V: PLACES OF PUBLICATION 345

110.266; 110.268; 111.5; 111.6; 111.7; 111.11; 112.6; 112.9; 112.10; 112.12; 112.13; 112.14; 112.16; 112.17; 112.19; 112.20; 112.23; 112.25; 112.26; 112.27; 112.28; 112.29; 112.33; 112.35; 112.36; 112.38; 112.40; 112.41; 112.42; 112.43; 112.45; 112.46; 112.47; 112.48; 112.51; 112.52; 112.53; 112.56; 112.58; 112.59; 112.60; 112.64; 112.66; 112.69; 112.70; 112.74; 112.75; 112.78; 112.79; 112.80; 112.81; 112.83; 112.85; 112.86; 112.87; 112.88; 112.89; 112.90; 112.91; 112.93; 112.94; 112.95; 112.96; 112.99; 112.101; 112.102; 112.106; 112.110; 112.111; 112.113; 112.114; 112.118; 112.120; 112.122; 112.123; 112.124; 112.128; 112.129; 112.130; 112.134; 112.137; 112.139; 112.141; 112.142; 112.145; 112.146; 112.148; 112.150; 112.152; 112.153; 112.154; 112.155; 112.156; 112.158; 112.161; 112.163; 112.164; 112.165; 112.166; 112.170; 112.172; 112.173; 112.174; 112.176; 112.177; 112.179; 112.180; 112.181; 112.182; 112.183; 112.184; 112.186; 112.190; 112.191; 112.192; 112.195; 112.196; 112.197; 112.198; 112.200; 112.201; 112.202; 112.203; 112.204; 112.207; 112.210; 112.211; 112.212; 112.213; 112.214; 112.215; 112.216; 112.217; 112.218; 112.219; 112.220; 112.221
Continent (probable): 88.4; 90.15; 90.21; 90.22; 90.83; 90.88; 90.92:1-6; 91.13; 91.21; 91.23; 92.94; 92.104; 92.111; 92.133; 93.63; 93.70; 94.4; 94.7; 94.15; 94.18; 94.22; 96.26; 96.51; 96.68; 96.84; 96.87; 96.90; 96.93; 97.44; 97.58:1-2; 99.34; 103.14; 103.61; 103.65; 103.75; 104.60; 104.62; 107.33; 107.46; 107.48; 107.60; 107.67; 107.109; 107.131; 108.4; 108.10; 108.13; 108.44; 108.58; 108.60; 108.70:2; 109.13; 109.19; 109.29; 109.39; 109.42; 110.42; 110.46; 110.64; 110.81; 110.88; 110.112; 110.115; 110.146; 110.148; 110.156; 110.158; 110.161; 110.201; 110.207; 110.218; 110.234; 110.237; 110.253; 110.258; 111.3; 111.4; 111.8; 112.5; 112.21; 112.31; 112.32; 112.37; 112.39; 112.55; 112.105; 112.131; 112.193

Emden (probable): 103.93

Florence: 92.7
Frankfurt am Main: 93.77; 104.19; 104.81; 110.27; 110.125
Frankfurt am Main (perhaps): 107.55

Geneva: 103.69; 103.94; 107.27; 110.39; 110.43; 110.44; 110.56; 110.57; 110.74; 110.101; 110.120; 112.121; 112.140

Heidelberg: 110.126; 112.138; 112.147

Ingolstadt: 93.56; 96.64

Jena: 107.73; 107.102

Lausanne: 110.69
Leipzig: 104.53; 104.74; 110.47; 112.199
London: 89.1; 90.35; 91.2; 91.34; 92.30; 93.6; 95.3; 96.65; 100.8; 103.2; 103.3; 103.6; 103.11; 103.12; 103.17; 103.20; 103.22; 103.25; 103.26; 103.27; 103.36; 103.59; 103.62; 103.83; 103.86; 103.87; 103.88; 103.90; 103.91; 103.96; 103.98; 104.1; 108.15; 108.37; 108.88; 109.16; 110.40; 110.60; 110.124; 110.137; 110.138; 110.147; 110.159; 110.249; 110.270; 112.4; 112.8; 112.34; 112.54; 112.62; 112.63; 112.65; 112.71; 112.73; 112.100; 112.107; 112.108; 112.115; 112.143; 112.144; 112.149; 112.175
Louvain: 90.37; 90.61; 90.84; 95.4; 104.89; 112.151
Lyon: 91.4; 92.17; 96.59; 97.50; 104.7; 104.55; 108.41; 108.47

Mainz (probable): 96.91
Marburg: 96.105; 107.112
Milan: 93.40

Nuremberg: 103.79

Oxford: 93.75

Paris: 90.56; 90.72; 90.80; 90.93; 92.20; 92.90; 93.45; 93.69; 96.21; 96.29; 96.60; 96.73; 96.74; 96.88; 96.104; 97.3; 103.21; 103.70; 103.80; 104.33; 104.52; 107.24; 107.49; 110.71; 110.168; 110.173; 110.187; 111.2; 111.9; 112.76; 112.77; 112.160; 112.206

Place not given: 93.58; 107.100

Place unknown: 90.18; 90.23; 90.82; 90.91; 91.25; 91.38; 92.28; 92.41; 92.44; 92.51; 92.125; 93.8; 94.6; 94.21; 94.29; 94.30:1-2; 94.38; 95.5; 96.67; 97.46; 97.51; 98.2; 98.18; 99.4; 99.5; 99.35:1-4; 101.6:1-4; 103.9; 103.74; 103.97; 104.40:1; 104.46; 104.75; 104.84; 104.93; 106.1:1; 106.1:3-15; 107.1; 107.13; 107.15; 107.16; 107.29; 107.38; 108.6; 108.12; 108.21; 108.29; 108.39; 108.43; 108.76; 108.83; 108.92; 108.93:1-5; 108.94:1-5; 109.5; 109.6; 109.28; 109.33; 110.7; 110.45; 110.54; 110.78; 110.86; 110.108; 110.122; 110.131; 110.142; 110.150; 110.171; 110.181; 110.199; 110.209; 110.212; 110.232; 110.239; 110.251:1; 110.251:2; 110.260; 111.12; 112.44; 112.49:1-3; 112.68; 112.159; 112.171; 112.222

Provenance unknown (manuscripts): 90.27; 90.55; 90.77; 92.38; 93.3; 94.41; 97.13:1-3; 100.11; 103.99; 104.87:1-3; 110.269:1-2; 111.10

Strassburg: 97.38; 99.30; 99.31; 104.68; 104.72; 107.101; 110.160; 112.189; 112.208

Strassburg (probable): 103.37

Venice: 90.2; 91.28; 92.9; 92.27; 92.110; 92.123; 93.9; 93.10; 93.49; 93.67; 109.1; 112.22; 112.209

Venice (probable): 107.52

Vienna: 100.5

Wittenberg: 96.66; 107.57; 107.59; 107.70; 107.87; 107.96; 107.97; 107.99; 110.83; 110.102; 110.114; 110.117; 110.119; 110.133; 112.82; 112.84; 112.119

Zürich: 96.46; 104.43; 107.54; 107.62; 110.5; 110.9; 110.13; 110.14; 110.21; 110.26; 110.33; 110.38; 110.48; 112.3

Index VI
Dates of Publications

Date ranges are not included. The abbreviation *c.* derives from the bibliographical source consulted. The word *probable* is a PLRE qualification.

1483: 93.49
1489: 112.22
1492: 91.4

1509: 93.40
1514: 100.5
1518: 93.75
1524: 97.3
1526: 93.31
1527: 96.4; 96.26; 96.47; 96.85
1528: 90.67; 96.102
1530: 92.20; 96.102
1532: 104.52; 110.235
1532 (probable): 103.90
1533: 96.88
1535: 104.89
1536: 96.91; 107.10
1537: 93.45
1538: 108.41
1539: 112.76
1540: 98.12; 107.112
1541: 96.41; 107.84; 107.101
1543: 103.92

1544: 96.64; 103.79; 110.65
1545: 93.56; 110.157
1546: 93.77
1547: 91.28; 96.74
c.1547: 103.55
1549: 90.72
1550 (probable): 103.27; 103.84
1551: 96.21; 96.56; 103.11
1552: 91.34; 92.7; 109.16
1553: 90.37; 96.65; 110.187; 112.117
1554: 90.61; 90.93; 92.90; 97.50
1555: 90.56; 90.80; 92.33; 103.57; 110.129
c.1555 (probable): 103.93
1556: 96.59; 99.30; 103.37
1557: 91.17
1558: 103.94; 112.209
1559: 90.58
1560: 90.84; 104.43; 104.51:A; 104.51:B; 110.89; 112.206
1561: 112.65; 112.97
1562: 92.3; 92.27; 97.26; 103.86; 103.91
1563?: 108.15

1563 (probable): 112.199
1564: 92.9; 103.83; 104.79; 108.86; 110.211
1565: 91.2; 96.66; 103.87; 110.57; 112.144
1566: 92.95; 97.37; 108.88
1567: 97.38; 104.72; 108.20; 110.18; 110.259; 112.100; 112.140
1568: 100.8; 103.17; 104.29; 112.84
1569: 104.19; 110.14; 112.72; 112.151
1569 (probable): 103.98
1570: 103.2; 104.74
1571: 103.26; 104.20; 107.73; 107.97; 110.83; 110.124; 112.54; 112.103
1572: 104.7; 107.70; 107.100; 107.102; 107.106; 110.13; 110.47; 110.117; 110.125; 112.92; 112.149
1573: 103.3; 110.26; 110.60; 110.137; 110.240
1574: 110.126; 112.34; 112.63; 112.71; 112.147
1575: 110.192:A; 110.192:B; 112.108; 112.138
1576: 112.4; 112.115; 112.121

R. J. Fehrenbach, Professor of English at the College of William and Mary, has specialized in English Renaissance studies since taking his Ph.D. in English and History. His publications include works on historical bibliography, particularly as related to the drama, and on Tudor popular literature and culture. He was chief editor of the computer-generated *A Concordance to the Plays, Poems, and Translations of Christopher Marlowe* (Cornell University Press, 1982).

E. S. Leedham-Green, Deputy Keeper of the Archives and Fellow of Darwin College, Cambridge, holds the D.Phil., having specialized in the classical tradition in English literature, and is a Fellow of the Society of Antiquaries. She has published on archival history and on the history of the book, most notably as editor of *Books in Cambridge Inventories: Booklists from Vice-Chancellor's Court Probate Inventories in the Tudor and Stuart Periods* (Cambridge, 1986). She is General Editor of *Libri Pertinentes*, a bibliographical series relating to sixteenth- and seventeenth-century libraries.

MRTS

MEDIEVAL & RENAISSANCE TEXTS & STUDIES
is the publishing program of the
Center for Medieval and Early Renaissance Studies
at the State University of New York at Binghamton.

MRTS emphasizes books that are needed —
texts, translations, and major research tools.

MRTS aims to publish the highest quality scholarship
in attractive and durable format at modest cost.